THE S. MARK TAPER FOUNDATION

IMPRINT IN JEWISH STUDIES

BY THIS ENDOWMENT

THE S. MARK TAPER FOUNDATION SUPPORTS

THE APPRECIATION AND UNDERSTANDING

OF THE RICHNESS AND DIVERSITY OF

JEWISH LIFE AND CULTURE

The publisher and the University of California Press Foundation gratefully acknowledge the generous support of the S. Mark Taper Foundation Imprint in Jewish Studies.

What Animals Teach Us About Families

What Animals Teach Us About Families

KINSHIP AND SPECIES IN THE BIBLE
AND RABBINIC LITERATURE

Beth A. Berkowitz

UNIVERSITY OF CALIFORNIA PRESS

University of California Press
Oakland, California

© 2026 by Beth A. Berkowitz

All rights reserved.

Library of Congress Cataloging-in-Publication Data

Names: Berkowitz, Beth A. author
Title: What animals teach us about families : kinship and species in the bible and rabbinic literature / Beth A. Berkowitz.
Description: Oakland, California : University of California Press, [2026] | Includes bibliographical references and index.
Identifiers: LCCN 2025018439 (print) | LCCN 2025018440 (ebook) | ISBN 9780520405226 cloth | ISBN 9780520405233 paperback | ISBN 9780520405240 ebook
Subjects: LCSH: Animals in the Bible | Animals in rabbinical literature | Kinship—Religious aspects | Human-animal relationships—Religious aspects—Judaism
Classification: LCC BS663 .B47 2026 (print) | LCC BS663 (ebook) | DDC 296.3/693—dc23/eng/20250828
LC record available at https://lccn.loc.gov/2025018439
LC ebook record available at https://lccn.loc.gov/2025018440

GPSR Authorized Representative: Easy Access System Europe, Mustamäe tee 50, 10621 Tallinn, Estonia, gpsr.requests@easproject.com

34 33 32 31 30 29 28 27 26 25
10 9 8 7 6 5 4 3 2 1

Contents

	Introduction: What Animals Teach Us About Families	1
1.	Do Animals Love Their Children? The Science of Animal Families	24
2.	The Bible's Animal-Family Laws: What Are They, Are They Related, and Are They Humanitarian?	43
3.	Animal Grandmothers: The Prohibition Against Same-Day Slaughter	68
4.	Animal Mothers: The Prohibition Against Cooking a Kid in His Mother's Milk	87
5.	Animal Fathers and Other Caregivers: Sending Off the Mother Bird	103
6.	Animal Orphans: Keeping the Baby with the Mother for the First Week of Life	122
	Conclusion: What Families Teach Us About Animals	141
	Epilogue: Five Ways to Support Animal Families	153
	With Rabbi Melissa Hoffman	

Acknowledgments	159
Notes	163
Bibliography	219
Index of Sources	251
General Index	257

Introduction

WHAT ANIMALS TEACH US ABOUT FAMILIES

BAMBI: A JEWISH ANIMAL-FAMILY STORY

Disney's *Bambi* is a children's movie, but the book on which it is based, published in 1923 by Viennese Jewish author Felix Salten, is not a children's story.[1] The deer coming-of-age tale told by Salten has dread hanging over it from the start. The secluded forest glade into which Bambi is born gives way quickly to the alluring but dangerous open meadow, where, Bambi soon discovers, forest animals face the risk of being struck down by "Him," Salten's oblique way of referring to human hunters. After some early idyllic scenes in which Bambi frolics in the meadow with his mother, aunt, and cousins, winter comes, and soon we find the meadow filled with carnage, thanks to the hunter's "third hand," which is how the animals perceive his gun. Bambi thinks he sees the hunters shoot his mother. The scene is near apocalyptic: "The thunder crashed around them on all sides. It seemed as if the earth would split in half."[2] *Bambi* is more *Saving Private Ryan* than *The Tale of Peter Rabbit*.

The loss of the beloved mother is the drama for which Bambi is best known, but Bambi's struggle to develop a relationship to his father is just as critical to the narrative arc, which begins with the mother-baby cocoon but closes with a late-blooming intimacy between father and son. Neither relationship is idealized. Bambi's mother nourishes and protects him and teaches him about the forest, but she also periodically abandons him and rebuffs him when he tries to cuddle with her. She fails to protect Bambi when, famously, she falls prey to hunters. Bambi is not aware of even having a father until his aunt reveals to him that the stag passing by is his father. The first words to Bambi from the "old stag," as Salten calls him, are to chide him for crying: "Can't you stay by yourself? Shame on you!" While the mother is a figure of attachment—Bambi's life begins with his mother licking and nursing him, the two oblivious to all but each other—the father stands for individuation and invulnerability. As the story unfolds, however, the old stag becomes more available. Their relationship reaches a turning point when the old stag takes Bambi under his wing, teaches him to avoid the traps and deer calls of the hunters, and then saves Bambi's life when he is wounded by a bullet. The relationship, and book, end with the old stag bidding farewell to Bambi and going off into the forest to die: "Good-by, my son. I loved you dearly." Still, the story closes with Bambi shaming two young fawns, presumably his own children, in just the way the old stag had once shamed him: "'Can't you stay by yourself?' he asked. The little brother and sister were silent."[3] The two young fawns go on to become the protagonists of Salten's sequel, *Bambi's Children*.

If Salten's drama of attachment and separation has a Freudian feel to it, that is probably no coincidence. Salten was friendly with Freud and traveled in some of the same circles in fin de siècle Vienna. Salten was friendly also with Theodor Herzl, supported Herzl's early Zionist efforts, wrote and lectured in favor of Zionism, and visited Palestine in 1924.[4] It is not surprising, then, that the story of Bambi has been read as an allegory for the plight of Jews in early twentieth-century Europe and a cautionary tale about antisemitism.[5] The character of Gobo, Bambi's cousin who receives kind treatment from humans and advocates for trusting them only to wind up shot and killed, seems a stand-in for assimilationist Jews. Old Nettla's rebuttal would seem to represent Salten's own perspective: "Friends with Him! He's murdered us ever since we can remember, every one of us, our sisters, our mothers, our brothers! Ever since we came into the world He's given us no peace, but has killed us wherever we showed our heads. And now we're going to be friends with Him! What nonsense!"[6] The terrifying violence of the hunters—read Christian Europe—is, instead, the reality with which Jews should reckon. The Nazis themselves saw Bambi as a criticism of their policies and in 1936 banned and burned copies of the book.[7]

Salten himself never confirmed the allegorical reading, and, while he may have been a Zionist, he was also an avid hunter as well as conservationist.[8] The story might be an allegory about the Jews of Europe, but it is also more, or less, as a story about animals. The story anthropomorphizes the animals, but Salten also adheres to the knowledge about deer behavior that he would have picked up in the hunting preserve in the Danube lowland where he loved to spend time.[9] Bambi's mother secludes herself in a remote glade to give birth just as real deer mothers do.[10] Her licking the baby right after birth and massaging him are true to deer behavior, as is the critical role of smell in their first encounter. Salten's depiction of Bambi's absent father also reflects actual deer-breeding habits, in which the father provides no direct care to the young and has little relationship with them. Male deer often live alone, in the way Bambi's father and, later, Bambi do. The presence of Bambi's various deer aunts and cousins reflects the typical small social configuration of a deer herd. Salten's interest in animal-family dynamics extends to other species too: a grasshopper husband and wife can be found conversing at one point in the story; Friend Hare is devastated by the violent death of his son at the hands of crows; a disconsolate squirrel widow makes an appearance; and Bambi befriends two mother ducks, whom he watches teach their ducklings.

DO ANIMALS HAVE FAMILIES TOO?

Readers of Salten's story will find it compelling if they accept that animals have families too and that those families are rife with the same rich dramas as human families. That question—*Do animals have families too?*—is the one that animates this book and the reason that I begin with Salten's *Bambi*. How and why do animal families matter to us? What are the biggest challenges that animal families face? Are *we* the biggest challenge, like the mysterious and villainous "He" in Bambi who is, quite plausibly, a stand-in for Salten himself? What are the implications of animal families for them and for us?

We love animal families. That much is clear. Salten was a highly prolific fiction writer, playwright, and critic, but *Bambi* was his biggest hit. *Bambi* was translated into English several years after its original publication in German by the well-known American writer and Soviet spy and, later, anticommunist, conservative hero Whittaker Chambers and then turned into a movie legend with Disney's 1942 film. Only two movies, *Gone with the Wind* and *The Sound of Music*, earned more money in rental fees than Bambi did in the years between 1939 and 1969. But our love for animal families does not stop us, like the hunters in *Bambi* and like Salten, from visiting terrible violence on them. Even in its Disney version, Bambi's loss of his mother, no matter how occluded—her death at the hands of the hunters is not pictured in either the book or film—has haunted generations of moviegoing children, including Walt Disney's own daughter, who reportedly asked her father why Bambi's mother had to die, and Paul McCartney, who cites Bambi as the inspiration for his animal advocacy.[11] How do we humans negotiate the trauma we inflict on the animal families with whom we simultaneously empathize?

Untangling that paradox from the distinctive perspective of the Jewish experience is my purpose in this book. The story of Bambi has universal appeal, but it is also very much a Jewish story even if most people do not realize it. The precariousness of the animal family in Salten's *Bambi* echoes the precariousness of the Jewish family at the time that Salten wrote it. By a stroke of luck for Salten—thanks to a daughter in Switzerland, Salten was able to escape to Zurich in early 1939—his own immediate family was not broken up by deportation and destruction in the way millions of other European Jewish families would be.[12] The tragedy at the heart of Salten's *Bambi* proved an eerie harbinger of the fate of so many Jewish families in the twentieth century.

My book reaches back further in time, to the ancient traditions of the Hebrew Bible and classical rabbinic literature, to ask about the insights they too might yield about animal families. The people who gave us these works lived before the advent of big animal agriculture with its massive industrial pens far from population centers. Their perspective on animals is rooted in a more familiar and intuitive relationship with animals than most readers of this book are likely to have. This book's premise is that these ancient perspectives have the power to change us—our minds, our feelings, our relationships to animals, and our relationships to one another. Most people today who hold the ancient traditions dear have not noticed the presence of animal families in them. We are used to animal families in children's stories like *Bambi;* we are less used to seeing them in authoritative religious texts. This book's aim is to fix that.

THE BIBLE'S FOUR ANIMAL-FAMILY LAWS AND THE RABBIS WHO READ THEM

The task is not easy, as is illustrated by the trajectory of *Bambi*, with its many surprising twists. Its author hunted animals but also loved them. In addition to writing one of the most famous children's stories, Salten also wrote pornography.[13] He was a great success who struggled with poverty throughout his life. His most well-known work is associated with Walt Disney rather than with him. *Bambi*'s first translator is best known for being an ex-spy whom Ronald Reagan awarded the Presidential Medal of Freedom. The story can be read either as a tale of the forest or a foreshadowing of the Holocaust. Wrapping one's head around these incongruities is a good warm-up for the biblical laws about animal families that are this book's subject and for the surprising trajectory that they too take.

Four laws in the Pentateuch—for Jews, the Torah—focus on the parent-child bond among animals. The most well known is the prohibition against cooking a kid in his mother's milk. This law appears three times in identical form, first in Exodus 23:19, then in Exodus 34:26, and finally, again, in Deuteronomy 14:21. A second law related to animal families is the injunction to leave an infant animal with the mother for the first week of life. This law appears twice, in Exodus 22:29 and in Leviticus 22:27, in somewhat different formulations. The other two animal-family laws each appear only once in the Pentateuch, a prohibition against slaughtering an animal and their child on the same day, found in Leviticus 22:28, and a requirement to send off the mother bird before taking her eggs or chicks from the nest, found in Deuteronomy 22:6–7. These four laws are scattered through the Pentateuch but have been recognized since antiquity as thematically related. A standard approach to these four laws is to see in them a humanitarian rationale. The humanitarian approach is ancient, with first-century-CE Philo as the touchstone, but it runs through medieval Bible commentators and contemporary scholarship. The humanitarian approach has its attractions, but it also has serious limitations. In this book I argue that the ancient Rabbis, in *not* taking the humanitarian approach and, on the contrary, in certain instances actively rejecting it, are able to offer a different and provocative set of perspectives on animal families that deserves our attention.

It is easier to make the case first by clarifying what it is not. The ancient Rabbis—I give them a proper introduction later in this chapter—do not offer a single approach to these laws. Each of the four laws raises its own set of interpretive questions for the Rabbis. The Rabbis also do not generally read these four laws as linked to one another. The rabbinic treatment of each law does not tend to mention the others. The Rabbis also do not offer exhaustive or proportional coverage of the four laws. The Rabbis give enormous attention to cooking a kid in his mother's milk, only a small fraction of which I cover. They give surprisingly little attention to leaving a baby with the mother for the first week of life. The Rabbis also do not offer unmediated access to animal families—far from it. These are human legislations embedded in human literature representing human perspectives. Finally, the Rabbis do not offer an ethic that is easily usable today. The Rabbis' lives with animals and with their own human families were so different that it is impossible to draw a straight line from their experience to ours.

Having cleared that brush, I can lay out my case. In the Mishnah, Tosefta, and Babylonian Talmud, the main rabbinic works that I discuss, the Rabbis recognized and reflected on animal families in the course of interpreting the Bible's four laws about them. In developing terminology for animal ancestors and family trees and requiring a public announcement of animal-family relations (see chapter 3), the Rabbis explored parallels between human and animal families and made animal families publicly visible. In laws and stories related to animal udders (see chapter 4), the Rabbis brought animal mothers into view even though the Rabbis' dietary laws obscured their presence. In elaborating the mother-bird commandment (see chapter 5), the Rabbis envisioned the nest as an architecturally sophisticated and socially diverse space where species and biological lines mix. In tall tales that the Rabbis tell about giant animals in faraway places (see chapter 6), they imagined the plight of animal orphans.

In these wide-ranging and intriguing treatments of animal families, I show that rabbinic texts focus our attention on the kinship ties of animals and that there is intellectual and ethical payout for us in having them do so. The rabbinic texts invite us to notice features of animal life that we would otherwise likely ignore. They ask us to see our own family bonds as a shared animal experience. They may inspire us to become vegan, as I have, so as not to contribute to the trauma visited on animal families in modern agriculture. Biblical and rabbinic texts can get us thinking differently about animals and about families. In the remainder of this introduction, I explain how.

ANIMAL KINSHIP

Nature metaphors are often used to express kinship. We speak of "roots" and family "trees." The Bible describes semen and progeny as "seed." But the logic of kinship is far from organic. It is idiosyncratic and erratic, as these questions posed by sociologist Eviatar Zerubavel reveal: "Why do we consider Barack Obama a black man with a white mother rather than a white man with a black father? . . . Why did the Nazis believe that unions between Germans and Jews would produce Jews rather than Germans? Are sixth cousins still family?"[14] Whom we consider to *be* blood is not in fact determined *by* blood. Advances in reproductive technologies and the phenomenon of fictive and chosen kin—think of adoption, foster care, monastic orders, fraternities and sororities, and military units—have brought a more expansive and flexible notion of kin into American public discourse and private life, where it sometimes generates anxiety for those accustomed to models of kinship that rely on biological relatedness.

This more elastic notion of kin has significant implications for animals. If genetic relationships are not inherent to kinship, then animals, who, according to Linnaean classification, are isolated from humans at a taxonomic level because of their inability to interbreed with us, can qualify as human kin. And that is precisely how humans often relate to the animals whom they live with or near. People who breed and train falcons have long-term intimate relationships with their falcons comparable to the relationships that people have with their human partners.[15] The Indigenous Dukha people of northern Mongolia develop kin relations with the reindeer whom they herd and consider them part of the Dukha household.[16] The men in rural Punjab who lavish attention on their pigeons, roosters, and dogs earn the resentment of their wives.[17] The documentary film *The Elephant Whisperers* features an Indigenous couple in southern India who adopt an orphaned baby elephant and love him like their own child.[18] Intimate long-term relationships between humans and animals have a long history. Members of the ruling Gonzaga family kept beloved companion cats and dogs at the Mantuan court in Renaissance Italy.[19] Early modern English wills mention individual cows by name.[20] These attachments are emotional and mutual (though we would have to ask the animals to know for sure) and survive even lengthy separation. Anyone who lives with an animal companion can confirm the power of such attachments. My dogs, Dulcie and Burt, feel like they are as much a part of my family as my children.

I speak here of the kinship that humans share with animals—such kinship is so enduring and vital that one cannot fathom human life without it—but what of the kinship that animals share *with one another?* My study of the Bible's animal-family laws focuses on the family ties that animals forge among themselves. To look at kinship from an animal perspective does not just mean add-animals-and-stir, though, or to claim that we know what kinship means for animals.[21] The biblical and rabbinic texts I study do not make any such claim, nor do I (though the next chapter reviews what modern scientists have discovered about animal parent-child bonds). The goal is, quite simply, to pursue an account of kinship that does not treat human kinship as the exclusive or primary form. The Bible and its readers, unlike most of us today, are attentive to the kinship bonds that animals build with one another and to the impact of human interference with those bonds.

It would be a mistake to think, however, that the Bible and the Rabbis somehow "beat us there." The treatment of animal families by the Bible and rabbinic literature leaves intact a world of anthropocentric assumptions that critical animal studies—the set of scholarly challenges to the human/animal binary—have thankfully thrown into question. Still, the ancients are a step ahead of critical animal studies in giving their attention to animals' own kinship ties, which, I have found to my surprise, occupy very little real estate in this vibrant scholarly field. If anyone did beat us there it is the ethologists, the scientists of animal behavior, who have been revealing to us for quite a while now the rich texture of animal-family life. Ethologists have exposed the rivalries that explain why sharks, hyenas, and pelicans kill their siblings and why beetles and mice kill their children. They have guided us through the intricate architecture of mammalian child care, which relies on mothers, as we might expect, but also on siblings, aunts, fathers, and friends.[22] We have learned about baboon mothers, lion and langur dads, and the dazzling variety of parenting styles displayed by sheep, bats, whales, wasps, elephants, and frogs.[23] In this book I follow the lead of the ethologists in putting animal families first.

ANIMALS AND THE JEWISH FAMILY

It still may seem strange to speak of animals as part of the *Jewish* family, yet that is exactly what I am asking us to do. The story of the Jewish family begins in antiquity before the very existence of Jews, with the ancient Israelites. The narrative of Genesis is, in essence, a single family's story. Over the course of several generations, that family learns to live together without conflict and to keep its members from drifting away.[24] In Exodus that family becomes the basis for a nation. The "children of Israel" are, literally, the children of a man named Israel. The family is the framework in the Bible not only for narrative but also for law, which treats such topics as the sale of daughters as slaves and the punishment of the rebellious child.[25] Family bonds were protected by the Bible, but the biblical family was far from a safe space for children, who were valued as contributors to the household but were at the same time vulnerable to exploitation, negligence, and harsh discipline.[26] The central Israelite hero, Moses, was abandoned as a baby by his parents, under duress from Pharaoh's orders.

The family looms large also in rabbinic literature of late antiquity. Pure lineage was highly prized by the ancient Rabbis.[27] Great ambivalence was attached to the role of the father, however, which vied with that of the

Rabbi for authority and loyalty. The Rabbis were themselves ambivalent fathers, if the stories in the Babylonian Talmud are any indication, which describe Rabbis leaving their wives and children for long stretches of time to study Torah.[28] Mothers and motherhood evoked complex responses as well.[29] In biblical Israel mothers on the one hand were mostly excluded from the sacred routines of sacrifice but on the other hand formed the basis of a maternal kinship unit ("the house of the mother") and of the organization of the tribes.[30] No loss was considered greater than that of a mother grieving her child.[31] Jewish mothers are today the stuff of comedy, but in late antiquity and the Middle Ages and later in the United States, during the Shoah, and in the State of Israel, mothers have defined the very meaning of Jewishness.[32] The quintessential mammalian experience of breastfeeding is often when Jewish mothers first begin to transmit culture to the next generation and become enmeshed in obligations toward husbands and children.[33]

Many Jewish families suffered fragmentation and destruction in the course of the twentieth century, including my own—when my paternal grandfather came to America in the interwar period, he left his siblings and parents in Transylvania, where almost all were eventually killed by the Nazis. Traumatic histories like these have led "the Jewish community," which is something of an imaginative construct given how divided actual Jews tend to be, to become preoccupied with "Jewish continuity," another ideological term, this one reflecting Jewish anxiety about cultural and physical survival. That anxiety contributes to a phenomenon called "Jewish pronatalism," which is the promotion of biological reproduction between Jews and other Jews in the context of the nuclear family. Pronatalism is far from absolute, however, in Jewish canonical sources and in contemporary Jewish practices related to childbearing, child-rearing, and family.[34] The recent explosion of interest in Jewish ancestries and origins is likewise fueled by the trauma experienced by Jewish families in modernity to the extent that, for many lay practitioners, genealogy is a sacred activity and itself a form of contemporary religion.[35]

The contemporary interest in—and one could say obsession with—the Jewish family invites us to consider the role of animals in it. Animals have always been an essential part of the Jewish family as producers (of milk, meat, wool, skins, and dung); laborers (plowing the field and threshing grain); transportation (carrying people and cargo); ritual objects (sacrifice, horns for the shofar, leather for tefillin, parchment for scrolls); protection (dogs barking and biting); "pest" extermination (cats eating rodents); property (an animal's value would have depended on all these roles); housemates (living near or in the family compound); and companions (especially as pets in modern Jewish households). But Jews have always encountered animals not only as contributors to their human families but also as participants in their own animal families. Every sheep, goat, ox, cow, donkey, horse, camel, dog, cat, and bird who has left their mark in Jewish history is born to parents and usually siblings and has other kin relations and ancestors and sometimes descendants. These animal families, I show in the trajectory of the Bible's animal-family laws, are not a silent archive but rather an explicit part of Jewish thinking about the family. For Jews, family matters. Animal families, it turns out, mattered too.

ANIMALS IN THE HEBREW BIBLE AND RABBINIC LITERATURE

The family is one frame for this book, and animals are another. In my previous book, I looked at the Talmud's treatment of age-old questions about animals: What do animals know? Do animals plan for the future? Do animals understand right and wrong? What are our ethical obligations toward animals?[36] The aim of that study and of other animal studies on the Bible and rabbinic canon is to pose the "question of the animal" to that literature—namely, to explore the problems we create when we survey the infinitely complex world of living creatures and divide them all into two crude categories, the human and the animal, and declare the human to be superior.

When one starts to look for animals in the Hebrew Bible and rabbinic literature, one soon realizes how ubiquitous and essential they are. The primeval history of Genesis—the creation of animals and humans, the evil snake in Eden, Noah's two-by-two (or by-seven) recruitment of animal species onto his ark, the dove flying away once the flood has ceased—receives the greatest attention. But what would the story of Abraham be without the ram whom he substituted for his son? One rabbinic midrash credits the ram for eagerly volunteering for the Akedah—in fact, engineering the Akedah by getting Abraham's attention with his hoof—thereby ensuring that the Jewish people would one day come into existence.[37] That same miraculous ram went on to provide the sinews for David's harp, the skin for Elijah's loincloth, and the horn to blow when the Messiah comes, according to the midrash.[38] What would the story of Jacob be without the meat of the goats that Jacob used to serve his father and the goat's skin that Jacob used to trick him or without the sheep that facilitated his encounter with his future wife? What would the story of Joseph be without the starving and fat cows in Pharaoh's dream? What would the story of the Exodus be without the frogs, lice, flies, cattle disease, and locusts as well as the lambs' blood that let God know which houses to skip?

Without these key animal figures, the story of Israel's beginnings would unravel. If Bilaam's donkey had not seen the angel, Bilaam might never have blessed the Israelites and helped them to win their battle with Moab. One can hardly imagine biblical law and ritual without the red heifer, the goring ox, the prohibitions on consuming animal blood and many animal species, the impurity of animal carcasses, and animal sacrifices and donations. One can hardly imagine biblical prophecy, poetry, and wisdom without the wolf dwelling with the lamb in Isaiah, the big fish in Jonah, "all creatures great and small" in Psalms, Behemoth and Leviathan in Job, and the lions' den in Daniel. Similarly, one would be left with a fraction of the rabbinic work known as the Mishnah were one to eliminate animals from it. One would lose some of the Talmud's best stories, such as the story in Tractate Gittin about the fly who enters Roman emperor Titus's head and kills him or the one in Tractate Avodah Zarah about Rabbi Meir magically protecting a Roman guard from attack dogs or the one in Tractate Berakhot about the deposition of Rabban Gamliel, in which some of the central drama revolves around the status of first-born animals.[39]

Western religious traditions are easy to blame for climate crisis and for what philosopher Peter Singer called "speciesism," which Singer defines as a prejudice in favor of the human species over and against all other species.[40] That is certainly what we find when we focus on texts like Genesis 1:26–28 and Genesis 9:2–3, in which God grants to humans dominion over animals. But when one reads the Hebrew Bible more carefully, one finds complexity and subtlety in its treatment of animals. The Bible often challenges speciesism and the simplistic binary of human versus animal on which it is based. Genesis 9 is a good example. God declares all the creatures of the earth to be given over into human hands, true, but God also makes a covenant not just with humans but with animals too. The rainbow in Genesis 9:15–17 is a sign of the covenant for "every living creature." One Bible scholar has argued that the Hebrew Bible provides a solid foundation for animal rights.[41]

Rabbinic and later Jewish literature likewise features animals in a multitude of ways. The Rabbis of the Roman Empire saw many resemblances and intersections between humans and animals.[42] Rabbis in the Persian-held East dedicated a chapter of their masterpiece, the Babylonian Talmud, to exploring differences among Jews, non-Jews, and animals.[43] Rabbis of medieval Christian Europe were fascinated by werewolves, dragons, and other wondrous creatures that defy the expected species categories.[44] Jewish writers of modernity—Heinrich Heine, Franz Kafka, Shmuel Yosef Agnon, Devorah Baron—featured animals centrally in their work as they negotiated what it means to be Jewish and human in the modern era. Kafka's stories are well known for playing with the boundaries between human and animal: the human who wakes up as a bug, the ape who turns into a human, the jackal who speaks.[45] Animals have played a significant role in the modern Jewish nation-building project in Israel as military dogs and companion animals, as the focus of vegan activism, and as exhibits in the Biblical Zoo in Jerusalem and in the Ramat-Gan Safari.[46]

It makes sense, then, that to fully appreciate the biblical and Jewish heritage, one must consider the animal. Why the animal family, though, specifically, and why these four laws? Animals are too often the sideshow to the human main event, and that is especially true when it comes to the family. The Bible helps to illustrate. In the second creation story, God seeks a "fitting counterpart," an *ezer kenegdo* (Genesis 2:18), for the man God has just created. The land animals and birds will not do; only a creature made from man's own body satisfies the need. The story does not entertain the possibility that the various animals and birds whom the man names but then discards might each possess their own "fitting counterpart" nor that animals might themselves someday, like the man, "leave [their] own father and mother" (2:24) to begin their own families. It is also left unclear why, if painful childbirth is the punishment for the woman's transgression, animal mothers should have to experience that punishment too. Family is conceived of by the story as a strictly human experience—and a fundamental one at that. To grant other species that same experience is a radical but entirely necessary move if the Bible's anthropocentrism and human exceptionalism—two key terms in the new thinking about animals that point to humans' outsized sense of their own importance—are to be mitigated. The notion that animals too might have "flesh of their flesh" (a common biblical idiom for kin relationship) and bear children who might end up killing one another, as Adam's children do, or whom they might either favor or abandon, as Abraham does Isaac and Ishmael, respectively, or who might bring them sadness, pleasure, and a whole range of other emotions and who might care for them in their old age, as Joseph does for Jacob, does not register on the biblical radar. Yet animal kinship is present in the Bible in its four animal-family laws even if the Bible's dominant speciesism might obscure it.

WHAT ANIMALS TEACH US ABOUT FAMILIES

One could raise objections. Does talking about animal families just project our own ideas about family onto animals? Does it romanticize the family in a way that makes our own lives worse and animal lives no better off? Philosopher Brian Massumi helps us with the first problem, while critical theorist Jack (Judith) Halberstam, with some help from Pixar, helps us with the second. My title, *What Animals Teach Us About Families*, is a riff on Brian Massumi's *What Animals Teach Us About Politics*. The answer to Massumi's question is something he calls "mutual inclusion," which refers to the continuum that links humans to other species.[47] All social species—Massumi uses the examples of wolf cubs playing and herring gull birds feeding their chicks—produce their own intricate politics filled with intrigue, conflict, and alliances, as primatologist Frans de Waal proposed back in 1982 when he published his landmark *Chimpanzee Politics*.[48] Massumi admits that the notion of a cross-species politics seems to fall into an "anthropomorphic trap" that fails to respect our difference from other species.[49] Applying that argument to animal families, one might say that that talking about animal mothers, fathers, children, and families is a form of projecting human constructs onto animals. Any conversation about animal families is bound by our own assumptions and expectations regarding the family. It is more respectful of animal difference *not* to speak of animal families, according to this line of thinking.

Massumi's rebuttal is that the criticism posits a false choice between utter sameness and radical difference. The "piety"—that is what Massumi calls it—of presuming radical difference is, in the end, worse for us and for animals: "Is it not the height of human arrogance to suppose that animals do *not* have thought, emotion, desire, creativity, or subjectivity?" I would add, family, and repeat Massumi's exclamation: "But is not to remain silent on the nature of differences dangerously close to silencing difference? What lack of respect!"[50] Massumi calls into question the longstanding search to find the thing that makes humans unique. People have tried rationality, language, tool use, shame, culture, consciousness, morality, memory, intentionality, individuality, reflexivity, religion, and the very need to claim uniqueness.[51] None have worked. All these capacities have been found in animals. Family is another feature of human life that humans have claimed as a distinguishing feature that does not work either. Animals teach us that family, too, is an experience shared among species. To paraphrase Leo Tolstoy, every family is alike in possessing kinship bonds, though every family within and across species enacts those bonds in its own way. In investigating biblical traditions about the animal family, I hope, as Massumi does for his animal politics, that these traditions can coax us out of our human exceptionalism, which has us believing that we are the only species that experience family, even if that experience is bound to be endlessly diverse.

We should be wary, though, along with Jack Halberstam, of sentimental appeals to the family that rely on animals. Stories about animal families tend to embrace the traditional nuclear family and try to make it seem ingrained in nature. Halberstam recommends animal stories that instead "forget the family." Halberstam brings the example of the 2003 animated Pixar/Disney movie *Finding Nemo*, which follows the saga of a clownfish family in Australia separated when a scuba diver captures the son, Nemo, and places him in a fish tank in a dentist's office in Sydney. Like *Bambi*, *Finding Nemo* is the coming-of-age tale of a young son whose mother has died—Nemo's mother, Coral, is eaten by a barracuda at the beginning of the story—and whose father, Marlin, is, at least for the duration of most of the plot, unavailable. *Finding Nemo* tells the simultaneous stories of Nemo learning to fend for himself and his father's anxious journey to reunite with him, aided by a fish friend named Dory who suffers from short-term memory loss. Halberstam focuses on the comic-relief figure of Dory, voiced by the queer Ellen DeGeneres. Dory's queer sense of time and unexpectedly wise guidance offer a model of no-strings attachment that is at once ephemeral and transformative, proposes Halberstam.[52] *Finding Nemo* shows that our stories about animal families do not need to ooze traditional family values.

A comparison between *Bambi* and *Finding Nemo*, both enormous popular hits, is instructive. *Finding Nemo* dispatches the mother more quickly than does *Bambi*, but both stories are propelled by the mother's untimely and violent death, showcasing the disastrous impact of human interference in animal families. Take away the hunters from *Bambi*, and there is no coming-of-age tale; take away the scuba diver and dentist's office from *Finding Nemo*, and there is no need to find him. In other words, animal-family stories do not have to whitewash or sidestep the exploitative relationship that humans have with animals. Neither *Bambi* nor *Finding Nemo* is looking to blow up the system, nor are the Bible's animal-family laws, but these treatments of animal families offer the makings of a critique simply by featuring animal families in the first place. Seeing animal-family relationships is the first step toward recognizing the human impact on them.

At the end of this book, I suggest things you can do to support animal families, but let me spell out here at the start the most obvious ramification of recognizing animal families, which relates to industrial animal agriculture. As a longtime vegetarian now turned vegan, I was surprised to find when I was doing research for this book that the dairy industry is even worse than the meat industry when it comes to the animal family since dairy cows are separated from their calves almost instantly after birth for them to produce more milk. This book has particular implications for veganism and choices around eating the bodies and products of animals raised in industrial settings, but this book also has implications for the use of animals in any condition of captivity—zoos, laboratories, our own homes—that requires them to be forcibly separated from their kin.

Recognition of animal families is consequential, finally, also for the broader environmental crisis in which we find ourselves, as human development and pollution disrupt animal families as much as they disrupt human ones.

I might seem to be presuming that talking about animal families will get us to treat them better. But that is not necessarily so. *Finding Nemo* generated a rush on clownfish that resulted in the devastation of clownfish populations. Felix Salten did not stop hunting after he wrote *Bambi*. The Bible's animal-family laws have not stopped everyone from slaughtering animal parents and children or taking eggs from birds' nests. On the contrary, an entire industry has emerged to furnish religious Jews with bird nests precisely so they can take the eggs and, those people believe, get good luck from having fulfilled the biblical commandment. Nevertheless, I believe that the Bible's animal-family laws can get us a little closer to a world in which humans do not see themselves as a priori dominant or sui generis different. Family has come to be associated with middle-class moral panic, but in this age of family separations due to war, incarceration, border control, and climate crisis, forgetting the family has its risks. The biblical and rabbinic texts featured in the following chapters offer resources for a perspective on family that cuts across species lines and that presents family in ways we might not before have imagined—with strange temporalities, in spaces not normally associated with families, and with family members not typically noticed—to expand what we might think we know about both families and animals.

CHAPTER GUIDE

The chapters move one by one through the Bible's animal-family laws, starting with the prohibition on same-day slaughter, proceeding to the prohibition on cooking kids in their mother's milk, then to sending off the mother bird, and finally to the requirement to keep the baby with the mother for the first week of life. The sequence of the chapters at the same time follows different members of the family: grandmothers, mothers, fathers, other helpers, and orphans. There is also a movement through ancient literature, with earlier chapters treating the Bible, Second

Temple-period Jewish literature, and early rabbinic literary corpora and subsequent chapters treating the relatively late rabbinic compendium of the Babylonian Talmud.

Chapter 1, "Do Animals Love Their Children? The Science of Animal Families," takes up the science of animal families to show that animals have emotional lives as complex as ours. I explain that animals not only have feelings but also have distinctly parental and filial feelings. When animal parents are separated from their children, it has a disastrous impact. I look at the realities of animal agriculture in antiquity and today, explaining how, when, and why animal families are separated and what it means for them.

Chapter 2, "The Bible's Animal-Family Laws: What Are They, Are They Related, and Are They Humanitarian?," introduces the animal-family laws in their original literary setting in the Torah and offers a reconstruction of how the laws developed. I turn to the dominant explanation for these laws, the humanitarian rationale, as it has been formulated with varying emphases from antiquity to modernity. I start with Philo's concern with Jewish philanthropy, move to medieval Jewish commentator Rashbam's focus on civilized behavior and Maimonides's on the animal mother's traumatic witness, and conclude with modern scholars' articulation of "humaneness" and *"rahamim."* I close the chapter with the main objections that have been raised against the humanitarian rationale before segueing to the classical Rabbis.

With the relevant science and biblical basics covered, I turn to rabbinic treatments that offer an alternative to the humanitarian rationale. Chapter 3, "Animal Grandmothers: The Prohibition Against Same-Day Slaughter," takes up Leviticus 22:28's prohibition against slaughtering an animal parent and child on the same day as it is elaborated in the rabbinic work known as the Mishnah. I explore in Mishnah Tractate Hullin Chapter Five the configuration of animal-family generations from grandparent to grandchild and look at rabbinic kinship terminologies and their social significance. I look at the Mishnah's instruction to owners, when they sell their animal, to announce, "I sold her mother for slaughter!" "I sold her daughter for slaughter!" and consider the demands such an announcement would have placed on those who buy, sell, and slaughter animals to know an animal's lineage and confer a biography on them.

Chapter 4, "Animal Mothers: The Prohibition Against Cooking a Kid in His Mother's Milk," lays out the theories that have been offered to explain the prohibition against cooking a kid in his mother's milk and zeroes in on the distinctive rabbinic approach, which generalizes the prohibition so that the mother-child pair at its center virtually disappears. This chapter looks at rabbinic discussions of the consumption of animal udders in Babylonian Talmud Hullin 109a–110b to argue that the animal mother shadows rabbinic thinking about this prohibition.

The commandment to send the mother bird from her nest before taking her eggs or chicks, known in Jewish tradition as *shiluach haken*, is found in Deuteronomy 22:6–7. Chapter 5, "Animal Fathers and Other Caregivers: Sending Off the Mother Bird," addresses dominant perspectives on the mother-bird mitzvah—its association with good fortune and virtuous behavior—before showcasing rabbinic texts from Mishnah and Babylonian Talmud Hullin Chapter Twelve that offer a "bird-centric" approach. The Rabbis portray birds as brilliant architects who build nests in a variety of locations with a wide array of materials, as parents with complex and cooperative caregiving arrangements, as moral actors who cleverly resist human repression, and as neighbors who live right alongside humans, sharing with them the same intimate spaces.

The Mishnah groups together the animal-family laws, except for one. The Mishnah devotes chapters to all but the commandment to keep the animal with the mother for the first week of life, found in Exodus 22:29 and Leviticus 22:27. Chapter 6, "Animal Orphans: Keeping the Baby with the Mother for the First Week of Life," proposes that the Rabbis, rather than develop this requirement, instead gave their energies to defining, legislating, and telling stories about the animal orphans who have lost their parents to slaughter.

The conclusion, "What Families Teach Us About Animals," reverses the terms of the title to reflect further on the two big ideas in this book: the animal and the family. I share several ancient texts about animal families and urge us to explore animal kinship there and in the many other places, both ancient and modern, that animal families appear. In an epilogue, I and coauthor Rabbi Melissa Hoffman of the Center for Jewish Food Ethics recommend specific strategies people can use in their own lives today to support animal families.

INTRODUCTION TO KEY WORDS AND WORKS IN RABBINIC LITERATURE

For those unfamiliar with rabbinic literature, I offer here a brief orientation.[53] The Rabbis trace their lineage back to Moses himself, with Mishnah Tractate Avot telling a story of the transmission of Torah from Mount Sinai to elders, prophets, and the "members of the Great Assembly," on to a series of "pairs," and then to the Rabbis, who depict themselves as emerging in the first century CE at about the time of the destruction of the Second Temple in Jerusalem. Scholars in recent years have shifted their position on the question of the Rabbis' power and influence among the Jewish population of Roman Palestine and the degree of their integration into the Roman cultural world. The current consensus is that the early Rabbis held limited and largely informal legal authority and that they were Romanized provincials who possessed a complicated relationship to imperial culture.[54] The impact of the Roman Empire's Christianization and of the Sasanian Empire's "state of mixture," as historian Richard Payne puts it, are the major lines of inquiry for the later rabbinic movement as it split into eastern (Babylonian) and western (Palestinian) branches and, ultimately, developed a greater degree of institutionalization, particularly in the East with the rise of Islam.[55]

The literary output of the Rabbis can be divided between the early works authored by the Tannaim (literally "repeaters" or "teachers"), the term for the Rabbis who lived until the turn of the third century CE, and the later works that cite the Amoraim (literally "sayers"), which refers to the Rabbis who lived in the third through fifth centuries. The early works, composed in Hebrew, include the Mishnah, Tosefta, and collections of midrash halakhah, or legal exegesis (even though some of the material is not of a legal nature). The major difference between the Mishnah and Tosefta on the one hand and the midrash halakhah collections on the other is their organization and internal structure, with the Mishnah and Tosefta arranged according to legal topic and the midrash halakhah arranged exegetically as a commentary, with collections dedicated to the books of Exodus, Leviticus, Numbers, and Deuteronomy, respectively. Which of these genres came first, midrash or Mishnah, or whether they developed in tandem remains a question, as does the main mode of transmission, whether oral or written or some combination.[56]

The question of oral versus written transmission becomes more pronounced for the relatively elaborate literary productions of the later period, the "amoraic" midrash collections and the two Talmuds, one from Byzantine Palestine and the other from Sasanian Babylonia (modern-day Iraq), both organized as commentaries on the Mishnah. The two Talmuds but especially the Babylonian Talmud possess a rich literary texture composed of biblical, tannaitic, amoraic, and anonymous editorial literary strata that are each marked out as distinct, with frequent language shifts between Hebrew and Aramaic.[57] Whether and to what extent these strata are in fact historically distinct and, beyond that, whether the various Rabbis mentioned were living historical figures are the subject of scholarly debate. The most hotly debated questions surround the authorship of the voluminous anonymous editorial material, the so-called Stam or Stammaim (literally "anonymous one/s"), that gives the Babylonian Talmud its distinctive flavor. When and where did they live? How many were there? How much material did they inherit, and how much did they invent? What was their aim? How did they work? Even the earliest partial manuscripts of the Talmud do not appear until well into the medieval period, leaving the period of composition shrouded in mystery.

In this book I follow what I consider to be the consensus position on key questions such as the Romanization of the Rabbis (it's complicated) and the degree of invention to attribute to the Babylonian Talmud's anonymous editors (it's also complicated). I take an agnostic position on the historicity of specific rabbinic figures, whom I describe in the book as "putatively" of whatever generation and period the Talmud itself assigns them. The main corpora that I discuss are the Mishnah, Tosefta, and Babylonian Talmud, with some reference to tannaitic and amoraic midrash collections and somewhat less to the Palestinian Talmud. The Palestinian Talmud does not feature commentary for the main Mishnah and Tosefta sections that I discuss in the order of Kodashim ("Sacred Things," referring to sacrificial offerings), mainly tractate Hullin, which treats several of the scriptural laws that are the subject of this book. Because critical editions for the Mishnah and Babylonian Talmud have so far been difficult for scholars to produce, I cite the Kaufmann manuscript of the Mishnah, considered to be the best witness, and the standard Vilna printed edition of the Babylonian Talmud, with reference to significant manuscript and printing variants.[58] For midrash halakhah I cite standard critical editions, and for the Tosefta I cite Moses Zuckermandel's edition.[59] English translations of rabbinic literature are my own, though I consult and sometimes cite the new Oxford translation of the Mishnah and Adin Steinsaltz's translation of the Babylonian Talmud.[60] I follow the Society for Biblical Literature's general-purpose transliteration style for Hebrew and Aramaic, with a few exceptions.[61] I use the Jewish Publication Society's English translation of the Hebrew Bible, also with some of my own alterations.

NOTE ON GRAMMAR: WHO DESERVES A "WHO"?

Grammar checks tend to think that animals are objects and that they have no gender. "Who" gets corrected to "that" and "he" and "she" to "it." The same is true for standard translations of the Bible and rabbinic canon, which usually use the grammar of "things" when translating animal subjects. In this book I do it differently, using the same rules for animals that I do for humans. That means, when I am speaking of animals in my own voice, I use whatever grammar I would normally use for humans. This gets tricky, admittedly, around gender, since it is not clear how to give animals the same care we give to ourselves and one another when it comes to grammatical choices for gender (animals aren't going to share their pronouns with us). It feels strange, then, to use masculine and feminine grammar in a straight-up biological way for animals when I no longer do that with people. Still, it feels stranger, and less respectful, to use the genderless, neuter language of things for animals. With those problems in mind, I tend to use "they" for animals to be gender-inclusive or gender-agnostic. When translating, I try to reflect the grammatical gendering in the ancient texts. When using family terms for animals, I use the same terms that I would use for humans (e.g., mother, father, parent, daughter, son, child, grandmother), and, when translating family terms, I follow the usage of the original text (e.g., if the original text uses the same term for a human mother and an animal mother, so do I) to accurately reflect ancient family discourse. For brevity I use the term "animal" instead of "nonhuman animal," which many animal studies scholars have adopted to make the important point that we humans are animals too, so I ask my readers each time they encounter the word "animal" to imagine a phantom "nonhuman" preceding it.

1 Do Animals Love Their Children?

THE SCIENCE OF ANIMAL FAMILIES

THE FAMILY MYTH

Do animals love their children? One wonders why the question needs to be posed in the first place, but a long tradition exists of denying that animals feel love or, indeed, anything at all. The Cartesian perspective is that animals are like machines, driven by instinct to do what it takes to survive.[1] The absence of parental love is only remarkable, in fact, if one assumes that it is natural. That assumption belongs to what biologist Scott Forbes calls the "family myth."[2] According to the family myth, families are nurturing and harmonious. Parents love their children and distribute that love equally. As an expression of that love, parents care for their children, feed them, teach them, and sometimes risk their lives for them. Parental neglect, abandonment, and abuse are signs of dysfunction. Incest and infanticide are severe pathologies or simply inexplicable.

Forbes points out, though, that in reality much of family life in the animal world, including the world of humans, is a "story of Darwinian live and let die." Parents can be loving but they can also be selfish and cruel and everything in between. Families are "forums for rival evolutionary agendas where brothers and sisters, parents and offspring, cooperate, compete, deceive, and nurture. . . . There is strategy, counterstrategy, and layers of intrigue."[3] So while animal parents, including human ones, do often love their children and devote themselves to their care, love is not the only emotion one should expect to see (as anyone with a parent or child already knows). Parents also habitually harass, abuse, and abandon their children and in some cases kill them and even eat them.[4] They play favorites among them and tolerate or foster sibling rivalries (read *King Lear*). Parents often have more children than they can provide for and so will choose which child to support and which to not. Parents naturally love their children, but they also naturally feel a lot of other things too.

If we are to fully understand animal families, it is worth asking whether animal parents love their children just as long as we remember that love is not the only emotion that characterizes the parent-child relationship. This chapter's premise is that modern scientific data about the animal parent-child bond can illuminate the realities that the Bible's animal-family laws were grappling with and that we are still grappling with today. I start with two fundamental questions: Do animals even have feelings in the familiar sense? The follow-up question, assuming that animals do have feelings, is whether they are able to recognize their parents and children to possess distinctively *parental* or *filial* feelings. That data lays the groundwork for my main subject in this chapter, which is animal parent-child love and its loss, both in antiquity and today. How are the Bible's animal-family laws trying to manage or mitigate the costs of the parent-child separation that occurs in animal agriculture?

DO ANIMALS HAVE FEELINGS?

In René Descartes's own time, his notion of the "beast-machine" (*bête-machine*) had many detractors, who called it an "impossible and ridiculous claim" and an "internecine and murderous view."[5] It was not until Charles Darwin, the first scientist credited with a systematic study of emotions in animals, that the Cartesian view was countered with empirical data. In his best-selling 1872 book *Expression of the Emotions in Man and Animals*, which started out as a chapter in his *Descent of Man* but grew long enough to become its own monograph, Darwin argued that other species are capable of having emotions.[6] Darwin's aim in the book was to support his theory of evolution by showing the continuities in emotional expression across human races and animal species. Storks get sexually excited, observed Darwin; bees get angry, and monkeys get irritated. Darwin's conclusion was that emotions are critical to the welfare of humankind and that we should study them in both humans and animals.[7]

The behaviorist paradigm of animal science that emerged in the twentieth century rejected Darwin's call. While not entirely a throwback to Descartes's animal-machine, the behaviorist model considered the attribution of emotions to animals to be anthropomorphic projection and "mentalist extravagance."[8] "Experiment much and speculate little" was psychologist Robert Yerkes's motto.[9] But Darwin's approach ultimately won the day. In Austria, at around the same time in the 1920s and 1930s that Yerkes was running his famous experiments on chimpanzees, zoologist Konrad Lorenz was unabashedly ascribing psychological states to the animals, primarily birds, whom he was beginning to study. By the time the careers of Lorenz and his future partner in the Nobel prize, Niko Tinbergen, were in full swing, the Americans had come round, and the field that Lorenz and Tinbergen pioneered, ethology, the study of animal behavior, had become common in the United States even if it still provoked controversy.

Ethology turned toward questions of animal mind, consciousness, and complex thinking in the 1940s and 1950s with the work of American zoologist Donald Griffin, founder of the field of cognitive ethology.[10] Griffin and his American colleagues still resisted talking about animal emotions, however.[11] That changed in the 1960s, when a number of European scientists immigrated to the United States, and the two groups began to mix more, leading the American scientists to become just as interested in animal emotions as their colleagues across the sea. Philosophers jumped on board, with Thomas Nagel publishing his influential essay "What Is It Like to Be a Bat?" in 1974.[12] Also critical to the new inquiry was the work of Estonian American neuroscientist Jaak Panksepp, who coined the term "affective neuroscience" for the study of the neural basis of emotions.[13] Panksepp became famous for experiments in which he tickled rats and got them to laugh. While still riven with debate, the study of animal emotions has entered the scientific mainstream and reached popular audiences through the work of scientists such as Marc Bekoff, Frans de Waal, Jane Goodall, Barbara King, and Carl Safina.[14] It has also become fully integrated into the humanities in the form of affect theory and the history of emotions.[15] My guess is that if philosopher Peter Singer were writing *Animal Liberation* today, his classic of animal rights, he would not find it necessary to spend five pages in the introductory chapter arguing that animals are capable of having feelings.[16]

Why wouldn't animals have emotions? (I will here sidestep difficult questions regarding what exactly an emotion is; what the difference is between an emotion, a feeling, and a mood; how many basic emotions there are; how emotion is related to consciousness and cognition; in what way emotion is rooted in the brain and body; and, the sixty-four-thousand-dollar question, the extent to which emotions are socially constructed.) It makes good evolutionary sense for animals to have emotions. Emotions are the social glue that bonds individuals with one another and catalyze a wide variety of social encounters.[17] Biologist Jonathan Balcombe observes that animals would not survive without pleasure impelling them toward certain experiences and pain discouraging them from others.[18]

But how do we humans know what animals are feeling if we are unable to ask them? "Anthropodenial," a term coined by primatologist Frans de Waal to refer to the human tendency to deny continuities between humans and other species, may lie behind our resistance to recognizing animal emotions, but the question of how to identify those emotions with scientific rigor is nevertheless a legitimate one.[19] The first clue is behavioral flexibility. When faced with new situations, animals make choices based on past experience. Such flexibility, Marc Bekoff explains, is the hallmark of emotion and consciousness.[20] Also pointing to the presence of emotion in animals (at least vertebrates) are their sensory systems and neural circuits, which are essentially the same as those that supply emotions in humans. It stands to reason those systems supply other species with emotions too. The final clues are the ones we use with our fellow humans to discern their emotions: facial expression, vocalization, posture, movement, and smell. A scientist familiar enough with an animal population will be able to read these clues (as will any human sufficiently attentive to an animal companion). Noninvasive neural imaging techniques such as functional magnetic resonance imaging (fMRI) and positron-emission tomography (PET) scans make it possible for scientists in the lab to test the intuitions about animal emotions that they develop in the field.

DO ANIMALS RECOGNIZE THEIR PARENTS AND CHILDREN?

One of the seven primary emotional systems that Panksepp identified in mammals is care or, one might call it, love. But does that necessarily mean that animal parents love their children and vice versa? How do we know that animals can even recognize their children and parents? Oedipus did not do a very good job of it, and neither did Isaac in Genesis. Hospitals would not need to put wristbands on newborns if we humans excelled at identifying our young. The problem of kin recognition belongs to the scientific field known as kinship selection theory, in which a critical line of inquiry is kin recognition or discrimination—how an individual recognizes their kin to provide advantages to them and avoid mating with or harming them.[21] Because investing in nonkin detracts from an individual's ability to invest in their kin and maximize their genetic contribution to the next generation, parent-child recognition is a key piece of the evolutionary puzzle. That is especially the case for mammals, for whom lactation and nursing constitute an enormous investment of time, energy, and resources.

The first step of parent-child recognition is called the maternal recognition of pregnancy, which refers to the mother's bodily response to the embryo that establishes and maintains the pregnancy.[22] The question of mother-child recognition in the sense of behavioral discrimination—*this* one and not *that* one is mine—comes into play once the mother gives birth to the baby and they interact postpartum. It would seem obvious that mothers would very soon after that point recognize their child and vice versa, especially if the relationship unfolds predictably in time and space. New settings inevitably present themselves, however, such as when a cow and a calf interact in the context of the herd.[23] In high-mobility species, the young are likely to spend substantial time separated from parents and in mixed social groups. The periods of separation make mechanisms of parent-child recognition important—something akin to the hospital wristbands that let parents know which baby is theirs.

Such mechanisms begin operating already in the prenatal phase, with auditory cues from the mother's vocalizations and chemical cues from the mother's physiology, diet, and environment.[24] Rats prenatally exposed to apple juice in their amniotic fluid drank more apple juice than water when given the choice, whereas rats not exposed showed no preference. The learning that takes place in utero facilitates recognition after birth. At that point all the major sensory modalities—vision, audition, olfaction, and touch—are set into motion to support the mutual recognition of mothers and infants. Mothers of many species have been shown to recognize their infant's visual appearance, vocalizations, and smell. Infants, in turn, discriminate between their mothers and strangers based on the same sensory modalities that mothers use to recognize the infants. The release of peptides and neurotransmitters in both mother and child facilitates the sensory capacities.

Examples abound. Sow and guinea pig mothers have been found to recognize their children when their children call to them.[25] Among farmed Iberian red deer, mothers and calves responded more strongly to recorded calls of each other than to others.[26] Northern fur seal mothers and pups use a well-developed multimodal recognition system to routinely find each other within sometimes very large groups.[27] Australian sea lion mothers and pups also use a combination of olfactory, acoustic, and visual cues—each type of cue offers advantages but also has environmental limitations—to recognize each other.[28] Mother sheep and goats bond with their infants on the basis of olfactory recognition, but even when olfactory cues are removed, it has been shown, the animals are able to identify each other.[29] When both olfactory and visual exposure are removed, mother goats are able to recognize their newborns by their bleats alone.[30] In other words, redundancies are built into recognition systems so that animal mothers and infants have many different media through which to identify each other.[31]

Mother-child recognition has been established across species that include wood lice, honeybees, cockroaches, fish, bats, monkeys, cats, and cattle.[32] That is not to say that the recognition mechanisms do not sometimes fail or that infant welfare is dependent solely on animal mothers; fathers, siblings, alloparents, and other helpers all play significant roles as complements or substitutes.[33] My Instagram algorithm is keen on showing me the caregiving relationships that form across species lines—a group of bears who adopt a lost dog, a sheep who raises a baby elephant. Still, in mammals, biological mothers have a distinctive role to play due to their bearing and nursing of babies. "Indisputably, for mammals, mothers matter."[34]

WHAT ARE THE SIGNS OF ANIMAL PARENT-CHILD ATTACHMENT?

I turn from the many different means by which parents recognize their children to the many different ways parents care for them.[35] Zoologist David Gubernick lays out six criteria for parent-child attachment in mammals: (1) preferring the attachment figure over others; (2) seeking and maintaining proximity to that figure; (3) responding to a brief separation from that figure; (4) responding to extended periods of separation; (5) responding to a reunion; and (6) (this one is from the perspective of the child) using the attachment figure as a secure base from which to explore the world.[36] Another criterion (this one from the perspective of the parent) is "mama bear"-style aggression in the face of threats to the child.[37]

Just as recognition begins in utero, so too does care. Maternal responsiveness is associated with estradiol and progesterone produced by the ovaries, prolactin and oxytocin released by the brain and pituitary gland, and elevated levels of corticosterone and cortisol during the late stages of pregnancy.[38] Then, during birth (called "fetal expulsion" in the literature or, less evocatively, "parturition"), a mother's hormone ratios continue to fluctuate to prepare them physiologically for maternal care. An important element in the process is what scientists call "vaginocervical stimulation," VCS for short, which refers to the stimulation of the genital tract that takes place during birth—scientists Lorel Mayberry and Jacqueline Daniel call it "birthgasm."[39] VCS causes dramatic changes in the release of hormones and neurotransmitters and is critical for triggering the mother's attraction to the newborn infant.[40]

The mother-child bond in mammals is evident immediately after birth. Biologists speak of parental care, expenditure, investment, effort, and effect, each of which refers to a different feature of the parent-child relationship.[41] The mother usually displays rapid interest in the newborn infant, cleaning the baby by licking them, in the process consuming the placenta, fetal membranes, and amniotic fluids and stimulating the baby's breathing, urination, and defecation.[42] The mother also vocalizes and shows behaviors of retrieving, gathering, herding, and carrying that protect the young and keep them close.[43] Marsupials spring to mind, the mother's body equipped with its own built-in baby carrier. Biologists call the mother's affiliative behaviors "maternal acceptance," which is predicated on what scientists call "maternal motivation," which describes the neural processes that mediate the mother's attraction to the newborn and their interactions.[44] The newborn in turn experiences an activation of systems that facilitate development of a preference for the mother and motivate behaviors to attract the mother's attention.[45] The bonding behaviors between mother and child have documented physiological rewards such as reduced heart rate and release of opioids.[46] Mother and child feel physically better when they are together. These behaviors and states of being are essential for socializing young animals and teaching them information critical to survival.[47]

The most important care behavior on the mammal mother's part is nursing. The infant's ingestion of colostrum and oral sucking behaviors are significant factors in the formation of the filial bond.[48] Some ruminants such as goats are "hiders"—mothers leave their infants for several hours, who "hide" while the mother is gone and nurse once the mother returns. Others such as sheep are "followers"—the lambs nurse while they move around with the ewe, and when the ewe rejoins the flock, so do they.[49] Cyclical patterns govern the time that mother and child spend together. Feeding periods are frequent at first, lasting from one and a half to three minutes, and get progressively shorter until they are down to about twenty seconds—a quick suck.[50] Without interference lambs normally stop nursing between four and six months of age, goats between three and six months, and calves between nine and eleven months.[51] In large-bodied mammals, the rule is that weaning occurs when the infant has grown to four times its birth weight, at which point the mother animal will produce less milk and begin to reject the child's nursing attempts.[52] The nursing cycle has at this point run its course.

The weaning of the child and the birth of subsequent children do not necessarily mark the dissolution of the mother-child bond.[53] We humans are not the only species in whom parents and children continue to have contact after childhood. Cows prefer their own calves even after weaning, and ewes associate with their lambs even after younger siblings are born.[54] In species who live in social groups with overlapping generations, mothers and their children may remain together in the same social group not only for the initial bonding period but throughout their lives.[55]

WHAT HAPPENS TO ANIMAL FAMILIES IN MODERN AGRICULTURE?

The animal mother-child relationship I have just described—from maternal recognition to motivation to acceptance, through pregnancy, birth, nursing, weaning, and after—looks very different in most modern agricultural settings. Cows are first inseminated usually when they are two years old; sheep and goats (females are called ewes and does) are first inseminated within the year they are born.[56] In cows the gestation period is about nine months; in sheep and goats, it is about five.[57] Dairy cattle farms, both conventional and organic, typically separate the cow and calf from each other shortly after birth, within a few hours. The mother is returned to the stall, while female calves are placed either by themselves in individual housing or with other calves in a group. Male dairy calves, because they are less profitable, are in most places immediately killed.[58] In the meat industry, calves are usually separated from their mothers later, at around six months of age. Sheep and goats raised for meat and wool are generally forcibly weaned between thirty and ninety days of age.[59] When bred for the dairy industry, sheep are separated from their newborns twenty-four to thirty-six hours postpartum, though they are sometimes allowed to suckle their lambs for up to thirty days since the short nursing period has been proven to increase the growth rate of the lamb.[60] Goats raised for dairy are not permitted to nurse their newborns, who are removed right after birth.

A raft of reasons is offered for why mother and infant must be separated and why the separation should be done early.[61] The main economic reason for early separation in dairy animals is that it maximizes saleable milk. If the infant is fed through "artificial rearing," as the mechanized feeding system is known, the amount of milk administered can be controlled. Early separation also accelerates the reproductive cycle of the mother. The earlier the separation from the newborn, the sooner the mother is ready to bear another baby (and the shorter her expected lifespan becomes).[62] There are also constraints of space. The industrial farm is not built to accommodate mother-child pairs.[63] Other reasons cited for early separation are the fear that infants who suckle from their mothers will be harder to handle and the hypothesis that artificial rearing reduces risk of infection and allows for better control of the quality and quantity of colostrum.[64] There are ethical reasons cited too, which is that the delay in weaning only increases the distress that the inevitable separation will produce. Better to rip off the Band-Aid. These rationales for early separation have been disputed and in some cases disproven by research but they continue to drive modern industrial agricultural practices.[65]

WHAT HAPPENS WHEN AN ANIMAL MOTHER IS SEPARATED FROM HER CHILD?

The effects of separation on animal mother and child are well documented in modern veterinary research. The bond is compared by scientists Ruth Newberry and Janice Swanson with addiction and separation between the mother and infant with withdrawal. The frenetic desperation that an addict experiences when deprived of access to the intoxicating substance is not unlike the state of acute agitation that mother animal and baby experience when separated. Drawing on psychiatrist John Bowlby's attachment theory, Newberry and Swanson describe the states brought on by premature separation between mother and infant as "protest" and "despair," each of which is associated with behaviors designed to increase the odds of reunion.[66]

Newberry and Swanson describe a wide range of distress responses by mutually strongly bonded animal mothers and children: altered feeding and sleep patterns, suspension of play, elevated corticosteroid levels, changes in heart rate and core body temperature, increased and frequent high-pitched vocalization, and potentially injurious escape attempts. Separated cows and calves were found to have increased display of the whites of their eyes.[67] Greater incidence of disease, worse reproductive success, and higher mortality are all linked with stress in farmed animals, with forced weaning identified as one of the main stressors.[68]

The stress on the children is particularly pronounced. It can impede young animals' growth by causing them to eat less and impairing their digestive function. It can impair their learning, which may lead later in the animals' life to difficulty identifying opponents and recalling the outcome of fights, which in turn results in prolonged aggression.[69] Maternal loss and artificial rearing have been linked also to heightened fearfulness, worse coping strategies, and less interactiveness.[70] Separation can cause abnormal behaviors such as pacing, repetitive biting, and sucking the navel or scrotum of pen mates.[71] These abnormal behaviors can last long after the frustration of separation wanes or if conditions improve. Some stereotypic behaviors may manifest only later in adulthood. Less attention has been paid to the impact of separation on the mother, but some known effects are "reinstatement behaviors"—that is, efforts to reunite with the child, decreased milk production, higher heart rate, and less lying down.[72]

Animal handlers have experimented with techniques to reduce the negative impact of separation. Keeping mother with child especially in the early "sensitive period" is an obvious solution but one not normally considered feasible in the context of modern industrial agriculture.[73] Farmers who try to delay separation for as long as possible report that the standard barn design is a major obstacle.[74] Preventing the mother and infant from forming a bond in the first place is a common alternative. Immediate removal of the newborn baby short-circuits maternal responsiveness, which fades within a few hours and is not immediately sparked even when the mother is reunited with the infant.[75] A review of studies found that immediate removal has worse long-term outcomes, however, not better, even if it avoids an acute distress response.[76]

Modern agriculturalists have devised a host of in-between strategies that entail neither total separation nor unconstrained bonding. These include delayed separation, such as at fourteen days; intermittent or gradual separations, such as half-day contact or allowing suckling only at the time of milking; and fenceline contact, which permits cows and calves to see each other through the fence but not to have physical contact. These modified separations (called "progressive," "two-stepped," or "mixed regime" weaning) have been shown to lead in some cases to better welfare outcomes but in other cases to increased susceptibility to mood and anxiety disorders, infections, and poor weight gain.[77] Some agriculturists have experimented with foster cow systems, in which calves nurse from a "wet-nurse," a lactating cow who is designated for this purpose.[78] Housing arrangements have a major impact. Weaned animals kept in a familiar environment adjust more easily to the separation than those who have been moved to a new space or mixed with new peers, according to studies of pigs, guinea pigs, lambs, and primates.

Methods for alleviating the anxiety of separation for young animals will sound familiar to human parents.[79] Infants may be offered an artificial teat, similar to a pacifier, as a substitute for the udder. Infants may be temporarily fitted with an antisucking device that prevents them from nursing and encourages them to eat solid food. The udder might be covered with what is called a nose flap, which makes the infant unable to suck. Much the way nursery school teachers comfort their pupils when upset, human handlers have been instructed to groom and stroke baby animals to replace the mother's bonding and consoling behaviors.[80] Other pacification strategies that have been tried are meditation music or white noise (a study showed that piglets in fact find silence more calming[81]); mirrors (it worked better in cows than in sheep); play opportunities and novel stimuli (akin to a good preschool environment[82]); and pharmacological intervention such as opioids, oxytocin, and prolactin.[83]

HOW WAS ANCIENT AGRICULTURE DIFFERENT?

These practices characterize modern industrial farming and not the more sustainable systems of the past. Ancient Israelites were, in some periods and places, sedentary herders—that is to say, settled farmers whose animals supplemented and supported the grains, olives, grapes, and other produce that they grew. In other cases Israelites were nomadic or "transhumant" (seminomadic) herders whose animals played a more central role in supporting them. (While herders and farmers are often seen as pitted against each other, in fact there was an overlap as well as a symbiotic relationship between the two.)[84] Herders kept small cattle—sheep and goats—at changing ratios, which they raised for wool or hair, milk and dairy products, meat, skins, hooves, horns, fats, sinews, bones, and dung.[85] They kept fewer large cattle—cows, bulls, oxen, and donkeys—who were more costly to maintain and used primarily for labor and transportation.[86]

The biblical laws about animal families are premised on the separation of animal parents from children, but the laws do not shed much light on the practices that surround that separation. The law in Exodus 22:29 and Leviticus 22:27 prohibiting the separation of mother from child in the first week of life implicitly permits separation immediately after the first week, but the biblical passages do not indicate whether early separation would have been routine the way it is in the modern dairy industry, which is able to feed the infants formula or refrigerated milk, an option that ancient farmers did not have. The laws prohibiting cooking kids in their mother's milk (Exodus 23:19, 34:26; Deuteronomy 14:21) and killing an animal parent and child on the same day (Leviticus 22:28) imply separation through slaughter, but the laws do not shed light on the question of when animal mothers and children would typically have been separated and what kind of contact they may have continued to have. The law in Deuteronomy 22:6–7 requiring the mother bird to be removed before taking her eggs or chicks explicitly thematizes separation, though that law deals with wild animals rather than domesticated ones and birds rather than mammals.

Features of life in biblical Israel that point to the relatively early separation of domesticated animal mothers from their children are the regular use of milk (the promised land is repeatedly characterized as flowing with milk and honey), the serving of young animals as a delicacy, and the command to sacrifice year-old animals, usually male.[87] The optimal age from an economic perspective for slaughter of the child is either right after weaning, at two to six months of age, or at a year old, since that timing places the mother at the height of her milk production without the farmer having had to put significant investment into the child.[88] The zooarchaeological record from Iron Age Levant features many juvenile (less than one-year-old) and subadult (one- to three-year-old) animals.[89]

The evidence taken together suggests that in ancient Israel mother animals would have been separated from their daughters, who could produce their own milk and offspring, less frequently than from their sons, who were considered less valuable because they produced neither milk nor offspring and therefore would have been killed young, minus the few males who would have been needed to replenish the herd. That does not mean that animal mothers and daughters would have lived in uninterrupted harmony. When mother animals reached the end of their reproductive lives, they too would have been "culled," just as their young sons had been.[90] Animal mothers would have also been temporarily separated from their infants while they were nursing them so that ancient Israelite herders could siphon off milk for their own family. The names of the matriarchs Rebecca and Rachel point to a system of constraint: Rachel means "ewe" and Rebecca *(rivkah)* refers to a row of tied animals.[91] The ewes— the "Rachels"—would likely have been tied up together into a "Rebecca" while they were being milked each morning and evening.[92]

Moving into later antiquity, we have more evidence for animal agriculture. Second-century-BCE Roman writer Varro, in his agricultural manual, advises against milking mother animals while they are still nursing their babies. Mother and baby sheep should be kept together in their own separate pen for the first two or three days after birth, recommends Varro, so that the babies learn to recognize their mother and can get their first nourishment from the mother undisturbed. After that, mother sheep should feed their lambs each morning and evening but rejoin the herd for grazing during the day. Mothers should still be separated from lambs during sleep, however, to protect the infants from being crushed during the night. Varro gives lactation tips for a lamb who does not latch on properly to the nipple. After about two weeks, lambs should be given solid food. At four months they should be weaned. Varro is attentive to the psychological stress of weaning, saying that "care must be taken that they do not sicken from the separation" and instructing the herder to restore the lamb to the flock "only after they no longer miss the dam, because they have forgotten the taste of milk." Varro does not repeat the instructions for goats, but presumably it would be the same, though Varro does specify that the weaning time for kids is three months rather than four.[93]

Echoing Varro, first-century-CE Roman writer Columella recommends that the mother be kept together with the baby for the first two days after birth "so that she may cherish her offspring, and that it may learn to know her."[94] When the lambs reach full strength, their mothers should be brought to them midday and released with them to get them used to grazing. Columella makes similar recommendations for goats, saying that nannies should be kept together with their kids, though only if they had been of the right childrearing age and only until the kids are ready to be sold.[95] In some cases Columella clearly presumes early separation, such as when he recommends buying cows from a particular town near Venice because they nurse other cows' young if their own are taken, and the calves, for their part, can make do with beans and wine (a strange diet for a baby animal!) if no cow is available to nurse them.[96] Columella speaks of killing males at a relatively young age.[97] All told, Roman agricultural writers seem highly attuned to the bond between animal mother and child and to the risks of interfering with that bond to the psychological and physical welfare of the animals. At the same time, Roman writers allow for such interference when it is to the farmer's economic advantage.

When we turn to the Rabbis of Roman Palestine, we find various hints within the Mishnah regarding the experience of animal families. Mishnah Bava Kamma 7:7's ban on raising sheep and goats has long surprised readers, given how central small cattle are to many economies especially in the Middle East.[98] The ban notwithstanding, the Mishnah points to the pervasive presence of sheep and goats among the Jews of Roman Palestine.[99] That presence is confirmed by the archaeological record.[100] Herds of sheep and goats, raised primarily for wool and milk, would likely have been kept out in the desert or at the periphery of the settlement during the summer and then confined within the settlement in the winter.[101] Some sheep and goats would have been kept singly or in small groups in or near the settlement year-round, with professional shepherds sometimes hired to take them out for grazing.[102] The average smallholder would have also owned a donkey for transportation and a cow for threshing.

Like the Roman agricultural writers, the Rabbis show concern for the successful birthing and rearing of animals, as reflected in Mishnah Hullin 4's discussion of difficult animal labor and deliveries and Tosefta Shabbat 15:2's treatment of acts permitted during a festival to assist a newborn animal ("One blows into his nostrils and places the nipple into his mouth and holds the baby so that he does not fall"). Tosefta Parah 2:3 speaks of a cow placed together with the mother while she threshes so that she can nurse.[103] Mishnah Bava Metzia 5:5 refers to different local customs regarding the separation of cows and donkeys from their children. In some places, according to the Mishnah, mother and child animals are divided immediately.[104] Mishnah Makkot 3:12 and Mishnah Avodah Zarah 1:6 imply that Jews slaughtered and sold lambs (though Jews must not sell lambs to gentiles, according to Avodah Zarah). Mishnah Bava Kamma 10:9 speaks of commerce with kids and calves. Mishnah Shabbat 16:5 speaks of kidskin being used to put out a fire. These passages, along with the predominance of young animals among the sheep and goat remains at several Roman period sites in Palestine, suggest that, on the Jewish farms of Roman Palestine, a substantial number of young animals would have been taken from their mothers, if not very soon after birth, then at least not long after, while they were still immature.[105]

The picture that emerges from ancient Israel and Roman Palestine of the mother-child bond among domesticated animals is that it was generally protected until the time of weaning and sometimes until the age of one year, at which point the mother-daughter bond had a far better chance of lasting than the mother-son bond did. Separation very soon after birth would have happened in some cases, as would separation at annual cullings, when flock numbers were regulated according to the capacity of the land and the needs of the people farming it. Ancient Israelites and Jews were concerned with the welfare of their animal families since the welfare of their own families depended on them. Still, when those interests clashed, it was the welfare of their own families that they prioritized.

WHAT HUMANS HAVE IN COMMON WITH SHEEP

Many modern consumers of animals and animal products do not even know that animal agriculture separates animal families, often immediately after birth.[106] Ancient urban or semiurban dwellers, by contrast, were likely to encounter farm animals right in their houses, the first floors of which were often dedicated to the household animals. People living in rural environments would have interacted with flocks and herds in the cold weather and then seen them head out to greener pastures in the summer.[107] Shepherds would have had the greatest familiarity with the flocks and herds, though some farmers liked to take their own animals out to graze rather than hire someone else for the job.[108] None of these ancient populations could have read the modern scientific research, however, and only very elite ancient people would have studied the Roman agricultural manuals or the Mishnah. That being the case, would the ancients necessarily have understood the power of the animal parent-child bond any better than most of us do today?

To answer that question, I turn back to science. Here is Raymond Nowak and his team from the French National Institute for Agriculture: "Social attachment functions to facilitate reproduction and social cohesion, provides a sense of security and reduces the feeling of stress and anxiety. In that sense, in terms of the mother-infant attachment process, the sheep is rather similar to humans." Nowak goes on to name the similarities: both lambs and human babies are fully developed at birth, both form multisensory mental images of their attachment figure, and both species possess hypothalamic-limbic-cortical circuits that activate the parent's response.[109] Both sheep and humans also give birth singly or at most to several young and thus have an exclusive relationship with them, unlike pigs and many other mammals who have large litters. In sum it is not a big jump for us to understand the kinship bonds of sheep and other cattle. Ours are not very different. Anyone even superficially familiar with cattle is likely to pick up on the features of the parent-child bond that we have in common with them. For many of us today, the reality of animal families is a remote one. We do not experience it even with our pets, who usually come to us singly, already separated from kin. For ancient farmers, herders, and even urbanites, animal-family bonds would have been palpable in the voices, smells, and physical movements of the animals around them. When people broke those bonds, they knew it. Human handlers could see the distress of their animals literally in the whites of their eyes.

That distress has a very long history. Fossilized cattle remains date back two million years. Cattle drawings from France date back fifteen thousand years.[110] Archaeology shows two independent domestications of cattle, one in the Near East approximately ten thousand years ago, the *Bos taurus*, and another in Asia and Africa a couple of millennia later, the *Bos indicus*.[111] While human and animal interests were more aligned at earlier points in history than they are in contemporary industrial agriculture, the alignment was never perfect.[112] Human use of animal milk generally requires some form of separation between animal mother and child, relies on the exploitation of the animal maternal body, and marginalizes the male animal's role in the herd. Animal-milk consumption by humans dates back to Neolithic times, according to the analysis of pottery residue, human dental plaque, and animal-bone assemblages. The use of animal dairy was responsible for a revolution in human subsistence strategies that facilitated human population growth and spread.[113] It likely drove natural selection for people in Asia, Europe, and Africa who possessed lactate persistence, which allows for the digestion of milk into adulthood.[114]

People from the earliest period of milk consumption until today have had to grapple with their impact on the animals they raise for this purpose. As historian Deborah Valenze writes in her history of milk, "Anthropologists tell us that human consumption of animal milk and its products constitutes an aberration of animal nature that our ancient ancestors had to rework in their own minds. Denying young animals nourishment of their mother's milk puts progeny at risk; it requires inserting human agency where it does not belong."[115] Or, as political theorist Steve Cooke puts it, "It is an unavoidable part of animal agriculture that it requires disrupting, controlling, and eliminating many of the relationships that matter most to those animals."[116] Domestication and especially dairy use have animal-family trauma built into them.

When confronted with the trauma to the animal family caused by agriculture, people do not tend to like it.[117] Canadian researcher Lara Sirovica found in a sample of about 300 Canadians and 1,500 Americans that, when asked about severing the mother cow-calf bond, people considered it a breach of care.[118] One participant in Sirovica's study commented, "It's cruel to take a baby away from mother regardless of human or animal."[119] Some said the study's information about the early separation of mother from calf made them reconsider their decision to buy dairy products. A similar study by American animal-welfare specialist Beth Ventura found that "the idea of severing the bond provoked strong reactions, in part because the cow-calf bond was seen as similar to the human mother-child relationship."[120]

Farmers who really get to know their animals may, ironically, be more able to manage their animals' distress because it comes up in the context of a textured relationship. In her investigation of the commercial dairy industry in Washington State, Kathryn Gillespie found that workers developed an emotional distance from the animals, which Gillespie saw as a survival strategy for dealing with the large-scale daily trauma to animals that the workers witness.[121] Farmers of the past who did not tend to a thousand cows, supervise mechanized milking, and face the pressures of a global market were likely to have had a more comfortable emotional connection with their animals. James Rebanks observes that change happening in the course of his own lifetime on his family's farm in Ireland: "It was becoming clear to me that the way we thought about and interacted with our animals was changing. Our farm animals had never been pets, and we were rarely sentimental about them, but there was a lot of care involved and a kind of intimacy that vanished as things got bigger and more industrial. The farm animals' characters were well known to us: they all had backstories."[122]

Farmers used to know their animals' backstories. When they separated animal families, they understood the impact.[123] It is that sort of understanding—of the powerful bonds that animals have with one another and of the trauma it causes when those bonds are broken—that we can see reflected in the biblical laws about animal families, to which I now turn. By studying the biblical laws, we gain insight into those bonds and the way that people of the past approached them.

2 The Bible's Animal-Family Laws

WHAT ARE THEY, ARE THEY RELATED, AND ARE THEY HUMANITARIAN?

ANIMALS IN BIBLICAL LAW

The vegan paradise of the creation story in Genesis is, after the flood, replaced by a meat-eating world. God tells Noah and his children that animals are now fair game for food: "Every creature that lives shall be yours to eat; as with the green grasses, I give you all these" (9:3).[1] Humans must not eat animal blood, though, and they definitely should not spill one another's blood: "You must not, however, eat flesh with its life-blood in it. But for your own life-blood I will require a reckoning: I will require it for every living thing; of the human, too, will I require a reckoning for human life, of every human for that of his fellow human!" (9:4–5). Even animals—"every living thing"—can be guilty of homicide. One could describe God's sanction for murder—"Whoever sheds the blood of man, by man shall his blood be shed" (9:6)—as measure-for-measure, a life for a life, but that is only technically true for humans, since animal lives can be taken at will. This passage, in which animals are first the objects of divine legislation and then its subjects, illustrates the variety of ways in which animals feature in biblical law, alternately as objects and subjects, sometimes protected, at other times exploited with divine imprimatur, almost always depicted as pieces of property that form the medium for human conflicts and who are at the same time living creatures with unpredictable wills of their own who share many resemblances to humans.

Animals appear with frequency in biblical law, but they raise more questions than they answer regarding the Bible's thinking about them.[2] Are biblical authors concerned about animal welfare? The Bible may have been unique in the ancient Near East for evincing such a concern.[3] The Talmudic Rabbis were not so sure. They debated whether the Bible prohibits people from inflicting animal suffering (which is not quite the same as requiring people to promote animal welfare).[4] The laws requiring Sabbath rest for animals (Exodus 20:10, 23:12; Deuteronomy 5:14) and aid for an ox or donkey who has fallen (Deuteronomy 22:1-4, parallel in Exodus 23:4-5) and the prohibitions on muzzling an ox while treading grain (Deuteronomy 25:4) and yoking together an ox with a donkey (22:10) have been seen as evidence for such a concern. Do biblical authors have a concept of animal rights? Some biblical laws have been read this way.[5] Does biblical law presuppose that animals possess agency, subjectivity, and moral accountability? The laws of the goring ox in Exodus 21:28-32 imply that the ox has committed murder.[6] How does biblical law approach different species differently? The dietary laws make many distinctions among animal species. The rationale behind those distinctions has been the source of much speculation from antiquity to the present.[7]

The four biblical laws that address parent-child relationships among animals pose all these questions and more. Whether the laws are concerned with animal welfare, hold a concept of animal rights, presuppose animal agency and subjectivity, and apply differently to different species are all open to dispute. The answer may well vary for each law. The Bible furnishes no explanation for any of them, though it does in one case offer a reward: the person who sends off the mother bird before taking her chicks or eggs is promised a long life and prosperity. That reward might motivate a person to fulfill the law—it has that effect today when people in Israel and Brooklyn and elsewhere seek out opportunities to shoo mother birds away from their nests and take the eggs—but it does not reveal the reason God wants Israel to do it in the first place.[8] And it is God, one might keep in mind, who is making the demand, since, unlike in other ancient Near Eastern cultures, in which legislation represented the will of the king, the narrative of the

Pentateuch presents the four animal-family laws, along with the many other laws that the Bible features, as emanating directly from God. To violate these laws is not just to cross the king but to sin against the Lord.

In this chapter I take readers on a guided tour of the Bible's four animal-family laws. After looking at the laws in their literary context, I proceed to the explanation that has dominated their interpretation—the so-called humanitarian rationale. I use the term "humanitarian" to describe this rationale because it is the term, along with "humane," that many modern Bible scholars use and because the emphasis on the "human"—*human*itarian—in the context of *animal* compassion speaks to the larger paradoxes at work in this rationale. With those paradoxes in mind, I turn at the end of the chapter to criticisms of the humanitarian rationale.

DO NOT COOK A KID IN HIS MOTHER'S MILK

The most famous and also the most puzzling of the Bible's four animal-family laws is the prohibition against cooking a young goat in his mother's milk:

> You shall not cook a kid in his mother's milk.
> (Exodus 23:19, 34:26; Deuteronomy 14:21)

No explanation accompanies this thrice-repeated law, nor are certain features of the law clear, such as exactly what sort of cooking preparation is intended (boiling? roasting? frying? all of the above?) and whether the prohibition applies only to goats as specified or to all commonly eaten animal species such as sheep and cows.[9]

The context does not offer many clues. The prohibition against cooking kids in their mother's milk that appears in Exodus 23:19 caps off a miscellany of laws that includes prohibitions against sorcery, bestiality, apostasy, exploitation of vulnerable people, judicial malpractice, depletion of the land, and Sabbath labor. (This miscellany of laws also includes one of the other animal-family laws, to be discussed shortly.) The prohibition against cooking kids in their mother's milk forms part of a brief appendix to the festival calendar (Exodus 23:14–17), in which the prohibition is partnered with rules about animal sacrifice and first fruits:

> ¹⁸You shall not offer the blood of My sacrifice with anything leavened; and the fat of My festal offering shall not be left lying until morning. ¹⁹The choice first fruits of your soil you shall bring to the house of the ETERNAL your God. You shall not cook a kid in his mother's milk.
>
> (23:18–19)

The prohibition's appearance here in connection with laws about sacrifice and donation and then later again in Exodus 34:26, when the covenant is renewed after the episode of the golden calf and the same grouping of laws is repeated, would suggest that the ritual calendar is the proper context in which to understand it. The rules may have functioned as a set that covers the three pilgrimage festivals: the sacrifice of the paschal lamb on Passover (note the mention in Exodus 23:18 of leavening), the first fruits on the Festival of Weeks (Shavuot), and then the goat-cooking rule for the Festival of Booths (Sukkot).[10] But just how and why the prohibition against cooking a kid in his mother's milk would belong to the celebration of Sukkot is uncertain.

When the prohibition appears for the third time, in Deuteronomy 14:21, it is no longer in connection with festivals but instead stated as part of Deuteronomy's dietary laws. The prohibition concludes the list of animal species forbidden for consumption and follows immediately after a prohibition on eating animals who died a natural death. The prohibition against cooking kids in their mother's milk fits somewhat more naturally into the context in Deuteronomy as a rule that governs the consumption of animals but is awkward there too since it is about how to cook the animal rather than the animal itself and seems to dangle at the end of the chapter.[11] Deuteronomy's presentation of the prohibition as a part of everyday eating habits is somewhat more intuitive than the one in Exodus but still enigmatic.

KEEP THE BABY WITH THE MOTHER FOR THE FIRST WEEK OF LIFE

A second biblical law featuring the mother-child relationship among animals is the requirement to keep a newborn animal with the mother for the first week of life. This law appears twice in the Pentateuch, the first time in the same legal section of Exodus, called the Book of the Covenant, in which the goat-cooking rule appears:

> [28]You shall not put off the skimming of the first yield of your vats. You shall give Me the first-born among your sons. [29]You shall do the same with your cattle and your flocks: seven days he shall remain with his mother; on the eighth day you shall give him to Me.
> (22:28–29)[12]

This rule dealing with "firsts"—first produce, firstborn human sons, firstborn animals—is part of a loosely organized series of instructions that follows the core of law in Exodus 21–22.[13] There shall be no delays ("you shall not put off") in offering first fruits to God. But in the case of animals and possibly people too, one should wait out the firstborn's first week of life.[14] Only on (or, in some interpretations, any time after) the eighth day should the baby be donated.[15]

Biblical literature favors sevens: seven days of creation, seven days of the week, the seventh-year sabbatical, seven-day festivals, seven days before circumcision. Some or all these associations may lie behind the seven-day waiting period for animals, possibly accompanied by a practical concern that seven days are necessary to confirm that the animal being given to God is healthy or to stimulate the mother's milk production so that the farmer can use her for dairy. The delay may also reflect the fraught nature of maternal grief in the Bible.[16] Leaving aside the big question of whether donation in this passage refers to sacrifice and, if it does, whether the passage could be demanding human sacrifice ("You shall give Me the first-born among your sons"), one might note the parallel between plants, humans, and animals and the disruption of that parallel for the purposes of protecting the initial period of attachment between mother and baby.[17] The infant belongs to God as of day eight, but for the first week the baby belongs with the mother.

Leviticus appears to be adapting Exodus when it repeats the requirement to leave the baby animal with the mother for the first week of life:

> When an ox or a sheep or a goat is born, he shall stay seven days with his mother, and from the eighth day on he shall be acceptable as an offering by fire to GOD.
> (22:27)

The seven-day requirement—along with a rule prohibiting the slaughter of animal parent and child on the same day, to be discussed next—closes out the list of qualifications for sacrificial animals found in Leviticus 22:17–25, part of the Holiness Legislation, called "H" by Bible scholars.[18] Leviticus is here transferring the seven-day requirement from the context of firstlings to that of general votive and freewill offerings. When ancient Israelites respected the initial week of animal infancy—for *all* animals and not just firstborns donated to the priests, as the earlier law in Exodus dictates—they would have been building cosmological order into their regular sacrificial practices.[19] The "creation" of every animal mirrored the creation of the world.

DO NOT SLAUGHTER AN ANIMAL PARENT AND CHILD ON THE SAME DAY

Another way that Leviticus revises Exodus's seven-day requirement is to couple it with a new prohibition against slaughtering animal parents and their children on the same day:

> [27]When an ox or a sheep or a goat is born, he shall stay seven days with his mother, and from the eighth day on he shall be acceptable as an offering by fire to GOD. [28]But a herd or flock animal, him and his child, you shall not slaughter on the same day.
> (22:27–28)

By combining the seven-day rule with a new prohibition on the slaughter of animal parent and child on a single day, Leviticus produces an animal-family theme found nowhere else in the Pentateuch. The paired verses have a push-pull dynamic: at birth the child must remain with the mother; at slaughter the child must be separate. Leviticus may be innovating also by expanding the animal-family concern beyond the animal mother to include the father: the language it uses for the parent in Verse 28 is masculine, *oto ve-et beno*, literally, "him and his child."[20] Some ancient Jewish readers understood the prohibition to refer also to pregnant animals (slaughter of a pregnant animal means that parent and *fetus* are slaughtered on the same day).[21]

SEND OFF THE MOTHER BIRD

Finally, Deuteronomy features its own unique animal-family law:

> ⁶If, along the road, you chance upon a bird's nest, in any tree or on the ground, with fledglings or eggs and the mother sitting over the fledglings or on the eggs, do not take the mother together with the children. ⁷Send off the mother, and take only the young, in order that you may fare well and have a long life. (22:6-7)

When a person happens upon a mother bird roosting in her nest, they must not take her together with her chicks or eggs. The person may take the chicks or eggs, but only after first chasing away the mother bird.

Deuteronomy's law is different from the other three animal-family laws in several ways: the animal in question is not a mammal but a bird; the animal is not domesticated but one whom "you chance upon"; and the law is justified or motivated—that is, you chase away the mother bird "that you may fare well and have a long life." That motivation—reward of prosperity and long life—connects this law with a more famous one, the fifth of the Ten Commandments:

> Honor your father and your mother, as the ETERNAL your God has commanded you, that you may have a long life, and that you may fare well, in the land that the ETERNAL your God is assigning to you. (5:16)

The repetition of the same reward using the same language (though in reverse order) suggests that honoring the bird's mother-child relationship secures a good and long life in just the way that, according to Deuteronomy's decalogue, honoring one's own parents does.[22] The parent, whether human or animal, must be accorded respect.[23]

The mother-bird law may be linked also to another law in Deuteronomy, one of the rules of warfare:

> When in your war against a city you have to besiege it a long time in order to capture it, you must not destroy its trees, wielding the ax against them. You may eat of them, but you must not cut them down. Are trees of the field human to withdraw before you into the besieged city? (20:19)[24]

Like Deuteronomy 22:6–7, this law limits the damage that a human may inflict on the natural world. Here Israelites attacking an enemy city are prohibited from cutting down its trees, but they are permitted to take the fruit. The verse offers a rationale through the rhetorical question that it poses: "Are trees of the field human to withdraw before you into the besieged city?" Trees are not able to protect themselves from human violence in the way that humans (at least theoretically) can. In both laws the reproductive figure—in Deuteronomy 20, the fruit tree; in Deuteronomy 22 the mother bird—is shielded from harm while the produce (fruit and children) is permitted for food. The connection between the two laws suggests some similarity between the two scenarios: invading a city and invading a nest. That connection is strengthened by the expression that the mother-bird mitzvah uses for taking "the mother together with the children," used elsewhere in the Bible to refer to a brutal massacre.[25]

THE EVOLUTION OF THE ANIMAL-FAMILY LAWS

The animal-family laws present a striking series of patterns, permutations, and adaptations as they unfold across the major documentary sources of the Pentateuch. The earliest material in Exodus features a prohibition against cooking kids in their mother's milk in the context of the festival calendar (23:19, 34:26) and a requirement to keep the newborn animal together with the mother in the first week of life in the context of firstling donations (22:28–29). The two laws complement each other in their mutual concern for the relationship of young animals to their mothers. That concern is not found in the Code of Hammurabi, which was likely an inspiration for Exodus's Covenant Code. In giving consideration to the mother-child relationship among animals, the Bible appears to make a distinctive and original contribution to the culture of the ancient Near East.[26]

Deuteronomy broadens the scope of the concern by presenting the prohibition against cooking kids in their mother's milk as a general dietary law (14:21) rather than one related to the festival calendar and by composing a new law that prohibits a person from taking a mother bird along with her chicks or eggs (22:6–7). That law too relates to general everyday practice rather than to special events such as festivals or firstling donations. Deuteronomy explicitly connects that law to the high-profile command to honor one's parents (5:16) and knits it into a broader concern with the damage that humans inflict on the natural world (20:19).

Leviticus's prohibition against slaughtering an animal parent and child on the same day (22:28) recapitulates the themes of the mother-bird law and the mother's-milk law.[27] In combining the prohibition on slaughtering animal parent and child on the same day with a requirement to keep mother and baby together in the first week of life, Leviticus 22:27–28 offers a minipack of animal-family laws that resonates with the various earlier ones scattered across Exodus and Deuteronomy. The pair of laws participates in the Holiness Legislation's broader program of extending holiness from priests to laity and making holiness a dynamic quality to which the everyday Israelite might aspire.[28] In creating this couplet of laws, the Holiness Legislation also remedies the absence of legal treatment of animal families in the Priestly source, the sole Pentateuchal source with no animal-family laws.[29] In doing so the Holiness Legislation takes up the ancient Israelite interest in animal families and integrates it together with Priestly sacrifice, making the interest in animal families an enduring part of the biblical heritage.

THE HUMANITARIAN RATIONALE IN PHILO:
THE BARBECUE PIT TALKS BACK

I have covered the what, where, and when of the Bible's four animal-family laws but not the biggest question, the why. These laws have long presented a conundrum to interpreters. Each law respects and in certain ways protects the bond between animal parents and children yet at the same time presumes a violation of that bond through separation or slaughter. In the discussion that follows, I review the dominant approach to these laws going back to antiquity that sees in them a "humanitarian" concern. The oldest, most complete formulation of the humanitarian approach is from first-century Jewish philosopher Philo in his *On the Virtues*.[30] Philo's aim in the essay is to refute a negative stereotype of the Jews as misanthropes and of their laws as miserly and selfish. Philo's argument uses the logic of "all-the-more-so." If Israelite scripture shows compassion for animals—the implication being that animals are the creatures least deserving of it—then all the more so must Israelite scripture be dedicated to that virtue when expressed toward humans.[31] As evidence, Philo invokes the four animal-family laws along with several other biblical laws having to do with animals.[32]

Philo begins with the law that requires the baby animal to be left with the mother for the first week of life. Philo declares it a "cruel soul" who would separate animal mother and child immediately after birth merely to gratify the belly. Philo lays out a number of ethical problems: one causes the animal mother emotional distress; one causes her physical distress by interfering with her milk flow and causing her breasts to become swollen and painful; and one thwarts God's will, who endowed animal mothers with the capacity to bear and nurse children. Philo takes a moment to sing the praises of mother's milk for its capacity to satisfy both thirst and hunger and to keep the delicate newborn alive. Philo advises his readers to learn "family love" from lambs and kids.[33] (Elsewhere, in his discussion of the Ten Commandments, Philo says that animals are a good model for honoring parents and gives the example of birds who care for their elderly parents.[34]) In a bold rhetorical strategy, Philo adopts the voice of the Torah, Moses, or perhaps God himself when he reformulates the seven-day requirement as, essentially, a gifting suggestion: "Make a present . . . of the child to its mother, if not for all time, to be suckled, at least, for the seven first days."[35] The ideal in Philo's vision is for the animal family to stay intact, with the seven-day minimum a concession. Note, though, that while Philo's discussion relies throughout on the value of respect for the natural order, here he imagines the integrity of the animal family to be not endemic to the natural world but rather a human prerogative, a gift that God instructs Israelites to bestow at least temporarily on their flocks and herds.

Philo takes a similar approach to two of the other animal-family laws, the prohibitions on same-day slaughter and cooking kids in their mother's milk. He denounces the gluttony and savagery he sees in the two acts, both of which entail, in Philo's estimation, an incongruous and ethically abhorrent mixing of life with death.[36] In the most vivid passage, Philo conjures up the unnerving image of severed animal limbs speaking out from the barbecue pit:

Indeed, if one should mix the limbs of the two and fix them on the spits to eat of the roast, these limbs, I think, would not remain mute, but break out into speech, indignant at the enormity of the unexampled treatment which they suffer, and hurl a host of invectives against the greediness of those who prepare these meats, fitter for a fast than for a feast.[37]

The mother and child animals talk back, as it were, to the human roasting them on the same spit. It is not their slaughter that the animals object to (though one could imagine them making that objection as well) but rather the gross disregard for their intimate relationship. Philo's defense of Jewish philanthropy relies on the virtues of gentleness (in the case of the animal-family laws, by showing sensitivity to the distress of the animal mother); moderation (regarding food); respect for nature (exemplified by maternal attachment and lactation); honor of family (as modeled by lambs and kids); and regard for life (by not mixing it with death). But what sticks is less Philo's rational argumentation than the image he conjures of animals cursing out the barbecue master as they lie, kebabbed, on the callous man's grill.

THE HUMANITARIAN RATIONALE IN RABBINIC MIDRASH: *IMITATIO DEI*

Further on in this chapter I discuss the objections made within rabbinic literature to the humanitarian reading of these laws, but some Rabbis did espouse it, as one sees in the following passage from the midrash collection Leviticus Rabbah:

> Rabbi Berekhiah in the name of Rabbi Levi: It is written, "A righteous one knows the soul *[nefesh]* of his animal, but the compassion of the wicked is cruel" (Proverbs 12:10).
>
> "A righteous one knows"—this is the Holy One Blessed Be He, as it is written in His Torah, "Do not take the mother together with the children" (Deuteronomy 22:6).
>
> "But the compassion of the wicked is cruel"—this is Sennacherib the Wicked, as it is written, "Mother together with children were dashed to death together" (Hosea 10:14).

> Another interpretation: "A righteous one knows the soul of his animal"—this is the Holy One Blessed Be He, as it is written in His Torah, "However, you shall not slaughter an animal from the herd or from the flock on the same day with his child" (Leviticus 22:28).
>
> "But the compassion of the wicked is cruel"—this is Haman the Wicked, as it is written about him, "to destroy, massacre, and exterminate, etc. (all the Jews, young and old, children and women, on a single day)" (Esther 3:13). (27:11)[38]

Rabbi Berekhiah, a fourth-century figure from Roman Palestine to whom many homilies are attributed, transmits this piece of exegesis in the name of Rabbi Levi, a Rabbi from the previous generation famous for his inspirational homilies exhorting Jewish audiences to observe the Torah's commandments. The target verse of Rabbi Levi's exegesis is one from Proverbs that exhibits the typical one-line, two-verset structure, designed to contrast righteousness with wickedness using semantic parallels that together produce an ethical principle: "A righteous one knows the soul of his animal, but the compassion of the wicked is cruel" (12:10). In this proverb the implied ethical principle would appear to be some version of "real compassion is hard to find," with the righteous person's compassion extending even to his animal but the wicked man's "compassion," in quotes, a fraud, in truth a form of cruelty.

The word *nefesh* in the first verset, which I have translated as "soul," has a wide range of meanings—life, living being, breath, needs, person, personality.[39] The verse requires the translator to weigh in on the long-standing question of whether animals have souls.[40] How the translator handles *nefesh* will affect how they approach the verb in the verse, *yode'a*, which typically would be translated as "knows" but could here also mean "is concerned for, takes care of" or even "loves"—the righteous person loves his animal.[41] The second verset is in some ways the more difficult in that it is essentially nonsensical, saying literally that "compassion is cruel." The effect appears to be ironic, inviting readers to consider the paradoxes that different kinds of compassion entail.

Rabbi Levi corrects with his midrash what Bible scholar Robert Alter has called the "untheological orientation" of Proverbs by identifying the righteous person of the first verset with God.[42] The concern that God shows for the mother bird in Deuteronomy 22:6 is proof positive for Rabbi Levi that, in the Proverbs verse, God is the one who knows or loves his animal. Rabbi Levi associates the second verset's cruel faux compassion with the brutal violence described in Hosea 10:14, a prophecy of the fall of the Northern Israelite Kingdom in the mid-eighth century BCE to Assyria. Rabbi Levi identifies Sennacherib, Assyria's evil king, as the "wicked" of the proverb. Prophetic visions of Israel's fall to the wicked are not hard to find in the Bible, but Hosea's vision is uniquely suited to Rabbi Levi's context in its depiction of the murder of mothers and children, framed in almost the same language—"mother together with children"—that the mother-bird commandment uses.[43] Rabbi Levi's reading of the Proverbs verse combines Jewish theology and history as it contrast God's compassion for animal families with the Israelite enemy's obliteration of human families.

In the alternative homily appended to the first one, the structure is identical, but the verses have been swapped out—Leviticus 22:28 for Deuteronomy 22:6 (trading one family law for another) and Esther 3:13 for Hosea 12:10 (trading a depiction of the eighth-century-BCE decimation of Israelite mothers and children with an equally grim depiction of fifth-century-BCE murderous plans for Jewish mothers and children). The repetition of verbs in Esther 3:13, "to destroy, massacre, and exterminate," highlights Haman's genocidal designs, as does the plan spelled out in the rest of the verse to kill "young and old, children and women, on a single day." The reference to mass destruction on a single day, *beyom ehad*, to an attentive Bible reader such as Rabbi Levi, would bring to mind the very same expression in Leviticus 22:28, *beyom ehad*, with both verses expressing horror at the killing of parents and children, the young and the old, on the same day.

The creative connections that Rabbi Levi makes in these paired homilies, which bring together two animal-family laws (mother-bird and same-day slaughter) with two violations of Israelite families (Hosea 10:14; Esther 3:13), all under the umbrella of the target verse (Proverbs 12:10), leave the reader with the lesson that God's righteousness is reflected in God's protection of animal families, while the wicked, by contrast, show gross disregard for human families. A series of parallels scaffolds the midrash—God and people, people and animals, Israel and other nations—

as do contrasts between the righteous and the wicked and between compassion and cruelty. The midrash's presentation of the animal-family laws, which it reads in connection with biblical wisdom, prophecy, and narrative, creates something of an orchestral prelude to the Bible that highlights themes of kinship, care, and violence as they play out among God, Israel, and its enemies and among the divine, human, and animal.[44]

THE MEDIEVAL HUMANITARIAN RATIONALE: RASHBAM AND MAIMONIDES

I skip ahead to the humanitarian rationale as it surfaces in the medieval period in the Bible commentary of Rashbam (Rabbi Samuel ben Meir, ca. 1080–1160), the grandson of Rashi.[45] Like Philo and Rabbi Levi, Rashbam groups the animal-family laws together even though they appear in scattered parts of the Pentateuch. Also like Philo—though not like Rabbi Levi—Rashbam considers gluttony to be the vice that the animal-family laws are designed to combat:

> It is disgusting, voracious, and gluttonous to consume the mother's milk together with its young. This law is comparable to "it and its young" and to "letting the mother go." The text gave this commandment in order to teach you how to behave in a civilized manner [comment on Exodus 23:19].[46]

For Rashbam the aspiration of the animal-family laws is "civilized behavior" *(derekh tarbut)*, a neologism that developed in Rashi's school.[47] Evoking medieval Latin idioms of civility, Rashbam implies that the ideals of Western Christian society are the very same ones encoded in the animal-family laws.[48]

Moving from Ashkenaz to Sefarad and from Christian to Islamic realms, we turn to the humanitarian rationale as it is found in the *Guide for the Perplexed*, written in Judeo-Arabic by the towering figure of medieval Jewish thought, Maimonides (1138–1204). It is worth quoting the passage in full:

> It is also prohibited to kill an animal with its young on the same day, in order that people should be restrained and prevented from killing the two together in such a manner that the young is slain in the sight of the mother; in these

cases animals feel very great pain, there being no difference regarding this pain between man and the other animals. For the love and the tenderness of a mother for her child is not consequent upon reason, but upon the activity of the imaginative faculty, which is found in most animals just as it is found in man. This law applies only to ox and lamb, because of the domestic animals used as food these alone are permitted to us, and in these cases the mother recognizes her young. This is also the reason for the commandment to let [the mother] go from the nest. For in general the eggs over which the bird has sat and the young that need their mother are not fit to be eaten. If then the mother is let go and escapes of her own accord, she will not be pained by seeing that the young are taken away. In most cases this will lead to people leaving everything alone, for what may be taken is in most cases not fit to be eaten. If the Law takes into consideration these pains of the soul in the case of beast and birds, what will be the case with regard to the individuals of the human species as a whole?[49]

For Maimonides in the *Guide for the Perplexed* (I speak later of his commentary on the Mishnah and of his legal work the Mishneh Torah), the key to understanding the animal-family laws is concern about what the animal mother might see. Maimonides presents the prohibition against slaughtering parent and child animals on the same day as a precautionary strategy, its purpose to ensure that an animal mother does not see her child slaughtered. Why does the Torah wish to avoid such a scenario? Maimonides claims that maternal feeling is shared across most species. A mother's love is rooted in the "imaginative faculty" rather than intellect, which, Maimonides implies, is unique to human beings, unlike the imaginative faculty, which other animals possess.

Here Maimonides echoes a number of strains within medieval Islamic thought. In *Governance of the Solitary (Tadbīr al-Mutawaḥḥid)*, Ibn Bājja (known in Latin as Avempace), whom Maimonides elsewhere cites and praises, argues that animals grasp "particular spiritual forms" and mentions mother animals as an example.[50] Maimonides also here evokes Avicenna's claim that animals possess *wahm*, usually translated as "estimation." Avicenna says that *wahm* generates desire like that of the animal mother to be with her newborn child.[51] Further context for Maimonides can be found in the depiction of animals as loving parents found in the widely circulated "Case of the Animals" of the *Epistles of the Brethren of Purity* (though elsewhere Maimonides criticizes that work).[52] Also relevant from the Islamic milieu is a hadith tradition that appears in different versions in which the Prophet Muhammad castigates his companions for taking young birds (or eggs) from a nest while heartlessly ignoring the hovering mother bird. The Prophet orders his companions to return what they have taken.[53]

Maimonides proposes here in the *Guide for the Perplexed* that an animal mother whose child is killed before her eyes experiences great suffering. In line with that reasoning, Maimonides points out that the prohibition on same-day slaughter specifies herd and flock animals because they are species in which mothers recognize children (Maimonides here addresses what would become in modern times a major question for evolutionary biologists—kin recognition).[54] Maimonides's reading may at first glance seem straightforward but is in fact quite a creative elaboration of the biblical prohibition against same-day slaughter of animal parent and child, which neither specifies the mother nor expresses concern for what the animal parent sees.

The inspiration for Maimonides's understanding of the law about same-day slaughter may be the law about the mother bird, to which Maimonides turns next, which does specify the mother and does seem worried about what she sees. Maimonides seems closer to scripture's plain sense when he characterizes the purpose of shooing away the mother bird to be that "she will not be pained by seeing that the young are taken away." The trauma to parents of having their children taken away from them is not, of course, strictly a visual problem. Maimonides himself seems to recognize this when he goes on to say that "in most cases this will lead to people leaving everything alone." The law's ideal, in Maimonides's understanding, is for the passerby simply to let the mother bird be. At the root of Maimonides's explanation appears to be a genuine solicitude for the experience of animal mothers and for the integrity of animal families, yet Maimonides closes on an anthropocentric note: "If the Law takes into consideration these pains of the soul in the case of beast and birds, what will be the case with regard to the individuals of the human species as a whole?" Ultimately, Maimonides says, the law's value lies not in its concern for the well-being of animals but for that of the human species—"the human species as a whole"—his totalizing language emphasizing a binary between humans and all other animals.

In Maimonides's reading the animal-family laws are designed to minimize the harms that humans do to the animal family by keeping the animal mother from directly seeing those harms and by discouraging those harms in the first place.[55] If Philo's identification of the purpose of these laws is modest consumption, Leviticus Rabbah's is imitation of God's righteousness, and Rashbam's is civilized behavior, then Maimonides's is consideration for the feelings of the animal mother, a theme found also in Islamic traditions of the time.

THE MODERN HUMANITARIAN RATIONALE:
HUMANENESS AND *RAHAMIM*

I skip ahead again, this time to modern Bible scholarship. In his 1979 study of the prohibition on cooking kids in their mother's milk, Russian-born Israeli Bible scholar Menahem Haran comes to the conclusion that "all these commandments [the four animal-family laws] are based on humane considerations" and that they are "a deliberate reminder of humane behavior."[56] Haran does not elaborate on what he means by "humane," nor do most of the other Bible scholars who use similar language.[57] Jeffrey Tigay offers a somewhat fuller articulation when he says that the four animal-family laws "have the humanitarian aim of preventing acts of insensitivity against animals."[58] Even scholars who criticize the humanitarian rationale subscribe to the language, which has a curious application in this context given that the subject is animals. "Humanitarian" according to the *Oxford English Dictionary* refers to concern with *human* welfare. "Humane," the other term used by Bible scholars, is perhaps a better fit, which, according to the *OED*, entails "feeling or showing compassion towards humans *or animals.*"

What likely lies somewhere in the background of scholars' use of this language for the animal-family laws is the American Humane Society, a network of animal- and child-advocacy organizations whose origins are mingled with those of the American Society for the Prevention of Cruelty to Animals (ASPCA), both of which hark back to the late 1800s.[59] By the 1970s, when Haran's article came out, the American Humane Society had been instrumental in passing the Humane Methods of Slaughter Act and was just celebrating its centennial. A Peanuts cartoon showed Snoopy making out his will to the American Humane Society.[60] "Humane" was by then a word with firm associations with kindness to animals, and not a small degree of Christian supersessionism, given long-standing characterizations of the Old Testament, especially its laws, as lacking in mercy. When Jewish Bible scholars in the 1970s, 1980s, and 1990s characterize the animal-family laws as "humane," they not only evoke the modern history of animal advocacy but also slide into ancient grooves of Jewish-Christian apologetics. They also participate in a twentieth-century Jewish orientation toward humanitarianism and human rights, which gained unprecedented global prominence around the time of Haran's article's publication in the 1970s.[61]

Contemporary religious studies scholar and animal activist Aaron Gross uses the more native term *rahamim* to characterize the impetus of the animal-family laws (though those laws do not themselves use the term). Gross calls the Bible's four animal-family laws the "*rahamim* traditions." Gross understands rahamim in terms of its Hebrew root *rehem*, meaning "womb," and the associations with motherly concern, nurture, attachment, and empathy. Gross sees the rahamim traditions as lacing together "concerns about animal death and birth, a mandate not to cause animals to suffer, respect for animal bonding with mothers, a valorization of human and divine *rahamim*, and the meaning of being a Jew." Gross describes a cascading flow of rahamim set into motion by the animal-family laws. The laws presume that animals are capable of rahamim in their parent-child bonds; the laws require humans to show rahamim in the face of those bonds; God in turn shows rahamim to Israelites who show rahamim. Rahamim begets rahamim, which begets more rahamim. Gross points out that contemporary animal science confirms the biblical hypothesis that other species have the same capacity for rahamim—we might call it empathy or even a theory of other minds—that we humans do.[62]

These approaches to the animal-family laws from antiquity to the present have in common, first—and this may seem obvious but it should not be—reading the four laws together, in tandem, as a unit, even though they are dispersed throughout the Pentateuch (though not every approach I have reviewed mentions all four laws). These approaches all take some version of civility, compassion, empathy, or humaneness to be the main motive of the laws, though each writer in each period gives the motive different shading and speaks within and to a different context. Philo's agenda is to prove the philanthropic character of the Jews, but he is also concerned, as any good Stoically minded philosopher would be, with avoiding gluttony and with acting in accordance with nature. Rashbam likewise expresses a concern with gluttony but within the broader framework of Christian "civilized" behavior. Echoing Islamic traditions, Maimonides understands the purpose of the animal-family laws to be saving the animal mother from seeing the most harrowing moment of separation from her child. Modern Jewish Bible commentators use the language of humaneness and humanitarianism, tapping into modern animal and human rights trends, while Aaron Gross takes up the native Jewish term *rahamim* to convey the concern of the animal-family laws with the cultivation of empathy.

CLASSICAL RABBINIC OBJECTIONS TO THE HUMANITARIAN RATIONALE: "THEY DO NOT ACT WELL"

The humanitarian rationale has a long and varied history, I have shown, but so too do objections to it. The classical Rabbis are thought to largely reject the humanitarian rationale, but the relevant material is in fact ambiguous. The Mishnah mentions several formulas that a person leading public prayer must not say, one of which mentions a bird's nest:

> One who says, "May Your mercy reach the nest of a bird," or "May Your name be mentioned for the good," "[We] give thanks, [we] give thanks," they silence him.[63]

The prayer formula "May Your mercy reach the nest of a bird" does not refer explicitly to the mother-bird commandment in Deuteronomy 22:6–7 but seems to have that law in mind. Censorship of the formula ("they silence him") would seem to entail a rejection of the humanitarian rationale for the mother-bird commandment and possibly for the other animal-family laws too.[64]

But the subjunctive mood of the verb "*May* Your mercy reach" is at odds with the imperative of Deuteronomy's instruction. God's mercy has *already* reached the bird's nest, given the issuance of the law. Moreover, the prayer formula says nothing about *mother* birds per se. The prayer leader wishes for mercy on the *nest*. With those discrepancies in mind, one might read the Mishnah's censorship as bearing no relationship to the animal-family laws but instead as registering a general theological concern. The bird's nest may signify, as it does elsewhere in the Mishnah as well as in the Gospels (Matthew 6:25, 10:29; Luke 12:24), a trivial entity undeserving of God's attention.[65] That being the case, the prayer formula expresses a wish for God's mercy to extend *very far, even* to a bird's nest. Why the Mishnah would censor such a wish remains a mystery.[66]

Ambiguity over whether the prayer formula refers specifically to the mother-bird commandment or to more general matters of divine providence also surrounds the explanations of this Mishnah by the Talmudic Rabbis.[67] There are only two passages that clearly connect the Mishnah's nest to the animal-family laws. One is a story from the Babylonian Talmud:

> A particular individual descended [before the ark as prayer leader] in the presence of Rabbah, saying: "You have shown mercy to a bird's nest, you should show mercy and pity for us. You have shown mercy to 'him and his child,' you should show mercy and pity for us." Rabbah said, "How much does this Torah scholar know to appease the glory of his Lord!" Abaye said to him, "But we learned that one silences him." But it is not so! Rabbah sought to sharpen Abaye.[68]

The prayer leader in the story pronounces the formula censored by the Mishnah but puts God's mercy for the bird's nest in past tense—"you have shown mercy" rather than the Mishnah's "may your mercy reach." The prayer leader speaks not only of the bird's nest but also of the same-day slaughter prohibition in Leviticus 22:28, using that law's distinctive phrasing, "him and his child." The prayer leader seems to identify the bird's nest of the Mishnah with the mother-bird commandment of Deuteronomy since otherwise it would not make much sense for him to mention it in conjunction with the Leviticus law (on the assumption that the prayer leader is grouping apples with apples, biblical law with biblical law). The prayer leader thus speaks of the animal-family laws and attributes to them a humanitarian rationale. Similar to Rabbi Levi in

Leviticus Rabbah, the prayer leader views the laws as a reflection of divine compassion.

The story's coda attests to a rabbinic rejection of that rationale. The prominent Babylonian Rabbi named Rabbah first compliments the prayer leader for his elegantly articulated praise of God. Rabbah's student Abaye is taken aback. Does not the Mishnah explicitly censor this very form of prayer? The Talmudic composer's rebuttal is, essentially, that Rabbah was "just kidding," that Rabbah did not sincerely intend the praise but was only testing Abaye. It is hard to know what the composer wants readers to take away from this anticlimactic and, frankly, implausible ending to the story. Was there more sympathy for the humanitarian rationale among the Rabbis than the Talmud would care to admit?[69] One imagines, yes, and that the Talmud was not trying too hard to hide it.

Another piece of evidence is a statement cited in the Palestinian Talmud:

> Rabbi Yosi son of Rabbi Bun said: They do not act well, those who make the attributes of the Holy One Blessed Be He mercy. Those who translate [into Aramaic] "My people, the children of Israel, just as I am merciful in Heaven, so you should be merciful on earth—a cow or sheep, she and her child, do not slaughter them on the same day" (Leviticus 22:28)—do not act well because they make the attributes of the Holy One Blessed Be He mercy.[70]

Rabbi Yosi son of Rabbi Bun here quotes the tradition of the ancient Targum commentary, which understands Leviticus's prohibition on same-day slaughter through the lens of divine mercy: "Just as I am merciful in Heaven, so you should be merciful on earth."[71] To observe the prohibition against same-day slaughter is, according to the Targum, to mimic God's mercy. Rabbi Yosi is not a fan of the Targum. He declares anyone voicing that tradition to be "not act[ing] well" because they "make the attributes of the Holy One Blessed Be He mercy," apparently an objection to presumptuous explanations of the divine will.

Both Talmudic traditions, the one from the Palestinian Talmud criticizing the Targum and the other from the Babylonian Talmud about Rabbah and Abaye and the prayer leader, explicitly feature the animal-family laws, unlike the Mishnah, which may well have nothing to do with them. Both Talmudic traditions mention the prohibition against same-day slaughter from Leviticus, though the Palestinian Talmud passage does not directly link that prohibition with the mother-bird commandment in the way that the Babylonian Talmud's story does. Both traditions feature a version of the humanitarian rationale focused on divine compassion. In both traditions that humanitarian rationale is denounced. The Palestinian Talmud is more straightforward in its denunciation than is the Babylonian Talmud, which features a prominent Rabbi initially praising that rationale. In sum, the two Talmuds each feature one passage in which the humanitarian rationale is rejected, but otherwise the materials are ambiguous regarding whether they are referring to the animal-family laws at all. The most accurate claim one can make about the humanitarian rationale in the Mishnah and Talmuds is that it is on the whole ignored.

MAIMONIDES'S OBJECTION TO THE HUMANITARIAN RATIONALE: "GOD WOULD NOT HAVE PERMITTED SLAUGHTER AT ALL"

A full-throated rejection of the humanitarian rationale appears in the medieval period. In commenting on the Mishnah's censored prayer formula, Rashi associates its bird's nest with the one in Deuteronomy, as does Maimonides, and the reading sticks. In his commentary on Mishnah Tractate Berakhot, Maimonides explains what is wrong with the humanitarian rationale:

> In mentioning the formula, "Your mercies extend to a bird's nest," they are referring to one who says, "As you have shown compassion upon a bird's nest and commanded, 'You shall not take the mother with the fledglings' (Deuteronomy 22:6), so too show mercy upon us." Whoever says this in his prayer is to be silenced, since he is making the reason for this command dependent upon God's compassion for the bird. This is not really true, for if it were actually an expression of mercy, then He would not have commanded to slaughter beasts or birds at all. Rather, this is a traditional law, for which there is no reason.[72]

If God were merciful to birds, Maimonides reasons, God would not have commanded Israel to slaughter them and other animals, such as in the laws of sacrifice. In his commentary on Mishnah Tractate Megillah,

Maimonides again makes the connection to Deuteronomy and explains concisely that "it is *gezerat ha-katuv*," a decree of scripture.[73] In his Mishneh Torah, Maimonides mentions both the mother-bird command and the prohibition on same-day slaughter, saying rather than that "God would have not *commanded*" the slaughter of animals if God had mercy on them, as he says in his commentary on the Mishnah, that "God would not have *permitted* slaughter at all."[74] A God who allows us to kill animals for food would not, at the same time, tell us to be merciful toward them.

Maimonides's logic is hardly airtight, as philosopher Roslyn Weiss points out: "Is it really impossible for a merciful God to permit animal slaughter yet also enjoin the sending away of the mother bird?"[75] Moreover, Maimonides himself has no qualms in his *Guide for the Perplexed*, as we saw earlier, attributing to these commandments a concern with animal suffering. I leave it to scholars of Maimonides to hash out why Maimonides rejects the humanitarian rationale in his Mishneh Torah and Mishnah commentary but embraces it in the *Guide for the Perplexed*.[76] What is important to highlight, though, is that the rejection of the humanitarian rationale is really a product of medieval rather than ancient rabbinic literature.

MODERN OBJECTIONS TO THE HUMANITARIAN RATIONALE: IT DOESN'T HELP ANIMALS

Modern Bible scholars have also pointed to problems with the humanitarian rationale. Jacob Milgrom gives the most thorough articulation in his commentary on Leviticus:

> The main argument against the humanitarian theory challenges its very use as the rationale for the kid law and the other cited animal prohibitions. It may be true that one may not slaughter the dam and its young on the same day (22:28) but it surely is permitted on successive days. The newborn must be permitted to suckle for seven days (22:27; Exod 22:29), but on the eighth day it may be brought to the altar—even though it is still suckling. The mother bird and her fledglings or eggs may not be taken together (Deut 22:6), but surely they may be taken separately. By the same token, the mother goat can in no way be aware that her kid is boiling in her milk. . . . In any event, the humanitarian theory must give way to another.[77]

One by one Milgrom shoots down the possibility that the animal-family laws demonstrate compassion. Regarding same-day slaughter, Milgrom points out that one may still slaughter the mother on Monday and child on Tuesday. Where lies the compassion in that? Regarding the seven-day requirement, Milgrom observes that eight-day-old babies are still nursing when they are removed from their mother and sacrificed on the altar. Sacrifice on day eight is no kinder to either baby or mother than it is on day seven. The mother-bird law appears equally arbitrary: the mother may not be present at the exact moment that her chicks or eggs are stolen from her, but they still are stolen. Milgrom's final argument, about not cooking kids in their own mother's milk, is that the mother would be entirely unaware of it. Whether her baby is cooked in her milk, another goat's milk, water, or on a roasting spit is immaterial to her; what matters is her child's removal in the first place. If compassion is the rationale for these laws, then it seems at best an empty performance, at worst hypocrisy, or simply nonsensical. Some might say the aim of the laws is not to help the animal but to inculcate virtue in humans. That is the thrust of Philo and Rashbam.[78] Yet it seems a strange and attenuated lesson in compassion if the recipient in no way experiences it.[79]

ALTERNATIVES TO THE HUMANITARIAN RATIONALE

The humanitarian rationale nevertheless won the day. Clement of Alexandria recapitulated much of Philo's argument on the animal-family laws.[80] Saint Augustine, Thomas Aquinas, Martin Luther, and John Calvin all adopted Clement, in turn, which means that the humanitarian approach became Christian normative and thus the main perspective through which most of the world's Bible-reading population has come to know the Bible's animal-family laws. The problem of the humanitarian approach is, in short, pressing, particularly because the challenges to it are so persuasive, and the main solution offered—essentially, don't ask—is likely to satisfy only the most pious among us.

Classical rabbinic literature offers an alternative. In the main sections of the Mishnah and Talmud where the Rabbis treat the animal-family laws, the Rabbis do not get snagged up in the convoluted moral logic of the humanitarian rationale. Instead, the Rabbis draw out the legal implications in their typical technical style. Perhaps to some modern readers' chagrin, they generally do so without explicit reference to ethical or theological ideas. The Rabbis do not even speak of the animal-family laws together, with a few exceptions, and even there the connection is formalistic.[81] Still, the Rabbis' legal articulations are hardly devoid of meaning or message even if the Rabbis ask not *why* these laws exist but what they *do*. I suggest, as we read the Rabbis in the upcoming chapters, that we follow suit. What do the animal-family laws do for animals?

3 Animal Grandmothers

THE PROHIBITION AGAINST SAME-DAY SLAUGHTER

HOLY LINEAGE

I begin with the Bible's prohibition against slaughtering an animal parent and child on a single day. My discussion in this chapter relies on the simplest of points, which is that everybody who considers themselves bound by scriptural law and wishes to observe the prohibition against slaughtering an animal parent and child on the same day will need to know, in the first place, who their animal's parent and child are. They must know the family history of their animals. If one wishes to understand this law, then one must enter the world of genealogy. Fortunately, for us today, that is not hard. In the contemporary United States, genealogy is practically a religion.

"Holy leisure" is what historian Rachel Gross calls the practice of family history by American Jewish amateur genealogists. They see themselves as "frontiersmen of the soul," seeking spirituality and meaning in the records of the past.[1] Their family tree networks are sites of lived religion that facilitate their sacred relationships with living family members and with Jews from other times and places. The reconstruction of family trees plays other roles too, for Jews and for the millions of others swept up in the roots craze of DNA tests, memberships in family-history companies and genealogical societies, and registration on Ancestry.com, which boasts over one hundred million families and whose online traffic is surpassed only by shopping and porn.[2] Genealogical research can be motivated by a practical need to verify lines of property inheritance or by a nativist ideology intent on showing a family's long-lasting presence in a particular place.[3] Genealogy can be a form of resistance to trauma through the preservation of the memory of ancestors lost to war, epidemics, or enslavement. Genealogy can produce a sense of continuity in the face of mobility and migration.[4] Genealogy can reveal either noble or notorious ancestors whose appearance in a lineage changes a person's sense of self. Black activist Angela Davis found out that she was descended from a passenger on the Mayflower.[5] Ben Affleck tried to suppress the discovery of slave-owning ancestors.[6] Genealogical research satisfies curiosity about the age-old question: Where did I come from?[7] American Jews trace their penchant for genealogies back to Genesis, its famous "begats" not holy leisure but holy lineage, highlighting the divine plan of history and lending to the biblical story an aura of authenticity.[8]

The Bible does not offer any such genealogies for animals. No chapter of the Bible begins with "This is the line of Bilaam's donkey. Bilaam's donkey was five years when she begat . . ." But it would be wrong to conclude that the biblical composers were indifferent to animal genealogies. The premise of Leviticus 19:19's prohibition against breeding together animals of different species is that people deliberately crafted animal lineages, presumably to improve their animal's fitness or other qualities that increased the animal's desirability. Just why the Bible would prohibit crossbreeding was debated by the medievals, with Rashi calling the prohibition a divine decree with no discernible reason, and Ibn Ezra and Nahmanides attributing it to the need to respect God's natural order.[9] The early Rabbis proposed that the Bible forbids breeding together only animals of different species. Breeding together animals of the same species— the Sifra's formulation is "grabbing the [female] animal and putting her before the male"—is permitted, the Rabbis inferred.[10] Later Rabbis cited in the Babylonian Talmud rule similarly that for "a species with its own species, one is permitted to insert like a brush into a tube, and there is not even [a concern for] arousal." The author of this legislation, Rav Yehudah, uses the standard rabbinic "mascara tube" metaphor for genital penetration and suggests, in dismissing a concern about human sexual arousal, that the sexual intercourse that people engineered for their animals did in fact generate some anxiety.[11] These rabbinic rulings reflect a world in which people clearly cared quite a bit about animal genealogies and were intimately involved in practices designed to manipulate them.

The broader Roman culture to which the Rabbis belonged shared their interests. Roman agricultural manuals praise certain cattle breeds for their beauty, "noble head," size, milk production, or draft strength and criticize some breeds for their flaws.[12] Nearly two millennia before Mendelian genetics, the Romans had sufficient knowledge of selective breeding to produce animal breeds that maximized profitability and utility.[13] Columella tells a story about his uncle Marcus, an eminent agriculturalist, who purchased beautifully colored wild rams imported from Africa, mated them with local coated ewes to produce sheep of the color he desired but whose wool was still coarse, and then mated those with Tarentine ewes to eventually produce sheep with both beautiful color and fine wool.[14] Zooarchaeologist Michael MacKinnon speculates about the various forces that would have impelled ancient Romans to "improve" their livestock: profit, competition, curiosity, ingenuity.[15] Agriculturalists were proud of the excellent breeds they created, which could command a fortune in the marketplace. Varro describes a pair of pigeons that went for 1,000 sestertii in the market in Rome. Some breeders were celebrated for their expertise in pedigree and performance.[16] These ancient practices culminate in today's global animal-genetics market, which in 2021 was valued at nearly seven billion dollars and is projected to grow to nearly twelve billion by 2029.[17]

There is much here to find unsettling. The "improvement" of animal breeds sounds very much like human eugenics. It also relies on forcible sex or insemination and impregnation—*The Handmaid's Tale* for cows, sheep, and goats. The Mishnah had a particular reason for its interest in animal genealogies, which was not producing beautiful or strong animals, though presumably the Rabbis would have valued those too, but rather conforming to biblical law.

LEVITICUS 22:28 AND THE NEED TO KNOW YOUR ANIMAL'S FAMILY

Located within the section of Leviticus known as the Holiness Legislation, Leviticus 22:17–25 lists a series of bodily conditions that disqualify an animal from sacrifice. Leviticus 22:27–28 is an addendum to that list:

> [27]When an ox or a sheep or a goat is born, he shall stay seven days under his mother, and from the eighth day on he shall be acceptable as an offering by fire to GOD. [28]But a herd or flock animal, him and his child, you shall not slaughter on the same day.

The passage features two laws, the first formulated as a positive command, the second negative (as discussed in chapter 2). The first law requires newborn oxen, sheep, or goats to be left with their mother for a week. Only after that time may they be offered as a sacrifice. The second law prohibits slaughtering animals and their children on the same day. The animal parents and children in verse 27 must be kept together immediately after birth, while the animal parents and children in verse 28 must be kept separate upon slaughter. I describe in this chapter how the Mishnah's treatment of the law in verse 28 engages in its own version of holy lineage—for animals. Ancestry matters for animals too, it turns out, in Mishnah Hullin Chapter Five's treatment of the prohibition on same-day slaughter, its animal genealogy not "memorial work" as it is for American Jewish family historians but "legal work," a primary mode of piety for the ancient Rabbis.[18]

Leviticus 22:28 was not the only piece of scripture motivating interest in animal genealogy on the part of the Bible's followers, nor were the other three animal-family laws (cooking kids in their mother milk, keeping a baby with the mother, and the mother-bird mitzvah). Leviticus 19:19's prohibition against crossbreeding directly addresses animal lineages. Deuteronomy 22:10's prohibition against yoking an ox and ass together also requires people to pay attention to animal genealogies since they must know the species lineage of their animals if they are going to keep different species apart.[19] The requirement to donate firstborn animals found in numerous places in the Pentateuch requires farmers to know whether a particular animal has ever given birth if they are to know whether the child needs to be donated (Exodus 13:1, 11–15, 22:28–29,

34:19–20; Leviticus 27:26–27; Numbers 18:15–18; Deuteronomy 15:19–23). To observe any of these laws, the pious Israelite or Jew needed to be able to locate animals within their "geographies of relatedness."[20]

Still, Leviticus 22:28 has certain unique features that led the Rabbis to track the specific genealogies of individual animals in a manner analogous to some of the human genealogical practices popular today. The biblical laws that deal with crossbreeding, firstborn donation, birds in the nest, and newborn animals focus on reproduction, birth, or the period immediately after. The prohibition in Leviticus 22:28 focuses instead on the act of slaughter.[21] That focus has several implications. First, whenever people go to slaughter an animal, they must first know who that particular animal's parents and children are. Second, for the slaughterers to hold such information, they must keep track of each animal parent-child pair. Third, the owners must also keep track of the family trees within the herd or flock since each individual animal occupies a slot within a broader lineage. Large-scale kinship geographies became necessary. Finally, those kinship geographies must be known not only to the current owner but to all potential future owners. We will see that the prohibition against same-day slaughter, for all these reasons, pressed the Rabbis to create practices of public accounting for all their animals' genealogies.

THE GRANDMOTHER HYPOTHESIS

The Bible's presumption about genealogy is that it is constituted by three generations or more.[22] That definition gives special significance to grandparents, whose role has attracted the interest of social scientists and public policy experts in recent years due to the lengthening of life expectancies and the shrinking social safety nets that grandparents' care and resources often come to replace.[23] Evolutionary biologists, for their part, have also shown great interest in the grandmother since humans are the only species, aside from several types of whales, in whom females experience menopause—that is to say, their reproductive potential ceases well before their lifespan does. According to the "grandmother hypothesis," menopause was an evolutionary adaptation that contributed to long-term fitness.[24] The nonreproductive grandmother increases the survival of her genetic heritage by taking care of her children's children more so than by bearing further children of her own.

In the ancient world and still today, many people do not get to meet or know their grandparents. In Roman Egypt children had an 80 percent chance that any of their grandparents would be alive at the time of their birth and a 50 percent chance by the age of ten. It was twice as likely at that point for a grandmother still to be alive (two-in-five chance) than a grandfather (one in five).[25] That demographic reality may help to explain the relative sparsity of references in rabbinic literature to grandparents. The rabbinic terms *zaqen/zeqenah, sav/savta, av/em,* and *rabah/rabtah* can refer to an elderly parent, any elderly person, any ancestor, or specifically to a grandparent. Only about half a dozen passages in the Mishnah speak unambiguously of grandparents or grandchildren, in contexts that range from levirate marriage to consumption of tithes, confirmation of lineage, and incestuous rape.[26]

Even animal grandparents appear in rabbinic literature, such as Babylonian Talmud Bekhorot 17a's reference to an animal grandmother and grandchildren, Hullin 75b's reference to the grandparentage of a male "koy" (a hybrid deer/goat), and Bava Kamma 80b's discussion about the dangers of a black cat born to a white mother and grandmother.[27] We will see that animal grandmothers also play a role in Mishnah Hullin Chapter Five's treatment of the same-day slaughter prohibition. Since common domesticated animals give birth earlier than humans do, living animal grandparents would have been a more common phenomenon than human ones. With animal genealogies in mind, and animal grandmothers in particular, I turn then to Mishnah Hullin Chapter Five's treatment of the prohibition in Leviticus 22:28 against the slaughter of an animal parent and child on the same day.

THE MISHNAH'S TECHNICAL APPROACH TO THE TORAH

Mishnah Hullin Chapter Five begins,

> "Him and His Child" applies in the land and outside the land, in the presence of the Temple and not in the presence of the Temple, for unconsecrated and consecrated animals.[28]

The Mishnah's first step in treating the biblical prohibition is to create a shorthand label for it, *Oto ve-et Beno* (Him and His Child), using the phraseology from Leviticus 22:28, "But a herd or flock animal, *him and his child*, you shall not slaughter on the same day." That label, which as far as I know is an innovation of the early Rabbis, sticks until today. The relevant chapter of the Jewish law code Shulhan Arukh is called "The Law of 'Him and His Child.'"[29] As the first words of the Mishnah chapter, the label also became the reference point for any topic that appears within the Talmudic chapter.

Chapter Five is the first of a trio of Mishnah chapters that feature nearly identical openings:

> 5:1 *Oto ve-et Beno* (Him and His Child) applies in the land and outside the land, in the presence of the Temple and not in the presence of the Temple, for unconsecrated and consecrated animals.
>
> 6:1 *Kisui ha-Dam* (Covering the Blood) applies in the land and outside the land, in the presence of the Temple and not in the presence of the Temple, for unconsecrated but not for consecrated animals.
>
> 7:1 *Gid ha-Nasheh* (Sciatic Nerve) applies in the land and outside the land, in the presence of the Temple and not in the presence of the Temple, and for unconsecrated and consecrated animals.

Each chapter's opening sentence begins with a shorthand label: *Oto ve-et Beno*, *Kisui ha-Dam*, and *Gid ha-Nasheh*. "Covering the Blood" refers to Leviticus 17:13's requirement to drain and cover the blood of an animal upon slaughter, the subject of Mishnah Hullin Chapter Six. "Sciatic Nerve" refers to the prohibition against eating the sciatic nerve, which is found in Genesis 32:33 and is the subject of Mishnah Hullin Chapter Seven. In each case the labels are followed by the same binary legal applications: in/outside the land of Israel; Temple/no Temple; meat/sacrifice. The formula picks up again in Mishnah Hullin Chapter Ten after a two-chapter hiatus, with "Shoulder, Cheeks, and Stomach" (which Deuteronomy 18:3 requires to be given to the priest) introducing Chapter Ten, "First of the Fleece" (which Deuteronomy 18:4 requires also to be given to the priest) introducing Chapter Eleven, and "Sending Forth the Mother Bird" (before taking her chicks or eggs) introducing Chapter Twelve (which I treat in my chapter 5).

I use uppercase in my translation to convey the technical feel of these labels. The label converts the biblical passage into a subject heading that governs the Mishnah chapters and creates parallels among them.[30] The labels also depersonalize (or one might more appropriately say "de-animalize") the law such that one forgets the fleshly realities it describes. When the technical terms are translated back into meaningful memes, the chapter headings seem either jarringly grisly or comically nonsensical. "Covering Blood," "Sciatic Nerve," and "Shoulder, Cheeks, and Stomach" sound more like the butcher's section of the supermarket than clauses in a legal tract.

The Mishnah's clinical approach to the prohibition is apparent also in the puzzle of slaughter scenarios with which Chapter Five begins:

> 5:1 *Oto ve-et Beno* (Him and His Child) applies in the land and outside the land, in the presence of the Temple and not in the presence of the Temple, for unconsecrated and consecrated animals.
> How so? One slaughters *Oto ve-et Beno* [and both are]:
> (1) unconsecrated animals, [slaughtered] outside [the Temple], both of them are valid, but the second [slaughterer] incurs the forty [lashes].
> (2) consecrated, outside, the first is liable for extirpation, and both of them are invalid, and both of them incur the forty.

Ten more scenarios follow. Each of the twelve same-day slaughter permutations is determined by two variables: (1) whether the slaughter is for ordinary meat or sacrifice and (2) whether the slaughter takes place inside or outside the Temple precincts. Three possible legal outcomes are laid out for the slaughterer who violates the biblical prohibition: punishment with divinely meted-out death; punishment with forty lashes, which is the standard rabbinic penalty for violating a negative commandment ("you shall not" versus "you shall"); or exemption from any penalties.[31] Two outcomes are possible for the animal: valid or invalid status, where validity makes it either edible meat or a valid sacrifice, depending on the scenario. (From the animal's point of view, there is only one possible outcome, and that is death.)

The scenarios seem designed to teach two principles: (1) violation of the prohibition on same-day slaughter does not invalidate the animal as ordinary meat, and (2) violation of the prohibition does, on the other hand, invalidate the animal for sacrifice.[32] These themes of edibility, validity, and liability continue into Mishnah Three:

> 5:3 One who slaughters and it is found to be *terefah* [i.e., invalid for slaughter]; one who slaughters for idolatry; one who slaughters the heifer of the sin-offering, or an ox who is to be stoned, or a calf whose neck is to be broken: Rabbi Meir says one holds [him] liable; Rabbi Shimon exempts.[33]

The question that opens Mishnah Three is no longer: If you violate the prohibition, can you still eat the animal? It is now: If you cannot eat the animal, are you still violating the prohibition? Mishnah Three considers whether a person who slaughters an animal that is prohibited for consumption—the red heifer whose ashes are used for purification (Numbers 19), the ox who has murdered a person (Exodus 21:28-32) or had sex with a person (Leviticus 18:23, 20:15-16), and other animals whom the Rabbis have banned eating—is liable for violating the same-day slaughter prohibition. The Mishnah features a dispute between Rabbi Meir and Rabbi Shimon, with Rabbi Meir ruling that the slaughterer is still liable, and Rabbi Shimon ruling that he is not.

The Mishnah's next subject is a variation on this one:

> One who slaughters and it becomes *nevelah* [improperly slaughtered] by his hand; one who stabs or one who tears [the two throat organs], he is exempt from "Him and His Child." (5:3, continued)

What if one cannot eat the animals not because they are prohibited, as in the previous case, but because one did not slaughter them properly? Is a person violating the same-day slaughter rule if the slaughter did not really happen, in legal terms?[34] The Mishnah's answer is no: "He is exempt from 'Him and His Child.'"

The series of cases in these first three Mishnahs play with the relationship between slaughter, sacrifice, and consumption. What is the effect of the prohibition against same-day slaughter on the validity of normal meat and sacrifice, and, conversely, what is the effect of invalid meat and slaughter on accountability for the prohibition? These questions, along with the answers the Mishnah provides, would seem to preclude the so-called humanitarian rationale. If the Rabbis in the Mishnah thought that the prohibition's purpose is to foster compassion for animals, they would not likely have ruled that one can still eat animals if one violates the prohibition or that one is not liable for violating the prohibition if one does not slaughter the animals properly or cannot eat them.[35] On the contrary, the Mishnah's introduction of shorthand labels; its focus on liability, validity, and edibility; and its limitations on the scope and impact of the prohibition all serve to blunt the humanitarian dimensions that readers such as Philo, Rashbam, and modern Bible scholars find in the biblical law.

ANIMAL FAMILY TREES

The Mishnah discards the humanitarian rationale, but so far it must seem a poor alternative—all technicalities, with no discernible vision or purpose other than mechanistic conformity to law. But as Mishnah Hullin Chapter Five progresses, a language of family emerges that accentuates animal kinship, though in a different way from the humanitarian rationale. Mishnah Hullin 5:3 next turns to questions of timing:

> Two bought a cow and her child: The one who bought first may slaughter first; but if the second preceded [the first], he has gained the right.
>
> One who slaughters a cow and [afterward] her two children, he incurs eighty [lashes].
>
> One slaughtered her two children and afterward slaughtered her, he incurs forty.
>
> One slaughtered her, her daughter, and her daughter's daughter, he incurs eighty.
>
> One slaughtered her and her daughter's daughter, and afterward he slaughtered her daughter, he incurs forty. Sumakhos said in the name of Rabbi Meir: He incurs eighty.[36]

This Mishnah presents scenarios that hinge on the temporal sequence of the slaughter. In the first scenario ("two bought a cow and her child"), one person buys a cow and another person buys that cow's child, presumably on the same day. Which of them has priority in slaughtering their newly purchased animal? To avoid violation of the prohibition, one of the buyers must wait a day. The Mishnah's ruling is that it is first-come-first-served, for the most part. The first buyer technically has the right to slaughter his animal first, but if the second buyer gets the jump on him, so be it.

Notice, however, that in the four subsequent scenarios it is not only temporality that is at stake but also the family relationships among the animals. The four scenarios read almost like a detective story. Three cows end up dead in all four scenarios, and one man has killed them. The variables are the relationship of the cows to one another, the order in which the person slaughters them, and the severity of the punishment for the slaughterer. The scenarios come in couplets. Within the first two scenarios, the same cows die, a mother and two children. Also within the second two scenarios, the same cows die, in that case a mother, daughter, and granddaughter.

The timing makes all the difference. In the first scenario, a person slaughters the mother and then the two children. Because the slaughter of each child constitutes its own violation of the prohibition on slaughtering a cow and her calf on the same day, the slaughterer receives a whopping eighty lashes. The second scenario is identical to the first except that the order is reversed: first the two calves are slaughtered and then their mother. The slaughterer receives only forty lashes (more than anyone would wish for but not as bad as eighty). The slaughterer is held accountable for only one violation, not two, because, as Talmud commentator Rashi explains, "here there is only one prohibited act of slaughter."[37] When the person slaughtered each of the two children, they triggered no prohibition. When they proceeded to slaughter the mother, at that moment they triggered the prohibition. Two mother-child pairs have been slaughtered on the same day, but one act of prohibited slaughter incurs only one set of lashes.

In the third scenario, the slaughterer proceeds by descending generations: mother, then daughter, then granddaughter. That person triggers the prohibition twice, first when he slaughters the daughter, then again when he slaughters the granddaughter. He incurs two sets of lashes, totaling eighty. In the fourth scenario, the slaughterer skips generations: first mother, then granddaughter, and then, backtracking, the daughter. This person has slaughtered two mother/daughter pairs in total, just as in the third scenario, but neither their first nor the second act of slaughter triggered the prohibition. Only the third of the three slaughters was, technically, a prohibited act. Thus, according to the consensus opinion of the Rabbis, this person incurs only the one set of forty lashes.

Intriguingly, even though the fourth case is essentially parallel to the second case within the two couplets, only the fourth case features a disagreement in which Sumakhos, in the name of Rabbi Meir, argues that the slaughterer is liable on two counts and receives eighty lashes.[38] We might speculate that the fourth case is controversial in a way that the second case is not because it features a spread of three generations rather than two. Rabbi Meir may balk at the idea of holding the slaughterer responsible on only one count when the slaughterer has destroyed three generations of an animal's family—a bona fide genealogy. In the first couplet, by contrast, only two generations of the cow's family tree are cut down.

This third Mishnah is as full of puzzles as the first two. Liability remains the central concern. The same animals die at the end of the day, and the only real change that transpires is the slaughterer's degree of liability. An important difference, though, is that the set of scenarios in Mishnah Three brings the cow's family tree to the foreground. Mothers, daughters, maternal granddaughters, and siblings are all featured. Compare Mishnah Yevamot 1:1:

> Fifteen [categories of] women exempt their rival wives and the rival wives of their rival wives and so on ad infinitum from *halitzah* [ceremonial release from levirate marriage] and from *yibum* [levirate marriage]: his daughter, and the daughter of his daughter, and the daughter of his son, and the daughter of his wife, the daughter of her daughter and the daughter of her son.[39]

Putting aside this Mishnah's concern with polygamy and levirate marriage, we might note that the language it uses for human family trees is the same that Hullin uses for animals—mothers, daughters, maternal granddaughters.[40] We find the same similarities in other Mishnah passages that refer to human genealogies. Mishnah Ketubbot 3:2 and Keritot 3:5 use the same terms as Hullin for daughters and maternal granddaughters. Parallel passages in the midrash collection Sifra and the Mishnah's partner work, the Tosefta, offer further examples of animal-family language. Like the Mishnah, the Sifra speaks of animal mothers, daughters, and maternal granddaughters. The Sifra mentions also animal brothers and maternal grandmothers.⁴¹ Tosefta Hullin adds filial granddaughter, and it also uses the language of *dorot* (generations) to describe animal family trees.⁴² Through their language the Mishnah, Tosefta, and Sifra implicitly compare animal and human families and consider both types to be legal subjects.

THE DRAMA OF FAMILY

The family language continues into the Mishnah's next legislation:

> At four times of the year, one who sells an animal to his fellow must announce: "I sold her mother for slaughter," "I sold her daughter for slaughter."
>
> And these [times] are:
>
> (1) The eve of the final festival day of the Festival [of Sukkot];
> (2) the eve of the first festival day of Passover;
> (3) the eve of Atseret (Shavuot);
> (4) and the eve of Rosh Hashanah;
>
> And, according to [the opinion of] Rabbi Yosi the Galilean:
> Also on the eve of Yom Kippur in Galilee.

If a person selling an animal has already sold that animal's parent or child, there are four times of the year when the seller must divulge that information: "'I sold her mother for slaughter,' 'I sold her daughter for slaughter.'"⁴³ Because on the eve of a festival people are preparing their celebratory feasts, the chance that buyer one and buyer two would slaughter their animals on the same day is high.

What if the seller is putting the daughter up for sale now, on the eve of one of these festivals, but sold the mother several hours, days, weeks, or even months ago? Is the concern for same-day slaughter still strong enough to require an announcement? That is the implicit question behind Rabbi Yehudah's subsequent limitation on this law:

> Rabbi Yehudah said: When [must the seller announce it]? If there is no interval of time [between sales]; but [if] there is an interval of time, one does not need to announce.

But Rabbi Yehudah agrees that if one sells the mother to a groom and the daughter to a bride that he must announce, since the matter is known that both of them slaughter on the same day.

Rabbi Yehudah here restricts the scope of the requirement to announce the sale of an animal parent or child, saying that if an interval of time has elapsed between the two sales (he does not say how long), an announcement is no longer necessary, presumably because the likelihood is less that the two buyers will still slaughter on the same day.[44] The consensus position, by implication, is that the seller must publicly announce the sales of a mother and daughter even if quite a lot of time has elapsed. Rabbi Yehudah himself withdraws his restriction in the case of wedding sales, when even he requires the seller to make the announcement, presumably no matter how much time has elapsed between the two sales and no matter what time of year it is. The chance of same-day slaughter is too high. (Call it a special burden for wedding caterers.)

I am interested in the language of this Mishnah and its impact. The Mishnah presents a first-person script for the seller's announcement: "I sold her mother for slaughter; I sold her daughter for slaughter." The animal's seller brings attention to the animal's family relations using the language of family normally associated with human beings. I hear a certain drama in the announcement. The Mishnah could just as easily have formulated the law in the third person, with less theatrics. The midrash collection Sifra supplies more drama by featuring a public crier to announce the sale.[45] The Sifra reads scripture's phrase *be-yom ehad* ("on the same day," literally, "in one day") as *yom meyuhad*, a distinct day, or special day.[46] The announcement of animal sales has almost a ceremonial quality. Animals are property for purchase, but their family relations must be accounted for, in dramatic and public fashion on a specially marked day, precisely at the moment of purchase.

WHY GRANDMAS AND NOT GRANDPAS?

Readers who have affection for their grandfathers or who are themselves grandfathers may take umbrage at the name I have given to this chapter on animal genealogies: "Animal Grandmothers." I never got to meet my own grandfathers but have the highest regard for my father as a grandfather, beloved by his grandchildren and now great-grandchildren. The Mishnah, lamentably, does not show such regard: it mentions only the animal grandmother and seems utterly indifferent to the grandfather. Even the status of fathers is precarious. The first two Mishnahs of Hullin Chapter Five, which use masculine grammar to describe parent and child animals, project a father-son pair. But the third Mishnah shifts back and forth between masculine and feminine grammar. Somewhere in the middle of that Mishnah, it settles on feminine grammar for the parent animal, and that grammar stays in place until the end of the chapter. The parent is a *parah*, a "female bovine" or "cow." Another Mishnah that touches on the same-day slaughter prohibition, Mishnah Hullin 4:5, likewise presumes an animal mother, though a Mishnah elsewhere, Bekhorot 7:7, seems to presume an animal father when it brings up the same-day slaughter prohibition.[47]

The ambiguity surrounding the animal parent's gender can be traced back to the biblical verse itself. I have translated the Bible's expression for the animal parent and child, *oto ve-et beno*, as "him and his child," using the masculine for the parent ("But a herd or flock animal, *him and his child*, you shall not slaughter on the same day"), to reflect the expression's masculine grammar. The grammar would seem to suggest that the prohibition on same-day slaughter relates primarily or exclusively to animal fathers and their children. Most interpreters, however, have understood the prohibition to apply primarily or exclusively to animal mothers. The crux of the question is whether "him and his child" is grammatically masculine only to match the pair of masculine collective nouns at the beginning of the verse that refers to cows, sheep, and goats *(ve-shor o'seh)*. If so, the prohibition may refer to animal mothers. Alternatively, *oto ve-et beno* is grammatically masculine because it is intended to reflect the male gender of the actual animal parent. If so, the prohibition would apply to animal fathers.[48] Factors weighing in the direction of the mother are the explicit reference to the animal mother in the prior verse requiring the baby to be left with her for the first week of life, and the relative sparsity of male animals that would have been raised into adulthood (see my discussion in chapter 1). Weighing in the direction of the animal father are the masculine grammar and the preference in biblical sacrifice for male animals.[49]

That ambiguity led ancient Jews to take a variety of positions on whether the animal mother or father is the subject of the same-day slaughter prohibition. The Temple Scroll, one of the major sectarian writings in the Dead Sea Scrolls, is nearly as ambiguous as the Bible itself when it features Leviticus's same-day slaughter prohibition along with two other laws about animal parents and children.[50] The context in the Temple Scroll may imply a mother animal. Another passage in the Dead Sea Scrolls, from *Miqsat Ma'aseh Ha-Torah*, seems to identify the Bible's prohibition on same-day slaughter with a prohibition on sacrificing pregnant animals, implying that the prohibition refers to mother animals.[51] The Septuagint, the ancient Greek translation of the Bible, is more definitive that the mother is the parent to whom the prohibition applies when it replaces the masculine grammar of the verse with feminine.[52] The Aramaic Targum traditions do the same.[53] First-century-CE Jewish philosopher Philo is even more explicit when he describes the parent animal in the prohibition using the Greek word for mother.[54] First-century-CE Jewish historian Josephus, by contrast, presents the same-day prohibition in gender-neutral terms.[55] The early rabbinic Sifra asks pointedly about the gender of the animal parent: "Could it be that 'him and his child' applies to males (fathers) as it does to females (mothers)?"[56] The Sifra here presumes that mothers are the main subject of the prohibition but considers whether fathers might also be included. The Sifra concludes that the verse applies only to mothers based on an analogy with Deuteronomy's mother bird or, alternatively, on a claim that the prohibition applies only to the parent "to whom the child clings." That parent is, according to the Sifra, the mother.

The Babylonian Talmud cites the mothers-only tradition but offers also a dissenting opinion that animal fathers are included, pointing to the masculine grammar in Leviticus.[57] That dissenting opinion, attributed to a Rabbi named Hananiah, is declared definitive law.[58] In his Mishneh Torah, Maimonides rules that the prohibition technically applies only to animal mothers but says that in a case where the father is known with certainty, the prohibition applies to him too, though with less legal force than to the mother.[59] The Shulhan Arukh recapitulates Maimonides, making his approach the legal touchstone.[60] Mothers are the main subject of the prohibition, but fathers may be marginally included.

The bias toward animal mothers is so pronounced in ancient Judaism that historian Shaye Cohen has argued that it is the basis for the famous Jewish matrilineal principle, which makes the mother the basis for Jewish status.[61] It is tempting to say that the emphasis on an animal's maternal genealogy is a response to biological realities. The mammalian mother, who has the job of bearing, feeding, and raising the child, is the far more identifiable parent. In most mammal species, fathers do not actually do very much as fathers.[62] The father may well not be known. We would not need paternity tests if it were easy to tell.[63] But the biology is not as simple as it seems. Among domesticated animals, the father is often known with certainty, especially in boutique breeding. Moreover, as zoologists Devra Kleiman and James Malcolm point out, a large number of mammal species show indirect paternal investment such as antipredator behavior and resource maintenance.[64] Paternal care is at any rate a moot question for domesticated animals, whose relationships are highly constrained by their human owners. Even if a domesticated animal wanted to be a great father, they likely would not get the chance. The Mishnah's emphasis on animal mothers rather than fathers is best seen as a choice and not a necessity of biology. The Mishnah chooses not to feature animal grandfathers the way it does animal grandmothers, and it chooses not to offer public announcements about the sales of fathers and sons. That being said, the Mishnah never outright excludes animal fathers and grandfathers the way some other ancient readers of the Leviticus prohibition did.

WHEN THE BUTCHER SHOWS UP

Civil rights historian Charles Payne once said that history "is something that happens when the White Folks show up and stops when they leave."[65] We might say, along similar lines, that animal-family history for the Mishnah is something that happens when the butcher shows up and stops when he leaves. Animal grandmothers and grandchildren and sisters matter, but they matter only when and because they are meat. "Genealogy is not free of power relations," observes Rachel Gross. Or, as anthropologist

Janet Carsten writes, "The history of kinship is always, among other things, a political history."[66]

That is no less true for the animal genealogies announced in the Mishnah. The Mishnah makes animal families publicly visible, but, as I have shown, there is little affect or empathy in these legislations about animals.[67] Whiffs of feeling sometimes waft up: people feasting together during their festivals, brides and grooms preparing for their wedding. But these hints of affect, if they are that, attach only to the humans of the Mishnah chapter and not to the many animals who appear in it. The Mishnah's shorthand labels, abstract categories, and brainteaser scenarios instead depersonalize the animals whose lives are at stake, draining the law, and with it human-animal and animal-animal relationships, of anything that resembles ethics. The Mishnah's principle that violation of the same-day slaughter prohibition does not invalidate the animal as meat seems to sever that law from lived relationships and to preserve the status quo of human power over animals.

The Mishnah's approach to animal genealogies is echoed in contemporary times in the pedigree certificate that can be purchased online from the American Kennel Club. The certificate "displays the lineage of an AKC dog and important information about the ancestors in a dog's family tree."[68] The date that appears next to the dog's registration number is not a birthday but the issue date of the "Stud Book Register" that shows the "sire and dam." The pedigree certificate shows AKC title wins for the dog's "stud" and "bitch" and certifications for the quality of the dog's hips, elbows, and eyes. The AKC certificate assesses the value of an animal in the way a jeweler would rate the carats of a diamond. The AKC, Uncle Marcus in Columella's sheep-breeding anecdote, and the Mishnah may each have different reasons for their concern with animal genealogies, but common to all of them is the manipulation of those genealogies to accord with human interest, whether that interest be best-in-show prize, fine wool and color, or loyalty to scriptural law.

But genealogies can also subvert power relations.[69] In Australia, family-history research helped to break down the "collective amnesia" that had developed around the deportation of many thousands of English convicts in the eighteenth and nineteenth centuries.[70] The descendants of those convicts had changed their names, fabricated family trees, and "lost" government records. Australians who decided to embrace their authentic family histories were able to contest the national narrative that had concealed Australia's past and shrouded it in shame. In his popular PBS television show *Finding Your Roots*, Henry Louis Gates Jr. uses genealogy to uncover the intertwined histories of Black and white Americans and to show that most of us were, at some point, immigrants to these shores, whether by choice or by force.[71] We might see the Mishnah, in parallel, as a recouping of kinship with liberatory potential. The Mishnah's language of family and its requirement for public recognition of animal kinship recover animal personhood and at least unconsciously remind people of it in a way that the English language resists when it refers to studs and bitches and sires and dams. Any time people wish to slaughter or sell an animal, they must first, according to the Mishnah, recall that animal's biography and family tree, asking themselves, Who is this cow's mother? Who are her daughters? Who are her granddaughters?

The attentiveness to animal families found first in biblical law emerges from an agrarian setting in which those relationships would probably have been readily known. In the urban commercial context of the Mishnah, which reflects robust economic exchange of cattle, it would have been more difficult to keep track of animal kin. Yet the biblical injunction prevented marketplace logic from triumphing completely. The prohibition against same-day slaughter inspired the Mishnah to recuperate animal-family relations. Following the model of the Mishnah, so too might we today take inspiration from biblical law and find ways to break out of our own collective amnesia about animal families. Those families deserve recognition.

4 Animal Mothers

THE PROHIBITION AGAINST COOKING A KID IN HIS MOTHER'S MILK

MILK AND MEAT

The Bible features many puzzling laws and rituals: using the ashes of a burnt red cow to remedy corpse impurity (Numbers 19), hacking apart a calf in response to an unsolved homicide (Deuteronomy 21:1–4), and not combining linen and wool in a garment (22:11). One of the more mysterious is the prohibition against cooking young goats in their mother's milk that appears in Exodus 23:19, Exodus 34:26, and Deuteronomy 14:21. Bible readers through the ages have tried to crack this nut. One solution is the "humanitarian" rationale that I discuss in chapter 2, embodied in Philo's proposal that cooking young animals in the fluid meant to sustain them is callous and cruel.[1] A second is a cultic explanation, associated with Maimonides, that cooking kids in their mother's milk was an idolatrous Canaanite practice that the biblical authors considered taboo.[2] Other theories are that the law prohibits removing baby goats from their mother while they are still nursing; that it prohibits cooking kids in their mother's fat (rather than milk); that it falls under the prohibition of eating blood, which mother goat's colostrum might have looked as though it contained; and that it reflects an ancient belief in a divine nursing animal figure.³ Some have suggested that the prohibition has nothing to do with animals at all and is actually about leaving first fruits to ripen in the field or about discouraging incest.⁴

Some ancient Jews understood the prohibition in yet another way. The ancient Aramaic translation of the Bible Targum Onkelos translates the Hebrew "Do not cook a kid in his mother's milk," saying, "Do not eat meat in milk." The brevity of the Targum should not conceal its enormous innovation to the verse, which the Targum extends from cooking to eating, from goats to all animals eaten for meat, and from the mother-child pair to any meat with any milk. The early rabbinic midrash Mekhilta de-Rabbi Yishmael further expands on this approach, proposing that the prohibition extends not just to cooking and eating meat with milk but also to deriving benefits from it; that the prohibition applies to cooking an animal of one species in the milk from an animal of another species (for example, cooking a sheep in goat's milk); that it prohibits cooking an animal in milk that the animal herself produced; and that it applies to the meat of fowl, who do not even produce milk.⁵ Contemporaneous material from Mishnah Hullin Chapter Eight makes similar generalizations from the prohibition. The mother-child pair at the center of the prohibition recedes and is replaced by abstract categories of milk and meat.⁶ That the separation between all milk and all meat is a "weird" new prohibition not well rooted in scripture is recognized in the rabbinic writings themselves, which call it a *hiddush* (novel law).⁷

The story of this strange biblical prohibition is almost the opposite of the one told in my previous chapter about the prohibition against same-day slaughter. When the Rabbis read the Bible's prohibition against same-day slaughter, they brought animal families to the fore. When they read the prohibition against cooking kids in their mother's milk, they pushed animal families into the background. If the central question of the previous chapter was what happens when we pay attention to animal families, the central question of this chapter is what happens when we don't.

THE ABSENT REFERENT

To get at that question, I look at rabbinic discussions about the consumption of udders. It is harder to forget about the mother when discussing the organ through which the infant attaches to her. The central image of the scriptural prohibition—the mother-child pair—reasserts itself through the udder and recalls scripture's original concern. The udder thus brings to the surface some fairly inconvenient truths about the labyrinthine logics of rabbinic law that allow it to stray so far from scripture and also about the practices of animal agriculture that habitually break the bond between animal mothers and their children. The udder makes it difficult to deny those dual realities of rabbinic life. In this chapter I take readers through the Talmud's treatment of the udder and suggest that the catalyst for its complex laws and lively stories about the udder is, first, the exegetical gap between the biblical prohibition on cooking kids in their mother's milk and the rabbinic laws about milk and meat and, second, the ethical gap that forms when the mother-child pair of the biblical prohibition gets lost from view. The Rabbis' encounter with the udder has implications for the treatment of animals and for the Jewish interpretive project as a whole.

I employ the standard feminist methodology of recovering female voices from texts in which they are normally marginalized.[8] You will hear the voices of women in the street and in the household who pose challenges to standard rabbinic practice. But in this chapter I also take a more unusual and admittedly more arguable approach to the Talmud in identifying there an "absent referent," a notion I take from Carol Adams's feminist writing about meat: "The absent referent is the literal being who disappears in the eating of dead bodies. The absent referent functions to put the violence under wraps: there is no 'cow' whom we have to think about."[9] A routine example would be a package of ground beef in the meat section of the supermarket. Even the name—"beef" instead of "cow"—deflects attention from the animal. One could easily not know that a Big Mac or Whopper came from a cow. The naming, the chopping and broiling, the fixings, the quick purchase, the Happy Meal, all "keep *something* from being seen as having been *someone*."[10] It is difficult to establish the presence of the absent referent because it is an argument from silence. I take to be our guides the women we meet in the Talmud who flout or skirt the laws of milk and meat; they alert us to who or what is missing. The missing person in this Talmudic discussion is no person at all, though, but the animal mother, buried beneath the sediment of rabbinic law.

THE MISHNAH'S UDDER PROBLEM

Mishnah Tractate Hullin Chapters Five to Ten treat a series of scriptural commandments related to *hullin* (meat outside the context of sacrifice). Chapter Eight is dedicated to the prohibition against cooking kids in their mother's milk. As I show in the previous chapter, Tractate Hullin is not interested in the law's rationale but in its application. The first four Mishnahs of Hullin Chapter Eight address the mixing of milk and meat as it relates to food preparation, cooking, serving, and eating. The udder appears within that section:

> A drop of milk that fell on a piece of meat: if there is in it a sufficient amount to impart flavor to that pot, it is forbidden.
>
> If he stirred the pot, if it is sufficient to impart flavor to that pot, it is forbidden.
>
> The udder: he tears it open and removes its milk.
>
> If he did not tear it open, he does not transgress on its account.
>
> The heart: He tears it open and removes its blood.
>
> If he did not tear it open, he did not transgress on its account.
>
> One who brings up fowl with cheese on the table does not transgress a negative commandment.[11]

This Mishnah starts with the problem of milk falling into a pot of cooking meat, moves to the procedure for permitting the consumption of an udder or heart, and closes with the case of poultry being served together with cheese. This Mishnah pairs eating the udder with eating the heart since both are "meat" organs that contain troubling fluids that are best extracted before cooking—milk, because it cannot be mixed with meat, and blood, because it cannot be eaten at all.[12]

The Mishnah's interest in the udder can be thought to follow four tracks: legal, symbolic, conceptual, and moral. The udder is legally interesting because it is simultaneously milk and meat and therefore presents the kind of category problem cherished by legal thought. The udder is of symbolic interest because the breast is the first node of affect for a mammal, offering nourishment, comfort, and attachment but also generating frustration and aggression. The udder is of particular interest in its being like the human breast but also different in its position, singleness, and multiple nipples.[13] The udder is conceptually interesting in the boundary problems it poses. The breast is a transitional space, an idea developed by psychoanalyst Donald W. Winnicott, between infant and world, with the milk flowing directly from the mother's body to the infant's, with periodic drips, spurts, or spit-ups finding their way into the external environment. The milk is doubly "inside": inside the udder, which is itself within the body of the mother cow, goat, or sheep, and then inside the baby's stomach, which is itself within the body of the baby. The udder suggests layers of insideness and outsideness. Udders are, finally, morally interesting in that they suggest that family attachments transcend the human. The dietary system makes animals into meat, but the udder pushes back as a reminder of the intimate lives of animals. The udder, in sum, invites a variety of lenses as the Rabbis grapple with its many meanings.

IS COOKING MEAT IN MILK EVER PERMITTED?

The ambiguity of the udder as both milk and meat is resolved, seemingly, by the tearing instruction in Mishnah Three: "He tears it open and removes its milk."[14] Getting rid of the milk inside the udder seems to make it just like any other organ. At the same time, tearing seems not to be entirely necessary from a legal point of view: "If he did not tear it open, he does not transgress on its account." Why is it okay for a person not to tear the udder and empty it of milk if the Mishnah first instructs people to do just that? The opening of the Babylonian Talmud's commentary raises this question:

> Rabbi Zeira said that Rav said: He does not transgress on its account, and it is permitted.
> But we learn: "He does not transgress on its account"—
> He does not transgress, but there is a prohibition![15]

Rav spells out the implications of the Mishnah. One may still eat the udder even if one does not first tear it. There must be some prohibition involved, objects the editorial voice in the Talmud, or the Mishnah would not say to do it. It cannot be that the udder truly is permitted to eat if one does not first take out the milk.

This problem occupies the entire opening section of the Talmudic discussion. Two approaches take shape, one permissive and one restrictive. On the permissive side, the voice of the Talmud suggests that one may eat the udder whether or not one tears it, either before or after cooking. On the strict side is the Talmud's proposal based on an alternative version of Rav's teaching ("and there are those that say, Rabbi Zeira said in the name of Rav: 'One does not transgress on its account, but it is forbidden'") that one must tear it beforehand, and afterward is too late. Without tearing prior to cooking and certainly eating, the udder is prohibited.

A teaching in the Mishnah's partner corpus, the Tosefta, is cited by the Talmud to support the permissive position:

> Let us say that [the following teaching] supports him: "The udder—one tears it and removes its milk. [If] one did not tear it, he does not transgress on its account. The heart—one tears it and removes its blood. [If] one did not tear it, one tears it after cooking it, and it is permitted."
> A heart is that which requires tearing, but an udder does not require tearing.[16]

The tradition represents essentially the same instruction as the Mishnah but with one key difference. The person who does not tear the heart before cooking is directed to do so afterward, at which point the heart becomes permitted to eat and only then. The implication, says the editorial voice, is that with the udder, one need not tear it even after cooking it. Not so with the heart, whose blood must be extracted at some point before eating it.

Which position on the udder does the Talmud implicitly support, the restrictive or permissive? A clue lies in the cap-off to this section, when the Tosefta is further quoted as support for the permissive stance:

> It is taught [in an early rabbinic tradition] in accordance with the first version of Rav: "An udder that one cooked in its milk is permitted. The stomach [of a suckling lamb or calf] that one cooked in its milk is prohibited." And what is the distinction between one and the other? The one is collected in his innards, but the other is not collected in his innards.[17]

The udder is contrasted here not with the heart, as in the prior teaching, but with the calf's full stomach, and the milk inside the one with the milk inside the other. The milk of the udder is "not collected in his innards" like the milk of the stomach, explains the Tosefta. Since the milk found inside the udder when the animal mother is slaughtered never left the udder, unlike the milk found inside her child's stomach, it "does not come under the category of milk," as Rashi comments.[18] When a person cooks the udder in its own milk, that meat is perfectly acceptable to eat. The section ends with the rather shocking idea, from a rabbinic perspective, that one can cook a piece of meat—the udder—in milk.

A FINE LINE

The rest of the passage is less about unraveling this mystery than wrapping it in additional layers. A story is told about Yalta, one of the few named women in the Talmud.[19] In it Yalta makes some astute observations about the relationship between law and desire:

> Yalta said to Rav Nahman: Now for anything that the Merciful One prohibited to us, He permitted to us something similar. He prohibited to us blood, yet He permitted to us liver; [He prohibited sexual intercourse with a] menstruating woman, [but permitted sexual intercourse with a woman who discharges] the blood of purity. [God prohibits] the fat of a *behemah* [domesticated animal] [but permits] the fat of a *hayah* [undomesticated animal]; pork, the brain of a *shibuta* fish; *giruta* [a nonkosher fish], a fish's tongue; a married woman, a divorced woman during the life of her [ex-]husband; one's brother's wife, his *yevamah* [his brother's widow when the brother dies childless; Deut. 25:5-10]; a gentile woman, a "beautiful woman" [who is a prisoner of war; Deut. 21:10-14]. We wish to eat meat in milk! Rav Nahman said to the cooks: "Blow up some udders for her!"[20]

For every item that the law forbids, something comparable is permitted, observes Yalta. These are the pairs with which Yalta illustrates her point:

Prohibited	Permitted
Animal blood	Animal liver
Menstrual blood	Blood of purification (nonmenstrual bleeding)
Fat of domesticated animal	Fat of wild animal
Pig	Shibuta brain
Giruta (eel-like fish)[21]	Fish tongue
Married woman	Divorced woman while ex-husband is alive
Brother's wife	Brother's widow when the brother dies childless
Gentile woman	Female prisoner of war

The pairs fall into the categories of either sex or food. The language shifts between Hebrew and Aramaic, with sex for the most part in Hebrew, food in Aramaic.[22] Though the voice is that of a woman, the perspective is male in claiming that the Torah forbids *us* a menstruating woman or the wife of another man. Yalta ends with her wish to eat meat in milk.

The punch line belongs to Rav Nahman, who orders up some udders for his wife. Really it belongs to students of the Talmud, who by the end of the story are primed, if they are as clever as this husband-and-wife team, with the solution to Yalta's seemingly unrequitable desire: the udder, the only "kosher" way to eat milk and meat together. Like the other items on the permitted list, the udder has the allure of the taboo, that which the Torah permits but which comes thrillingly close to the forbidden.

THE LAX LADIES OF TATTLEFUSH

The udder's air of taboo might help to explain Rav's stringency in the story to which I turn next. Rav pays a visit to the wonderfully named village of Tattlefush, where he overhears a couple of women chatting.[23] One is asking the other for cooking tips:

> When Rav arrived in Tattlefush, he heard a certain woman saying to her friend: How much milk does it require to cook a quarter-weight of meat? He said: They are not educated in [the prohibition of] meat in milk. He tarried and prohibited udders to them.[24]

Rav does not like what he hears. He infers from their conversation that they are not versed in the prohibition of milk and meat. Whether that is the case, or the women know of it but choose not to adhere to it, Rav takes extreme action. Rather than teach the prohibition itself, Rav goes a few steps further and issues a total prohibition on udders. Even the restrictive position attributed to Rav, cited here, permits udders if they are properly torn.

The Tattlefush tale is told in connection with a debate over the origins of Rav's restrictive position:

> When Rabbi Elazar ascended [from Babylonia to Palestine] he found Zeiri. He said to him: Is there a *tanna* [an early Rabbi] who taught Rav an udder? He showed him Rav Yitzhak bar Avudimi. He said to him: I did not teach Rav an udder at all; rather, Rav found a valley and fenced it in with a fence.
> ... Rav Kahana teaches thus; Rabbi Yose bar Abba teaches: I taught him the udder of a nursing mother. And due to the sharpness of Rabbi Hiyya, he taught an unspecified udder.[25]

Rabbi Elazar wants to know from Zeiri which transmitter is responsible for Rav's prohibition. Rav Yitzhak bar Avudimi chalks up Rav's stance to his hardline legal philosophy, expressed in the eloquently redundant "fenc[ing] it in with a fence."[26] Even if udders technically are permitted, better to prohibit them in case people get the wrong idea that milk and meat can be mixed. Rabbi Yosi bar Abba attributes Rav's prohibition on udders instead to Rav's misunderstanding of Rabbi Hiyya, who, being too smart for his own good, assumed Rav would understand that only in certain cases—an actively nursing animal mother "whose breasts have a great deal of milk collected in them," comments Rashi—is the udder a problem. Rav needed Rabbi Hiyya to spell it out; Rav incorrectly inferred a universal ban on udders from Rabbi Hiyya's carelessly vague ruling. By the section's end, one is left to wonder what went wrong in this rabbinic game of telephone. As in a Talmudic story about a dangerous cat that I have written about in another context, Rav reacts to a problem with an outsize ruling, a disproportionate and likely-to-be ineffective response that conceals and distracts from deeper tensions—tensions that I explore in this chapter's conclusion.[27]

The Tattlefush story bears resemblances to the one about Yalta. In both, women defy the prohibition against milk and meat. Yalta brazenly declares her appetite for meat cooked in milk, while the female friends of Tattlefush casually converse about it. The consequences are diametrically opposed. For Yalta the udder redirects the wish for the forbidden into licit channels. For the women of Tattlefush, the udder itself becomes forbidden. It is the difference between bending the law to desire—Yalta has a keen eye for this—and bending desire to the law, which Rav does with a little too much law-and-order enthusiasm. In both stories men make the ultimate call. The impression left by the sequence is that Rav's stringent stance on the udder reflects the flaws of rabbinic transmission. The informal communication of women in the marketplace conveys specific, clear, and useful information (a quarter-weight of meat, how much milk does one need for cooking?), while the formal communication of Rabbis, by contrast, seems filled with glitches and results in draconian measures.

DINNER AT RAV PAPPI'S

The next episode—set in a later rabbinic era, the fourth and fifth generations of Talmudic Rabbis rather than the first, second, and third, as the prior stories were and subsequent story will be—is a dinner at Rav Pappi's. The udder continues to be divisive, here getting in the way of Rabbis enjoying a meal together:

> Ravin and Rav Yitzhak bar Yosef arrived at the house of Rav Pappi. They brought before them a dish of udder. Rav Yitzhak bar Yosef ate. Ravin did not eat. Abaye said: Bereaved Ravin *[Ravin takhla]*, why do you not eat? After all, Rav Pappi's wife is the daughter of Rabbi Yitzhak Nappaha, and Rabbi Yitzhak Nappaha was a master of good deeds. If she had not heard it in her father's house, she would not have made [it].[28]

Ravin is called by the moniker *takhla*, a possible wordplay on udder *(kehal)* and a reference, according to Rashi, to having buried his children, an apt association for a story about a disemboweled udder. The total ban on udders introduced by Rav in Tattlefush appears to have had its influence, with Ravin refraining from eating a supper of udders with his colleagues.

How is the division among Rabbis adjudicated? Through the woman of the house. Abaye notes that Rav Pappi's wife is the daughter of Rabbi Yitzhak Nappaha, said to be a man of upstanding behavior. If Rav Pappi's wife had not learned in her father's model household to eat udders, she would not be serving them in her own, says Abaye.[29] Abaye highlights the role of women in transmitting legal standards in a mimetic model that offers an alternative to formal rabbinic transmission.[30] Women's informal modes of transmission come across once again—recall the women of Tattlefush—as effective and unifying, while the Rabbis get gummed up in their disagreements. Once again the female figures in the story are associated with cooking and eating udders.

GORGING BEFORE YOM KIPPUR

The climactic story of the sequence features the trickster figure Rami bar Tamarei, named also Rami bar Dikulei, satisfying his appetite for udders:

> In Sura they do not eat udders; in Pumbedita they do eat udders. Rami bar Tamarei, who is Rami bar Dikulei, from Pumbedita, arrived in Sura on the eve of Yom Kippur. Everyone brought out their udders and threw them away. He went and gathered them and ate them.[31]

The story begins with background information. The town of Sura's custom is not to eat udders—Rav's ban in Tattlefush must have taken hold there—while Pumbedita's is. Rami bar Tamarei arrives in Sura on the eve of Yom Kippur, just as all the Suran Jews are discarding their udders while they prepare their pre-fast feasts. Rami bar Tamarei takes the opportunity to scoop up the discarded udders and make for himself a meal of udders.

Rami bar Tamarei's dinner draws the attention of Rav Hisda, to whom Rami is brought.[32] The two Rabbis engage in a tête à tête about Rami's questionable behavior:

> They brought him before Rav Hisda. He said to him: Why would you do this? He said to him: I am from the place of Rav Yehudah, which eats. He said to him: And do you not hold [by the principle that] they impose upon him the stringencies of the place that he left and the stringencies of the place

to which he went? He said to him: I ate them outside the boundaries [of Sura]. And with what did you roast them? He said to him: Grapeseeds. Perhaps they were from wine used for a libation to idolatry? He said to him: They were [there] for twelve months. Perhaps they were stolen? He said to him: There would have been despair of the owners, as grass was growing among them. He saw that he had not put on tefillin. He said to him: What is the reason that you have not put on tefillin? He said to him: He is [i.e., I am] suffering from intestinal illness, and Rav Yehudah said that one who has intestinal illness is exempt from tefillin. He saw that he had not placed [*rami*] threads [of tzitzit]. He said to him: What is the reason that you do not have the threads? He said to him: It is a borrowed robe, and Rav Yehudah said with regard to a borrowed robe that during all of the [first] thirty days one is exempt from tzitzit.[33]

Rav Hisda's first challenge is direct and simple: "Why would you do this?" How could you eat udders in a town that forbids them? Rami's response is to identify himself as hailing from "the place of Rav Yehudah." Rami's association with Rav Yehudah's residence resurfaces at the end of the story.

When Rav Hisda objects to Rami's disrespect for local customs, Rami claims to have had his pre-fast meal on the outskirts of Sura, where town customs do not apply. When accused of using grapeseed oil derived from idolatrous libation wine or, alternatively, stolen seeds, Rami declares his grape seeds to be too old to be prohibited on those counts. When Rav Hisda asks Rami why he is not wearing tefillin, Rami notes that his stomachache (from all those udders?) has absolved him of the obligation, according to the opinion of Rav Yehudah. When Rav Hisda asks Rami why he does not place tzitzit on his garments (a Rami who does not *rami!*), Rami has an answer for that too. His garment is borrowed and so tzitzit are not required, again according to the opinion of Rav Yehudah.[34]

Did Rami really use aged grape seeds to roast his udders and then eat them outside the town limits? Did he not bother with tefillin because he had a stomachache and was his garment in fact borrowed? We are probably not meant to find Rami's excuses persuasive. The point is Rami's capacity to deflect any legal argument thrown (Aramaic: *rami!*) his way. The coup de grâce for Rav Hisda comes when a man is hauled in for having dishonored his mother and father. As Rav Hisda's henchmen prepare to flog the offender, Rami tells them to back off:

ANIMAL MOTHERS 99

> Meanwhile, they brought in a certain man who would not honor his father and mother. They tied him up. He said to them: Leave him alone, as it is taught [in an early rabbinic tradition]: With regard to any positive commandment whose reward is stated alongside it, the earthly court is not meant to enforce it.[35]

Rami stops them with an authoritative teaching. Only the heavenly court punishes a sin whose rewards are explicit in the Torah, as is the case for honoring parents, which is said to merit long life (Exodus 20:12; Deuteronomy 5:16).

Whether the man is flogged or not, we will never know, but Rami finally earns the grudging respect of Rav Hisda:

> He said to him: I see that you are very sharp. He said to him: If you were in the place of Rav Yehudah, I would show you my sharpness![36]

You're quite the smart aleck, says Rav Hisda to Rami. Just you wait, Rami responds. Go to Rav Yehudah's residence, and I'll show you smart.

Rami's sparring with Rav Hisda indexes a variety of rabbinic legal topics: legal pluralism, libation wine, loss and theft, tefillin, tallit, borrowed items, honor of father and mother, and fair penalties. Like the Yalta story, this story celebrates the legal workaround.[37] One may need to eat on the outskirts of town or make do with fish brains instead of pork, but one can get fairly close to fulfilling one's wishes, whatever the law is. Rav Yehudah, whom Rami invokes at the beginning, middle, and end of his repartee, embodies the power of legal wit to achieve one's desired results, and Pumbedita, Rav Yehudah's "place," provides its locus. The Rabbi named Rav from Sura, a central figure throughout the larger passage, represents an alternative type of legal power, that of "finding a valley and fencing it in."[38] The udder is the battleground over which these two models vie with each other.

GOT MILK?

The image of the Rabbi gorging on udders on the outskirts of the city as the Day of Atonement arrives captures the uncanny tone of the passage as a whole. The udder's ambiguity—milk and meat at the same time, permitted by some and prohibited by others—highlights competing models of legal reasoning and ruling. On the one hand is the repressive stringency of Rav, who reflects a tradition that is misunderstood, broken, or reactionary, while on the other hand is the playful tricksterism of Rami and Yalta. Alongside these models is one of women trading information in their daily domestic lives. The anonymous authors of the Talmud do not so much side with either stance as expose the strategies by which Rabbis navigate the exegetical and ethical gaps that are opened up by their project.

Joining recent efforts to recover the Jewish mother in the narration of Jewishness, I look here to the animal mother as an even less heralded yet still powerful figure.[39] The repressed mother, I propose, appears in various guises throughout the Talmudic passage on the udder in Hullin 109a–110b. The animal breast as it emerges in the Talmud's treatment divides men from women, some Rabbis from other Rabbis, and Jews in one Babylonian city from Jews in another. It comes dangerously close to causing a violation of the Torah's commands. The animal mother, symbolized by the udder, resists her invisibility within rabbinic law and challenges the mechanisms and media through which that law works.[40]

If we are to eat animals, we must not see their attachments, which bear uncomfortable resemblances to our own. The Torah appears to have been troubled by those resemblances; its prohibition on cooking kids in their mother's milk seems to reflect such discomfort. The Rabbis tried to put the resemblances out of mind when it came to interpreting this prohibition. But the mother—and female perspective—prove difficult to forget when thinking about the udder. The Talmudic treatment of the udder invites those accustomed to rabbinic practices to see the irony in them: Yalta with her legal loopholes, the ladies of Tattlefush with their casual disregard for this entire area of law, Rav Pappi's wife with her mimetic traditions, and Rami bar Tamarei with his tricksterism. These stories have a gotcha quality; there is a knowingness to them. The stories seem to say that, in using our exegetical ingenuity, we have concealed even from ourselves the true meaning of the Torah.

But what the Talmud misses is the violence behind its interpretive games—a gender-based violence, Carol Adams would say, pointing out that meat and masculinity usually go hand in hand.[41] Yalta and Rami may be funny, but the udder is no joking matter. A twenty-first-century reader, schooled by Peter Singer and PETA, can't but take seriously the suffering that farm animals experience when mother and child are separated at birth and deprived of the bonds of intimacy and sociality, to say nothing of the pure brutality that animals today endure in industrial livestock production.[42] We readers of the Talmud's treatment of the udder may realize somewhere along the way that the animal mother, *her* relationship to *her* child, and not the generic abstractions that the Rabbis call "meat" and "milk," is the concern that brought these laws into being in the first place. When read with Carol Adams and other contemporary critics of meat culture, the Talmud teaches about the damage done when rabbinic lines of transmission are privileged and female traditions are ignored and when all the traces of motherhood are destroyed even as we are contemplating one of its central symbols—milk—and the organ that produces it: the udder.[43]

The udder invites reflection on rabbinic tricksterism, on the capacity of the Rabbi to argue nearly anything. This is Yalta's point when she shows how little daylight there is between the permitted and the prohibited. The female figures in this Talmudic material, along with this animal organ, the udder, betray the fiction on which the law rests. They resist the displacement of the mother and child both in the Rabbis' legal substance (milk and meat) and the Rabbis' legal form (male-to-male formal instruction). Female modes of production, reproduction, attachment, and transmission prove more reliable, less brittle, than the ones adopted by the Rabbis and especially by Rav in his restrictive position. The repressed female returns in the women of this Talmudic material, in the female body and its fluids, and most of all in the udder. The Talmud opposes laxity with stringency, tricksterism with dimwittedness, women with men, and humans with animals and demonstrates, with respect to all of them, the power of appetite and the ambivalence of attachment. The Talmud almost but not quite succeeds in suppressing the intimate lives of animals that we try to forget.

I return to a question I posed earlier in this book: What do the animal-family laws do for animals? In the case of the prohibition on cooking kids in their mother's milk, the answer is, regrettably, *not very much*. Through the marvel of their exegetical skill, the Rabbis managed to suppress the concern with animal families that animates this biblical law, even if the precise contours of that concern will remain forever mysterious to the

Bible's readers. And, yet, in the Talmud's discussions about the udder, female perspectives and practices percolate up. Animal mothers do not themselves appear, but resistance to the way rabbinic law treats them does. This chapter shows that, try as we might, forgetting the animal family never fully works.

5 Animal Fathers and Other Caregivers

SENDING OFF THE MOTHER BIRD

BIRDS, BUBBIES, AND BEAUTIFUL MITZVAHS

The video "Yonis Mom Does Shiluach Hakan" did not go viral, and neither did "Bubby Does Shiluach Hakan"[1] The YouTube videos show women shooing birds off their porches and picking up the eggs left behind in the nest. In "Yonis Mom," the featured woman (presumably the mother of someone named Yoni) struggles to scare the pigeon off her porch. Yoni's mom is the one who looks scared, though, as she stamps her feet in the pigeon's direction, saying worriedly, "Where's it going to go, in my face?" In "Bubby Does Shiluach Hakan," a woman's family coaches her as she opens her porch's sliding door with purple plastic gloves. Fortunately for Bubby (Yiddish for "grandma"), the bird flies away as soon as she steps onto the porch ("See, it's shooing away already," says her daughter) so all that is left to Bubby to do is to lean over and grab the eggs from the nest in the corner. Bubby clutches the eggs in her hand, murmuring a prayer as she ignores pleas from her family to turn around and face the camera. A grandchild outside the video frame exclaims, "Bubby, what a beautiful mitzvah!"

Yoni's mom and Bubby are performing the commandment known as *shiluach haken* (literally, "sending of the nest").[2] I turn in this chapter to a third animal-family law, sending off the mother bird. The mitzvah's origin is in Deuteronomy:

> ⁶If you happen upon a bird's nest along the road, in any tree, or on the ground, with chicks or eggs, and the mother is sitting over the chicks or on the eggs, do not take the mother with her children. ⁷Send off the mother, and take the children for yourself, in order that you may fare well and have a long life.
>
> (22:6-7)

One must first shoo away the mother bird before taking her chicks or eggs from the nest. Found in a miscellany of criminal, civil, and family laws, the command is immediately preceded not, as one might expect, by the instruction to restore lost and fallen animals that comes a few lines earlier (22:1-4) but with a prohibition on cross-dressing (22:55), and it is followed by the requirement to surround one's roof with a guardrail to make sure that no one falls off (22:8). The bird commandment's concern with respect for parents evokes the law of the insubordinate son found in the preceding chapter (21:18-21) but is even more explicitly connected to the decalogue's "honor thy father and mother" (5:16), which offers the same promise of prosperity and long life that this command does.³

It is that reward that Yoni's mom and Bubby are seeking, as are the other people performing this commandment featured on YouTube, mostly ultra-Orthodox Rabbis in the company of their followers. The mitzvah has generated something of a cottage industry, with charges of up to five or six hundred dollars for a home pickup and drive to a nesting spot.⁴ It is an awkward, even comical mitzvah. People shake sticks and screwdrivers at pigeons nesting in the crevices of urban landscapes. They climb rickety ladders to reach nests whose contents may be a surprise. In one video a Rabbi who has climbed a ladder to take a nest from the eaves of a building exclaims when he finds a fully hatched chick there. One of the boys to whom the Rabbi shows the chick looks alarmed. As the Rabbi turns to the assembled boys and blesses each one, the fearful boy shouts, "You're going to kill her [the bird]!" On another video in which a father pulls out a bird's nest from behind a light affixed to a wall and asks his children, "Who wants to see the eggies?," someone on YouTube comments, "Where's PETA?"⁵

The path from Deuteronomy to Bubby's porch is plotted through a passage in the Babylonian Talmud:

> The Sages taught (in an early rabbinic teaching): "If you happen upon a bird's nest" (Deuteronomy 22:6). What teaching [does the verse] convey? Since it is stated "Send off the mother, and take the children for yourself" (22:7), is it possible that one should search in the mountains and hills in order to find a nest? The verse states "If [you] happen upon"—when it befalls you.[6]

This commentary on Deuteronomy 22:6 poses a rhetorical question: Should one seek out a bird's nest to perform the mitzvah? Of course not, answers the midrash.[7] One performs the mitzvah only should it become relevant, in the same way that one returns one's neighbor's lost ox only if the ox gets lost (Deuteronomy 22:1). The midrash's intentionally implausible reading of the verse, through a fluke, ends up being taken by modern audiences to be the Talmud's, and the biblical verse's, intended meaning. This counterintuitive reading of Deuteronomy—that one should go out of one's way to find bird nests just to be able to fulfill the mitzvah—was inspired by the Jewish mystical work the Zohar, which envisions the suffering of the mother bird catching the notice of the divine Shekhinah, who then fills with compassion and redeems the suffering people of Israel.[8] By the eighteenth century it had evidently become popular to seek out opportunities to perform the mitzvah, though most rabbinic decisors objected to the practice. Contemporary writers on the mitzvah—promoter of Jewish rationalism Natan Slifkin and eco-kabbalah scholar David Seidenberg—critique the practice, Slifkin calling it a pursuit of personal reward rather than service of God, and Seidenberg describing it as "truly perverse" and contrary to "common sense, and to ethical human development."[9]

A BIRD-CENTRIC APPROACH TO THE MOTHER-BIRD MITZVAH

In this chapter I showcase the bird-centric approach to this mitzvah taken by the ancient Rabbis. Along with the three other commandments in the

Torah treated in this book—do not cook a kid in his mother's milk (Exodus 23:19, 34:26; Deuteronomy 14:21); leave a baby animal with the mother for the first week of life (Exodus 22:29; Leviticus 22:27); and do not slaughter an animal parent and child on the same day (Leviticus 22:28)—the law of sending off the mother bird is concerned with animal kinship ties. Often, though, the reading of these laws makes them about people, not animals. The mother bird's relationship to her chicks is merely the pretext for people to pursue their own ends.

I begin this chapter with the dominant anthropocentric perspective on the mother-bird mitzvah that sees it as offering good luck, as in the YouTube videos, or a lesson in theology and ethics. But I then proceed to materials from the Mishnah and Babylonian Talmud Tractate Hullin that have been underrepresented, materials that feature neither good luck nor bad luck, nor theology nor ethics, nor anything human at all. The rabbinic texts that I discuss from Hullin Chapter Twelve evince interest in birds as ingenious builders, as fathers and not just mothers, as caregivers and altruists, as rebel spirits who resist captivity even unto death and, finally, in birds as coinhabitants of the earth whose lives are parallel to as well as enmeshed with our own. I present here a reading of the mitzvah in a spirit of antianthropocentrism.

To help me, I draw on philosopher Matthew Calarco's notion of indistinction.[10] According to Calarco, indistinction is a "zone of profound identity" and "shared, exposed embodiment among human and animal."[11] Indistinction begins with seeing animals as similar to people, such as when we see elephants bury their dead or chimpanzees wage war to expand their territory. But it also entails the reverse, seeing people as similar to animals, such as when we watch toddlers play and think that they look remarkably like a litter of clumsy puppies or note that the girl braiding her friend's hair at summer camp is engaging in a grooming behavior found in many social animal species. "Indistinction" means not taking the distinction between humans and animals as the chief point of departure for our thinking.[12]

In the case of the mother-bird mitzvah, indistinction means not reading the mitzvah strictly in light of human interests and goals. It means taking some genuine interest in birds. Mishnah and Talmud Hullin Twelve are a model for such a reading. As the Rabbis delve into the details of this mitzvah, they are led to dwell at some length on the lives of birds and to give those lives rich description. The mitzvah has the salutary effect of shaking the Rabbis, and us, out of our ingrained anthropocentrism and pushing us toward the zone of indistinction that Calarco envisions.

A THEOLOGY FOR THE BIRDS

The powers of the mother bird are plentiful according to rabbinic traditions. People such as Bubby and Yoni's mom who seek her out for the mitzvah believe she can confer on them a good life. Philo and Rashbam, who explain the mitzvah with the humanitarian rationale (see my discussion in chapter 2), believe she can teach people to be virtuous. The medieval Spanish Rabbi Nahmanides says this succinctly in his comment on Deuteronomy 22:6: "Thus these commandments with respect to cattle and fowl are not [a result of] compassion upon them, but they are decrees upon us to guide us and to teach us traits of good character." Aaron Gross has called the mother-bird mitzvah one of the *rahamim* traditions, designed to cultivate *rahamim* (compassion), from the Hebrew word for "womb" *(rehem)*.[13]

The ancient Rabbis believed that the mother bird has the power to harm as well:

> Rabbi Yaakov says: There is no commandment in the Torah in which the reward for its performance is right by its side, and resurrection of the dead is written with respect to it, except "Send off the mother bird, etc." This person ascended to the top of a tree, fell, and died, or to the top of a building, and fell and died. Where is this man's prosperity and long life? Say as a consequence "in order that good come to you"—in the world that is good, "and your days be long"—in the world that is long.[14]

The Torah promises that performance of the mother-bird mitzvah ensures long life and prosperity. In the story recounted here in the early rabbinic work the Tosefta, the mitzvah instead brings disaster. The person who climbs up a tree or building to perform the mitzvah falls to his death. No good deed goes unpunished, as the saying goes.[15]

Rabbi Yaakov does not leave it there, though. He supplies a theodicy that restores the mother bird as a force for good. The person who attends to the mother bird may not experience the prosperity and long life promised by the Torah in this life, but they will in the world to come. Rabbi Yaakov's theodicy comes across as a quick fix, however, for an uncomfortable problem. In the Babylonian Talmud's version of the story, the person who climbs the tree to fulfill the mitzvah is doing so under the instruction of his father, to honor him as the decalogue demands.[16] When he falls and dies, he does so in the course of fulfilling not one but two commandments, both of which promise long life.

In the subsequent back-and-forth, the Talmud gives voice to the discomfort that the story's readers are likely to feel:

> But perhaps this never occurred? Rabbi Yaakov saw the incident. But perhaps he was contemplating sin? The Holy One, Blessed be He, does not link a bad thought to an action.... Rather, there is no reward for commandments in this world.

The editorial voice of the Talmud first suggests that perhaps the tragic events never transpired ("But perhaps this never occurred?"). When that proposal backfires ("Rabbi Yaakov saw the incident"), the Talmud suggests that the man's death must have been a punishment ("But perhaps he was contemplating sin?"). That proposal does not fly either. The Talmud claims that God does not strike people down for evil thoughts. After several more attempts to explain how a man performing a double mitzvah with a double reward could have died as a consequence, the Talmud comes to the deflating conclusion that "there is no reward for commandments in this world." It is this conclusion, the Talmud goes on to propose, that led to the heresy of the notorious Aher (Other), or Elisha ben Abuya.[17] The enthusiastic exclamations of Bubby's grandchild give way here to the darkest heresy of the ancient Rabbis.

While these perspectives on the mother bird might appear to be diametrical opposites—according to the Torah, she confers long life; according to the Talmud, she brings about an untimely end—in fact they occupy a shared conceptual framework, which is an overarching anthropocentrism. Whether the mother bird brings good luck, trains people to be better, or sends them off to an untimely death, she is teaching people some lesson about how to be and what to believe. In the subsequent discussion I turn to rabbinic treatments of the mother-bird mitzvah that offer an alternative approach, one that teaches people not how to think about themselves, one another, and God, but how to think in new ways about birds.

BIRDS AS BUILDERS

Nests are having a renaissance. In a trend known as biomimicry, architects look to nature for inspiration.[18] Any structure we make is a nest, says Janine Benyus, a biologist who studies biomimicry.[19] Some architects design buildings that actually look like bird nests, such as South African designer Porky Hefer's human tree nests, New York architect Michael Perry's affordable apartments attached to the side of a building, and the gargantuan Beijing National Stadium, which locals dubbed the "Bird's Nest."[20] Even though birds spend relatively little time in their nests—nests are essentially containers for eggs and chicks and are abandoned outside breeding season—and have only their beaks and bodies to use as equipment, bird nests are ingenious in design, diverse in size and location, eclectic in materials, and extraordinarily adapted to their environments.[21]

The architectural talent of birds does not go unnoticed in rabbinic treatment of the mother-bird commandment. Tosefta Hullin 10:13 speaks of multiple locations in which birds build nests:

> One who finds a nest in pits, ditches, or caves, it is permitted with respect to [the laws of] theft and they are liable for sending.[22]

The concern in the Tosefta passage is the applicability of the mother-bird mitzvah to nests found not specifically "along the road, in any tree, or on the ground," which is the phrasing of Deuteronomy 22:6. According to Peter Goodfellow's survey of nest construction, the sites mentioned in the Tosefta—pits, ditches, and caves—are in fact selected by many bird species for building their nests.[23] Shore-nesting plovers and the common eider gouge shallow scrape nests out of the ground in open habitats. Eastern meadowlarks conceal their dome nests in depressions in the ground. Bee-eaters, great hornbills, and burrowing owls dig or find holes and tunnels in which to build their nests to protect their young from predators and bad weather. The Tosefta rules that a nest in any of these sites falls within the scope of the mitzvah. A person must send off a mother bird they find nesting there.

The Babylonian Talmud explores other bird nesting locations and habits:

> Pigeons of a dovecote or pigeons of an attic who nested in wall crevices or in buildings, and geese or chickens who nested in an orchard, one is obligated in sending. But those who nested inside the house, and likewise Hardisean pigeons, one is exempt from sending.[24]

The legal principle here is that birds who reside more or less within the household—birds one does not "happen" upon, as the verse formulates it, and are instead *mezuman* (available), the term Mishnah Hullin 12:1 uses—do not fall within the scope of the mother-bird mitzvah. Should certain birds nest freely in locations like a wall crevice, nearby building, or orchard, however, they become subject to mother-bird treatment according to this Talmudic teaching. Even if these sites are human-made and not exactly natural, they still qualify for the purposes of the commandment.

The Talmud also mentions nests on the sea and in the air:

> As Rav Yehudah said [that] Rav said: If one found a nest in the sea, one is obligated in the mitzvah of sending, as it is stated: "So said the Lord, who makes a way *[derekh]* in the sea" (Isaiah 43:16).
>
> If that is so, one found a nest in the sky, about which it is written: "The way of an eagle in the sky" (Proverbs 30:19), one should also be obligated in sending away from the nest.
>
> [The sky] is called "the way of an eagle," but it is not called a way in an unspecified manner.[25]

The Rabbi Rav questions whether nests in the sea and sky fall within the scope of the mother-bird mitzvah. The Talmud concludes that the sea but not the sky counts as "the road" mentioned in Deuteronomy 22:6, which the Talmud reads in conjunction with verses from Isaiah and Proverbs that use the same term.

One who thinks that these scenarios are the product of rabbinic imagination will find Goodfellow's book instructive. Some bird species—jacanas, marsh terns, grebes, and rails—are "specialist architects" who build nests that rest on a waterbed, float as islands, or roam as rafts.[26]

Ornithologist Howard Saunders in 1899 recorded an aquatic nest firm enough to support a seated man up to his knees in water.[27] Nests in the air are even more impressive. Species like the osprey take years to build nests up on platforms and repair them when needed, while the white stork builds nests on chimneys and utility poles. Some weavers and orioles build their nests dangling, as if by magic, in the air.[28] Careful binding, weaving, and knotting provide the support for these pensile nests.

The Talmud also discusses the materials that birds use to pad the nest:

> Rabbi Yirmiyah poses a question: A rag, what is [the law]? Does it interpose? Feathers, what is [the law]? Do they interpose?[29]

The mother must be "sitting over the chicks or on the eggs" according to Deuteronomy 22:6. What if there is something in between, asks Rabbi Yirmiyah—does the command still apply? It is a technical point, but the question of interposition motivates Rabbi Yirmiyah to consider the materials with which birds build their nests.[30] When read aviancentrically, the texts shed light on the rich and diverse nesting habits of birds. Located in pits, ditches, cisterns, caves, gardens, residential interiors, and hospitable spots in walls, corners, and crevices and made up of found objects like rags and their own bodies' feathers, the nests that appear in Tractate Hullin testify to the ingenuity, agility, and versatility of their builders.

FATHER BIRDS

The mother bird plays the starring role in Deuteronomy 22:6–7 ("the mother sitting over the chicks . . . do not take the mother . . . send off the mother"), but what about the father? He does not make even a cameo appearance. Yet in the lived reality of bird families, the father is far from an absent figure. One of the distinguishing features of birds among vertebrates is their biparental care norm.[31] In 90 to 95 percent of bird species, both parents are involved in direct care of the young.[32] Male and female birds are equally able to build a nest and incubate and feed chicks. If bird fathers do not help out, the chicks have a greatly diminished chance of survival. In some bird species—kiwis, cassowaries, and moorhens—males are the exclusive or dominant caretaker.[33]

The ancient Rabbis ask about the father's role. Mishnah Hullin 12:2 features a dispute about whether the male *qore*—according to Yehuda Feliks, the *ammoperdix heyi*, commonly known as the sand partridge—is subject to the command of sending off the "mother" bird:

> A male *qore:* Rabbi Eliezer obligates, while the Sages exempt.[34]

What happens when the "mother" bird is a father?[35] Then the mitzvah no longer applies, say the Sages, but Rabbi Eliezer dissents, saying the male partridge qualifies.

The Mishnah elsewhere implies that the mother bird is the primary if not solo caretaker:

> Just as eggs need their mother, so too do fledglings need their mother—excluded [from the scope of the commandment] are young birds who have already fledged.[36]

The Mishnah rules that when the nest contains young birds who are already able to fly, the mother-bird commandment ceases to apply. Even though scientific data suggests that bird survival is generally dependent on both parents, the Mishnah's representation of bird parenthood privileges the mother and "invisibilizes" the father. The same rhetoric of maternal dependency is used by Mishnah Sukkah 2:8 with respect to humans:

> Women, slaves and minors are exempt from the sukkah [the fall festival booth]. A minor who does not need his mother is obligated in the sukkah.

Once children no longer need their mother, they become obligated to dwell in the sukkah. The father, siblings, and other caretakers fall away entirely in this narrative of development, in which the mother is the figure on whom the child depends (similar to the image of the mother as the parent "to whom the child clings," discussed in chapter 3).

The male partridge does not fade into the background as other bird fathers do, however. The Talmud asks why Rabbi Eliezer includes him in the mitzvah:

> A male *qore:* Rabbi Eliezer obligates, while the Sages exempt. Rabbi Abbahu said: What is the reasoning of Rabbi Eliezer? [A verbal analogy between] brooding [stated with regard to a male *qore*] and brooding [with regard to a mother bird] is derived. It is written here: "As the *qore* that broods over young that he has not brought forth" (Jeremiah 17:11); and it is written there: "[There shall the great owl *[kipoz]* make her nest, and lay,] and hatch, and brood under her shadow" (Isaiah 34:15).[37]

The shared use of the verb for "brooding" or incubation *(degirah)*, in Jeremiah 17:11, where it refers to the male *qore*, and Isaiah 34:15, where Rabbi Abbahu takes it to be referring to a nesting female bird, is said to be the inspiration for Rabbi Eliezer.[38] The incubating male partridge is not a positive image in Jeremiah, where he symbolizes ill-gotten gains, nor is the image of the owl (or, possibly, a type of snake) in Isaiah, where she forms part of an apocalyptic fantasy of vengeance against the Edomites.[39] Rabbi Abbahu here establishes an equivalence between mother and father birds, but it is shadowed (literally, in Isaiah: "brood under her shadow") by the sense of a world gone wrong.

According to the Tosefta and Babylonian Talmud, the male *qore* is an exception even for Rabbi Eliezer. All other male birds fall outside the scope of the mitzvah:

> A male: one is exempt from sending, but with a male *qore:* Rabbi Eliezer obligates, while the Sages exempt.[40]

Even though the male bird may incubate the eggs, feed the chicks, and protect them, he does not satisfy the requirements of the commandment according to the Tosefta and Talmud. The Mishnah, whatever may be its reasons, keeps the father's status more ambiguous, mentioning only the male partridge and presenting him as the subject of dispute.

Still, the father bird is not so easily booted out of the nest, even within the Talmud:

> Rabbi Yirmiyah asks . . . a male on top of the eggs and a female bird on top of the male, what is [the law]? [The dilemma] shall stand.[41]

In this passage Rabbi Yirmiyah poses the same problem of interposition we saw earlier, though there the question was about rags and feathers. In this scenario it is the father bird who interposes himself, lying on top of the eggs, forming a barrier between the mother and the chicks. The question of whether the mitzvah still applies is left to stand, as is the father bird's precarious status within the bird family. But the image is suggestive: the nest is not a place of splendid isolation of mother with chicks but is populated by a variety of other characters. It is to some of these other characters that I turn next.

BIRDS AS BABYSITTERS

Like many social species, birds are cooperative or communal breeders. Various "aunties" and "uncles" help out with child care. The phenomenon of cooperative breeding—referring to when three or more individuals collectively raise a single brood or litter—has been recognized by naturalists for over two centuries, but, with the rise of behavioral ecology in the 1960s, scientists became more curious about the evolutionary benefit of cooperative formations. "Helpers at the nest," as naturalist Alexander Skutch called them, posed a paradox to evolutionary theory because of the apparent self-sacrifice or altruism they seem to show.[42] In the less common but related phenomenon of "brood parasitism," the helper at the nest is the mother bird herself, who incubates and raises the egg of another species—cuckoos and cowbirds are well known for dropping their eggs off in other birds' nests—or an egg of the same species whose own biological mother has dropped it off there.[43]

In addition to creative nest design and active paternal care, cooperative breeding and brood parasitism are features of bird life that the ancient Rabbis address. Rabbinic discussions refer repeatedly to nests in which the eggs are not the biological offspring of the parent sitting on top:

> An impure bird: one is exempt from sending. An impure bird lies on the eggs of a pure bird, a pure lies on the eggs of an impure bird, one is exempt from sending.[44]

The Mishnah exempts the nest in which a mother bird sits atop eggs born from a mother of a different bird species when one species is pure and the other impure. If mother and child are both of impure species the nest is unambiguously exempt. The midrash collection Sifre Deuteronomy rules that the mother and eggs must be of the same species for the commandment to apply: "until they are all of one species."⁴⁵ The Tosefta similarly instructs that when "an impure bird lies on the eggs of a pure bird who is not of his species, one is exempt from sending."⁴⁶

The Talmud further probes the scope of difference between "mother" and child:

> Rabbi Zeira asks: A pigeon is upon the eggs of a *tasil*, what is [the law]? A *tasil* on the eggs of a pigeon, what is [the law]?⁴⁷

What if the mother bird and the eggs on which she sits are both from pure species, asks Rabbi Zeira—here the pigeon and *tasil*—but still not from the same species?⁴⁸ Is the relationship between caretaker and child close enough to trigger the mother-bird requirement?

Abaye says yes, drawing an inference from the Mishnah, though the editorial voice of the Talmud pokes a hole in his argument:

> Abaye said: "Come and hear [that which is taught in a Mishnah]: An impure bird lies on the eggs of a pure bird, a pure lies on the eggs of an impure bird, one is exempt from sending. Behold a pure on a pure, one is obligated." Perhaps it is regarding a *qore!*⁴⁹

Abaye highlights the Mishnah's concern with purity and impurity. Beyond that distinction, Abaye infers, "mother" and eggs should be taken as a package deal. So long as they are both from a pure species, they should be considered a pair for the purposes of the commandment. The Talmud brings up the *qore* in response, somewhat elliptically, apparently suggesting that, with the exception of the *qore*, who typically "babysits" other species, the mother bird and her eggs must be of the same species, even if both species are pure.

In these passages the Rabbis ask what it means for a mother and child to count as such. The Rabbis surprisingly take for granted that an adult and child of the same species, when found together in the nest, count as mother and child when in reality they may not be biologically related, as is the case with a helper "auntie." Perhaps the Rabbis figured that a passerby could not be expected to tell if birds of the same species are biologically related, or they did not consider biology to be the sole or even primary basis for the relationship. Whatever the case, the Talmud takes as its premise that nests might be occupied by any number of biologically unrelated individuals. The nest, as the Rabbis understand it, is what we might today consider a queer space, one in which mothers need not be breeders, and families need not be made of biological relations.[50] Queer bird families are a remarkably unremarkable feature of rabbinic discussions.

BIRDS AS REBELS AND KILLERS

The cooperative breeding patterns of birds reflect complex behavioral norms. In the human world, we might call it morality.[51] A good indicator of the presence of a moral code is when individuals feel pressure to hide certain behaviors. Australian ornithologists Michael Double and Andrew Cockburn have documented female superb fairy wrens flying off in secret in the early morning hours to engage in quick sexual liaisons.[52] White-winged choughs in Australia helped to feed their compatriots' chicks, but, as soon as those compatriots were not looking, they snatched the food back and gulped it down themselves.[53] These birds "pay to stay," says Sarah Blaffer Hrdy, "and occasionally they only pretend to pay at that."[54]

A moral universe in which birds sometimes play by the rules and sometimes flout them, whether brazenly or on the down-low, appears also in the rabbinic texts. The flouting is explicit in rabbinic passages that use the rhetoric of rebellion—the Hebrew root is *m-r-d*—to describe birds who leave human domestic spaces. Note Tosefta Hullin 10:9:

> Geese, chickens, and doves who rebelled *[mardu]* or made a nest in an orchard, one is obligated in sending.

As domesticated birds, all geese, chickens, and doves would normally be exempt from the mother-bird mitzvah because they are not birds one "happens" or "chances" upon, as Deuteronomy would have it. The Tosefta rules here that the mother-bird mitzvah applies to those birds once they leave the household, however, and nest, for example, in a nearby orchard. The rebellion rhetoric that the Rabbis use to describe such bird behavior reflects a series of assumptions: birds are properly controlled by human beings; when they leave human domiciles they "revolt" against the natural hierarchy; and such rebellion is akin to the rebellion of a Jew against rabbinic norms. When a Jew flouts rabbinic law, they are punished with *makkat mardut* (a flogging for disobedience), which uses the same Hebrew root as the one that the Tosefta uses for birds.[55] The same root is used to describe the domestic "rebellion" of a wife against husband *(moredet)* or husband against wife *(mored)*.[56]

Bird rebellion might even reach the level of homicide:

> Ravina said: Therefore, a pure bird who killed a person, one is exempt from sending. What is the reason? As the verse states: "You shall send the mother"—it refers to one whom you are commanded to send, which excludes this one whom you are not commanded to send but to bring him to court.
>
> What are the circumstances? If this is a case where his verdict was issued, he is subject to being killed. Rather, it is a case where his verdict was not yet issued, and one is required to bring him to the court to fulfill through him "and you shall eradicate the evil from your midst" (Deuteronomy 13:6).[57]

The Talmud presents a case where a bird has murdered a human being. That bird need not be shooed away, says the Rabbi Ravina, since other consequences await the bird: judicial trial. The Talmud expresses puzzlement over Ravina's scenario: If the bird had in fact killed a person, would the bird not immediately be tried and possibly executed? If so, how would she have time to incubate eggs such that the question of shooing her could even arise, and why raise the legal question? Rather, the Talmud proposes, Ravina has in mind the very specific case of a bird who has committed homicide but whose verdict has not yet been issued by the court. In such a case, do not shoo her away. Bring her to court to fulfill the scriptural mandate to eradicate evil from your midst.

The Talmud's scenario raises many questions. Does the Deuteronomy verse really intend to exclude the very unusual case of a homicidal bird who has not yet been tried by the court? Even the staunchest Talmudist is likely to admit that the verse did not have homicidal birds in mind. Then there is also the matter of bird trials; much scholarship has been devoted to the fascinating phenomenon of judicial trials for animals.[58] The most interesting question perhaps is how a bird could commit homicide in the first place. There are recorded instances of birds killing people. Cassowaries have gained a reputation for it, as have ostriches to a lesser extent, but it is rare and tends to be in response to provocation.[59] When my dog once startled a swan in Prospect Park, the swan spread enormous wings and hissed and growled threateningly at her. I doubt the swan was planning to kill my dog, but the swan certainly wanted her to think so and seemed to have succeeded, judging from my dog's frightened response.

In a tragic-comic tale in the Talmud, a bird acts like a human rebel and is punished as one. The story is inspired by wordplay on a pigeon breed that appears in the Mishnah called the Hardisean dove, and in other versions the Hadrisean dove, named possibly after the Syrian island of Arwad or the Greek island of Rhodes.[60] By the time of the later generations of Rabbis, the dove breed was clearly no longer familiar and became associated with King Herod because of the similarity to his name:

> Rabbi Hiyya and Rabbi Shimon: One teaches "Hadrisean doves," and the other teaches "Hardisean doves." According to the one who teaches "Hardisean doves," it is on account of King Herod, and according to the one who teaches "Hadrisean doves," it is on account of their location.
>
> Rav Kahana said: I myself saw them, and they were standing in sixteen rows, each a *mil* wide, and they were calling out "My master, my master." There was one of them who was not calling out "My master, my master." Her companion said to her, "Blind one, say 'My master, my master.'" She said to her, "Blind one, say, 'My master, my slave.'" They brought her and slaughtered her.
>
> Rav Ashi said: Rabbi Hanina said to me: It is mere words.
>
> Can it enter your mind that it is mere words? Rather, say, through words.[61]

This story is a riff on one told about Herod in Babylonian Talmud Bava Batra 3b-4a. The story in Bava Batra calls into question Herod's pedigree and undermines his claims to authority by introducing him as a "slave of the Hasmonean house" who brutally kills all those who surround him except a single Sage, whom Herod blinds but does not kill.[62] In the story here in Hullin, it is a bird who proclaims Herod's illegitimate roots ("Blind one, say, 'My master, my slave'") and pays a bloody price for it ("They brought her and slaughtered her").[63] Ultimately the story ponders the meaning of language: Is this just a fanciful tale ("It is mere words"), or is this, on the contrary, the account of a lone bird in an avian army who speaks truth to power ("Rather, say, through words")?

The story highlights the moral calculus through which Mishnah and Babylonian Talmud Hullin frame the mother-bird commandment. The bird in this story offers a lesson not in compassion but in power and pain. Birds rebel and are killed, just as people rebel and are killed.[64] Birds are not vectors for morality but agents within it as murderers, traitors, heroes, or martyrs. This is how Jason Hribal urges us to view animals who resist or escape captivity and suffer death as a consequence:

> These animals understand that there will be consequences for incorrect actions. If they refuse to perform, if they attack a trainer, or if they escape their cage, they know that they will be beaten, have their food rations reduced, and be placed in solitary confinement. Captive animals know all of this and yet they still carry out such actions—often with a profound sense of determination. This is why these behaviors can be understood as a true form of resistance.[65]

When animals act defiantly, they may very well know what it is they are risking.

BIRDS AS HATS

Rabbinic treatment of the mother-bird mitzvah features birds who are builders, fathers, helpers, rebels, and victims. The last text to which I turn features birds in yet another role, as—and it may sound strange—hats:

> The Pappunyans said to Rav Mattana: One found a nest on the head of a person, what is the law? He said: "And earth upon his head" (2 Samuel 15:32).[66]

People from the village of Pappunya pose a strange question to Rav Mattana: Does the mother-bird commandment still apply if the nest is located on top of someone's head?[67] Does the nest still qualify as being "on the road," as Deuteronomy specifies? Like the passage about homicidal birds, this one inspires a host of questions. Why would people let a bird build a nest on their head? How would the nest stay on? The Talmud's answer to the question is terse, citing without elaboration or explanation a snippet of 2 Samuel 15:32, "And earth upon his head," which describes King David's mourning upon encountering his son Absalom's rebellion. According to commentator Rashi's explanation, the fact that the dust on David's head is called "ground" suggests that a human head, however far off the actual ground it may be, qualifies too as ground. The answer, then, is yes, the mother-bird mitzvah applies even when the nest is on top of someone's head.

In the continuation of the Talmud, the Pappunyans pose a series of outlandish questions to Rav Mattana, asking him to find a foreshadowing of major characters in the Bible—Moses, Haman, Esther, Mordecai—before they are explicitly introduced by the narrative. The dialogue's fantastical tone suggests that the head-bird-nest is intended in a similar spirit. Nevertheless, a serious insight lies therein regarding the entanglement of human and animal lives. In this entangled world, the human being is no longer at the center. In the image of the nest as a hat, the human head becomes the ground, the foundation for animal families and homes, serving their needs rather than the animals serving them. When the chicks hatch, the human head is left behind, its purpose served. Alternatively, the human being and the bird retain the relationship that the conjoining of their lives has created.

The Talmud's head-bird-nest creates a zone of indistinction of the kind that Matthew Calarco describes, as does the Talmud's appreciation for avian architecture, its interest in the eclectic caregivers that hover at the nest, and the laws and stories it relays about freedom-seeking birds. The very notion of the mother bird challenges the human/animal binary by imagining a motherhood that transcends species. "We need new ideas," says Calarco, "new practices ... that resist the status quo but also that allow for other forms of life and relation to emerge."[68] Mishnah and Talmud Hullin Twelve offer new ideas, we have seen, that go beyond the theology and ethics usually associated with the mother-bird mitzvah. No image better captures Calarco's zone of identity and shared embodiment than the Talmud's nest-head.

That is not to deny the anthropocentrism of the mother-bird mitzvah, which presupposes human exceptionalism (the idea that humans are exceptional among animals), human-animal dualism (there is the human on one side and all the other species on the other), and a strong moral hierarchy (in which humans always come out on top). These are the three defining features of anthropocentrism, according to Calarco.[69] The mitzvah presumes that baby birds are there for the taking, that our obligation to the bird family extends no further than a brief act of deception or concealment, and that human families are different from and superior to bird families.

But if we humans are so vain that we probably think this mitzvah is about us, that is only partly true for the Rabbis. When the Rabbis discuss the mother-bird mitzvah, they show real affinity for other animals and genuine curiosity about them. The mitzvah gets them out of their own heads or, as is the case with the head-bird-nest, gets them to use their heads in new ways. From the Mishnah's partridge dad to the Talmud's head-bird-nest to Nahmanides's lesson in compassion to Bubby's porch, the mother-bird mitzvah is, like the mother bird herself, on the move, inspiring legal and exegetical elaboration, moral and theological reflection, fantastical stories, popular practices, and, not least of all, appreciation for all that birds can do.

6 Animal Orphans

KEEPING THE BABY WITH THE MOTHER
FOR THE FIRST WEEK OF LIFE

ORPHAN LAWS AND ORPHAN ANIMALS

Jewish and Christian Bible readers from antiquity to today have viewed the four animal-family laws as a unit. The Mishnah groups them together too—with one exception. Mishnah Tractate Hullin Chapter Five is dedicated to Leviticus 22:27's prohibition against slaughtering animal parents and their children on the same day. Mishnah Hullin Chapter Eight is dedicated to the prohibition on cooking kids in their mother's milk, transformed into a more general prohibition on mixing meat with milk. Mishnah Hullin Chapter Twelve treats the mother-bird mitzvah, the "sending of the nest," in Deuteronomy 22:6-7.[1] But what of the fourth animal-family law, the commandment to keep the animal with the mother for the first week of life? No chapter of Mishnah Hullin exists for that law.

In this chapter I show that the requirement in Exodus 22:29 and Leviticus 22:27 to keep mother and baby together in the first week of life has a curious "orphan" status within rabbinic literature. The animal orphan, literally, becomes the focus of rabbinic attention instead. In the first part of this chapter, I treat the relative sparsity of rabbinic traditions on the first-week-of-life requirement. In the second part, I treat the material on the animal orphan that seems to take its place. That material, in turn, inspires a story in the Talmud, narrated by an obscure Rabbi, about a faraway city with phantasmagoric features. It is a short passage, but its subject is of colossal scale. These are literal tall tales, where the lettuces grow to the size of trees and the trees to the size of roads. I take up the fantastic features of the story one by one: the ghostly practice of taxidermy that the story describes, the story's geography, the colossal scale of the flora and fauna, and, finally, the mass destruction with which the story closes. Putting the pieces together, I show that the tall tales in the Talmud convey the haunting of rabbinic culture by animal orphans.

Most people today do not think much about agriculture's impact on animal families. The Talmudic materials I discuss in this chapter, by contrast, put the fragmentation of animal families front and center. What are the consequences when an animal parent is taken from the child? How does the child manage to survive? What are the ripple effects? The Talmud poses these questions through its laws and stories about animal orphans. The dystopian world that the Talmud ends up envisioning, in my reading of it, offers fresh perspectives on human and animal lives. In the way that the dystopia of *Wall-E* delivers an environmentalist critique and that of *The Handmaid's Tale* a feminist critique, the strange and disturbing images in the Talmudic stories cast a critical eye on the treatment of animals.

The plight of the orphan has long generated pathos within Jewish culture. "Uphold the rights of the orphan," exhorted Isaiah (1:17). The orphan's cry goes straight to God because it has no parents to hear it, said the early Rabbis.[2] The traumas of war, persecution, migration, and disease made orphanhood all too common within Jewish history. "'Hear Their Cry': Understanding the Jewish Orphan Experience" was the theme of a recent working group at the Center for Jewish History. But the animal orphan has drawn little attention even though, we will see, that figure is far from absent in ancient Jewish literature. The bereaved baby animal, on the contrary, sparked the rabbinic imagination. Anthropologist Claude Lévi-Strauss said that animals are good to think with.[3] For the Rabbis, animal families are also good to think with and to make laws and tell stories about.

CHAPTER SIX

BAD TIMING

The requirement to keep animals with their mother for the first week of life appears in two places in the Pentateuch, Exodus 22:29 and Leviticus 22:27. In Exodus's Book of the Covenant, the requirement forms part of the laws of first offerings:

> ²⁸You shall not put off the skimming of the first yield of your vats. You shall give Me the first-born among your sons. ²⁹You shall do the same with your cattle and your flocks: seven days he shall remain with his mother; on the eighth day you shall give him to Me.
> (22:28–29)

One should be neither too late nor too early with first offerings. "You shall not put off," on the one hand, regarding the new produce, but wait until the eighth day of life for firstborn animals, on the other.

In Leviticus's Holiness Legislation, the seven-day requirement is an addendum to the laws that qualify animals for sacrifice:

> ²⁷When cattle or sheep or goats are born, he shall be seven days under his mother, and from the eighth day on he shall be acceptable as an offering by fire to GOD. ²⁸But cattle or flock animals, him and his child, you shall not slaughter on the same day.
> (22:27–28)

For Leviticus too, timing is the central concern. The person who brings a sacrifice must wait in certain cases: when the animal is too young or if the animal's parent or child has already been slaughtered on that day.

It seems strange that Mishnah Tractate Hullin would devote a chapter to the law about same-day slaughter but not the one about the seven-day wait given that the two laws are paired by Leviticus. One possible reason is that the Rabbis thought that the seven-day law was relevant only to sacrifice. Mishnah Tractate Hullin—*hullin* means "nonsacral things"—is about everything *but* sacrifice. The shift in verb phrases from the seven-day rule in Leviticus 22:27, "he shall be acceptable as an offering," to the same-day rule in Leviticus 22:28, "do not slaughter," may have signaled to the Rabbis that the seven-day rule does not belong in a discussion of everyday meat in the way that the same-day rule does. The hitch in that proposition is that Leviticus 22 presents both laws, *seven*-day and *same*-day, plainly in connection to sacrifice. If the Mishnah could change the context for one of the laws from the sacred to the profane, surely it could have changed the context for the other. Tractate Hullin seems as good a place as any in which to put a discussion of the seven-day law, but the composers of the Mishnah opted against it.

So where did the Rabbis put it, if not Tractate Hullin? The seven-day law is a straightforward and explicit injunction that appears not just once but twice in the Torah. One would expect it to appear somewhere in the Mishnah, a rabbinic work that does not cite the Torah very much but is nevertheless grounded thoroughly in its laws.[4] A likely candidate is Tractate Zevahim, whose main subject is animal sacrifice. And, in fact, the seven-day rule does appear there, but only in passing rather than as a subject in its own right. The concern in the relevant passage is with people sacrificing animals in the proper location of the Temple precincts. If a person sacrifices in the wrong spot—anywhere outside those precincts—they are to be punished. In exceptional cases, however, such as when the animal is disqualified from sacrifice, the person is exempted from punishment. In these cases, since the sacrifice does not count anyway, sacrifice in the wrong place does not even register as a problem.

One of the disqualified animals on Mishnah Zevahim's list is the animal "lacking time":

> "Him and his child" (who were slaughtered on the same day), and the one lacking time: Rabbi Shimon says: This [falls] within [the scope of] a negative commandment, for Rabbi Shimon used to say: Any [animal] who is fit to come [to the altar] after [a period of] time, this [falls] within [the scope of] a negative commandment, and it does not have in it the category of *karet* [excision]. And the Sages say: Any [animal] that does not have in it the category of *karet* does not [fall] within [the scope of] a negative commandment.
>
> "Lacking time"—whether intrinsically [premature], or whether [premature] for their owner. And which is the one lacking time for their owner? [The animal] of a man who experiences a gonorrhea-like discharge *[zav]*, and a woman who experiences a discharge of uterine blood after her menstrual period *[zavah]*, a woman after childbirth, and a leper [whose period of impurity is not yet complete], where they sacrificed their sin offerings or guilt offerings outside [the Temple courtyard], they are exempt.[5]

Rabbi Shimon and the Sages here disagree over two cases: a person who sacrifices an animal parent and child on the same day, violating Leviticus 22:28, and a person who sacrifices an animal within their initial week of life, violating Leviticus 22:27.[6] In both cases the sacrificer has, in effect, struck too soon. If the sacrificer were to wait the appropriate time, in the first case, a day, and in the second case, a week, their animal would be a legitimate sacrifice. The cases are of legal interest for precisely this reason: the disqualifications are only temporary. The sacrifices are close to being valid but do not quite make it. Rabbi Shimon legislates that the rules of sacrifice—here regarding location—still to some extent apply even if the sacrifice did not technically count as one. Rabbi Shimon's logic is summed up at the end, when he says that regarding any animal "fit to come [to the altar] after [a period of] time, this [falls] within [the scope of] a negative commandment." Even if animals are not currently valid for sacrifice, if at some point they will become so, then penalties apply if the proper procedures are not observed. The Sages, by contrast, eliminate the act entirely from the scope of sacrifice.

Sacrifice is all in the timing, it seems, though in different ways for Exodus, Leviticus, and the Mishnah.[7] The one lacking time, the Mishnah goes on to say, refers not only to infant animals in their first week of life but also to various persons who lack time. The examples given are the man or woman who experiences genital discharge, the woman who has just given birth, and the leper. In these cases the subject, now human rather than animal, has at some point in the past been qualified to bring a sacrifice or will be at some point in the future, but in their present state their disqualification from bringing a sacrifice excludes them from the field of liability. Lacking time, then, according to Mishnah Zevahim, is not specific to the seven-day rule nor even to animals and is part of a larger set of legislations around problems of timing in sacrifice.

DIFFICULT BIRTHS

While Leviticus 22:27 presents the seven-day rule in the context of animal sacrifices, Exodus 22:29 does so in the context of firstborn donations. The other place in the Mishnah that one might therefore expect to find the seven-day rule is in Tractate Bekhorot, whose main subject is firstborn animals and people. The seven-day rule is indeed found there too but, surprisingly, in the context not of firstborn donations but of animal tithes:

> All enter to be tithed except the cross-bred, and the *terefah*, and the one born by Caesarian section [literally "one who emerges from the side"], the one lacking time, and an orphan.[8]

The animal lacking time is grouped here not, as in Mishnah Zevahim, with other sacrificial animals where proper timing is at issue, but with the animal bred from mixed species, the *terefah* (an animal invalid for consumption due to a physical impairment), the animal born by cesarean section, and the orphan, all of whom are declared exempt from the tithe.[9] The common denominator among the animals listed here is less clear than in Tractate Bekhorot, though three of the categories—the animal born of a C-section, the one lacking time, and the orphan—relate to precarious circumstances in which the mother either experiences complications during delivery, is separated from the baby immediately after birth, or dies.

Not only is it unclear what principle unites these categories but also what the exegetical basis is for exempting them from the animal tithe. The relevant biblical passage, Leviticus 27:32–33, does not mention any exemption and, if anything, emphasizes that every tenth animal should be tithed no matter what their condition is. "All tithes of the herd or flock—of all that passes under the shepherd's staff, every tenth one—shall be holy to the Lord. One must not look out for good as against bad, or make substitution for it." The missing link for Mishnah Bekhorot's categories is supplied by a passage found in early midrash:

> "A bull or a sheep" excludes the cross-breed; "or a goat" excludes the one who resembles [another species, for example, a sheep who is the offspring of two sheep but who looks like a goat or vice versa]; "when . . . is born" excludes the one born by Caesarean section; "then he shall be seven days" excludes the one lacking time; "under his mother" excludes an orphan.
>
> Rabbi Yishmael son of Rabbi Yohanan ben Berokah says: It is stated here [with regard to the animal tithe]: "Whatever passes under the rod" (Leviticus 27:32), and it is stated there [with regard to all offerings] "under his mother" (Leviticus 22:27). Just as "under" stated here excludes the

cross-bred, the one born of C-section, the one lacking time, and the orphan, so too "under" stated there excludes the cross-bred, the one born of C-section, the one lacking time, and the orphan.[10]

This midrash is multistep. The author reads Leviticus 22:27 as invalidating from sacrifice not only the newborn animal infant, as the simple sense of the verse dictates, but also the hybrid-species animal, the animal "who resembles" (shorthand for an animal who resembles a different species than the one he was born from), the animal born by C-section, and the orphaned animal.[11] The author associates each exemption—rather arbitrarily—with a different phrase from the verse.[12] Then, through a textual bridge, known in rabbinic terminology as a *gezerah shavah*, Rabbi Yishmael son of Rabbi Yohanan ben Berokah extends the disqualifications from animal sacrifices to animal tithes based on the common use of the word *tahat* (under) in Leviticus 22:27, where it refers to the baby animal remaining "under" the mother, and in Leviticus 27:32, where it refers to the animals passing "under" the staff as they are counted for the tithe.[13]

The picture that emerges from the early rabbinic works is a strangely piecemeal and oblique treatment of the seven-day requirement in Exodus 22:29 and Leviticus 22:27. While the Mishnah dedicates full chapters to each of the other three animal-family laws, it gives only scattered mentions to the seven-day rule, within the vague and nonspecific rubric of a person or animal lacking time. The seven-day rule is subsumed in Tractate Zevahim within its treatment of sacrificial timing and in Tractate Bekhorot within its treatment of animal tithes.[14]

A CURIOUS DEFINITION OF ORPHANHOOD

One of the animals whom Tractate Bekhorot exempts from the tithe is the orphan. The Mishnah digresses to define the animal orphan:

> What is an orphan? Anyone whose mother has died or has been slaughtered. Rabbi Joshua says: Even if his mother was slaughtered, if the hide is intact, this one is not an orphan.[15]

The animal orphan never appears in biblical law, unlike the animal mother and baby in the first week after birth, who appear twice. Why is the Mishnah more concerned, then, with the former than the latter?

Let us look more closely at the definition of the orphan: "Anyone whose mother has died or has been slaughtered." The Mishnah implies that an animal becomes an orphan only when the mother dies, but not the father. If so, the Mishnah's definition of orphanhood for an animal contrasts with that for a human, for whom the father's death was considered to be of equal or greater weight than the mother's.[16] The Rabbis generally privilege the father over the mother, but, when it comes to animals, they flip the order of importance. In this Mishnah, the Rabbis once again sideline the animal father (see chapters 3 and 5 for other cases).

The Mishnah's definition mentions both natural death and slaughter. A related passage in Babylonian Talmud Hullin 38b shrinks the scope of animal orphanhood only to cases when the mother dies right at the moment of birth ("this one withdrew for death and this one withdrew for life" is the language used). But, in fact, the Mishnah's definition theoretically includes an animal of more mature age and not only the newborn, the way orphanhood for humans can happen at any age even if we tend to associate the term with early childhood (think Oliver Twist). Animals who lose their mother to disease or slaughter at any point in their lives could presumably qualify as orphans according to the Mishnah's definition.

Rabbi Joshua makes a curious exception. He says that an animal is not considered an orphan when the mother's hide exists after she is slaughtered. That the mother's disembodied skin should be considered a substitute for the mother herself and, by law, stand in for her is surely a strange claim on Rabbi Joshua's part that requires explication.[17] The term found in Rabbi Joshua's ruling, *shelah*, is an uncommon word for skin in early rabbinic literature that is used in cases when the skin is no longer part of the living body and is stripped off and put to some other purpose.[18] Rabbi Joshua does not mention any purpose, but the Talmud's commentary on the Mishnah suggests that it is to wrap the newborn animal:

> Rabbi Yishmael ben Satriel from Arkat Leveinah testified before Rabbi: In our locale, they flay the dead and clothe the living. Rabbi said: The reason for our Mishnah is revealed.[19]

Rabbi Yishmael ben Satriel, who hails from a city named Arkat Leveinah, testifies to a practice of flaying the dead—presumably the animal mother who has been slaughtered—and using the fresh hide to "clothe" the survivor, presumably the vulnerable infant. In point of fact, Rabbi Yishmael does not explicitly mention animals, mothers, or children, only "the dead" (*ha-metah*, feminine grammar) and "the living" (*ha-hai*, masculine grammar). It is the response of Rabbi, the great Rabbi named simply as such ("the reason for our Mishnah is revealed") that connects Yishmael's testimony to the Mishnah.[20] Exploring that connection is my next task, and it takes me to contemporary art's turn to taxidermy.

THE TALMUD AND TAXIDERMY

Though seemingly remote from rabbinic texts, the practice of taxidermy helps to illuminate Rabbi Joshua's strange approach to animal orphanhood.[21] Whether one speaks of the history of the practice or its recent referencing in modern art, taxidermy—the Greek refers literally to the arrangement (taxi-) of skin (-dermy)—takes some element of a deceased animal's body, usually the outer layer of skin, fur, feathers, or scales, to "resurrect" it and make it seem alive and real.[22] Out of all bodily organs, the skin is especially effective for achieving this reality effect since, as art historian Steve Baker observes, the skin possesses a distinctive "aura of authenticity" and bears more than any other part of the body "the trace of a life lived."[23]

The Talmud's practice of clothing the newborn baby in the dead mother's hide evokes the uncanny quality of a taxidermied animal.[24] The hide on the one hand is a testament to the mother's death, a "ghostly object."[25] Death is, after all, the precondition of taxidermy.[26] The animal skin speaks also to the animal's transformation into a thing, a surface. Many of the contemporary artists who use taxidermy are also animal rights activists whose work exposes the treatment of animals as things to be exploited or trophies to be displayed. But at the same time, the animal skin, which taxidermy manipulates to mimic the animal's live form, participates in an emotional story that in some sense honors the animal and exists in a relational state with it.[27] Taxidermy is perhaps the ultimate objectification, but it is also an everlasting tribute.

In the practice from Arqat Leveinah attested by Rabbi Yishmael ben Satriel and associated by Rabbi with Rabbi Joshua's position in the Mishnah, the animal mother is said to be brought back to life through her hide. The reanimated hide works similarly also to the relic—a body part or possessed object that embodies the person who once lived and confers on them continuing life—or even to the souvenir, which points to a lived experience now lost to the past.[28] The hide, according to Rabbi Yishmael ben Satriel, becomes at the most basic level an item of clothing, a layette for the lamb, kid, or calf. The hide is said to clothe or dress the newborn like a swaddling blanket. Unlike the transitional object of the baby blanket, however, the mother's hide both substitutes for the mother and, according to Rabbi Joshua's legislation, *is* the mother. Where the skin exists, Rabbi Joshua says, so too does the mother.

RABBINIC GEOGRAPHY

The zombification of the mother—her resurrection from the dead into a pseudo-living state—is offered to Rabbi as testimony, but it is received by him as revelation ("Rabbi Yishmael ben Satriel from Arqat Leveinah testified before Rabbi: In our locale, they flay the dead and clothe the living. Rabbi said: The reason for our Mishnah is revealed.")[29] Indeed, Rabbi Yishmael ben Satriel, who appears in rabbinic literature only here, sounds like a mystical master one would expect to encounter in the classical kabbalistic work the Zohar. The Hebrew root *s-t-r* refers to hiding or overturning, and the ending *-el* to an association with the divine. Satriel is found among the angel names inscribed on the ancient Aramaic magic bowls.[30]

That which Yishmael ben Satriel offers to Rabbi sounds less like a revelation, however, than a lively piece of rabbinic folklore about the faraway land from which he comes.[31] Arqat Leveinah is elsewhere known as Arca Caesarea, or Caesarea Libani, and lies at the northwestern foot of Mount Lebanon.[32] Today it is known as Tel Arqa near the Mediterranean coast, twenty miles southwest of Arod and seventy-seven miles northwest of Sidon. The city is mentioned in old Egyptian records.[33] The rabbinic midrash collection Genesis Rabbah links the city of Arqa to the Arqites mentioned in the Table of Nations in Genesis 10:17 and 1 Chronicles 1:15, where Arqa is one of five city names used to refer to an offshoot of the primeval family.[34] The city of Arqa thus has resonances of hoary antiquity for the Rabbis, but it was also known as the birthplace of the last of the Severan emperors, who was born there in 208 CE, and as the seat of a Christian bishop in the 300s CE. Arqa is biblical, Roman, and Christian all at once.

Arqa is even somewhat magical. Josephus mentions it as part of Agrippa's territory:

> In the course of his march he [Titus Caesar] saw a river, the nature of which deserves record. It runs between Arcea, a town within Agrippa's realm, and Raphanea, and has an astonishing peculiarity. For, when it flows, it is a copious stream with a current far from sluggish; then all at once its sources fail and for the space of six days it presents the spectacle of a dry bed; again, as though no change had occurred, it pours forth on the seventh day just as before. And it has always been observed to keep strictly to this order; whence they have called it the Sabbatical river, so naming it after the sacred seventh day of the Jews.[35]

Josephus reports that Arqa's river flowed only on the Sabbath—a religiously sensitive river! Arqa is clearly no normal place when it comes to the workings of nature.

COLOSSAL FAUNA, FLORA, AND MARASCHINO CHERRIES

The unusual impression of Arqa left by Josephus is amplified by the Talmud. After the initial account of Arqa's infant animal care, Rabbi Yishmael ben Satriel's report continues:

> The lettuces in our locale have 600,000 leaves in their omasum [the core]. Once one cedar tree fell in our locale, and sixteen wagons passed over its back [as] one. Once an egg of *bar yokhani* fell and drowned sixty cities and broke 300 cedar trees.[36]

Rabbi Yishmael ben Satriel regales Rabbi with tales of Arqa, describing lettuces with six hundred thousand leaves, cedars the width of superhighways, and a giant bird whose eggs can kill cities and forests. Most Talmud manuscripts add giant mosquitoes, strengthening the already dark tone of Arqa's marvels. Just what relevance any of these features bear to the original one mentioned by Yishmael ben Satriel—the taxidermied mother—is a subject to which I will return.

Impossible physical dimensions such as the ones found in Yishmael ben Satriel's report are not uncommon in rabbinic tall tales.[37] The giant proportions of ancient Canaan are a theme already in the Bible, in Numbers 13:21–24, which describes a single cluster of grapes found by the spies needing to be mounted on poles to be transported (pictured in the logo of modern Israel's Ministry of Tourism). The grapes are large but not of colossal proportions, but a little later in the Numbers narrative (13:25–33), the spies spread fearful reports of giant people who inhabit the land. The Babylonian Talmud expands on the motif of colossal Canaan, such as in Hullin 60b, which pictures sixteen rows of teeth possessed by the Avvim, gigantic inhabitants of Canaan; in Ketubbot 111b, which describes Canaan's turnips weighing sixty litra and mustard branches that produce nine kavs of mustard; and in Hullin 59b, which depicts ancient Canaan inhabited by giant animals.[38]

The Talmud does not reserve colossal-scale flora, fauna, and people for the land of Israel alone. Megillah 6b describes the gigantic proportions of the city of Rome and the colossal scale of its produce. In a nautical-themed story cycle in Bava Batra 73–75, Rabbah bar bar Hanah recounts giant waves, antelopes, snakes, frogs, ravens, trees, fishes, and birds, along with the mythological monsters Behemoth and Leviathan. Rabbah bar bar Hanah's tall tales share particular similarities with Rabbi Yishmael ben Satriel's in their number scheme of threes and sixes. Both story cycles feature the destruction of sixty cities: Rabbah bar bar Hanah in Bava Batra reports sixty districts destroyed by a giant fish, while Yishmael ben Satriel in Bekhorot describes the drowning of sixty cities by the yolk of the *bar yokhani* bird.[39] Rabbah bar bar Hanah in Bava Batra even has his own version of a giant bird, the Ziz, which some identify with the *bar yokhani* (if for no other reason than that it would be strange for the Talmud to speak of two different colossal birds).

Pop artist Claes Oldenburg's sculptures provide some insight into the colossal imagination. Oldenburg plays with scale in his fifty-one-foot spoon cradling a maraschino cherry in Minneapolis, thirty-eight-foot-tall flashlight in Las Vegas, and forty-five-foot-tall clothespin in Philadelphia. Oldenburg's sculptures challenge the viewer's sense of location within the world, evoking in the viewer both pleasure and disquiet. Colossal sculptures put the viewer in their place.[40] Philosopher Herbert Marcuse saw in Oldenburg's sculptures revolutionary potential: "People cannot take anything seriously; neither their President, nor the Cabinet, nor the corporation executives."[41] In the colossal imagination, the human body is no longer the measure of things.[42] Rabbi Yishmael's report about Arqat Leveinah, which interrupts the Talmud's sober legal discussion, produces that same sense of disorientation.[43] His stories of colossal plants, trees, birds, and eggs make people and their vehicles seem miniscule next to the awesome, awful flora and fauna said to dominate the Lebanese landscape.

BIG BIRDS

After the initial testimony about "clothing the living with the dead," Yishmael ben Satriel's report about Arqat Leveinah features three items:

1. A description of lettuces with six hundred thousand leaves
2. An anecdote about a cedar tree that fell and sixteen wagons rode side by side on it
3. An anecdote about a *bar yokhani* egg that fell and drowned sixty cities and broke three hundred cedars

One might note that the list moves from static description to dynamic narrative: the lettuce is characterized by its six hundred thousand leaves, but the single cedar tree is described in action, as falling, and so too is the egg.[44] The report also moves from absolute to relative size, a distinction that art critics consider essential to scale, which is defined as the relationship between physical magnitude and the way in which magnitude is represented.[45] In Yishmael ben Satriel's narration, the lettuce is described by its absolute size—six hundred thousand leaves—while the giant size of the cedar tree and the egg is illustrated through their relationship to other things: the sixteen wagons that can roll side by side along the width of the fallen tree, and the egg yolk capable of drowning sixty cities and breaking three hundred cedar trees. Rabbi Yishmael's anecdotes move also from the productive to the destructive. The fallen cedar turns into a mass transportation hub, but the fallen egg inflicts carnage and chaos. Rabbi Yishmael's anecdotes also, finally, move from colossal to supercolossal scale. A single cedar can accommodate sixteen wagons, but a dropped *bar yokhani* egg can, in turn, break three hundred cedars (if one does the math, that's a lot of wagons that the egg yolk can destroy).

Let me at this point "drop" into the discussion a subtext for the *bar yokhani* bird: the mother-bird mitzvah in Deuteronomy 22:6–7. According to Deuteronomy, a person should shoo away the mother bird before taking her eggs. Here the mother bird drops her own egg. It is she who harms people with her egg rather than people who harm the bird and her eggs. In the two other places in the Talmud in which the *bar yokhani* appears, the *bar yokhani* exemplifies a large bird but not a colossal one.[46] In these other passages, the *bar yokhani* is essentially similar to an ostrich or eagle or some other large but perfectly realistic bird whose size exemplifies for the Talmud the difficulties of speaking of objects as having an average size. The two other Talmudic references to the *bar yokhani* recall the ancient Roman writer Pliny's treatment of the ostrich, whom Pliny describes as exceeding in height a man sitting on horseback and whose eggs are prized on account of their large size.[47] In Rabbi Yishmael ben Satriel's tall tales, by contrast, the *bar yokhani* has grown into a monstrous creature whose eggs are not just larger than those of other birds but are supernaturally colossal.[48]

The Talmudic storyteller may be inspired here by Iranian myth, which features an entire cast of colossal birds: the simorg, sen, camros, karsift, baskuc, zorbarag, and rukk.[49] The *bar yokhani* bears some similarity to the camros, who is said to make periodic forays into non-Iranian lands to pluck up people like specks of grain. It is the story of the rukk, however, known from the Arabian tales of *1,001 Nights*, that comes closest to that of the *bar yokhani* in also featuring a colossal egg and horrific destruction.[50] After sailors break the rukk's egg and steal and hide the chick aboard their ship, the rukk retaliates by dropping an enormous rock on the ship.[51] Closer to the Talmud's place and time are the demonic eggs described in the writing on Aramaic magical bowls and the eggshells on which the spells were sometimes written.⁵² Then as now, eggs carry rich symbolism (consider the expressions "nest egg," "good/bad egg," or "chicken and egg"). Eggs were associated with fertility, as one might expect, but also with supernatural powers.

ANGRY BIRDS

The Talmud ironically associates the *bar yokhani*'s giant egg with sterility, as we see in the final segment of the Talmud's discussion:

> And does [the *bar yokhani*] throw it? But it is written: "The *kenaf renanim* rejoices" (Job 39:13)? Rav Ashi said: That [egg] was rotten.⁵³

The dialogue here is brief but dense. The Talmud cites a notoriously obscure biblical passage from the book of Job about a bird called the *kenaf renanim*. Here is the biblical passage in full:

> ¹³The *kenaf renanim* rejoices;
> Are her pinions and plumage like the stork's?
> ¹⁴She leaves her eggs on the ground,
> Letting them warm in the dirt,
> ¹⁵Forgetting they may be crushed underfoot,
> Or trampled by a wild beast.
> ¹⁶Her young are cruelly abandoned as if they were not hers;
> Her labor is in vain for lack of concern.
> ¹⁷For God deprived her of wisdom,
> Gave her no share of understanding,
> ¹⁸Else she would soar on high,
> Scoffing at the horse and its rider.
> (39:13–18)

Job's *kenaf renanim* is usually taken to be an ostrich, though one scholar has argued that it is a sandgrouse.⁵⁴ Job takes the bird's placement of her eggs on the ground to be a sign of grievous maternal neglect ("She leaves her eggs on the ground . . . / Forgetting they may be crushed underfoot . . . / Her young are cruelly abandoned").⁵⁵ Unlike the mother goats and hinds at the beginning of Job 39 who are the object of wonder and the father eagle at the end of the chapter who builds his nest on high and feeds his young, the ostrich portrayed in these verses does not demonstrate the procreative drive and care for offspring that characterize the rest of the animal world. She is, rather, "deprived" "of wisdom," and given "no share of understanding." The poet's depiction of the ostrich as an enigma of nature forms part of God's climactic speech to Job in chapters 38 and 39 about what Bible scholar Robert Alter has called "the great panorama of creation."[56]

The Talmud's treatment of Job 39:13 is riddled with irony. First, the Talmud identifies the *kenaf renanim* bird of the Job verse, whose concern is the observable zoological world, with the giant *bar yokhani* bird of folkloric fantasy. Second, the Talmud takes the *kenaf renanim* of Job to be paradigmatic not of a bad mother who abandons her children—that seems to be Job's intention—but of a good mother who protects them.[57] With that understanding in tow, the Talmud challenges Rabbi Yishmael ben Satriel's account of the *bar yokhani*: "And does [the *bar yokhani*] throw it?"[58] The *kenaf renanim* bird, far from abandoning her eggs, takes painstaking care of them, argues the Talmud, objecting to Rabbi Yishmael ben Satriel's depiction. The *bar yokhani* is not the sort of mother to drop her egg in flight.[59] That is what the Talmud claims, but, paradoxically, the Job verse in fact seems to give excellent *support* for Rabbi Yishmael ben Satriel's tale. Two contradictory ways of thinking about the *bar yokhani* bird emerge from the Talmud's back-and-forth about her: the careless mother portrayed by Rabbi Yishmael ben Satriel, on the one hand, versus the attentive mother (but not!) portrayed by Job on the other. Which is correct? That is the Talmud's question.

Rav Ashi evades the dilemma altogether with his proposal that the egg was rotten.[60] (Just how the *bar yokhani* mother would have known that her egg was rotten is clearly not a question the audience is meant to ask; perhaps she saw her other eggs hatch first, and this was the only one left in the nest.)[61] The mother bird tossed it away because she knew no chicks would be born from it, explains Rashi.[62] While the language that Rabbi Yishmael ben Satriel uses is that of dropping—"the egg dropped"—the language used by the Talmudic challenge is that of throwing—"did she throw?!" The implicit answer to that last question is yes, she did throw the egg, but she had a reason. The *bar yokhani* proves to be neither the neglectful mother bird we may have originally thought nor the attentive one of the Talmud's ironic reading of Job. One might call her, inspired by the video game, an angry bird, hurling her egg down to earth and drowning the people below, frustrated that it will not bear fruit for her.[63]

EMPTY SHELLS AND EMPTY NESTS

Rabbi Yishmael's report gives new meaning to the metaphor of the empty shell. His stories begin with the disembodied skin of a slaughtered animal and end with the colossal cracked egg of the *bar yokhani*. Are these strange stories meant to make us laugh or cry? Are they comedy or horror or something else entirely? Colossal proportions convey overwhelming emotions, art historians have said. What overwhelming emotions might be conveyed by the colossal flora and fauna recounted by Rabbi Yishmael?

The key to making sense of the stories, I believe, is the animal orphan. The question that launches the stories—"What is an orphan?"—points to the animal orphan's ghostly presence at the margins of the rabbinic world. The stories told by Rabbi Yishmael ben Satriel supply an answer to the uncomfortable question implicitly posed by Deuteronomy's mother-bird mitzvah: *What happens when the mother bird returns to her nest?* The Talmud's answer is, in essence: she goes ballistic. Colossal flora and fauna turn against humans in Rabbi Yishmael ben Satriel's dystopian stories, revealing to the audience the skeletons in the Jewish ritual closet, even though the practice of reanimating the slaughtered mother through her skin tries to deny her death.

The requirement to keep the baby animal with the mother for the first week of life that appears twice in the Torah is treated only tangentially by the Mishnah. But the Mishnah does display interest in the animal orphan. Other rabbinic passages suggest a surprisingly significant role for the animal orphan. The Talmud cites one early rabbinic teaching about the performance of the animal tithe:

> How do they tithe? They place the mothers outside, lowing, and the children exit towards them.[64]

Any schoolteacher or camp counselor knows the difficulty of getting a group of children to stand in line. Here the task is to move the young animals along so that every tenth can be tapped and removed, as per Leviticus 22:32's instruction that "all that passes under the shepherd's staff, every tenth one, shall be holy to the Lord." The strategy developed by the farmers to direct their young flocks, according to this teaching, was to hold the bleating mothers on the other side of the fence. While effective for keeping the line moving, the strategy would have created some palpable anguish when, on the tenth tap, the young animal was taken off to be tithed rather than reunited with the anxiously waiting mother.

Perhaps with that problem in mind, the Talmud directs, "Throw them a vegetable and let them go out towards it!"[65] Why didn't they just use vegetables to lure the animals—a literal carrot versus stick—rather than generate a terrible family drama that neither the animals nor the farmers would have much wanted to experience. The answer offered by Babylonian Rabbi Rav Huna is that the mother-and-stick method was instituted to make sure that orphan animals, who are exempt from the tithe, were not accidentally counted.[66] With no mothers to call to them, the orphan animal would have just stayed in the pen. When the farmer ushered the young animals along and made his count, he did not have to worry that the orphans would join the line. Here concern for the orphan animal is shown to be the impetus for the design of the annual tithe ritual.

The Talmud refers again to that same teaching from Rav Huna to explain why the animal tithe was abolished after the destruction of the Temple in Jerusalem:

> "In the presence of the Temple and not in the presence of the Temple" (quoting Mishnah Bekhorot 1:1 on animal tithes): If so, now too!
> It is like Rav Huna, as Rav Huna said: It is a decree because of the orphan.[67]

The Mishnah declares the animal tithe to be operative regardless of the Temple's existence. That being the case, the Talmudic commentary asks why the animal tithe is no longer practiced. We should still be counting out animals today and donating every tenth. The Rabbis instituted a halt on animal tithes, explains the Talmud, citing Rav Huna, so as not to risk accidentally including animal orphans. Animal orphans are featured here as the reason for the ritual rift between the Temple era and the subsequent period in which the Rabbis lived. Concern about the animal orphan drives historical change in Jewish practice.

These rabbinic laws and stories that feature the animal orphan—orphaned in most cases presumably because the mother was slaughtered—are a way of processing the impact on animals of human agricultural practices. The animal orphan becomes the jumping-off point in this Talmudic material for a series of tall tales, which, when read through the lens of modern art and parallel literature from the Bible, Talmud, and Zoroastrian myths, emerge as fantasies of revenge—by the animals. Rather than humans dominating nature, plants and animals turn the tables and tower over tiny humans. Rabbi Yishmael ben Satriel's alternative universe is one in which humans are not the ones in control. The delight that the audience may take in Rabbi Yishmael's tales—who doesn't like a good dystopia?—suggests that the universe that we do inhabit isn't all it's cracked up to be. Making orphans may not ultimately make us very happy.

One scholar has said about the Talmud's tall tales that they call existing order into question.[68] If so, what is the existing order that Rabbi Yishmael ben Satriel's tall tales call into question? The topics treated in this part of the Talmud are the main ancient Jewish practices associated with animals: tithes, donations, sacrifice, slaughter. It is these practices—all the different ways that Jews use and misuse animals—that the tall tales of Arqat Leveinah might be said to call into question. Rabbi Yishmael ben Satriel's stories experiment with scale and play with perspective. They invite us into an encounter with the bereaved animal children that Jewish practices inevitably and perpetually leave behind. In this chapter I have shown that the idyllic image of baby animals nestled with their mother for the first week of life is not one to which the Rabbis are drawn. It is, rather, the animal orphans, left to cuddle only with their slaughtered mother's hide, that capture the Rabbis' attention.

Conclusion

WHAT FAMILIES TEACH US ABOUT ANIMALS

SUMMARY OF THE CHAPTERS

In this book I have guided you through the readings of the Bible's four animal-family laws left to us by the ancient Rabbis. After chapter 1's review of the science and natural history of animal families and chapter 2's analysis of the biblical laws in context and survey of the humanitarian rationale, the chapters go one by one through each of the Bible's four animal-family laws as the Rabbis read them. Chapter 3 looks at the animal family trees and kinship terminology that the Rabbis take up as they treat the Bible's prohibition against slaughtering an animal parent and child on the same day. Chapter 4's concern is with absence and presence in the Bible's prohibition against cooking kids in their mother's milk. The Rabbis read the animal mother almost entirely out of the prohibition, but, in considering whether and how to eat animal udders, they recognize the mother's presence along with their own legal contrivances. Chapters 5 and 6 are likewise concerned with absence and presence: in chapter 5 the presence of bird fathers and other "aunties" at the nest in rabbinic elaborations of the mother-bird mitzvah and in chapter 6 the absence of substantive rabbinic discussions of the requirement to keep the baby animal with the mother for the first week of life. That absence is filled, chapter 6 shows, with Talmudic tall tales about taxidermied animal skins and giant homicidal birds, envisioning a world in which animals dominate humans rather than the other way around. The chapters together have illustrated the variety of ways in which rabbinic readings complement and correct the so-called humanitarian rationale that has monopolized interpretation of the Bible's four animal-family laws.

But readers should be aware that these four laws are not the only instances in antiquity in which animal families appear. As I wrote this book, I kept a running collection of other ancient texts about animal kinship, mostly biblical and rabbinic, but also classical, Christian, and Persian, along with visual imagery and material culture. Here in the conclusion, I share several highlights from my collection with the aim of showing the riches that await those who pay attention to animal families. I present, first, the pair of mother cows who appear in 1 Samuel 6; second, the animal who is a "ben pekuah," found in the Babylonian Talmud, which uses the term to refer to a baby animal born during a difficult delivery; and, finally, an ancient Egyptian painting of a mother cow being milked while her calf stands beside her.

THE NURSING COWS AND THE DAVIDIC CROWN

In the ark narrative of 1 Samuel 4–7:1, the Israelites are at war with the Philistines, who at first have the upper hand. The Israelites fetch the Ark of the Covenant from Shiloh in the hopes that God's presence will protect them from further losses, but to no avail. Even worse losses ensue, including the death of the two sons of Eli the priest and the capture of the ark by the Philistines. Things turn around after that, though. As soon as the ark reaches the Philistine towns Ashdod and Gat, God strikes down the inhabitants with a plague of killer hemorrhoids.[1] When the ark is sent on to Ekron, the inhabitants balk, not knowing what to expect, and they decide to give the ark back. They ask their priests the best way to do so. The Philistine priests tell the Ekronites to prepare some golden statues, and then get a new cart ready and two milch cows that have not borne a yoke; harness the cows to the cart, but take back indoors the calves that follow them. ⁸Take the ark of the Lord and place it on the cart; and put next to it in a chest the gold objects you are paying Him as indemnity. Send it off, and let it go on its way.

(6:7–8)

The nursing cows harnessed to the cart will want to stay home with their calves. Follow the cart, instruct the priests. If the cows proceed to Beth-shemesh in Israelite territory, they must be driven by divine hand. The Philistines did as they were told, and, sure enough, "the cows went straight ahead along the road to Beth-shemesh. They went along a single high-road, lowing as they went, and turning neither to the right nor to the left" (6:12).[2] When the cart appears in Beth-shemesh, the people rejoice, split up the wood of the cart to make a sacrifice, and offer up the two cows. The war continues for the next twenty years, until Israel finally purges itself of foreign gods, Samuel sacrifices a suckling lamb and asks for God's help, and the Israelites rout the Philistines and take back their territory. At that point the elders of Israel ask Samuel to appoint a king and the rest, as they say, is history (or legend, depending on one's stance on the historicity of the Israelite monarchy). The ark narrative is but the prelude to the Shakespearian-style drama of King David that occupies the bulk of the Book of Samuel.

The Hebrew root *ayin-lamed-heh* ("go up") recurs throughout the Beth-shemesh episode, along with the similar *ayin-vav-lamed* ("suckle") and *ayin-lamed-lamed* ("act severely").[3] The episode kicks off in 1 Samuel 5:12 with the outcry of the Ekronites going up *(ta'al)* to heaven. The Philistine priests caution their people not to let God make a mockery of them *(hitalel)* the way God did to the Egyptians in the Exodus (6:6). The priests tell them to take two nursing cows—the participle for nursing is *olot*—who have not borne a yoke *(asher lo alah alehem ol)*, which repeats the *ayin-lamed* sound three times and also evokes the description of the red cow in Numbers 19:2 and makes clear that these cows have no experience as draft animals (6:7). If they pull the cart, it is truly the work of God. The priests tell the people to see whether the cart goes up *(ya'aleh)* to Beth-shemesh (6:9). When it does, the people of Beth-shemesh respond by bringing up the *olah* sacrifice *(he'elu olah)* (6:14). Then, later, the phrase repeats for Samuel's sacrifice of a suckling lamb (7:9).

The repetition of the *ayin-lamed* letter combination telegraphs the message that, for Israel to make the transition successfully from judges to kings—that is the grand narrative of the book of Samuel—the *parot olot* (nursing cows) must become *parot* who are an *olah* (cows offered up as a sacrifice). That is to say, the bond between parent and child, represented by the nursing cows, powerful as it is, must be severed and superseded by loyalty to God, represented by the sacrificed cows.[4] Just as the two cows must be separated from their calves to demonstrate God's power—the cows are propelled to Beth-shemesh almost as if under a spell, crying for their children all along the way—so too must Hannah at the beginning of the story give up her beloved Samuel (though she is able to wait until after he is weaned, unlike the two cows, who are still nursing).[5] So too must the various fathers in the story find successors other than their sons: Eli for the priesthood, Samuel for prophecy, and Saul for the monarchy. Not unlike in HBO's hit series *Succession*, there are interests, we are led to discover, that transcend the bonds of family.[6] God says as much to Eli when God's messenger reprimands him: "You have honored your sons more than me" (1 Samuel 2:29). The nursing cows and suckling lamb illustrate this point as much as do the priests, prophets, and kings whose foibles fill the narrative.[7] Robert Alter praises the narrator for crafting "this most searching story of men and women"—and animals, one might add, recalling that Saul first appears while searching for his father's donkeys, and David while tending his father's flocks.[8] The very word for cow, *parah*, means reproduction, making the cow the embodiment of childbearing and thus a flashpoint for problems of succession. The animal family is, in short, critical to the story of Israel's beginnings as scripture tells it.

THE FOREVER FETUS

Part of what makes the next topic a highlight of my collection is its utter independence from scripture. The ben pekuah demonstrates the rabbinic imagination at its most creative. The opening words of Mishnah Tractate Hullin Chapter Four provide the premise: "an animal who is having difficulty while giving birth."[9] The legal questions raised by this scenario relate to the status of the baby found inside her should her handlers decide to slaughter her while she is in labor, presumably because they expect her to die from childbirth anyway.[10] Does the fetus in such a case count as a firstborn for purposes of donation? Does the fetus impart impurity? What difference might it make if the fetus is alive or dead, not yet fully formed or already viable, or if the fetus has extended a limb or its head during the delivery? Does the kosher slaughter of the mother "count" for the fetus too, permitting both to be eaten? Mishnah Hullin 4:5 features a debate about this last question:

> If one found a living nine-[month]-old, it requires slaughter, and one is obligated regarding "him and his child" [the prohibition in Leviticus 22:28 against slaughtering animal parent and child on the same day]—the words of Rabbi Meir.
>
> But the Sages say: The slaughter of his mother purifies him.
>
> Rabbi Shimon Ha-Shezuri says: Even if he is five years old and is threshing in the field, the slaughter of his mother purifies him.[11]

Here the cow's owner or handler finds a fetus inside her who is alive, viable, and full-term. That fetus is, according to Rabbi Meir, considered a separate animal and requires its own act of slaughter to make it kosher to consume. Clinching the point is the application to the fetus of the same-day slaughter prohibition in Leviticus 22:28. If Rabbi Meir prohibits slaughter of that fetus on the same day with the mother, then clearly Rabbi Meir views that fetus as already an independent child.[12] The Sages take the opposite viewpoint, ruling that the slaughter of the mother covers the baby as well. The implication is that the Sages consider the fetus still to be part of the mother despite its capacity to exist as an independent entity. The final opinion from Rabbi Shimon Ha-Shezuri takes that view even further. When the baby grows up—five years old and working in the field is how Rabbi Shimon Ha-Shezuri pictures him—the act of slaughter that killed his mother during his birth continues to cover him as well.[13]

Those who study the first three chapters of Mishnah Hullin will, when they arrive at this ruling, register something of a shock. The laws of slaughter are elaborate. For a perfectly healthy five-year-old animal to bypass all those laws and be killed for consumption any which way would seem to land us in an enormous legal void. The Babylonian Talmud's commentary on Rabbi Shimon Ha-Shezuri's ruling at first pulls us back from the void, but then it plunges us further in:

> This is the "first tanna" [that is, the Sages' consensus position]!
>
> Rav Kahana said: The [difference] between them regards when [the fetus] stood on the ground.
>
> Zeiri said Rabbi Hanina said: The law is like Rabbi Shimon Shezuri, and thus Rabbi Shimon Shezuri would permit regarding his child and his grandchild, until the end of all the generations.
>
> Rabbi Yohanan said: He is permitted, but his child is forbidden.[14]

Rav Kahana stakes out a practical difference between the consensus position in the Mishnah—that full-term, living fetuses born from slaughtered mothers do not require their own slaughter for them to be lawfully consumed—and Rabbi Shimon Ha-Shezuri's statement that the exemption applies even once these animals have grown up. Rav Kahana proposes that for the Sages, once the babies' feet hit the ground, they require their own slaughter. For Shimon Ha-Shezuri, they never do. Rav Kahana thus restricts the scope of the Mishnah's consensus position, walking back its surprising leniency. Zeiri, on the other hand, extends Shimon Ha-Shezuri's position to a new area: the children's children.[15] Zeiri's teaching from Rabbi Hanina proposes that Shimon Ha-Shezuri's exemption from slaughter applies not only to these particular children as they grow up and throughout their own lifetime but also to their children and children's children, ad infinitum. Zeiri then establishes this position as definitive law.[16] Rabbi Yohanan disagrees, restricting the exemption to animals who are themselves born under these circumstances but not subsequent generations.

Whether we follow Zeiri or Rabbi Yohanan, we are left with the extraordinary position that an animal who for all intents and purposes looks and acts like every other animal does not require kosher slaughter. One need not go through the elaborate checking procedure for injuries, and one need not kill the animal with the appropriate knife using the appropriate methods. Traditions in the Talmudic chapter and subsequent decisors exempt animals born under these circumstances also from the prohibitions on consumption of the sciatic nerve and forbidden fats and on the mixing of meat with milk.[17] According to Rabbi Hanina, the ben pekuah animals can go on to have their own children, and those children their own children, and few of the strictures of kashrut will apply to any of them, theoretically forever.

Why on earth should this be so? Are these animals and their later generations, possibly entire herds, all somehow considered still a part of their mother's, grandmother's, or great-grandmother's body? Are they fetuses, in some technical sense, forever? Are they, as Rashi comments, not even considered animals at all?[18] The ben pekuah is a bold and bizarre legal invention, the term ben pekuah (literally, "child of a split one") a fabrication of the Babylonian Talmud, certainly not present in scripture but also not present in earlier rabbinic strata.[19] Both the Mishneh Torah and the Shulhan Arukh rule that the ben pekuah is exempt from kosher slaughter so long as they do not put their feet on the ground, and the Shulhan Arukh grants ben pekuah status to all future generations so long as the ben pekuah mates with a fellow ben pekuah (though the Shulhan Arukh adds that by rabbinic decree the animals should be properly slaughtered).[20]

A company called Ancient Kosher Ben Pekuah Australia came up with the idea in 2015 of creating ben pekuah herds that could be slaughtered and sold without the entire expensive apparatus that characterizes the kosher slaughter industry (careful lung checks, disposal of the many animals who do not pass inspection, excision of forbidden parts, close rabbinical supervision, specially trained slaughterers).[21] Faced by resistance from rabbinic legal decisors, the company failed, but contemporary efforts to capitalize on the ben pekuah concept demonstrates for my purposes the problems and opportunities that animal-family relationships continually pose to religious communities. The animal parent-child bond in the case of the ben pekuah pushes the limits of rabbinic logic and tests the boundaries of rabbinic law. The animal family in 1 Samuel forms part of the foundation of Jewish history; the animal family of the ben pekuah law stretches Jewish practice in new and unpredictable directions.

CONCLUSION

ANCIENT VEGAN ART

The third and final highlight of my collection takes us far back in time to the twenty-first century BCE, to a relief decoration on the sarcophagus of Kawit, royal companion of Mentuhotep II and daughter of Mentuhotep I of the eleventh dynasty in Egypt's Middle Kingdom.[22] The sarcophagus was originally stored in the burial complex of Deir el-Bahari on the Nile's shore in Thebes. Today one can see it at the Egyptian Museum in Cairo. Most of the images on Kawit's sarcophagus are of the queen luxuriating in her palace life, attended by maids who serve her drinks, style her hair, and offer her lotions and jewelry, but there is one image on the east side that features a milking scene (see figure 1). On the left stands a horned cow with a small calf next to her. Next to that calf is a second large cow, this one without horns, also accompanied by a small calf.[23] A kneeling human figure extracts the second cow's milk with both hands, squeezing her milk from the udder into a pouch suspended with straps. The second calf, presumably the child of the unhorned cow, has been tied to the cow's front leg with a rope. The line of the calf's head and neck slopes downward toward the rope, suggesting resistance by the calf to being restrained. The first calf, by contrast, stands erect.

The composition, in which the kneeling figure and second calf are the sole figures facing left while all the others face right, emphasizes the plight of the tethered calf. The drama at the heart of the tableau is captured in a single tear that drops from the mother's eye (see figure 2).[24] Is the viewer meant to see pathos, perhaps cruelty, in the separation of cow from calf during milking? Is the scene intended as critique? It is hard to interpret the tear otherwise. The grandeur of the horned cow and the freedom of her calf present to the viewer an alternative vision in which cows are not restrained by humans. The scale in the scene dwarfs the human, who appears to be of about the same size and bulk as the young calf.

I like to think of this relief as a form of ancient "vegan art."[25] It is, admittedly, a stretch, especially if the interpretation is correct that the milking scene is meant to reveal the origin of the fluid that the queen is shown drinking in the scene opposite.[26] Clearly the viewer is meant to accept the queen's claim to the milk. If anything, the cow's tear may demonstrate just how strong that claim is.[27] Whatever the case, this image

Figure 1. Sarcophagus of Queen Kawit at the Egyptian Museum in Cairo. Photo from Shutterstock, asset ID 2435043315.

Figure 2. Detail of the sarcophagus of Queen Kawit. Photo © Andrea Jemolo, Bridgeman Images.

and many others like it from ancient Egypt, Syria-Palestine, and Mesopotamia show a vivid interest in animal maternity.[28] The popularity of the motif goes beyond the ancient Near East. Images of sheep, goats, cows, and other animal mothers, either nursing their own animal children or being milked by people while their animal children stand by, and even images of humans shown suckling straight from an animal's udder, have been found in Hellenistic mosaics, early Christian frescoes, medieval illuminated manuscripts, and countless depictions of the Hindu god Krishna. One finds a human child nursing straight from a cow, with the calf nursing too, all perched on a rooftop, in Marc Chagall's 1911 surrealist masterpiece *To Russia, Asses, and Others*.[29] A video of a chihuahua mother nursing her puppies got over six million views on YouTube.[30] A video of a stray dog who lost her own litter of puppies and nursed kittens instead got eighteen million.[31]

BIG MAMA AND HER FUZZY LITTLE FAMILY

Many more images of animal families remain to be tapped. There is, from the Hebrew Bible, Job 39's vision of animals bearing and raising children. From the first century CE, there is 4 Maccabees 14:14–18's encomium of parental love among birds. There is Genesis Rabbah 86:2's comparison of the patriarch Jacob following his son Joseph to Egypt to a cow following after her calf. There is the Mishnah's treatment of an ox goring a pregnant cow, a person stealing a pregnant cow, and a person selling a female animal and her child.[32] From the Babylonian Talmud come traditions that describe assisting in the delivery of an animal's baby during a festival; the desire of a cow to suckle and a calf to suck; the biblical Ninevites cruelly separating animal mothers from their children; parental care among jackals and ravens; attachment between mother and daughter doves; and discussions of whether animal mothers ever nurse the babies of other mothers.[33] Second- and third-century CE Roman writer Aelian offers copious information about animal families, describing storks who tend to their elderly parents; pigeons, cocks, donkeys, catfish, and hares who are caring fathers; mother elephants and Libyan cows who risk their lives for their children; cows and ants who mourn their loved ones; and mares who nurse foals who lost their own mothers.[34] The popular ancient Christian *Physiologus* adapts these classical traditions so that the lioness and pelican mother stand in for God, the elephant mother becomes a surrogate for Mary, and the elephant father for Joseph.[35] The Zoroastrian *Videvdad* deems it a sin to fail to care for pregnant and postpartum dogs.[36] When we look, we find animal kin relations throughout human culture, right up until today.

The three highlights I discuss here are each fairly disturbing, I realize. All three feature animal bereavement, as does the story of Bambi with which this book began. The ark episode in 1 Samuel, the law of the ben pekuah in the Babylonian Talmud, and the limestone relief on Queen Kawit's tomb are all concerned with the traumatic separation that typifies the domesticated animal-family experience. While these texts are, admittedly, not exactly enjoyable, they are, I believe, deeply poignant. That poignancy has the power to transform our thinking—so too do the Bible's animal-family laws to which I have dedicated this book.

There is a happier side to the animal-family story. In one of the episodes in his podcast series *Animal*, New York Times journalist Sam Anderson travels to the Yucatán to learn about bats.[37] Anderson starts out afraid of bats, as most people are. Bats are the only mammals that fly, they come out at night, and they are associated with Halloween, haunted houses, and vampires. Anderson meets up with a Mexican ecologist who tries to convince him that bats are beautiful, smart, and good for the planet (they control pests and pollinate and disperse seeds). It doesn't really click for Anderson, though, until one particular moment in the trip. The ecologist and his students plunge into the depths of an ancient Mayan temple and bring out five bats, all struggling inside the cloth bags that the scientists have used to trap them. Anderson is freaked out. As the scientists pull the bats out of the bags, they discover that one of the bats is a mother—they name her "Big Mama"—and another is her baby boy. When Anderson sees the baby, he exclaims, "It's so freaking cute. It's fresh and fuzzy."

Anderson doesn't fully come round until the ecologist points to the milk inside the little pink belly of the baby, who has been nursing. Anderson explains to the podcast audience, "Because these bats are part of a little family. They're a family of bats." Anderson continues, "And seeing all this just unlocks my general feeling of love for all animals." He starts to see the darkness inside the ancient temple differently, not as a "horrifying void of death" but as the home of "Big Mama and her fuzzy little family." It is a conversion narrative. Anderson's encounter with the little bat family profoundly changes him, not only in his view of bats but in his capacity to connect with all animals. Anderson's account shows that the encounter with animal families does not have to be filled only with poignancy and pain. It can be filled also with pleasure and delight.

We cannot realistically eliminate the trauma endemic to animal domestication. That is utopian thinking. But we can recognize it and, to the extent that each of us can, reduce it. For ideas of how to do so, read on to the epilogue. While I began this book with the question of what animals teach us about families, I end by asking, What do families teach us about animals? They teach us that the lives of animals are complicated, intense, and dramatic—and as filled with joy and love as our own.

Epilogue

FIVE WAYS TO SUPPORT ANIMAL FAMILIES

With Rabbi Melissa Hoffman

What would an update of the Bible's animal-family laws look like? How can we today in our own lives support animal families? None of us has expert knowledge of the needs of every species or the power to protect every kinship bond, but there are things we can do to reduce our negative impact on the family lives of animals. This epilogue offers suggestions that cover five domains in which animals live: cities and suburbs, homes, farms, cages, and natural areas. The suggestions invite us to think differently about the animals living in each environment and to modify our daily habits so that both human and animal families can survive and thrive.

1. URBAN AND SUBURBAN ANIMALS

Animals seem to endlessly adapt to our human-made environment, yet we keep finding ways to eliminate them from it. Denver poet Suzi Q. Smith observes that our treatment of animals in cities and suburbs—such as the pigeons who were bred to live among people and to rely on them—reflects judgments about which lives matter and which don't.[1] Smith draws out a harsh truth: humans intentionally brought animals into our domestic worlds only to subsequently reject them. In a story in the Talmud, Rabbi Yehudah Ha-Nasi chides his housekeeper for sweeping young weasels out of his home.[2] Following the Rabbi's model, we can reach a compassionate compromise with the animals who live among us and pose challenges to human development, health, and quality of life but who are also an integral part of our urban and suburban spaces. As the percentage of the world human population that resides in urban and suburban environments continues to increase, our ability to experience nature within these environments becomes ever more important (and opportunities abound—from cracks in the pavement to urban wildlife refuges), says conservation biologist Jon Regosin. Not ten blocks away from where I live in Brooklyn is a historic cemetery, home to many bird, butterfly, native bee, and other insect families.[3] It's not just good for animals but it's good for us when we have quality nature experiences in our neighborhoods and backyards.

What you can do:

- Maximize biodiversity outside your home by reducing manicured lawns, planting trees and other native plants, and creating pollinator gardens.
- Appreciate local wildlife. Get to know the rhythms and habits of the creatures who share your space. Don't interfere too much, however: feeding animals risks skewing population balances, spreading disease, and habituating them to humans so that they are more likely to become "pests" whom humans will want to eliminate.[4]
- Take preventive measures not to attract unwanted animals into your home by keeping living areas clean, storing food in sealed containers, securing garbage and recycling, eliminating standing water, and plugging up holes and cracks in walls and doors. Never use methods of removal that result in prolonged suffering for animals such as glue traps and poisons (which in turn poison birds of prey who eat the rodents who eat the poison).[5]

2. COMPANION ANIMALS

In the United States, companion animals are usually considered members of the family. Yet hundreds of thousands of healthy, adoptable pets are still euthanized each year in our already inundated shelter system.[6] Adopting an animal from a public shelter or reputable rescue can save a life and make room for another animal to be given the same chance. Pets also come with a significant carbon footprint (largely because of meat-heavy diets), so breeding more of them only contributes to the sustainability problem. Animals who come from both breeders and shelters are typically separated from parents, children, siblings, and peers, sometimes prematurely. That separation may be inherent to keeping animals as companions in our homes, but there are still many ways to ensure that companion animals lead fulfilling lives alongside us.

What you can do:

- Adopt, don't shop—and do your research to find the right kind of companions so that you can provide a healthy and happy home for their entire life.
- Educate yourself about the needs of your pets. Make sure they get appropriate stimuli, exercise, and attention. Socialize them properly so that they learn to interact peaceably with visitors and household members.
- Feed them foods that are sustainably sourced and plant-forward after checking with your veterinarian about your pet's nutritional needs. Avoid having your companion animal eat less ethically than you do. Buy pet-related goods like bags, litter, tanks, and toys with an eye toward sustainability.[7]

3. FARMED ANIMALS

Farmed animals have become some of the most "successful" animals by sheer population thanks to humans, yet they suffer some of the worst abuses of our food system. No animals on factory farms remain tied to their original family. Though they still possess strong instincts to parent and be parented, form friendships, and learn from one another, animals are routinely separated from their parents, their peers, and their natural environments. Though people have raised and eaten animals (to a much lesser extent than now) for many generations, this separation feature is relatively recent and fueled by profit-driven capitalism. Normalizing a return to plant-based eating would in the short term reduce our reliance on this industrial farming model and in the long term benefit our entire planet. Making plant-based meals the default reduces greenhouse gas emissions and water and land use.[8] An exclusively plant-based diet is not possible for many people, including subsistence farmers, populations in the Global South, people disproportionately impacted by conflict and climate change, and communities in industrialized countries who suffer from food-access issues, but for the many who can make these choices freely and for institutions, corporations, and organizations, plant-forward shifts in food and product sourcing would have massive impact.

What you can do:

- Aim for a plant-forward diet that reduces consumption of meat, dairy, eggs, and fish. Try new plant-based recipes and restaurants. Make sustainable plant-based foods the norm by serving them as the default option or in higher quantities.
- Choose plant-based or synthetic fabrics rather than those for which animals are killed or unsustainably bred such as leather, suede, down, fur, silk, wool, feathers, and hair. Instead of the down coat or comforter, get the one stuffed with down alternative.
- Speak up! Encourage the schools, communities, organizations, places of worship, and social circles in which you take part to create a food policy, pact, or commitment.[9]

4. CAPTIVE ANIMALS

Zoos and aquariums that house and breed captive animals cannot replicate the access to space, freedom to express natural behaviors, and maintenance of kinship bonds that they need as wildlife, especially for large mammals. Unaccredited and roadside zoos, marine parks, and circuses with animals are inconsistently regulated across the United States, as anyone who has watched *Tiger King* on Netflix would know.[10] Major zoos and aquariums sometimes play an important role in species conservation and public education, though there are still many that do not meet their conservation potential. Even the best zoos that advocate for wildlife outside the zoo participate in the common practice of separating captive animals from parents and peers to maintain a genetically sound "assurance population," whether through moving the animals to different facilities or killing (culling) surplus animals that no longer contribute to the gene pool.[11] Quality of life is worse for laboratory animals, millions of whom continue to be used every year not only in medical and drug research but also to test cosmetics, toiletries, and household products even though sophisticated nonanimal methods of testing have emerged.[12] Lab animals are typically kept alone in cages, sometimes with their parents, siblings, or children similarly isolated in cages near them.

What you can do:

- Avoid establishments that keep animals captive for the primary purpose of human entertainment. Consider taking a hike to enjoy wildlife safely in their natural habitat.
- Look for cruelty-free logos and plant-based ingredients and certification when you are shopping for shampoo, laundry detergent, cosmetics, toiletries, and household products.[13]
- Volunteer and sign petitions with the Nonhuman Rights Project, the only civil rights organization in the United States fighting for the rights of nonhuman animals, which is suing to free seven chimpanzees held at a roadside zoo in Michigan, among other clients.[14]

5. ANIMALS IN NATURAL HABITATS

We are facing an unprecedented biodiversity crisis. Human development, natural resource extraction, and land clearing for agriculture cause the loss, fragmentation, and degradation of natural animal habitats and drive climate change, which compounds the problem. Animals who live in natural ecosystems are responding by modifying the times and places that they bear and raise their children, but shrinking habitats along with rising temperatures and sea levels, changes in water quality and quantity, severe weather events, and pollution are making it harder for animals to have children at all.[15] Some populations simply abandon breeding or experience large-scale mortality.[16] Even people who love animals may inadvertently harm them by trying to see them up close. If tour companies make their money by ensuring that you'll be able to see, hold, or photograph an animal, they are likely putting animals' welfare at risk and harming true sustainability efforts. As one *Lonely Planet* writer says, responsible ecotourism means watching wildlife interact in the wild while keeping your distance and avoiding opportunities to interact.[17]

What you can do:

- Contribute to effective conservation efforts that benefit wild populations of plants and animals, in particular at-risk species and their habitats, in an environmentally just framework that considers the needs of underresourced and underserved human communities.
- Support effective environmental education and nature literacy and access to nature for all people, with the notions that "nature is for everyone" and that experience is an integral part of the pathway to action.
- Plan eco-conscious travel with vendors and sites that support wildlife-friendly practices and disavow the commercial exploitation of animals for tourism.[18]

The Bible's animal-family laws do not protect animal families so much as sensitize us to their presence. In the culture of ancient Israel and the late ancient Rabbis, that meant keeping track of animal genealogies, learning about animal behaviors, and caring for animals who lost their parents to slaughter, as we have seen in this book. A twenty-first-century world presents new challenges but also new opportunities. Global capitalism produces misery for animals on an unprecedented scale, but it has also led to a wide variety of plant-based food options and cruelty-free products. Conservation programs help preserve animal habitats. By participating in these practices and programs and giving them our support, we can sustain the spirit of the animal-family laws today and make a positive difference for animal families.

Acknowledgments

I am grateful to the many people with whom I had the opportunity to share parts of this project and to the institutions that helped to support it. I thank Saul Olyan for inviting me to be the Elga K. Stulman Scholar at Brown University and for being a wonderful interlocutor and friend. I thank Ruth von Bernuth of the Carolina Center for Jewish Studies and the convivial group of Jewish studies faculty in the North Carolina Jewish Studies Seminar for their generous hosting and insightful feedback on chapter 4. Thanks go to Yaakob Dweck for inviting me to be the Mytelka Scholar at Princeton and to Shuli Shinnar for inviting me to give the John Priest Lecture at Florida State.

Thanks go to Julia Watts Belser, Ariel Mayse, Jonnie Schnytzer, and the other participants in the AJS seminar "Beyond the Human"—Mara Benjamin, Aaron Gross, Rafe Neis, and David Shyovitz—and Judith Plaskow for chairing. Working at the intersection of Jewish studies and animal studies, these scholars are creating a new field with their brilliant and beautiful work. Ariel Mayse and Deborah Barer created a community out of the AJS seminar "Reading the Talmud as Ethical Prompt." I want to thank them, the seminar participants, and especially Ariel and Jon Schofer for their comments on my paper. Alex Weisberg and I co-organized an AAR roundtable on critical animal studies and Jewish studies with a "celebrity" cast: Aaron Gross, Naama Harel, Noam Pines, David Shyovitz, Ken Stone, and Mira Wasserman, chaired by Carol Adams. I want to thank everyone who participated and especially Alex for our work together and for the invitation to contribute to the special issue of *Worldviews* on Jewish environmental ethics.

ACKNOWLEDGMENTS

The "Humanimal" team of Bible scholars, now also behind the SBL Animal Studies unit, is a model of creative collaboration: David Carr, Sébastien Doane, Jake Evers, Dong Jeong, Brian Kolia, Suzanna Millar, Megan Remington, and Brian Tipton. I am honored to have served as a keynote speaker at the first Humanimal conference and hope to participate in many more. I also thank David Carr for inviting me to join and present at the Columbia University Hebrew Bible Seminar and for always being up for reading and sharing work. I thank Karina Hogan too for the Bible seminar invitation and for joining the Morningside Heights workshop with Erez DeGolan, Sarit Kattan Gribetz, Marjorie Lehman, and Sarah Wolf. That group has heard about this project for years and has been a source of so much great feedback, conversation, support, and friendship as we weathered the pandemic and political upheavals.

Thanks go to former colleague Robbie Harris for inviting me to share work at the JTS/UTS lunchtime Bible seminar; to David Flatto and Benny Porat for inviting me to present at the Hebrew University Jewish Law workshop; to the Columbia University Seminar on Animal Studies for the opportunity to share work and especially to Naama Harel; to Dave Aftandilian, Barbara Ambros, and Aaron Gross for including me in their textbook *Animals and Religion* and offering valuable feedback on my contribution; to Carol Bakhos and Alyssa Gray for including me in their Festschrift and for being such great colleagues over the years; and to Michal Bar-Asher Siegal, Simcha Gross, Tzvi Novick, and Sara Ronis for giving me the chance to share work at Chris-Fest, with special thanks to Sara for her feedback on my paper.

Thanks to Todd Berzon and Jennifer Knust for including me in their collection honoring Elizabeth Castelli, who brings so many together in shared admiration for her scholarship, mentorship, and utter *menschlichkeit*. Barnard Religion has been a happy home with an almost weird level of cooperation and functionality. Thanks for being the best of colleagues: Elizabeth, Najam Haider, Tiffany Hale, Jack Hawley, Gale Kenny, Tim Vasko, the newly arrived Meghan Hartman, the soon-to-arrive Mike Chin, and our ultrareliable administrator, Anna Hotard. Thanks also go to my great colleagues at Columbia Religion and especially to Gil Anidjar for reading material along the way and for sharing an interest in mothers. Thanks go to Dakota Straub for diversifying my media footprint and making the IRCPL podcast episode. Columbia's Institute for Israel and Jewish Studies has offered unfailing support and collegiality; thanks go to directors Elisheva Carlebach and Rebecca Kobrin, to administrator Julie Feldman and the other wonderful staff, to Isabelle Levy for the annual invitations to talk about animals to her students, and to my other IIJS colleagues, along with librarian extraordinaire Michelle Margolis. Seth Schwartz is not only the best of colleagues in ancient Judaism but also the best of friends.

Thanks go to Miryam Segal for thinking to ask me whether I was working on anything related to families and for all that unfolded after—the feedback, the friendship, and the mentor-mentee exchange. I am grateful to Jordan Rosenblum for sending me his edition of Hullin in advance of publication, for including me in the ancient law and animals conference at Brown he co-organized with Saul Olyan, and for sharing my interest in rabbinic animals. Thanks go to Moshe Simon-Shoshan for lots of intriguing text tidbits about animals and to Monika Amsler for helpful references. Other great colleagues for whom I'm grateful at BC/CU, JTS, and beyond, including teachers and students, are Liz Alexander, Mira Balberg, Emmanuel Bloch, Daniel Boyarin, Jonah Boyarin, David Brodsky, Naftali Cohn, Andrea Dara Cooper, Krista Dalton, Celia Deutsch, Steven Fraade, Xandy Frisch, Gregg Gardner, Lisa Gordis, Max Grossman, Achsah Guibbory, Amit Gvaryahu, Chaya Halberstam, Chris Hayes, Amy Kalmanofsky, Richard Kalmin, Laura Kay, Gwynn Kessler, Naomi Koltun-Fromm, Yedidah Koren, Jenny Labendz, Lennart Lehmhaus, Sarra Lev, Ishai Mishory, James Redfield, Adele Reinhartz, Jeff Rubenstein, Joe Sakurai, Michael Satlow, Benjamin Schvarcz, Rachel Slutsky, Jessica Spencer, Elsie Stern, Max Strassfeld, Deborah Valenze, Moulie Vidas, Steve Weitzman, Barry Wimpfheimer, and Shmuly Yanklowitz. I am grateful to Rabbi Jonathan Bernhard and Jon Regosin for their help on the epilogue and to Rabbi Melissa Hoffman for agreeing to coauthor it. I learned so much from figuring out how to put the ideas of the book into action.

Many thanks go to Eric Schmidt, who took on the project at University of California Press; to Chloe Layman, who took it over; and to Chad Attenborough, who attended to all the nitty-gritty. I'm very grateful to all of them for their support for the book and great ideas for it.

I offer endless love and gratitude for this particular animal's wonderful family: Josh, Orly, and Tamar. I feel so lucky also to be part of a larger pack that includes my parents, Sharon and Jerry; my sister, Randi, and Jon, Talia, Greg, Nadav, Laya, Shachar, David, Daniel, Alisa, Sammy, Dahlia, Ariana, and Burt.

An earlier version of chapter 3 appeared as "A Genealogy of the Jewish Family, Animals Included," in *Jewish Law Association Studies XXXII: Jewish Law and the Family; Anatomies of Home and Disruption*, ed. Miryam Segal, 15–38 (New York: Jewish Law Association, 2023). An earlier version of chapter 4 appeared as "Appetite for Udders: The Return of the Repressed Mother in b. Hullin 109a–110b," *Journal of Textual Reasoning* 15, no. 1 (2024): 121–52. An earlier version of chapter 5 appeared as "Birds as Dads, Babysitters, and Hats: An 'Indistinction' Approach to the Modern Bird Mitzvah in Deuteronomy 22:6–7," *Worldviews: Global Religions, Culture, and Ecology* 26, nos. 1–2 (2022): 79–105. Parts of chapter 6 appeared in "The Tall Tales of Babylonian Talmud Bekhorot 57b: Zombie Mothers, Angry Birds, and Egg Drop Soup," in *Making History: Studies in Rabbinic History, Literature, and Culture in Honor of Richard L. Kalmin*, ed. Carol Bakhos and Alyssa M. Gray (Providence, RI: Brown Judaic Studies, 2024), 3–24.

Notes

INTRODUCTION: WHAT ANIMALS TEACH
US ABOUT FAMILIES

1. The book first appeared in a serialized version in the *Neue Freie Presse* in 1922.
2. Felix Salten, *Bambi: A Life in the Woods*, trans. Whittaker Chambers (New York: Simon and Schuster, 1928), 141.
3. Salten, 81, 287, 293.
4. Paul Reitter, *Bambi's Jewish Roots and Other Essays on German-Jewish Culture* (New York: Bloomsbury Academic, 2015), 88–90.
5. The allegorical reading appeared already in the 1940s, when Austrian Jewish writer Karl Kraus identified "Jewish dialect" in the hares of *Bambi* (Reitter, 91).
6. Salten, *Bambi*, 127.
7. Maya Balakirsky Katz, "'Bambi' Abroad, 1924–1954," *AJS Review* 44, no. 2 (2020): 286.
8. Beverley D. Eddy, *Felix Salten: Man of Many Faces* (Riverside, CA: Ariadne, 2010), 199.
9. Salten reportedly wrote *Bambi* in Salzkammergut, a mountainous region near Salzburg where Salten spent summers (Eddy, *Felix Salten*, 198).
10. On the breeding habits of deer, see George A. Feldhamer and William J. McShea, *Deer: The Animal Answer Guide* (Baltimore: Johns Hopkins University Press, 2012), 45, 67–77.

11. Ralph H. Lutts, "The Trouble with Bambi: Walt Disney's Bambi and the American Vision of Nature," *Forest and Conservation History* 36, no. 4 (1992): 168, 161; "Former Beatle 'Inspired by Bambi,'" BBC, December 12, 2005, http://news.bbc.co.uk/2/hi/entertainment/4520658.stm.

12. Hillary Hope Herzog, *Vienna Is Different: Jewish Writers in Austria from the Fin de Siècle to the Present*. Austrian and Habsburg Studies (New York: Berghahn Books, 2011), 44.

13. Simone Rebora and Massimo Salgaro, "Is Felix Salten the Author of the Mutzenbacher Novel (1906)? Yes and No," *Language and Literature* 31, no. 2 (2022): 243–64.

14. Eviatar Zerubavel, *Ancestors and Relatives: Genealogy, Identity, and Community* (New York: Oxford University Press, 2012), 3.

15. Sara Asu Schroer, "Breeding with Birds of Prey: Intimate Encounters," in *Domestication Gone Wild: Politics and Practices of Multispecies Relations*, ed. Heather Anne Swanson et al. (Durham: Duke University Press, 2018), 33–49.

16. Selcen Küçüküstel, *Embracing Landscape: Living with Reindeer and Hunting Among Spirits in South Siberia* (New York: Berghahn Books, 2021).

17. Muhammad A. Kavesh, *Animal Enthusiasms: Life Beyond Cage and Leash in Rural Pakistan* (Abingdon, Oxon: Routledge, 2021), 115–29.

18. *The Elephant Whisperers*, documentary (short), Netflix, 2022, www.imdb.com/title/tt23628262/.

19. Sarah D. P. Cockram, "Sleeve Cat and Lap Dog: Affection, Aesthetics and Proximity to Companion Animals in Renaissance Mantua," in *Interspecies Interactions: Animals and Humans Between the Middle Ages and Modernity*, ed. Sarah D. P. Cockram and Andrew Wells (London: Routledge, Taylor and Francis Group, 2018), 34–65.

20. Erica Fudge, *Quick Cattle and Dying Wishes: People and Their Animals in Early Modern England* (Ithaca: Cornell University Press, 2018).

21. My formulation is inspired by Damien W. Riggs and Elizabeth Peel, *Critical Kinship Studies: An Introduction to the Field* (London: Palgrave Macmillan, 2016), 11.

22. Sarah Blaffer Hrdy, *Mother Nature: A History of Mothers, Infants, and Natural Selection* (New York: Pantheon Books, 1999); Hrdy, *Mothers and Others: The Evolutionary Origins of Mutual Understanding* (Cambridge, MA: Harvard University Press, 2009).

23. Jeanne Altmann, *Baboon Mothers and Infants* (Cambridge, MA: Harvard University Press, 1981); Susan Allport, *A Natural History of Parenting: From Emperor Penguins to Reluctant Ewes, a Naturalist Looks at Parenting in the Animal World and Ours* (New York: Harmony Books, 1997).

24. Devora Steinmetz, *From Father to Son: Kinship, Conflict, and Continuity in Genesis* (Louisville, KY: Westminster John Knox Press, 1991), 30.

25. Joseph Fleishman, *Parents and Children in Ancient Near Eastern Law and Biblical Law* (Jerusalem: Magnes, 1999).

26. See these studies of children in ancient Israel: Julie F. Parker, *Valuable and Vulnerable: Children in the Hebrew Bible, Especially the Elisha Cycle* (Providence, RI: Brown Judaic Studies, 2013); Naomi A. Steinberg, *The World of the Child in the Hebrew Bible* (Sheffield: Sheffield Phoenix, 2013); and Laurel Koepf Taylor, *Give Me Children or I Shall Die: Children and Communal Survival in Biblical Literature* (Minneapolis: Fortress, 2013).

27. See Yedidah Koren, "'Look Through Your Book and Make Me a Perfect Match': Talking About Genealogy in Amoraic Palestine and Babylonia," *Journal for the Study of Judaism in the Persian, Hellenistic, and Roman Period* 49, no. 3 (2018): 417–48; and Koren, "Policing Lineage in Rabbinic Literature," *Journal of Ancient Judaism* 11, no. 1 (2020): 76–115.

28. On the story cycle with this theme in Babylonian Tractate Ketubbot 62b-63a, see references in Haim Weiss and Shira Stav, *The Return of the Absent Father: A New Reading of a Chain of Stories from the Babylonian Talmud*, trans. Batya Stein (Philadelphia: University of Pennsylvania Press, 2022), 93n1.

29. Marjorie Suzan Lehman et al., eds., *Mothers in the Jewish Cultural Imagination* (Oxford: Littman Library of Jewish Civilization/Liverpool University Press, 2017).

30. Nicole J. Ruane, *Sacrifice and Gender in Biblical Law* (New York: Cambridge University Press, 2013); Ruane, "Milk, Meat, and Mothers: The Problem of Motherhood in Some Ritual Food Laws," in *New Perspectives on Ritual in the Biblical World*, ed. Melissa Ramos and Laura Quick (London: T&T Clark International, 2022), 51–70; Cynthia R. Chapman, *The House of the Mother: The Social Roles of Maternal Kin in Biblical Hebrew Narrative and Poetry* (New Haven, CT: Yale University Press, 2016); Lea Jacobsen, *The Legal Status of the Mother in the Ancient Near East and the Bible* (Jerusalem: Magnes, 2017); D. Charles Smith, *The Role of Mothers in the Genealogical Lists of Jacob's Sons*, Contributions to Biblical Exegesis and Theology 90 (Leuven: Peeters, 2018).

31. Ekaterina E. Kozlova, *Maternal Grief in the Hebrew Bible* (New York: Oxford University Press, 2017).

32. See the collected essays in Leonard J. Greenspoon, ed., *Mishpachah: The Jewish Family in Tradition and in Transition*, Studies in Jewish Civilization 27 (West Lafayette, IN: Purdue University Press, 2016); and David Charles Kraemer, ed., *The Jewish Family: Metaphor and Memory* (New York: Oxford University Press, 1989). See also Joyce Antler, *You Never Call! You Never Write! A History of the Jewish Mother* (Oxford: Oxford University Press, 2007); Elisheva Baumgarten, *Mothers and Children: Jewish Family Life in Medieval Europe*, Jews, Christians, and Muslims from the Ancient to the Modern World (Princeton: Princeton University Press, 2004); Federica K. Clementi, *Holocaust Mothers and Daughters: Family, History, and Trauma*, HBI Series on Jewish Women

(Waltham, MA: Brandeis University Press, 2013); Tova Hartman Halbertal, *Appropriately Subversive: Modern Mothers in Traditional Religions* (Cambridge, MA: Harvard University Press, 2002); and Smadar Lavie, *Wrapped in the Flag of Israel: Mizrahi Single Mothers and Bureaucratic Torture*, rev. ed., Expanding Frontiers: Interdisciplinary Approaches to Studies of Women, Gender, and Sexuality (Lincoln: University of Nebraska Press, 2018).

33. Deena Aranoff, "Mother's Milk: Child-Rearing and the Production of Jewish Culture," *Journal of Jewish Identities* 12, no. 1 (2019): 1–17; Pratima Gopalakrishnan, "Domestic Labor and Marital Obligations in the Ancient Jewish Household" (PhD diss., Yale University, 2020).

34. Michal Raucher, "Jewish Pronatalism: Policy and Praxis," *Religion Compass* 15, no. 7 (2021): e12398.

35. Nadia Abu El-Haj, *The Genealogical Science: The Search for Jewish Origins and the Politics of Epistemology*, Chicago Studies in Practices of Meaning (Chicago: University of Chicago Press, 2012); Steven Weitzman, *The Origin of the Jews: The Quest for Roots in a Rootless Age* (Princeton: Princeton University Press, 2017). On modern Jewish genealogy as a form of religion, see chapter 3 of this volume.

36. Beth A. Berkowitz, *Animals and Animality in the Babylonian Talmud* (New York: Cambridge University Press, 2018).

37. Thanks to Moshe Simon-Shoshan for bringing to my attention this passage from Pirke de-Rabbi Eliezer 31:11.

38. Pirke de-Rabbi Eliezer 31:13.

39. Gittin 55b–56b; Avodah Zarah 18a–b; Berakhot 27b–28a.

40. Peter Singer, *Animal Liberation: The Definitive Classic of the Animal Movement* (New York: Ecco, 2009).

41. Saul M. Olyan, *Animal Rights and the Hebrew Bible* (Oxford: Oxford University Press, 2023).

42. Rafael Rachel Neis, *When a Human Gives Birth to a Raven: Rabbis and the Reproduction of Species* (Oakland: University of California Press, 2023).

43. Mira Beth Wasserman, *Jews, Gentiles, and Other Animals: The Talmud After the Humanities* (Philadelphia: University of Pennsylvania Press, 2017).

44. David I. Shyovitz, *A Remembrance of His Wonders: Nature and the Supernatural in Medieval Ashkenaz*, Jewish Culture and Contexts (Philadelphia: University of Pennsylvania Press, 2017).

45. See my "Jews and Animals," *Oxford Bibliographies in Jewish Studies*, www-oxfordbibliographies-com.ezproxy.cul.columbia.edu/view/document/obo-9780199840731/obo-9780199840731-0229.xml.

46. See the section on Israel studies in my "Jews and Animals."

47. See Brian Massumi, *What Animals Teach Us About Politics* (Durham, NC: Duke University Press, 2014), 1–54.

48. Frans B. M. de Waal, *Chimpanzee Politics: Power and Sex Among Apes* (New York: Harper and Row, 1982).

49. Massumi, *What Animals Teach Us*, 50.

50. Massumi, 51.

51. Massumi's first thesis on the animal is to "not presume that you have access to a criterion for categorically separating the human from the animal" (91). I thank Bernard Kabak for his suggestions here and elsewhere.

52. Judith Halberstam, "Forgetting Family: Queer Alternatives to Oedipal Relations," in *A Companion to Lesbian, Gay, Bisexual, Transgender, and Queer Studies*, ed. George E. Haggerty and Molly McGarry, Blackwell Companions in Cultural Studies (Malden, MA: Blackwell, 2007), 316, 322.

53. For further reading, see Christine Elizabeth Hayes, ed., *The Literature of the Sages: A Re-visioning* (Leiden: Brill, 2022).

54. Key works are Seth Schwartz, *Imperialism and Jewish Society, 200 B.C.E. to 640 C.E*, Jews, Christians, and Muslims from the Ancient to the Modern World (Princeton: Princeton University Press, 2001); and Hayim Lapin, *Rabbis as Romans: The Rabbinic Movement in Palestine, 100–400 CE* (New York: Oxford University Press, 2012).

55. Richard E. Payne, *A State of Mixture: Christians, Zoroastrians, and Iranian Political Culture in Late Antiquity* (Berkeley: University of California Press, 2015). On the Hellenistic, Christian, and Sasanian contexts of the Babylonian Talmud, see the relevant contributions in Christine Elizabeth Hayes and Jay Michael Harris, eds., *What Is the Talmud? The State of the Question* (Cambridge, MA: Harvard University Press, forthcoming).

56. On the priority of midrash or Mishnah, see the formulation in Dayid Halivni, *Midrash, Mishnah, and Gemara: The Jewish Predilection for Justified Law* (Cambridge, MA: Harvard University Press, 1986). On rabbinic orality, see Martin S. Jaffee, *Torah in the Mouth: Writing and Oral Tradition in Palestinian Judaism, 200 BCE–400 CE* (New York: Oxford University Press, 2001); and Elizabeth Shanks Alexander, *Transmitting Mishnah: The Shaping Influence of Oral Tradition* (New York: Cambridge University Press, 2006).

57. On the literary strata, see Moulie Vidas, *Tradition and the Formation of the Talmud* (Princeton: Princeton University Press, 2014). On the language shifts, see Willem F. Smelik, *Rabbis, Language and Translation in Late Antiquity* (Cambridge: Cambridge University Press, 2013).

58. "Dávid Kaufmann and His Collection," Mishnah, http://kaufmann.mtak.hu/en/ms50/ms50-coll1.htm; Saul Lieberman Institute for Talmudic Research and CDI Systems, eds., *Sol and Evelyn Henkind Talmud Text Databank* (Jerusalem: CDI Systems, n.d.); Friedberg Jewish Manuscript Society, "Hachi Garsinan: The Friedberg Project for Talmud Bavli Variants," https://bavli.genizah.org/Global/homepage?lan=eng&isPartial=False&isDoubleLogin=False&TractateID=0&DafID=0.

59. Moses Samuel Zuckermandel, ed., *Tosephta: Based on the Erfurt and Vienna Codices [Tosefta al-pi Kitve-yad ʿErfurṭ Vinah]* (Jerusalem: Wahrman, 1970).

60. Shaye J. D. Cohen et al., eds., *The Oxford Annotated Mishnah: A New Translation of the Mishnah*, 3 vols. (New York: Oxford University Press, 2022). The Steinsaltz translation is publicly accessible through "Sefaria: A Living Library of Jewish Texts Online," Sefaria, www.sefaria.org/texts. All biblical and rabbinic works referred to in this book are found in the original language also on Sefaria.

61. Billie Jean Collins, ed., *The SBL Handbook of Style*, 2nd ed. (Atlanta: Society of Biblical Literature Press, 2014), 58–59. Exceptions are the letter *tzade*, which I transliterate as *tz* rather than *ts* since *tz* seems to me to better reflect the phoneme, and the letter *kuf*, which I transliterate as *k* rather than *q* since *k* in my opinion looks more natural to the English reader.

1. DO ANIMALS LOVE THEIR CHILDREN?

1. Some philosophers dispute this view of Descartes; see Gary Hatfield, "Animals," in *A Companion to Descartes*, ed. Janet Broughton and John Peter Carriero (Malden, MA: Blackwell, 2008), 404–25.

2. Scott Forbes, *A Natural History of Families* (Princeton: Princeton University Press, 2005), 5.

3. Forbes, 6.

4. Scientists call it "filial cannibalism" when parents eat their children. See Hope Klug and Michael B. Bonsall, "When to Care For, Abandon, or Eat Your Offspring: The Evolution of Parental Care and Filial Cannibalism," *American Naturalist* 170, no. 6 (2007): 886–901.

5. Michael R. Miller, "Descartes on Animals Revisited," *Journal of Philosophical Research* 38 (2013): 89.

6. Paul Ekman, ed., *Emotions Inside Out: 130 Years After Darwin's "The Expression of the Emotions in Man and Animals"* (New York: New York Academy of Sciences, 2003).

7. Charles Darwin, *The Expression of the Emotions in Man and Animals* (London: Murray, 1904), 95, 115, 389.

8. Donald O. Hebb, "Emotion in Man and Animal: An Analysis of the Intuitive Processes of Recognition," *Psychological Review* 53, no. 2 (1946): 88.

9. Anne C. Rose, *In the Hearts of the Beasts: How American Behavioral Scientists Rediscovered the Emotions of Animals* (Oxford: Oxford University Press, 2020), 7.

10. Donald Redfield Griffin, *The Question of Animal Awareness: Evolutionary Continuity of Mental Experience* (New York: Rockefeller University Press, 1981); Griffin, *Animal Minds: Beyond Cognition to Consciousness* (Chicago: University of Chicago Press, 2013).

11. Rose, *Hearts of the Beasts*, 2, 4, 113–31.

12. Thomas Nagel, "What Is It Like to Be a Bat?," *Philosophical Review* 83, no. 4 (1974): 435–50.

13. Jaak Panksepp, *Affective Neuroscience: The Foundations of Human and Animal Emotions* (New York: Oxford University Press, 1998).

14. Marc Bekoff, *The Emotional Lives of Animals: A Leading Scientist Explores Animal Joy, Sorrow, and Empathy—and Why They Matter* (Novato, CA: New World Library, 2008); Frans B. M. de Waal, *Mama's Last Hug: Animal Emotions and What They Tell Us About Ourselves* (New York: Norton, 2020); Jane Goodall, *In the Shadow of Man* (Boston: Mariner Books, 2009); Barbara J. King, *How Animals Grieve* (Chicago: University of Chicago Press, 2013); Carl Safina, *Beyond Words: What Animals Think and Feel* (London: Souvenir, 2016).

15. For affect theory as it intersects with animal studies and religious studies, see Donovan O. Schaefer, *Religious Affects: Animality, Evolution, and Power* (Durham, NC: Duke University Press, 2015). On using affect theory to look at the Bible's animals, see Ken Stone, *Reading the Hebrew Bible with Animal Studies* (Palo Alto, CA: Stanford University Press, 2017), 140–63; and Sébastien Doane, *Reading the Bible amid the Environmental Crisis: Interdisciplinary Insights to Ecological Hermeneutics* (Lanham, MD: Lexington Books, 2024), 31–47.

16. Peter Singer, *Animal Liberation: The Definitive Classic of the Animal Movement* (New York: Ecco, 2009), 9–15.

17. Bekoff, *Emotional Lives of Animals*, xviii.

18. Jonathan Balcombe, *The Exultant Ark: A Pictorial Tour of Animal Pleasure* (Berkeley: University of California Press, 2011).

19. Waal, *Mama's Last Hug*, 50.

20. Bekoff, *Emotional Lives of Animals*, 31.

21. See the review of research in Michael D. Breed, "Kin and Nestmate Recognition: The Influence of W. D. Hamilton on 50 Years of Research," *Animal Behaviour* 92 (June 2014): 271–79.

22. Fuller W. Bazer, "History of Maternal Recognition of Pregnancy," in *Regulation of Implantation and Establishment of Pregnancy in Mammals: Tribute to 45 Year Anniversary of Roger V. Short's Maternal Recognition of Pregnancy*, ed. Fuller W. Bazer and Rodney D. Geisert (New York: Springer Berlin Heidelberg, 2015), 5–25.

23. See discussion in Bruce Waldman, "The Ecology of Kin Recognition," *Annual Review of Ecology and Systematics* 19, no. 1 (1988): 544.

24. Scott R. Robinson and William P. Smotherman, "Fetal Learning: Implications for the Development of Kin Recognition," in *Kin Recognition*, ed. Peter G. Hepper (Cambridge: Cambridge University Press, 2005), 308–34, 319.

25. Gudrun Illmann et al., "Acoustical Mother-Offspring Recognition in Pigs (Sus Scrofa Domestica)," *Behaviour* 139, no. 4 (2002): 487–505; Melanie Kober et al., "Vocal Mother–Pup Communication in Guinea Pigs: Effects of Call

Familiarity and Female Reproductive State," *Animal Behaviour* 73, no. 5 (2007): 917-25.

26. Olga V. Sibiryakova et al., "The Power of Oral and Nasal Calls to Discriminate Individual Mothers and Offspring in Red Deer, Cervus Elaphus," *Frontiers in Zoology* 12 (January 2015): 2.

27. Stephen J. Insley, "Long-Term Vocal Recognition in the Northern Fur Seal," *Nature* (London) 406, no. 6794 (2000): 404-5.

28. Kaja Wierucka et al., "Multimodal Mother-Offspring Recognition: The Relative Importance of Sensory Cues in a Colonial Mammal," *Animal Behaviour* 146 (December 2018): 135-42.

29. Pascal Poindron et al., "Early Recognition of Newborn Goat Kids by Their Mother: I. Nonolfactory Discrimination," *Developmental Psychobiology* 43, no. 2 (2003): 82-89.

30. Angelica Terrazas et al., "Early Recognition of Newborn Goat Kids by Their Mother: II. Auditory Recognition and Evidence of an Individual Acoustic Signature in the Neonate," *Developmental Psychobiology* 43, no. 4 (2003): 311-20.

31. Visual appearance, vocalization, and smell are "signatures" by which parents and infants identify each other. See Richard H. Porter, "Mutual Mother-Infant Recognition in Humans," in Hepper, *Kin Recognition*, 413-32.

32. See Waldman, "Ecology of Kin Recognition," 545-46.

33. Stacy Rosenbaum and Lee T. Gettler, "With a Little Help from Her Friends (and Family): Part I, The Ecology and Evolution of Non-maternal Care in Mammals," *Physiology and Behavior* 193 (September 2018): 1-11; Rosenbaum and Gettler, "With a Little Help from Her Friends (and Family): Part II, Non-maternal Caregiving Behavior and Physiology in Mammals," *Physiology and Behavior* 193 (September 2018): 12-24.

34. Rosenbaum and Gettler, "With a Little Help," pt. 1, p. 1.

35. For a helpful summary of the bonding process between mother and child, with sheep as the case study, see Isabelle Veissier et al., "Ontogeny of Social Awareness in Domestic Herbivores," *Applied Animal Behaviour Science* 57, no. 3 (1998): 235-36.

36. David J. Gubernick, "Parent and Infant Attachment in Mammals," in *Parental Care in Mammals*, ed. David J. Gubernick and Peter H. Klopfer (New York: Plenum, 1981), 246.

37. Bruce B. Svare, "Maternal Aggression in Mammals," in Gubernick and Klopfer, *Parental Care in Mammals*, 179-211.

38. Frédéric Lévy, "Neuroendocrine Control of Maternal Behavior in Nonhuman and Human Mammals," *Annales d'endocrinologie* 77, no. 2 (2016): 114-25.

39. Eric B. Keverne et al., "Vaginal Stimulation: An Important Determinant of Maternal Bonding in Sheep," *Science* 219, no. 4580 (1983): 81-83; Lorel May-

berry and Jacqueline Daniel, "Birthgasm," *Journal of Holistic Nursing* 34, no. 4 (2016): 331–42.

40. Keith M. Kendrick et al., "Importance of Vaginocervical Stimulation for the Formation of Maternal Bonding in Primiparous and Multiparous Parturient Ewes," *Physiology and Behavior* 50, no. 3 (1991): 595–600.

41. Mathias Kölliker et al., "What Is Parental Care?," in *The Evolution of Parental Care*, ed. Nick J. Royle et al. (Oxford: Oxford University Press, 2012), 7.

42. Alain Boissy et al., "Assessment of Positive Emotions in Animals to Improve Their Welfare: Stress and Welfare in Farm Animals," *Physiology and Behavior* 92, no. 3 (2007): 375–97.

43. Marina A. G. von Keyserlingk and Daniel M. Weary, "Maternal Behavior in Cattle," *Hormones and Behavior* 52, no. 1 (2007): 106–13; Lévy, "Neuroendocrine Control," 115.

44. Daniel E. Olazábal et al., "New Theoretical and Experimental Approaches on Maternal Motivation in Mammals," *Neuroscience and Biobehavioral Reviews* 37, no. 8 (2013): 1862.

45. Raymond Nowak et al., "Mother-Young Relationships in Sheep: A Model for a Multidisciplinary Approach of the Study of Attachment in Mammals," *Journal of Neuroendocrinology* 23, no. 11 (2011): 1042–53.

46. Eric B. Keverne et al., "Beta-Endorphin Concentrations in Cerebrospinal Fluid of Monkeys Are Influenced by Grooming Relationships," *Psychoneuroendocrinology* 14, no. 1 (1989): 155–61; Claudia Feh and Jeanne de Mazières, "Grooming at a Preferred Site Reduces Heart Rate in Horses," *Animal Behaviour* 46, no. 6 (1993): 1191–94.

47. Anna G. Thorhallsdottir et al., "The Role of the Mother in the Intake of Harmful Foods by Lambs," *Applied Animal Behaviour Science* 25, no. 1 (1990): 35–44; Jill M. Mateo and Warren G. Holmes, "Development of Alarm-Call Responses in Belding's Ground Squirrels: The Role of Dams," *Animal Behaviour* 54, no. 3 (1997): 509–24.

48. David Val-Laillet et al., "A Full Belly and Colostrum: Two Major Determinants of Filial Love," *Developmental Psychobiology* 45, no. 3 (2004): 163–73; Val-Laillet et al., "Nonnutritive Sucking: One of the Major Determinants of Filial Love," *Developmental Psychobiology* 48, no. 3 (2006): 220–32.

49. Timothy M. Caro, *Antipredator Defenses in Birds and Mammals*, Interspecific Interactions (Chicago: University of Chicago Press, 2005), 99; Pascal Poindron et al., "Sensory and Physiological Determinants of Maternal Behavior in the Goat (Capra Hircus)," *Hormones and Behavior* 52, no. 1 (2007): 100.

50. Leonard Hersher et al., "Maternal Behavior in Sheep and Goats," in *Maternal Behavior in Mammals*, ed. Harriet Lange Rheingold (New York: Wiley, 1963), 211.

51. Nowak et al., "Mother-Young Relationships," 1048.

52. Ruth C. Newberry and Janice C. Swanson, "Implications of Breaking Mother-Young Social Bonds," *Applied Animal Behaviour Science* 110, nos. 1–2 (2008): 9; Ungerfeld Rodolfo et al., "Minimising the Stress of Weaning of Beef Calves: A Review," *Acta Veterinaria Scandinavica* 53, no. 1 (2011): 28.

53. Newberry and Swanson, "Implications," 9–10.

54. Alistair B. Lawrence, "Mother-Daughter and Peer Relationships of Scottish Hill Sheep," *Animal Behaviour* 39, no. 3 (1990): 481–86; Geoff N. Hinch et al., "Long-Term Associations Between Merino Ewes and Their Offspring," *Applied Animal Behaviour Science* 27, no. 1 (1990): 93–103; Veissier et al., "Ontogeny of Social Awareness."

55. Newberry and Swanson, "Implications," 10.

56. John L. Lesmeister et al., "Date of First Calving in Beef Cows and Subsequent Calf Production," *Journal of Animal Science* 36, no. 1 (1973): 1–6; John Webster, *Management and Welfare of Farm Animals: The UFAW Farm Handbook* (Hoboken, NJ: Wiley and Sons, 2011), 191, 373.

57. Heide Schatten and Gheorghe M. Constantinescu, *Comparative Reproductive Biology* (Hoboken, NJ: Wiley and Sons, 2008), 130.

58. Matthias Placzek et al., "Public Attitude Towards Cow-Calf Separation and Other Common Practices of Calf Rearing in Dairy Farming: A Review," *Organic Agriculture* 11, no. 1 (2021): 45–47, 42–44.

59. Reid Redden and Jacob W. Thorne, "Reproductive Management of Sheep and Goats," in *Animal Agriculture: Sustainability, Challenges and Innovations*, ed. Fuller W. Bazer et al. (London: Academic Press, 2020), 226; Aline Freitas-de-Melo et al., "What Do We Know and Need to Know About Weaning in Sheep? An Overview of Weaning Practices, Stress and Welfare," *Frontiers in Animal Science* 3 (February 2022): 1–17.

60. Redden and Thorne, "Reproductive Management," 227.

61. Annabelle Beaver et al., "Invited Review: A Systematic Review of the Effects of Early Separation on Dairy Cow and Calf Health," *Journal of Dairy Science* 102, no. 7 (2019): 5784–810.

62. See Pedro L. P. Fontes et al., "Reproductive Management of Beef Cattle," in Bazer et al., *Animal Agriculture*, 63. According to Fontes and colleagues, "Cow-calf operations rely on their females to produce a healthy calf once per year to generate revenue and remain profitable" (57).

63. Beth A. Ventura et al., "Views on Contentious Practices in Dairy Farming: The Case of Early Cow-Calf Separation," *Journal of Dairy Science* 96, no. 9 (2013): 6105–16.

64. Jan Paul T. M. Wagenaar and J. Langhout, "Practical Implications of Increasing 'Natural Living' Through Suckling Systems in Organic Dairy Calf Rearing," *NJAS: Wageningen Journal of Life Sciences* 54, no. 4 (2007): 380.

65. See, for example, the conclusions from Beaver et al., "Invited Review," 5805.

66. Newberry and Swanson, "Implications," 11.

67. Agnethe-Irén Sandem and Bjarne O. Braastad, "Effects of Cow-Calf Separation on Visible Eye White and Behaviour in Dairy Cows: A Brief Report," *Applied Animal Behaviour Science* 95, no. 3 (2005): 233–39.

68. Pierre Orgeur et al., "Artificial Weaning in Sheep: Consequences on Behavioural, Hormonal and Immuno-pathological Indicators of Welfare," *Applied Animal Behaviour Science* 58, no. 1 (1998): 89; Eilish Lynch et al., "Weaning Management of Beef Calves with Implications for Animal Health and Welfare," *Journal of Applied Animal Research* 47, no. 1 (2019): 170.

69. Candace C. Croney and Ruth C. Newberry, "Group Size and Cognitive Processes," *Applied Animal Behaviour Science* 103, no. 3 (2007): 219.

70. Kathrin Wagner et al., "Effects of Mother Versus Artificial Rearing During the First 12 Weeks of Life on Challenge Responses of Dairy Cows," *Applied Animal Behaviour Science* 164 (March 2015): 1–11.

71. Fabio Napolitano et al., "Welfare Implications of Artificial Rearing and Early Weaning in Sheep," *Applied Animal Behaviour Science* 110, no. 1 (2008): 58–72.

72. Edward O. Price et al., "Fenceline Contact of Beef Calves with Their Dams at Weaning Reduces the Negative Effects of Separation on Behavior and Growth Rate," *Journal of Animal Science* 81, no. 1 (2003): 116–21; Sandem and Braastad, "Effects of Cow-Calf Separation," 234; Ilona Stěhulová et al., "Response of Dairy Cows and Calves to Early Separation: Effect of Calf Age and Visual and Auditory Contact After Separation," *Applied Animal Behaviour Science* 110, no. 1 (2008): 161–62.

73. On the sensitive period, see John P. Kent, "The Cow-Calf Relationship: From Maternal Responsiveness to the Maternal Bond and the Possibilities for Fostering," *Journal of Dairy Research* 87, no. S1 (2020): 103.

74. Hanna Eriksson et al., "Strategies for Keeping Dairy Cows and Calves Together: A Cross-Sectional Survey Study," *Animal* (Cambridge) 16, no. 9 (2022): 1–14.

75. Pascal Poindron et al., "Maternal Responsiveness and Maternal Selectivity in Domestic Sheep and Goats: The Two Facets of Maternal Attachment," *Developmental Psychobiology* 49, no. 1 (2007): 56.

76. Frances C. Flower and Daniel M. Weary, "Effects of Early Separation on the Dairy Cow and Calf," *Applied Animal Behaviour Science* 70, no. 4 (2001): 275–84; Newberry and Swanson, "Implications," 13–14; Beaver et al., "Invited Review."

77. Price et al., "Fenceline Contact."

78. Kent, "Cow-Calf Relationship."

79. Rodolfo et al., "Minimising the Stress"; Freitas-de-Melo et al., "What Do We Know?"

80. Steve Cooke, "The Ethics of Touch and the Importance of Nonhuman Relationships in Animal Agriculture," *Journal of Agricultural and Environmental Ethics* 34, no. 2 (2021): 12.

81. Sylvie Cloutier et al., "Can Ambient Sound Reduce Distress in Piglets During Weaning and Restraint?," *Journal of Applied Animal Welfare Science* 3, no. 2 (2000): 107–16.

82. Akaysha C. Tang et al., "Programming Social, Cognitive, and Neuroendocrine Development by Early Exposure to Novelty," *Proceedings of the National Academy of Sciences* 103, no. 42 (2006): 15716–21; Marek Spinka et al., "Mammalian Play: Training for the Unexpected," *Quarterly Review of Biology* 76, no. 2 (2001): 141–68.

83. The mitigation strategies point to the complex role of agriculture researchers, which is both to promote animal welfare and to maximize productivity. On the conflict between these goals, see Caroline Clarke and David Knights, "Milking It for All It's Worth: Unpalatable Practices, Dairy Cows and Veterinary Work?," *Journal of Business Ethics* 176, no. 4 (2021): 673–88; and Elein Hernandez et al., "Applied Animal Ethics in Industrial Food Animal Production: Exploring the Role of the Veterinarian," *Animals* (Basel) 12, no. 6 (2022): 678.

84. Oded Borowski, *Every Living Thing: Daily Use of Animals in Ancient Israel* (Walnut Creek, CA: AltaMira, 1998), 40–45, 14–15, 46–47.

85. Justin Lev-Tov, "Animal Husbandry: Meat, Milk, and More," in *T&T Clark Handbook of Food in the Hebrew Bible and Ancient Israel*, ed. Cynthia Shafer-Elliott et al. (London: T&T Clark, 2021), 77.

86. Borowski, *Every Living Thing*, 42.

87. Borowski, 52–58, 77. Biblical passages in which young animals are served as a delicacy include Genesis 18:6–8 and Judges 6:19, 13:15, and 15:1. Passages that call for sacrificing a yearling include Exodus 12:5, Leviticus 9:3, and Numbers 7. Regular milking of caprids is suggested also by the loss of bone detected in female animal remains, the inference of dairy production from kill-off patterns, and chemical analysis of ceramics; see Lev-Tov, "Animal Husbandry," 83.

88. Borowski, *Every Living Thing*, 57. Borowski says that optimal weaning would have been at age two to three months, leaving a milking period of three to four and up to five months (82n18).

89. See Aharon Sasson, *Animal Husbandry in Ancient Israel: A Zooarchaeological Perspective on Livestock Exploitation, Herd Management and Economic Strategies* (London: Taylor and Francis, 2016), 39–41; and Shyama Vermeersch et al., "Animal Husbandry from the Middle Bronze Age Through the Iron Age in the Shephelah: Faunal Remains from the New Excavations at Lachish," *Archaeological and Anthropological Sciences* 13, no. 3 (2021): 38.

90. Borowski, *Every Living Thing*, 57, 18–19. Sex ratios are rarely provided in the faunal reports, however, according to Lidar Sapir-Hen et al., "Environmental and Historical Impacts on Long Term Animal Economy: The Southern Levant in the Late Bronze and Iron Ages," *Journal of the Economic and Social History of the Orient* 57, no. 5 (2014): 713.

91. On the term *rivkah*, see Moshe Beer, *Amora'e Bavel: Perakim Be-ḥaye Ha-Kalkalah* [Babylonian Amoraim: Aspects of Economic Life] (Ramat Gan, Israel: Bar Ilan University Press, 1974), 117n2.
92. Borowski, *Every Living Thing*, 53–54.
93. Marcus Terentius Varro, *On Agriculture*, trans. Harrison Boyd Ash and William Davis Hooper, Loeb Classical Library 283 (Cambridge, MA: Harvard University Press, 2014), 340–41, 342–43, 348–49.
94. Lucius Junius Moderatus Columella, *On Agriculture*, trans. Edward S. Forster and Edward H. Heffner, Loeb Classical Library 361 (Cambridge, MA: Harvard University Press, 2014), 248–49. See, similarly, the fourth- or fifth-century Rutilius Taurus Aemilianus Palladius's *The Work of Farming (Opus Agriculturae) and Poem on Grafting*, trans. John G. Fitch (Totnes, UK: Prospect Books, 2013), 211. Palladius recommends allowing the lambs to drain the udder (and thus presumably not milking the ewe during this period), gradually introducing solid food, and bringing them into the flock with their mothers accompanying them.
95. Columella, *On Agriculture*, 250–51, 280–81.
96. Another passage that presumes early separation is when Columella directs his reader who lives near a town to bring the lambs to the town butcher before they are of age to join the flock. See *On Agriculture*, 246–47. In *Georgics* 3:398–99, Vergil describes early separation of mother goats (and sheep are implied) from their kids for the farmer to benefit from the milk supply. See *Eclogues and Georgics*, trans. James Bradley Wells (Madison: University of Wisconsin Press, 2022), 147.
97. Columella, *On Agriculture*, 258–59.
98. On the ban, see Asher Gulak, "Al ha-Ro'im u-Megadle Behemah Dakah bi-Tekufat Hurban Bayit Sheni [Shepherds and breeders of domestic cattle after the destruction of the Second Temple]," *Tarbiz* 12, no. 3 (1941): 181–89; Gedalia Alon, *The Jews in Their Land in the Talmudic Age, 70–640 C.E.* (Jerusalem: Magnes, 1980), 1:277–85. See my discussion of the ban and theories about it in Beth A. Berkowitz, *Animals and Animality in the Babylonian Talmud* (New York: Cambridge University Press, 2018), 132–38.
99. See, for instance, Mishnah Bava Kamma 2:3, which speaks of a kid jumping off a roof, implying that he is in the household.
100. On the presence of sheep and goats, see Justin Lev-Tov, "'Upon What Meat Doth This Our Caesar Feed . . . ?' A Dietary Perspective on Hellenistic and Roman Influence in Palestine." In *Signs of Text and Stone: Studies Towards an Archaeology of the New Testament*, ed. Stefan Alkier and Jürgen Zangenberg (Tübingen, Germany: Francke, 2003), 420–46; Lev-Tov, "Diet, Hellenistic and Roman Period," *The Oxford Encyclopedia of the Bible and Archaeology*, Oxford University Press, 2013, https://www.oxfordreference.com/display/10.1093/acref:obso/9780199846535.001.0001/acref-9780199846535-e-35.

101. Tosefta Bava Metzia 5:4 states, "Goats are evaluated in accordance with the fact that they are milked while ewes are evaluated in accordance with the fact that they are shorn." See Zeev Safrai, *The Economy of Roman Palestine* (London: Routledge, 1994), 96.

102. Safrai, 93–97; Zeev Safrai, "Agriculture and Farming," in *The Oxford Handbook of Jewish Daily Life in Roman Palestine*, ed. Catherine Hezser (New York: Oxford University Press, 2010), 256–58.

103. Moses Samuel Zuckermandel, ed., *Tosephta: Based on the Erfurt and Vienna Codices [Tosefta al-pi Kitve-yad ʿErfurṭ Vinah]* (Jerusalem: Wahrman, 1970), 631. The teaching is cited in Babylonian Talmud Pesahim 26a; Gittin 53a; and Bava Metzia 30a.

104. Based on other passages, Talmud commentator Rashi understands "immediately" to mean a month or two after the birth and not literally right after, but in my view the more likely reading is the latter.

105. Lev-Tov, "Upon What Meat?," 9.

106. "Hötzel et al. (2017) reported that 67% of citizens participating in their study (n=400) were unaware of this practice. This result coincides with the studies of Cardoso et al. (2017) and Ventura et al. (2016), who reported that 65% (n=296) and 37 out of 50 participants respectively were uninformed of cow-calf separation." Placzek et al., "Public Attitude," 45.

107. Borowski, *Every Living Thing*, 45.

108. Safrai, *Economy of Roman Palestine*, 94.

109. Nowak et al., "Mother-Young Relationships," 1050.

110. Rebecca Doyle and John Moran, *Cow Talk: Understanding Dairy Cow Behaviour to Improve Their Welfare on Asian Farms* (Clayton, Victoria, Australia: CSIRO, n.d.), 26.

111. Elizabeth Wright and Catarina Ginja, eds., *Cattle and People: Interdisciplinary Approaches to an Ancient Relationship*, Archaeobiology 4 (Columbus, GA: Lockwood, 2022), xxii.

112. Some veterinarians today are trying to create better alignment between human and animal welfare through an agenda called "One Welfare," modeled on the World Health Organization's initiative "One Health"; see www.who.int/news-room/questions-and-answers/item/one-health; and Rebeca García Pinillos et al., "One Welfare: A Platform for Improving Human and Animal Welfare," *Veterinary Record* 179, no. 16 (2016): 412–13.

113. Sophy Charlton et al., "New Insights into Neolithic Milk Consumption Through Proteomic Analysis of Dental Calculus," *Archaeological and Anthropological Sciences* 11, no. 11 (2019): 6183–96. Animal milk's capacity to nourish human infants allowed for the earlier weaning of human babies from their mothers and thus increased rates of human reproduction. On neolithic baby bottles, see Julie Dunne et al., "Milk of Ruminants in Ceramic Baby Bottles from Prehistoric Child Graves," *Nature* (London) 574, no. 7777 (2019): 246–48.

114. Madeleine Bleasdale et al., "Ancient Proteins Provide Evidence of Dairy Consumption in Eastern Africa," *Nature Communications* 12, no. 1 (2021): 632; Eva Rosenstock et al., "Cultured Milk," *Current Anthropology* 62, no. S24 (2021): S256-75.

115. Deborah Valenze, *Milk: A Local and Global History* (New Haven, CT: Yale University Press, 2011), 3.

116. Cooke, "Ethics of Touch," 12. See also Juliet Clutton-Brock, *Animals as Domesticates: A World View Through History* (East Lansing: Michigan State University Press, 2012), 6: "For animals that have been prey to be domesticated, they have to be incorporated into the social structure of the human community and become objects of ownership, inheritance, purchase, and exchange."

117. Ventura et al., "Views on Contentious Practices"; Beth Ann Ventura et al., "What Difference Does a Visit Make? Changes in Animal Welfare Perceptions after Interested Citizens Tour a Dairy Farm," *PloS One* 11, no. 5 (2016): e0154733; Gesa Busch et al., "American and German Attitudes Towards Cow-Calf Separation on Dairy Farms," *PloS One* 12, no. 3 (2017): e0174013; Maria J. Hötzel et al., "Citizens' Views on the Practices of Zero-Grazing and Cow-Calf Separation in the Dairy Industry: Does Providing Information Increase Acceptability?," *Journal of Dairy Science* 100, no. 5 (2017): 4150-60; Placzek et al., "Public Attitude"; Lara V. Sirovica et al., "Public Attitude Toward and Perceptions of Dairy Cattle Welfare in Cow-Calf Management Systems Differing in Type of Social and Maternal Contact," *Journal of Dairy Science* 105, no. 4 (2022): 3248-68.

118. Women tended to be more concerned than men, and people outside the industry more than people inside.

119. Sirovica et al., "Public Attitude," 3262.

120. Ventura et al., "Views on Contentious Practices," 6109.

121. Kathryn Gillespie, *The Cow with Ear Tag #1389* (Chicago: University of Chicago Press, 2018), 72.

122. James Rebanks, *Pastoral Song: A Farmer's Journey* (New York: HarperCollins, 2021), 136-37.

123. No research seems to exist on the impact today of animals' distress on their handlers (Janice Swanson, pers. comm.), but there is research on injuries that stockpeople sustain from aggressive animals and the safety benefits to stockpeople of positive relationships with their animals. See Susanne Waiblinger et al., "Assessing the Human-Animal Relationship in Farmed Species: A Critical Review," *Applied Animal Behaviour Science* 101, nos. 3-4 (2006): 185-242; Fabio Napolitano et al., "Human-Animal Interactions in Dairy Buffalo Farms," *Animals* (Basel) 9, no. 5 (2019): 246; and Fabio Napolitano et al., "The Human-Animal Relationship in Dairy Animals," *Journal of Dairy Research* 87, no. S1 (2020): 47-52.

2. THE BIBLE'S ANIMAL-FAMILY LAWS

1. On the primeval vegan diet envisioned in the creation stories, see Jonathan K. Crane, *Eating Ethically: Religion and Science for a Better Diet* (New York: Columbia University Press, 2018), 103–11.

2. For a survey of the literature, see Phillip Michael Sherman, "Animals," *The Oxford Encyclopedia of the Bible and Law*, Oxford University Press, 2015, https://www.oxfordreference.com/view/10.1093/acref:obso/9780199843305.001.0001/acref-9780199843305-e-5.

3. Idan Breier, "Animals in Biblical and Ancient Near Eastern Law: Tort and Ethical Laws," *Journal of Animal Ethics* 8, no. 2 (2018): 166–81.

4. See my discussion in Beth A. Berkowitz, *Animals and Animality in the Babylonian Talmud* (New York: Cambridge University Press, 2018), 89–119.

5. Saul M. Olyan, *Animal Rights and the Hebrew Bible* (Oxford: Oxford University Press, 2023).

6. Jacob J. Finkelstein, "The Goring Ox: Some Historical Perspectives on Deodands, Forfeitures, Wrongful Death and the Western Notion of Sovereignty," *Temple Law Quarterly* 46, no. 2 (1972): 169–290; Moshe Greenberg, "Some Postulates of Biblical Criminal Law," in *Studies in the Bible and Jewish Thought*, ed. Moshe Greenberg (Philadelphia: Jewish Publication Society, 1995), 25–42.

7. Jordan Rosenblum, *The Jewish Dietary Laws in the Ancient World* (New York: Cambridge University Press, 2016).

8. See chapter 5 of this volume.

9. On the method of cooking, see Menahem Haran, "Seething a Kid in Its Mother's Milk," *Journal of Jewish Studies* 30, no. 1 (1979): 31; Alan Cooper, "Once Again Seething a Kid in Its Mother's Milk," *Jewish Studies: An Internet Journal* 10 (2012): 124–27. On the species of animal, see William Henry Propp, *Exodus 19–40: A New Translation with Introduction and Commentary* (New York: Doubleday, 2006), 284–85. The Septuagint translates the Hebrew term *gedi* with the Greek *arna*, which normally refers to sheep.

10. This suggestion, which follows fifteenth-century Portuguese Bible commentator Isaac Abarbanel, is found in Haran, "Seething a Kid," 35; and Nahum M. Sarna, *Exodus = [Shemot]: The Traditional Hebrew Text with the New JPS Translation* (Philadelphia: Jewish Publication Society, 1991), 147. But see the critique in Cooper, "Once Again Seething," 112.

11. The prohibition should possibly read in conjunction with the subsequent material in Deuteronomy 14:22–29 about tithes, first fruits, and firstlings (Cooper, "Once Again Seething a Kid," 114). See also J. Webb Mealy, "You Shall Not Boil a Kid in Its Mother's Milk (Exod. 23:19b; Exod. 34:26b; Deut. 14:21b)," *Biblical Interpretation* 20, no. 1 (2012): 52–72. Carmichael thinks that the D source no longer understood the ancient law: Calum M. Carmichael, *The Laws of Deuteronomy* (Ithaca: Cornell University Press, 1974), 152.

12. On the legal material in the Book of the Covenant and various questions debated with respect to it, see Cynthia Edenburg, "The Book of the Covenant," in *The Oxford Handbook of Biblical Law*, ed. Pamela Barmash (New York: Oxford University Press, 2019), 157–76.

13. On the organization, see Edenburg, "Book of the Covenant," 158–60. Eckart Otto considers verses 28 and 29 to be part of the final section of case law; see "Book of the Covenant," *The Oxford Encyclopedia of the Bible and Law*, Oxford University Press, www.oxfordreference.com/display/10.1093/acref:obso/9780199843305.001.0001/acref-9780199843305-e-11.

14. On whether the eighth-day requirement refers to human sons also or exclusively, see Michael A. Fishbane, *Biblical Interpretation in Ancient Israel* (New York: Oxford University Press, 1985), 181–87; and John Van Seters, *A Law Book for the Diaspora: Revision in the Study of the Covenant Code* (New York: Oxford University Press, 2003), 146.

15. Whether an act of donation specifically on the eighth day is intended is related to the question of whether the donation means setting aside or sacrifice since not everyone would have been able to reach the priests by day eight. See Propp, *Exodus 19–40*, 272.

16. Ekaterina E. Kozlova, *Maternal Grief in the Hebrew Bible* (New York: Oxford University Press, 2017). Kozlova does not address animal mothers per se but does discuss ancient cultural analogies between human and animal mothers' bereavement (16–24).

17. *Ken-ta'aseh* ("Thus shall you do," translated here as "You shall do the same") links the instruction for animals to the instruction for humans, as does the repetition of the verb *titen* (give), which could suggest that both are sacrificed. See the discussions in Jon D. Levenson, *The Death and Resurrection of the Beloved Son: The Transformation of Child Sacrifice in Judaism and Christianity* (New Haven, CT: Yale University Press, 1993), 3–5; Van Seters, *Law Book*, 145–53; and Propp, *Exodus 19–40*, 264–71.

18. On the relationship of the Holiness Legislation to earlier materials, see Jeffrey Stackert, "The Holiness Legislation and Its Pentateuchal Sources: Revision, Supplementation, and Replacement," in *The Strata to the Priestly Writings: Contemporary Debate and Future Directions*, ed. Sarah Shectman and Joel S. Baden (Zürich: Theologischer, 2009), 187–204.

19. For a proposal along these lines, see Christophe Nihan, *From Priestly Torah to Pentateuch: A Study in the Composition of the Book of Leviticus* (Tübingen, Germany: Mohr Siebeck, 2007), 493. On the first creation story as a product of the Holiness Legislation, see Jacob Milgrom, "HR in Leviticus and Elsewhere in the Torah," in *The Book of Leviticus: Composition and Reception*, ed. Rolf Rendtorff et al. (Leiden; Boston: Brill, 2003), 33–36. But see the methodological cautions in David M. Carr, "Standing at the Edge of Reconstructable Transmission-History: Signs of a Secondary

Sabbath-Oriented Stratum in Genesis 1:1–2:3," *Vetus Testamentum* 70, no. 1 (2020): 26–28.

20. See my discussion of the animal parent's gender in chapter 3 of this volume.

21. A prohibition on sacrificing or slaughtering pregnant animals is found in the Temple Scroll (11QT 52:5–7); Miqsat Ma'aseh Ha-Torah (4QMMT B36–38); and Philo, *On the Virtues* 137–39, trans. Francis Henry Colson, Loeb Classical Library 341 (Cambridge, MA: Harvard University Press, 2014), 8:246–49. Rabbinic texts do not feature such a prohibition and, on the contrary, go so far as to say that even a fully formed and viable fetus, if found inside the mother when she is slaughtered, is considered a part of her body and does not require its own slaughter. See the discussion of the ben pekuah in my conclusion.

22. Inversion of clauses often indicates intentional allusion. See Jeffrey H. Tigay, *Deuteronomy = [Devarim]: The Traditional Hebrew Text with the New JPS Translation* (Philadelphia: Jewish Publication Society, 1996), 201. Exodus's version of the decalogue mentions long life but not prosperity. Long life and prosperity are each rewards typical to Deuteronomy, but the two phrases are used in conjunction elsewhere only in Deuteronomy 4:40, which shares with Deuteronomy 5:16 the extended formulation "in the land that the ETERNAL your God is assigning to you" but attaches it not to prosperity but to long life and, unlike Deuteronomy 5:16 or 22:7, expands the reward of prosperity to "your children after you."

23. On parental authority in Deuteronomy, see Joseph Fleishman, "Legal Innovation in Deuteronomy XXI 18–20," *Vetus Testamentum* 53, no. 3 (2003): 311–27; and Samuel L. Boyd, "Deuteronomy's Prodigal Son: Deut. 21:18–21 and the Agenda of the D Source," *Biblical Interpretation* 28, no. 1 (2020): 15–33.

24. On the link between the two laws, see Carmichael, *Laws of Deuteronomy*, 153–56; Rachel Muers, "Setting Free the Mother Bird: On Reading a Strange Text," *Modern Theology* 22, no. 4 (2006): 563–66; and Bernard M. Levinson, "Deuteronomy: Introduction and Annotations," in *The Jewish Study Bible: Featuring the Jewish Publication Society Tanakh Translation*, ed. Marc Zvi Brettler and Adele Berlin (New York: Oxford University Press, 2014), 395. Fifteenth-century Portuguese Bible commentator Isaac Abarbanel connects the two passages in his commentary on Deuteronomy 22:6.

25. Tigay, *Deuteronomy*, 201. See also Genesis 32:12 and Hosea 10:14. Genesis Rabbah 76:12 connects Genesis 32:12, Deuteronomy 22:6, and Leviticus 22:28 because of their common use of the phrase, while Leviticus Rabbah 27:11 and parallel Pesikta de-Rav Kahana 9:11 connect Hosea 10:14, Deuteronomy 22:6, and Leviticus 22:28. Julius Theodor and Chanoch Albeck, eds., *Berischit Rabba, mit Kritischem Apparat und Kommentar*, 3 vols (Jerusalem: Wahrmann Books, 1965), 2:904; see also Carmichael, *Laws of Deuteronomy*, 155; and Calum M. Carmichael, *Law and Narrative in the Bible: The Evidence of the Deuteronomic Laws and the Decalogue* (Ithaca: Cornell University Press, 1985),

165–68. Genesis 9:2 likewise uses militaristic language to describe the relationship between humans and nondomesticated animals ("they are given into your hand"). I thank David Carr for this observation.

26. David P. Wright, *Inventing God's Law: How the Covenant Code of the Bible Used and Revised the Laws of Hammurabi* (Oxford: Oxford University Press, 2009), 312, 286.

27. For the suggestion that the same-day prohibition recapitulates the mother-bird law, see Tigay, *Deuteronomy*, 200; Jacob Milgrom, *Leviticus 17-22: A New Translation with Introduction and Commentary*, The Anchor Bible (New York: Doubleday, 2000), 3A:1884; Levinson, "Deuteronomy," 395; and Nicole J. Ruane, "Milk, Meat, and Mothers: The Problem of Motherhood in Some Ritual Food Laws," in *New Perspectives on Ritual in the Biblical World*, ed. Melissa Ramos and Laura Quick (London: T&T Clark International, 2022), 67. For the suggestion that it recapitulates the mother's-milk law, see Erhard S. Gerstenberger, *Leviticus: A Commentary*, Old Testament Library (Louisville, KY: Westminster John Knox Press, 1996), 331; and Nihan, *Priestly Torah to Pentateuch*, 492.

28. Milgrom, *Leviticus 17-22*, 3A:1352–53. See also the approach to H taken by Julia Rhyder, *Centralizing the Cult: The Holiness Legislation in Leviticus 17-26*, Forschungen Zum Alten Testament 134 (Tübingen, Germany: Mohr Siebeck, 2019).

29. That curious absence may reflect the Priestly author's notion of what it means to be human. For the Priestly source, the human exists in grand isolation as a godlike figure, an "animated God statue," as David Carr describes it; see "Competing Construals of Human Relations with 'Animal' Others in the Primeval History (Genesis 1–11)," *Journal of Biblical Literature* 140, no. 2 (2021): 263. For an expanded discussion, see David M. Carr, *Genesis 1-11: International Exegetical Commentary on the Old Testament* (Stuttgart: Kohlhammer, 2021). For the non-Priestly sources, by contrast, the human is not wholly set apart but instead exists within a set of hierarchies, ethnic male Israelite at the top, and women, children, and foreigners ranked below, with the animal at the bottom of the pyramid. For the non-Priestly sources, animal families would exist lower on the scale of families, but still as one version. When the Holiness Legislation incorporates animal-family laws, the author brings animal families back into the Priestly fold, so to speak. That being said, the Priestly flood narrative does speak of animal "families" exiting the ark (Genesis 8:19). Most medieval Jewish commentators understand the term *mishpehot* here as a reference to the different species (e.g., David Kimhi), but a tradition in Babylonian Talmud Sanhedrin 108b, featured by Abraham ibn Ezra, understands it as a reference to actual animal families, parents with their children.

30. Katell Berthelot, "Philo and Kindness Towards Animals (De Virtutibus 125–147)," *Studia Philonica Annual*, no. 14 (2002): 49. Philo's essay appears to have been intended for a mixed Jewish and gentile audience.

31. Philo summarizes his agenda here: "Let those clever libellers continue, if they can, to accuse the nation of misanthropy and charge the laws with enjoining unsociable and unfriendly practices, when these laws so clearly extend their compassion to flocks and herds, and our people through the instructions of the law learn from their earliest years to correct any willfulness of souls to gentle behaviour." The logic is grounded in Philo's Stoic assumption that human beings have no obligation to act justly toward animals. See Philo, *Philonis Alexandrini de Animalibus: The Armenian Text*, trans. Abraham Terian (Chico, CA: Scholars' Press, 1981), 141.

32. Philo covers the seven-day requirement to leave the baby with the mother (*On the Virtues* 126–30, trans. Colson, 8:238–43); the prohibition on the sacrifice of a mother and her offspring on the same day (134–36, trans. Colson, 8:244–47); a prohibition on keeping pregnant animals in the sacred precincts and on slaughtering them (137–38, trans. Colson, 8:246–49); the prohibition against cooking a kid in his mother's milk (142–44, trans. Colson, 8:248–51); and the prohibition against muzzling the ox and yoking him together with the ass (145–47, trans. Colson, 8:250–55). First-century Jewish historian Josephus makes a similar though greatly condensed argument; see Flavius Josephus, *The Life; Against Apion*, trans. Henry St. J. Thackeray, Loeb Classical Library 186 (Cambridge, MA: Harvard University Press, 2014), 378–79. Josephus mentions Deuteronomy's mother-bird law and two other animal laws not explicit in the Pentateuch: a prohibition on killing animals one finds living in one's house (reminiscent of a story about Rabbi Judah the Prince told in Babylonian Talmud Bava Metzia 85a) and another prohibition on killing draft animals in an enemy country, which echoes Deuteronomy 20:19's prohibition on chopping down fruit trees when waging war. See the commentary in *Flavius Josephus: Translation and Commentary*, vol. 10, *Against Apion*, trans. John M. G. Barclay (Leiden: Brill, 2007), 293–94.

33. Philo, *On the Virtues* 126, 133, trans. Colson, 8:240–41, 8:244–45.

34. Philo, *On the Decalogue* 110–17, trans. Francis H. Colson, Loeb Classical Library 320 (Cambridge, MA: Harvard University Press, 1937), 7:62–67. See Maren Niehoff, *Philo of Alexandria: An Intellectual Biography*, Anchor Yale Bible Reference Library (New Haven, CT: Yale University Press, 2018), 158.

35. Philo, *On the Virtues* 129, trans. Colson, 8:240–41.

36. "It is the height of savagery to slay on the same day the generating cause and the living creature generated" (Philo, *On the Virtues* 134, trans. Colson, 8:244–45). With respect to cooking kids in their mother's milk, Philo says that it is prohibited so that the "substance which fed the living animals should [not] be used to season and flavour the same after its death." The cook "misuse[s] what had sustained its life to destroy also the body which remains in existence." A person who chooses the young animal's own mother's milk as cooking fluid "shows himself cruelly brutal in character and gelded of compassion, the most vital of

emotions and most nearly akin to the rational soul" (144, trans. Colson, 8:250–51).

37. Philo, *On the Virtues* 136, trans. Colson, 8:246–47.

38. One witness attributes the midrash to Rabbi Joshua of Sikhnin, who appears frequently as a transmitter of Rabbi Levi's homilies; see Mordechai Margalioth, ed., *Encyclopedia of Talmudic and Geonic Literature*, 2 vols. (Tel Aviv: Chachik, 1960), 2:618. One witness features Nebuchadnezzar rather than Sennacherib. One witness cites Leviticus 22:27 rather than Leviticus 22:28. Mordechai Margalioth, *Midrash Wayyikra Rabbah: A Critical Edition Based on Manuscripts and Genizah Fragments with Variants and Notes* (Jerusalem: Wahrmann Books, 1972), 644–45. For parallels in later midrashic works, see Margalioth's notes on line 4. A nearly exact parallel can be found in Pesikta de-Rav Kahana 9:11; see Bernard Mandelbaum, ed., *Pesikta de Rav Kahana: According to an Oxford Manuscript with Variants from All Known Manuscripts and Genizoth Fragments and Parallel Passages with Commentary and Introduction* (New York: Jewish Theological Seminary of America, 1962), 158.

39. Olyan translates *nefesh* here as "feelings." See his discussion of Proverbs 12:10 in *Animal Rights*, 100–106.

40. *HALOT Online*, s.v. "Nefesh," https://dictionaries-brillonline-com.ezproxy.cul.columbia.edu/search#dictionary=halothebrew&id=NUN.366. And see Paul Badham, "Do Animals Have Immortal Souls?," in *Animals on the Agenda: Questions About Animals for Theology and Ethics*, ed. Andrew Linzey and Dorothy Yamamoto (Urbana: University of Illinois Press, 1998), 181–89.

41. Joseph Tabory, "Shiluah ha-Ken: On the Relationship Between the Reason for the Mitzvah and Its Laws," in *Studies in Halakhah and Jewish Thought in Honor of Rav Menahem Immanuel Rackman on His 80th Birthday*, ed. Moshe Beer (Ramat Gan, Israel: Bar-Ilan University, 1994), 123.

42. Robert Alter, ed., *The Wisdom Books: Job, Proverbs, and Ecclesiastes: A Translation with Commentary* (New York: Norton, 2010), 185.

43. See note 25, on the literary motif of killing women and children, found in other formulations also in 2 Kings 8:12, Isaiah 13:16, Hosea 14:1, Nahum 3:10, and Psalms 137:9.

44. See the similar reading in Tal Ilan, *Massekhet Hullin: Text, Translation, and Commentary* (Tübingen, Germany: Mohr Siebeck, 2017), 96–97. A more explicit formulation of the humanitarian rationale is found in the later midrash collection Deuteronomy Rabbah Ki Tetze 6:1.

45. Perhaps Rashbam brought his own experience with livestock, from which he made a living, to his exegesis. See Ephraim Kanarfogel, "Shemu'el Ben Me'ir," in *The Oxford Dictionary of the Jewish Religion*, ed. Adele Berlin, 675–76 (Oxford: Oxford University Press, 2011).

46. Translation from Martin I. Lockshin, *Rashbam's Commentary on Exodus: An Annotated Translation* (Atlanta: Scholars' Press, 1997), 287–88.

47. The phrase evokes *bnei tarbut*, a term used by the Mishnah to describe trained animals (Bava Kamma 1:4). See Mordechai Z. Cohen, *Rashi, Biblical Interpretation, and Latin Learning in Medieval Europe: A New Perspective on an Exegetical Revolution* (New York: Cambridge University Press, 2021), 234. Rashbam's comment on Deuteronomy 22:6 uses the more common expression *derekh eretz*. French Tosafist Bekhor Shor, Rashbam's student, uses similar language of *derekh akhzariut* (the way of cruelty) in his commentary on Deuteronomy 14:2. Abraham ibn Ezra follows suit in connecting the animal-family commandments with one another and seeing in all of them a concern to avoid cruelty.

48. See the similar reading in Hanna Liss, *Creating Fictional Worlds: Peshaṭ-Exegesis and Narrativity in Rashbam's Commentary on the Torah* (Leiden: Brill, 2011), 216–17. Seeing the comment as taking a more polemical tone is Elazar Touitou, *"Exegesis in Perpetual Motion": Studies in the Exegesis of Rashbam on the Torah* (Ramat-Gan, Israel: Bar Ilan University Press, 2003), 44, 186. See also Yizhak Heinemann, *The Reasons for the Commandments in Jewish Thought: From the Bible to the Renaissance*, trans. Leonard Levin (Boston: Academic Studies Press, 2008), 49.

49. Moses Maimonides, *The Guide of the Perplexed*, trans. Shlomo Pines (Chicago: University of Chicago Press, 1963), 2:599–600.

50. Peter Adamson, "Human and Animal Nature in the Philosophy of the Islamic World," in *Animals: A History*, ed. Peter Adamson and G. Fay Edwards (New York: Oxford University Press, 2018), 109–10. See Ma'an Ziyadah, "Ibn Bajja's Book Tadbir al-Mutawahhid: An Edition, Translation and Commentary" (master's thesis, McGill University, 1968), 103–4.

51. Ahmed Alwishah, "Avicenna on Animal Self-Awareness, Cognition and Identity," *Arabic Sciences and Philosophy: A Historical Journal* 26, no. 1 (2016): 82; Adamson, "Human and Animal Nature," 105–6.

52. Lenn E. Goodman and Richard McGregor, eds., *The Case of the Animals Versus Man Before the King of the Jinn* (New York: Oxford University Press, 2012), 271. On Maimonides's criticism, see Sarah Stroumsa, *Maimonides in His World: Portrait of a Mediterranean Thinker*, Jews, Christians, and Muslims from the Ancient to the Modern World (Princeton: Princeton University Press, 2009), 97.

53. Richard Foltz, *Animals in Islamic Tradition and Muslim Cultures* (Oxford: Oneworld, 2006), 52–53; Aisha Y. Musa, "Raḥma: Universal Divine Mercy in the Qur'an and Hadith," *Journal of Islamic and Muslim Studies* 6, no. 1 (2021): 137.

54. Maimonides here once again echoes Goodman and McGregor, *Case of the Animals*, 114.

55. See, however, Josef Stern: "The reason that all commandments require the humane or merciful treatment of animals is not, then, the welfare of the

animals, but to perfect *us* so that we should not acquire moral habits of cruelty." *Problems and Parables of Law: Maimonides and Nahmanides on Reasons for the Commandments (Ta'amei Ha-Mitzvot)* (Albany: State University of New York Press, 1998), 54. My reading of Maimonides here is more like Roslyn Weiss's: "All of these expressions suggest that the object of the Torah's concern is the animals themselves." "Maimonides on 'Shilluaḥ Ha-Qen,'" *Jewish Quarterly Review* 79, no. 4 (1989): 357.

56. Haran, "Seething a Kid," 29, 35.

57. Sarna, *Exodus*, 141; Baruch J. Schwartz, "Leviticus: Introduction and Annotations," in Brettler and Berlin, *Jewish Study Bible*, 248–49; Tigay, *Deuteronomy*, 140. For reference to other Bible scholars who adopt the "humane" approach (Baentsch, Christensen, Gispen, Grünwaldt, Hartley, Isaacs, Nelson, von Rad), see Nihan, *Priestly Torah to Pentateuch*, 493n370; and Breier, "Ancient Near Eastern Law," 173–75. (Breier himself advocates for the humane approach.)

58. Tigay, *Deuteronomy*, 140; *Oxford English Dictionary*, s.v. "humane," September 2024, https://doi.org/10.1093/OED/1060225966; *Oxford English Dictionary*, "humanitarian," December 2024, https://doi.org/10.1093/OED/4289396434.

59. Janet M. Davis, *The Gospel of Kindness: Animal Welfare and the Making of Modern America* (Oxford: Oxford University Press, 2016), 1–25.

60. American Humane Society, "History," www.americanhumane.org/about-us/history/.

61. Jan Eckel et al., eds., *The Breakthrough: Human Rights in the 1970s* (Philadelphia: University of Pennsylvania Press, 2014); James Benjamin Loeffler, *Rooted Cosmopolitans: Jews and Human Rights in the Twentieth Century* (New Haven, CT: Yale University Press, 2018).

62. Aaron S. Gross, "Animals, Empathy, and Raḥamim in the Study of Religion: A Case Study of Jewish Opposition to Hunting," *Studies in Religion/Sciences Religieuses* 46, no. 4 (2017): 517–19, 518, 520–24. See also Gross, *The Question of the Animal and Religion: Theoretical Stakes, Practical Implications* (New York: Columbia University Press, 2015), 128–30, 169.

63. Mishnah Berakhot 5:3; Mishnah Megillah 4:9.

64. On interpretations of this Mishnah, see Natan Slifkin, "Shiluach haKein: The Transformation of a Mitzvah," Zoo Torah, www.zootorah.com/Rationalist Judaism/ShiluachHaKein.pdf, 10–16.

65. Mishnah Hullin 12:5.

66. A line of inquiry based on the context in Megillah (which may be the original context) regards whether the Rabbis deemed the formula to be heretical. See treatment in Alan F. Segal, *Two Powers in Heaven: Early Rabbinic Reports About Christianity and Gnosticism* (Leiden: Brill, 2002), 98–108.

67. In the explanations in the Palestinian Talmud (Berakhot 5:3 [9c]; parallel in Megillah 4:10 [75c]), the problem with the prayer formula is either that it

minimizes God's compassion by implying that it is issued *only* toward the bird and not toward others who are deserving or that it implies that God's mercy is finite. According to the explanations in the Babylonian Talmud (Berakhot 33b; Megillah 25a), the problem is either that the prayer formula seeds jealousy among God's creatures by implying that birds are lucky enough to receive God's compassion but other creatures may not be or that "one makes the attributes of the Holy One Blessed Be He mercy, when they are nothing but decrees *[gezerot]*," in other words, the very effort to explain God's actions is objectionable. See the discussion and references in Tabory, "Shiluah ha-Ken," 122; and Slifkin, "Shiluach haKein," 11. On *gezerot* in classical rabbinic literature, see Aaron D. Panken, *The Rhetoric of Innovation: Self-Conscious Legal Change in Rabbinic Literature* (Lanham, MD: University Press of America, 2005), 247–331.

68. Berakhot 33b (version from the Munich manuscript); Megillah 25a.

69. Dayid Halivni, *Sources and Traditions: A Source Critical Commentary on the Talmud: Seder Moed, from Yoma to Hagiga (Meḳorot u-Masorot)* (Jerusalem: Jewish Theological Seminary of America, 1974), 504–5. I cite the version of the story in the Munich manuscript of Berakhot since the part most relevant to my discussion, when the prayer leader mentions same-day slaughter, does not appear in the standard Vilna printed edition (it appears in parentheses in the Vilna edition of Megillah 25a). The Soncino and Pesaro printings have the expanded version for Megillah 25a but not for Berakhot 33b. Some manuscripts have Rava instead of Rabbah.

70. Palestinian Talmud Berakhot 5:2 (9c), based on the Leiden manuscript of the Yerushalmi; Yaacov Sussman, ed., *Talmud Yerushalmi According to Ms. Or. 4720 (Scal. 3) of the Leiden University Library with Restorations and Corrections* (Jerusalem: Academy of the Hebrew Language, 2001), 47. In Megillah 4:10 (75c), the statement is clipped and appears without the reference to the Targum and the law in Leviticus. The statement of Rabbi Yosi son of Rabbi Bun matches nearly verbatim the one in the Babylonian Talmud about "making the attributes of the Holy One Blessed Be He mercy," though the Palestinian Talmud's presentation offers a clear attribution to Rabbi Yosi son of Bun; does not add the explanatory phrase about divine decrees that the Babylonian Talmud does; and couches the Hebrew-language core within a broader Aramaic-language formulation in which the "bad" theology it describes is linked with the same-day slaughter prohibition in Leviticus.

71. Martin McNamara et al., *The Aramaic Bible: Leviticus* (Collegeville, MN: Liturgical Press, 1994), 3:190–91. See also Eliezer Segal, "Justice, Mercy and a Bird's Nest," *Journal of Jewish Studies* 42, no. 2 (1991): 182.

72. Mishnah Berakhot 5:3. Translation from E. Segal, "Justice," 186. Moses Maimonides, *Mishnah 'im Perush Rabenu Moshe Ben Maimon*, trans. Yosef Kafaḥ (Jerusalem: Rav Kook Institute, 1963), 1:42.

73. Mishnah Megillah 4:9. According to Josef Stern, Maimonides intends to say not that this law is arbitrary and has no reason but that the reason—which

Maimonides describes in the *Guide of the Perplexed* to be a precautionary measure—must not be revealed to the hoi polloi. See Stern, *Problems and Parables*, 65.

74. Laws of Prayer (Hilkhot Tefillah) 9:7. See the translation in Stern, 49. Maimonides refers also to "similar statements" that must not be made, in which he conceivably has in mind the other animal-family laws and perhaps other animal-related laws.

75. R. Weiss, "Maimonides on 'Shilluaḥ Ha-Qen,'" 54.

76. For attempts at reconciliation, see R. Weiss; E. Segal, "Justice," 186–90; and Stern, *Problems and Parables*, 49–66.

77. Jacob Milgrom, *Leviticus 1–16: A New Translation with Introduction and Commentary*, vol. 3, *The Anchor Bible* (New York: Doubleday, 1991), 739.

78. Nahmanides is explicit on this point in his comment on Deuteronomy 22:6: "Thus these commandments with respect to cattle and fowl are not [a result of] compassion upon them, but they are decrees upon us to guide us and to teach us traits of good character." Charles B. Chavel, *Commentary on the Torah by Nahmanides* (New York: Shilo, 1971), 271. A key text for both Nahmanides and Maimonides is Genesis Rabbah 44:1: "And what difference does it make to the Holy One, blessed be He, whether an animal is slaughtered from the front of the neck or the back? Surely you must say the commandments have been given only for the purpose of refining men through them, as it is said, 'Every word of God is refined' (Proverbs 30:5)."

79. See the critique of humanitarianism in Talal Asad, "Reflections on Violence, Law, and Humanitarianism," *Critical Inquiry* 41, no. 2 (2015): 390–427.

80. Clement, *Stromateis*, trans. John Ferguson, The Fathers of the Church (Washington, DC: Catholic University of America Press, 1991), 85:218–20. See also Annewies W. van den Hoek, *Clement of Alexandria and His Use of Philo in the Stromateis: An Early Christian Reshaping of a Jewish Model* (Leiden: Brill, 1988), 92–95.

81. Exceptions include Sifra Emor Parshata 8:9-12 and Babylonian Talmud Hullin 78b, which cites the Sifra. Isaac Hirsch Weiss, ed., *Sifra Deve Rav: Hu Sefer Torat Kohanim* (New York: Om, 1946), 117–18.

3. ANIMAL GRANDMOTHERS

1. Rachel B. Gross, *Beyond the Synagogue: Jewish Nostalgia as Religious Practice* (New York: New York University Press, 2021), 40, 47.

2. Susan Moore et al., *The Psychology of Family History: Exploring Our Genealogy* (London: Routledge, 2021), 1; Ancestry, "Searching Public Family Trees," https://support.ancestry.com/s/article/Searching-Public-Family-Trees?language=en_US.

3. R. Gross, *Beyond the Synagogue*, 48.

4. Radmila Švaříčková-Slabáková, ed., *Family Memory: Practices, Transmissions and Uses in a Global Perspective* (New York: Routledge, 2021), 15.

5. Kali Holloway, "Angela Davis's Family History Is Remarkable—and Unexceptional for Black Americans," March 2, 2023, www.thenation.com/article/society/angela-davis-pbs-genealogy/.

6. John Koblin, "A PBS Show, a Frustrated Ben Affleck, and a Loss of Face," *New York Times*, June 26, 2015, sec. Business, www.nytimes.com/2015/06/26/business/media/a-pbs-show-a-frustrated-ben-affleck-and-a-loss-of-face.html.

7. Catherine Nash, *Genetic Geographies: The Trouble with Ancestry* (Minneapolis: University of Minnesota Press, 2015); Angma Dey Jhala, introd. to *Genealogy, Archive, Image: Interpreting Dynastic History in Western India, c. 1090–2016*, ed. Angma Dey Jhala and Jayasinhji Jhala (Warsaw: De Gruyter Open, 2017), 1.

8. R. Gross, *Beyond the Synagogue*, 44. See also Hedda Klip, *Biblical Genealogies: A Form-Critical Analysis, with a Special Focus on Women* (Leiden: Brill, 2022).

9. Another approach is to see interspecies mating as symbolic of intermarriage. See Jacob Milgrom, *Leviticus 17–22: A New Translation with Introduction and Commentary, The Anchor Bible* (New York: Doubleday, 2000), 3A: 1659.

10. Sifra Kedoshim Perek 4:13; Isaac Hirsch Weiss, ed., *Sifra Deve Rav: Hu Sefer Torat Kohanim* (New York: Om, 1946), 89; Babylonian Talmud Bava Metzia 91b. The presence in biblical and rabbinic literature of mules, who are the product of crossbreeding a horse and a donkey and usually cannot themselves reproduce, likewise attest to purposeful breeding practices.

11. Babylonian Talmud Bava Metzia 91a, parallel in Avodah Zarah 20b. In Codex Florence of Bava Metzia 91a, Rav Yehudah transmits in the name of Rav. The addendum about arousal, which appears to be from the anonymous redactors, is ambiguous regarding whether the concern is that the human breeder would be tempted to have inappropriate sex with another human or with the animal. The Talmuds speak also of animals who have sexual intercourse of their own volition (Palestinian Talmud Kilayim 8:2:2 says, "When he ejaculates, he does so by himself") and of a middle ground in which people put animals together in a pen for the animals to have sex, but the people do not compel the intercourse (Babylonian Talmud Bava Metzia 91a). The Roman writers counsel against compelling animal intercourse. See Lucius Junius Moderatus Columella, *On Agriculture*, trans. Edward S. Forster and Edward H. Heffner, Loeb Classical Library 361 (Cambridge, MA: Harvard University Press, 2014), 182–83.

12. For references in Columella, Cicero, Varro, Vergil, and others, see Geoffrey Kron, "Animal Husbandry, Hunting, Fishing and Pisciculture," in *Oxford Handbook of Engineering and Technology in the Classical World*, ed. John Peter Oleson (Oxford: Oxford University Press, 2008), 179; and Idoia Grau-Sologestoa et

al., "Innovation and Intensification: The Use of Cattle in the Roman Rhine Region," *Environmental Archaeology: The Journal of Human Palaeoecology*, June 23, 2022, 2.

13. Kron, "Animal Husbandry," 177–80; Michael MacKinnon, "Cattle 'Breed' Variation and Improvement in Roman Italy: Connecting the Zooarchaeological and Ancient Textual Evidence," *World Archaeology* 42, no. 1 (2010): 71. Kron points out that even modern racehorse breeders rely on intuition and experience rather than on formal genetics (177).

14. *De Re Rustica* 7.2.4–5; Columella, *On Agriculture*, 234–37. See also Columella's discussion of how best to breed mules in 216–21.

15. MacKinnon, "Cattle 'Breed' Variation," 71–72.

16. *Rerum Rusticarum* 3.7.10; Marcus Terentius Varro, *On Agriculture*, trans. Harrison Boyd Ash and William Davis Hooper, Loeb Classical Library 283 (Cambridge, MA: Harvard University Press, 2014), 466–67. See also the discussion in Kron, "Animal Husbandry," 179.

17. Fortune Business Insights, "Animal Genetics Market Size and Growth: Global Report," www.fortunebusinessinsights.com/animal-genetics-market-105584. See also Margaret E. Derry, *Made to Order: The Designing of Animals* (Toronto: University of Toronto Press, 2022).

18. For the formulation "ancestry matters," see Nash, *Genetic Geographies*, 13. On the "memorial work" done by Jewish genealogies, see R. Gross, *Beyond the Synagogue*, 64.

19. Milgrom speculates that the Deuteronomic source changes the law, substituting "breeding" in the Holiness Legislation with "plowing," because the source intended to permit crossbreeding animals, reflecting a time when mules had become widespread; see *Leviticus 17-22*, 3A:1658.

20. Nash, *Genetic Geographies*.

21. The prohibition on cooking kids in their mother's milk also focuses on slaughter and its aftermath, but since the Rabbis generalized that law to mixing all meat with all milk, animal genealogies lost relevance. See my discussion in chapter 4.

22. Klip, *Biblical Genealogies*, 2.

23. Nitza Berkovitch and Shlomit Manor, "Between Familism and Neoliberalism: The Case of Jewish Israeli Grandmothers," *Feminist Theory*, February 28, 2022, 3–5.

24. Kristen Hawkes et al., "Grandmothering, Menopause, and the Evolution of Human Life Histories," *Proceedings of the National Academy of Sciences* 95, no. 3 (1998): 1336–39.

25. Ville Vuolanto, "Grandmothers in Roman Egypt," *Greek, Roman and Byzantine Studies* 57, no. 2 (2017): 375, 376.

26. Levirate marriage is in Mishnah Yevamot 1:1; the consumption of tithes is in Yevamot 7:5; lineage confirmation is in Kiddushin 4:4; and incestuous rape

is in Ketubbot 3:2 and Keritot 3:5. Other relevant passages include Genesis Rabbah 77:26, where it is clear from the context that *zaqen* and *zeqenah* refer to grandparents, and Babylonian Talmud Bava Batra 125b, where *savta* clearly refers to a grandmother. Julius Theodor and Chanoch Albeck, eds., *Berischit Rabba, mit Kritischem Apparat und Kommentar*, 3 vols (Jerusalem: Wahrmann Books, 1965), 2:913. A well-known Talmudic story that features grandchildren is that of Honi the Circle Drawer. See a treatment of that story's grandchildren motif in Marc Hirshman, "Changing Focuses of Sanctity: Honi and His Grandchildren," *Tura* 1 (1989): 109–18.

27. Babylonian Talmud Bekhorot 17a; Hullin 75b; Bava Kamma 80b.

28. Mishnah Hullin 5:1.

29. Yoreh Deah 16.

30. The labels are what Alexander Samely describes as "technical expressions for a particular subject matter." Samely covers this rhetorical device in section 2.4.4.1 of *Profiling Jewish Literature in Antiquity: An Inventory, from Second Temple Texts to the Talmuds* (Oxford: Oxford University Press, 2013), 39, 125. In the case of the Hullin chapter titles, the technical expressions are "linguistically opaque" and rely on knowledge of the relevant biblical sources, a phenomenon Samely describes as "biblicizing language." This is discussed in sections 2.4.4.4., 7.1.4.1, and 8.1.4.1; see pages 129, 260, and 291.

31. On the rabbinic punishments of divine death and lashes, see Aharon Shemesh, *Punishments and Sins: From the Bible to Rabbinic Literature [Onashim va-Hata'im: Min ha-Miqra le-Sifrut Hazal]* (Jerusalem: Magnes, 2003).

32. Maimonides puts the first principle simply in his opening to the relevant chapter of the Mishneh Torah: "One who slaughters him and his child on the same day, the meat is permitted for eating" (Laws of Slaughter 12:1).

33. The printed edition has a different version of the dispute: "Rabbi Shimon declares him exempt, but the Sages declare him liable." The Kaufmann manuscript's version is more similar to that of the Tosefta. See Tosefta Hullin 5:2; Moses Samuel Zuckermandel, ed., *Tosephta: Based on the Erfurt and Vienna Codices [Tosefta al-pi Kitve-yad 'Erfurṭ Vinah]* (Jerusalem: Wahrman, 1970), 507.

34. As Rashi says, "For behold there is no slaughter at all, and this is not like the slaughter mentioned above in any way, for there the slaughter is entirely fit, but some other factor produced the disqualification" (Hullin 81b, see the comment *"ve-ha-noher ve-ha-me'aqer"*). Jordan Rosenblum's explanation is helpful: "There are two important slaughter-related terms vital for understanding *Hullin*. In the Hebrew Bible, *nevelah* (carcass) is a technical term for an animal that has died a natural death, and *terefah* (lit. "torn") refers to an animal killed by another animal. However, in rabbinic texts, *nevelah* . . . refers to an animal that has been improperly slaughtered, while *terefah* refers to an animal that has been properly slaughtered but is declared invalid for another reason (see 2:4)." "Tractate Hullin," in *The Oxford Annotated Mishnah: A New Translation of the*

Mishnah, ed. Shaye J. D. Cohen et al., 3 vols. (New York: Oxford University Press, 2022), 3:121.

35. The Tosafot on Hullin 80a (see comment *"Hullin"*) propose that eating the meat should violate Deuteronomy 14:3's instruction not to eat something abhorrent. The Tosafot understand the Mishnah to be excluding precisely this possibility—the meat is valid even though its slaughter would seem to have made it abhorrent.

36. The line "One slaughtered her, her daughter, and her daughter's daughter, he incurs eighty" follows the standard printed edition instead of the Kaufmann manuscript, whose meaning is more opaque and seems potentially incorrect: "One slaughtered her, he incurs forty; he slaughtered her and her daughter, he incurs eighty".

37. Hullin 82a; see comment *"ve-ahar kakh shehatah."*

38. The restriction of Sumakhos and Rabbi Meir's position to only this case is likely an innovation that the Mishnah is making to earlier traditions. The Tosefta suggests that Sumakhos and Rabbi Meir's position is broader. See Tosefta Hullin 5:7; Zuckermandel, *Tosephta*, 507. The traditional commentators understand Rabbi Meir transmitted by Sumakhos to differ in both cases. See, for example, Bartenura, comment, *"Sumakhos omer sofeg shemonim."* But Rabbi Yehudah bar Pazi in the name of Rabbi Yohanan, in Palestinian Talmud Yevamot 11:1, comments that Sumakhos concedes his position in the first case.

39. On levirate marriage in rabbinic literature, see Dvora E. Weisberg, *Levirate Marriage and the Family in Ancient Judaism* (Waltham, MA: Brandeis University Press, 2009).

40. Palestinian Talmud Yevamot 11:1 explicitly connects the two contexts. Federico Dal Bo makes a similar observation about the same language being used for human and animal lineages in Mishnah Hullin; see *Massekhet Keritot* (Tübingen, Germany: Mohr Siebeck, 2013), 359.

41. Mishnah Ketubbot 3:2; Keritot 3:5; Parashat Emor Parshata 8, Pereq 8:4–5; I. Weiss, *Sifra Deve Rav*, 99.

42. Tosefta Hullin 5:6; Zuckermandel, *Tosephta*, 507.

43. Medieval commentators debate whether there is also an obligation on the part of the buyer to ask and whether such an obligation would apply if the seller is not Jewish. See the comment in the Maggid Mishnah's commentary on the Mishneh Torah, Laws of Slaughter 12:14. A putatively early rabbinic teaching on Babylonian Talmud Hullin 83a implies that the buyer need not ask.

44. Rashi gives the example of a day elapsing: "He sold the first yesterday and the second today" (83a, see comment *"aval yesh lo revah"*). Maimonides, however, interprets Rabbi Yehudah to be referring to a period of elapsed time on the same day of sale (Laws of Slaughter 12:15). See Abraham ben David of Posquières's critique, who follows a position more like Rashi's and brings the Tosefta as evidence. See comment *"aval im hayah revah."*

45. Parashat Emor Parshata 8, Pereq 8:9.

46. See the parallel in Babylonian Talmud Hullin 83b.

47. The scenario addressed by Mishnah Hullin 4:5 is a fetus who is already nine months old and is found alive inside the mother while she is being slaughtered, so the presumed parent is clearly a mother (see the discussion in my conclusion). Mishnah Bekhorot 7:7 presents the following puzzling teaching: "These are valid for a person but invalid for an animal: 'him and his son,' etc." The Mishnah probably means that while a parent and child animal must not be sacrificed on the same day, a parent and child priest may work together in the Temple on the same day. For the analogy to hold, the Babylonian Talmud observes (Bekhorot 45b), the figures would all be male, since priests who serve in the Temple are exclusively male. If so, then the authors of this Mishnah would appear to have a father-son animal pair in mind when they mention the same-day slaughter prohibition, though they could, on the other hand, simply not mind that the parallel requires gender-crossing.

48. The Brown-Driver-Briggs-Genesius lexicon, which defines *shor* as a "head of cattle, bullock, ox, etc.," claims that the word is normally used "without emphasis on sex," though occasionally it may refer specifically to the male or specifically to the female (the example given for the latter is in this verse). Francis Brown, *The Brown, Driver, Briggs Hebrew and English Lexicon* (Peabody, MA: Hendrickson, 1996), 1004. The Hebrew and Aramaic lexicon of the Old Testament says that *shor* is gender neutral but goes on to cite alternative definitions that make it specifically male. *HALOT Online*, s.v. "shor," February 2017, https://dictionaries.brillonline.com/search#dictionary=halothebrew&id=SHIN.212. The term *seh* appears to be more gender neutral than *shor*, with neither Brown-Driver-Briggs nor HALOT addressing gender at any point in the entry. Brown, *English Lexicon*, 961-62; *HALOT Online*, s.v. "seh," February 2017, https://dictionaries.brillonline.com /search#dictionary=halothebrew&id=SIN.32. David J. A. Clines says that *seh* can refer to a sheep, ram, or she-goat, suggesting that the gender can go either way. See "Seh," in *The Dictionary of Classical Hebrew* (Sheffield, England: Sheffield Academic Press, 1993), 8:115-16. See the discussion of the gender implications of the verse in *Ha-Ketav ve-ha-Kabbalah* by nineteenth-century German Rabbi Jacob Zvi Mecklenburg.

49. Nicole J. Ruane, "Milk, Meat, and Mothers: The Problem of Motherhood in Some Ritual Food Laws," in *New Perspectives on Ritual in the Biblical World*, ed. Melissa Ramos and Laura Quick (London: T&T Clark International, 2022), 68. If the biblical composer had wanted to indicate only female animals, Ruane points out, he could have done so by using specific terms for female animals, such as *parah, kisbah, ez*, and feminine possessives and pronouns. Moreover, the occasions on which multiple animals were sacrificed on the same day would have been important cultic events that called specifically for many males at once. S. Tamar Kamionkowski similarly concludes that the father is as likely as the mother to be

the verse's concern; see *Leviticus* (Collegeville, MN: Liturgical Press, 2018), 249. Jacob Milgrom leans toward the mother but similarly argues for inclusion of the father, citing the masculine language of *shor* and *oto;* see Milgrom, *Leviticus 17–22*, 3A:1884. Many scholars take the mother to be the sole referent and either do not mention the father or consider him to be excluded. See John E. Hartley, *Leviticus*, Word Biblical Commentary (Dallas: Word Books, 1992), 4:362; Erhard S. Gerstenberger, *Leviticus: A Commentary*, Old Testament Library (Louisville, KY: Westminster John Knox Press, 1996), 331; Samuel E. Balentine, *Leviticus* (Louisville, KY: Westminster John Knox Press, 2002), 171; and Christophe Nihan, *From Priestly Torah to Pentateuch: A Study in the Composition of the Book of Leviticus* (Tübingen, Germany: Mohr Siebeck, 2007), 492.

50. Temple Scroll 11QT^a Column 52:5–7; Yigael Yadin, ed., *The Temple Scroll* (Jerusalem: Israel Exploration Society, 1983), 1:312–14; Florentino García Martinez and Eibert J. C. Tigchelaar, eds., *Dead Sea Scrolls: Study Edition* (Grand Rapids, MI: Eerdmans, 1999), 1270–72; Lawrence H. Schiffman and Andrew D. Gross, *The Temple Scroll: 11q19, 11q20, 11q21, 4q524, 5q21 with 4q365a*, Dead Sea Scrolls Editions 1 (Boston: Brill, 2021), 147. In Beth A. Berkowitz, "Interpretation in the Anthropocene: Reading the Animal Family Laws of the Pentateuch," in *Studies in the History of Exegesis*, ed. Mark Elliott et al. (Tübingen, Germany: Mohr Siebeck, 2022), 39–52, I had more or less agreed with Lawrence H. Schiffman, "'Miqsat Ma'aseh Ha-Torah' and the 'Temple Scroll,'" *Revue de Qumrân* 14, no. 3 (1990): 449–50, who sees the Temple Scroll potentially including the father, but it now seems to me unlikely and I am closer to the reading suggested in James L. Kugel, *Traditions of the Bible: A Guide to the Bible as It Was at the Start of the Common Era* (Cambridge, MA: Harvard University Press, 1998), 697.

51. Miqsat Ma'aseh Torah 4QMMT^c B36–38 Column 1; Elisha Qimron and John Strugnell, eds., *Qumrân Cave 4: Miqṣat Maʿaśe Ha-Torah. V*, Qumrân Cave 45 (Oxford: Oxford University Press, 1994), 158; Martinez and Tigchelaar, *Dead Sea Scrolls*, 794–95. See the alternative reconstruction in Moshe J. Bernstein, "The Employment and Interpretation of Scripture in 4QMMT: Preliminary Observations," in *Reading and Re-reading Scripture at Qumran* (Leiden: Brill, 2013), 2:564. Schiffman and Bernstein take MMT to be referring to Leviticus 22:28 despite a number of differences between them. Schiffman, "Miqsat Ma'seh Ha-Torah," 449; Bernstein, "Employment and Interpretation," 2:564.

52. The Hebrew *oto ve-et beno* became "her and her children," or *autēn kau ta paidia autēs*. See Mark A. Awabdy, *Leviticus: A Commentary on Leueitikon in Codex Vaticanus*, Septuagint Commentary Series (Boston: Brill, 2019), 156, 379.

53. Onkelos translates *lah ve-livrah;* Neofiti and Pseudo-Jonathan translate *yata ve-yat berah*. The Targums also use female nouns for the animal species: in Onkelos *torata o' sita* and in Neofiti and Pseudo-Jonathan *torata o' rehela*. For Pseudo-Jonathan and Neofiti, see Martin McNamara et al., *The Aramaic Bible:*

Leviticus (Collegeville, MN: Liturgical Press, 1994), 3:87–88, 190–91. Neofiti omits the phrase "on the same day." On the Aramaic words chosen for the animal species, see Samuel David Luzzatto's commentary on the verse. Chanoch Albeck presents this targumic tradition as an illustration of the oral Torah departing from the plain sense of scripture (and then the early Rabbis disputing the meaning); see *Mavo La-Mishnah* [Introduction to the Mishnah] (Jerusalem: Bialik Institute, 1960), 13.

54. "He forbids them to sacrifice the mother and offspring *(mētera kai engonon)* on the same day." Philo, *On the Virtues* 134, trans. Francis Henry Colson, Loeb Classical Library 341 (Cambridge, MA: Harvard University Press, 2014), 8:244–45.

55. *Antiquities* 3.9.4; Flavius Josephus, *Jewish Antiquities*, trans. Henry St. J. Thackeray, Loeb Classical Library 242 (Cambridge, MA: Harvard University Press, 1930), 1:430–31. The term Josephus uses for the animal parent *(gegennēkotos)* has no clear gender (if any gender is implied, it would be male, since the term is grammatically either neuter or male). Josephus curiously flips the verse's perspective so that the prohibition is no longer against the same-day slaughter of animal and child but against the same-day slaughter of animal and parent. In his rendering of the requirement to keep the baby with the mother for the first seven days (which he places after the same-day slaughter requirement, not before as it appears in Leviticus), Josephus omits explicit mention of the mother and instead focuses on the time elapsed since the baby animal's birth.

56. Sifra Emor Parashah 8, Pereq 1 and 2, from the Vatican manuscript, Biblioteca Apostolica Ebr., 66, found in "Ma'agarim," Historical Dictionary Project of the Academy of Hebrew Language, https://maagarim.hebrew-academy.org.il/Pages/PMain.aspx?mishibbur=18000&mm15=011008001000.

57. Babylonian Talmud Hullin 78b–79a.

58. The law is stated both in Hullin and in Bekhorot 45b.

59. Laws of Slaughter 12:11.

60. Yoreh Deah, Laws of Slaughter 16:2. The medieval Jewish Bible commentators almost all take the prohibition to be referring exclusively to the mother, with Saadiah Gaon explaining that *shor ve-seh* means "cow and ewe," and Rashi saying simply that the prohibition applies to animal mothers but not to animal fathers and that it is permissible to slaughter an animal father and child on the same day. One notable exception is Abraham ibn Ezra, who writes that the command applies to both males and females. See an overview of the interpretive history in Schiffman, "Miqsat Ma'seh Ha-Torah," 451.

61. Shaye J. D. Cohen, *The Beginnings of Jewishness: Boundaries, Varieties, Uncertainties* (Berkeley: University of California Press, 1999), 308–40.

62. Stacy Rosenbaum and Lee T. Gettler, "With a Little Help from Her Friends (and Family): Part I, The Ecology and Evolution of Non-maternal Care in Mammals," *Physiology and Behavior* 193 (September 2018): 2.

63. See Nara B. Milanich, *Paternity: The Elusive Quest for the Father* (Cambridge, MA: Harvard University Press, 2019).

64. Devra G. Kleiman and James R. Malcolm, "The Evolution of Male Parental Investment in Mammals," in *Parental Care in Mammals*, ed. David J. Gubernick and Peter H. Klopfer (New York: Plenum, 1981), 351.

65. Charles M. Payne, *I've Got the Light of Freedom: The Organizing Tradition and the Mississippi Freedom Struggle* (Berkeley: University of California Press, 1995), 308.

66. R. Gross, *Beyond the Synagogue*, 42; Janet Carsten, introd. to *Ghosts of Memory: Essays on Remembrance and Relatedness*, ed. Janet Carsten (Malden, MA: Blackwell, 2008), 22.

67. On the significance of affect theory for understanding animals, religion, and the Bible, see Donovan O. Schaefer, *Religious Affects: Animality, Evolution, and Power* (Durham, NC: Duke University Press, 2015); Ken Stone, *Reading the Hebrew Bible with Animal Studies* (Palo Alto, CA: Stanford University Press, 2017), 140–63; and Sébastien Doane, *Reading the Bible amid the Environmental Crisis: Interdisciplinary Insights to Ecological Hermeneutics* (Lanham, MD: Lexington Books, 2024), 31–47.

68. American Kennel Club, "AKC Pedigree: How to Purchase a Document on Your Dog's Lineage," www.akc.org/register/pedigree/.

69. Švaríčková-Slabáková, *Family Memory*, 5; Nash, *Genetic Geographies*, 11.

70. Ashley Barnwell, "Convict Shame to Convict Chic: Intergenerational Memory and Family Histories," *Memory Studies* 12, no. 4 (2019): 405.

71. Henry Louis Gates Jr., *Finding Your Roots* (Arlington, VA: PBS, 2012–25).

4. ANIMAL MOTHERS

1. Philo, *On the Virtues* 142–44, trans. Francis Henry Colson, Loeb Classical Library 341 (Cambridge, MA: Harvard University Press, 2014), 8:248–51.

2. Moses Maimonides, *The Guide of the Perplexed*, trans. Shlomo Pines (Chicago: University of Chicago Press, 1963), 2:599. The cultic theory appeared to be confirmed in the 1930s by a Ugaritic text that was discovered, but in the end most scholars dismissed it as unrelated to the biblical prohibition. See Jacob Milgrom, "You Shall Not Boil a Kid in Its Mother's Milk," *Bible Review* (Washington, DC) 1, no. 3 (1985): 48.

3. For the theory that that the law prohibits removing a baby goat from the mother while still nursing, see Hans Goedicke, "Review of *Das Böcklein in Der Milch Seiner Mutter und Verwandtes* by Othmar Keel," *Journal of Near Eastern Studies* 42, no. 4 (1983): 302–3; and Stefan Schorch, "'A Young Goat in Its Mother's Milk'? Understanding an Ancient Prohibition," *Vetus Testamentum* 60, no. 1

(2010): 116–30. The interpretation that it refers to the mother's fat *(helev)* and not her milk *(halav)* is from Jack M. Sasson, "Ritual Wisdom? On 'Seething a Kid in Its Mother's Milk,'" in *Kein Land für sich allein: Studien zum Kulturkontakt in Kanaan, Israel/Palästina und Ebirnari für Manfred Weippert zum 65 Geburtstag*, ed. Manfred Weippert et al. (Freiburg, Germany: Universitätsverlag; Vandenhoeck und Ruprecht, 2002), 294–308. For the theory about blood and colostrum, see Casper J. Labuschagne, "'You Shall Not Boil a Kid in Its Mother's Milk': A New Proposal for the Origin of the Prohibition," in *The Scriptures and the Scrolls*, ed. Florentino García Martinez et al. (Leiden: Brill, 1992), 6–17. The divine nursing figure theory is from Othmar Keel, *Das Böcklein in Der Milch Seiner Mutter und Verwandtes: Im Lichte Eines Altorientalischen Bildmotivs* (Freiburg, Germany: Universitätsverlag/Vandenhoeck und Ruprecht, 1980); and Ernst Axel Knauf, "Zur Herkunft und Sozialgeschichte Israels: 'Das Böckchen in Der Milch Seiner Mutter,'" *Biblica* 69, no. 2 (1988): 153–69.

4. Arguing that the prohibition symbolizes incest is Jean Soler, "The Semiotics of Food in the Bible," in *Food and Drink in History: Selections from the Annales, Économies, Sociétes, Civilisations*, ed. Robert Forster and Orest A. Ranum (Baltimore: Johns Hopkins University Press, 1979), 5:126–38. Bekhor Shor and Karaite Anan ben David make the first-fruits suggestion; see William Henry Propp, *Exodus 19–40: A New Translation with Introduction and Commentary* (New York: Doubleday, 2006), 284.

5. Mekhilta de-Rabbi Yishmael Tractate Kaspa 20; H. Saul Horovitz and Israel Abraham Rabin, eds., *Mechilta d'Rabbi Ismael* (Jerusalem: Wahrmann Books, 1970), 335–38.

6. See also the discussion in Jordan Rosenblum, *The Jewish Dietary Laws in the Ancient World* (New York: Cambridge University Press, 2016), 95–97.

7. Babylonian Talmud Hullin 108a; parallels in Pesahim 44b and Nazir 37a–b. On why the Rabbis would have developed the prohibition along these lines, see David Charles Kraemer, *Jewish Eating and Identity Through the Ages* (New York: Routledge, 2007), 39–54.

8. The touchstone for this approach is Tal Ilan, *Mine and Yours Are Hers: Retrieving Women's History from Rabbinic Literature* (Leiden: Brill, 1997).

9. Carol J. Adams, *The Pornography of Meat* (New York: Bloomsbury, 2020), 50. For a brief encapsulation of the idea and its implications, see Matthew Calarco, *Animal Studies: The Key Concepts* (London: Routledge/Taylor and Francis, 2021), 2–4.

10. Carol J. Adams, "The Absent Referent," https://caroljadams.com/the-absent-referent.

11. Mishnah Hullin 8:3; Jordan D. Rosenblum, "Tractate Hullin," in *The Oxford Annotated Mishnah: A New Translation of the Mishnah*, ed. Shaye J. D. Cohen et al. (New York: Oxford University Press, 2022), 3:155.

12. See Mishnah Keritot 5:1. The liver is another organ filled with troubling fluids—like the heart, it is filled with blood—discussed in this chapter of Babylonian Talmud Hullin.

13. In his case study of Dora, Freud wrote that the udder is an "image intermediate between a nipple and a penis" because it hangs down from the undercarriage of the cow but appears to the human eye like a penis. Sigmund Freud, *Dora: An Analysis of a Case of Hysteria*, ed. Philip Rieff (New York: Simon and Schuster, 1997), 45. The association between udder, breast, and penis came up again for Freud nine years later in his study of Little Hans: "A cow's udder plays an apt part as intermediate image, being in its nature a mamma and in its shape and position a penis." Sigmund Freud, *The Standard Edition of the Complete Psychological Works of Sigmund Freud*, ed. James Strachey and Anna Freud (London: Hogarth/Institute of Psycho-Analysis, 1995), 10:7.

14. In what appears to be a strange coincidence, brought to my attention by Marc Brettler, Jeremiah 4:30 combines the language of tearing used by the Mishnah *(qeriah)* with the imagery of kohl (eye makeup), which is the more common meaning of the rabbinic word for udder *(kahal)*. The Hullin passage expands on tearing in a section that I do not discuss here, in which Rav Yehudah instructs that the udder should be torn crosswise, literally by warp and woof in a weaving motion, and then smeared against a wall. It is the first echo of the feminine—here, the quintessentially feminine labor of weaving—that runs through the passage. I thank Marc Brettler and Pratima Gopalakrishnan and the other members of the North Carolina Jewish Studies Seminar for the insights they brought to this material when I shared it with them. On the matter of tearing, it was also noted by those in the seminar that the cutting and smearing of the udder would have had the effect of making it unrecognizable.

15. Hullin 109b.

16. Hullin 109b; Tosefta Hullin 8:8.

17. Hullin 109b; Tosefta Hullin 8:9.

18. *"Zeh kanus be-me'av"* on 109b or, as he says later, "when it comes out it is fully milk *[halav gamur]*."

19. On the figure of Yalta, see Charlotte Elisheva Fonrobert, *Menstrual Purity: Rabbinic and Christian Reconstructions of Biblical Gender* (Palo Alto, CA: Stanford University Press, 2002), 118–27. On the named women of the Talmud, see Gila Fine, *The Madwoman in the Rabbi's Attic: Rereading the Women of the Talmud* (Jerusalem: Maggid, 2024).

20. Hullin 109b. Translation "blow up" is from Marcus Jastrow, "Dictionary of the Targumim, the Talmud Babli and Yerushalmi, and the Midrashic Literature," Tyndale Archive, www.tyndalearchive.com/TABS/Jastrow/, 389. The meaning is uncertain, according to Michael Sokoloff, *A Dictionary of Jewish Babylonian Aramaic of the Talmudic and Geonic Periods* (Baltimore: Johns Hopkins University Press, 2002), 405. Rashi understands the verb "blow up" in accordance with

37. On celebration of dialectical ability within the Babylonian Talmud, see Jeffrey L. Rubenstein, *The Culture of the Babylonian Talmud* (Baltimore: Johns Hopkins University Press, 2005), 39–53.

38. Amit argues, rightly in my opinion, for an "anti-Suran tone" to the story; "Halakhic Kernel," 190. On why within the story Rav Hisda represents the city of Sura and on why Rav Yehudah, in the guise of the obscure Rami, represents the city of Pumbedita, see "Halakhic Kernel," 194–95.

39. See, for instance, Elisheva Baumgarten, *Mothers and Children: Jewish Family Life in Medieval Europe*, Jews, Christians, and Muslims from the Ancient to the Modern World (Princeton: Princeton University Press, 2004); Ellen Davina Haskell, *Suckling at My Mother's Breasts: The Image of a Nursing God in Jewish Mysticism*, SUNY Series in Western Esoteric Traditions (New York: State University of New York Press, 2012); Marjorie Suzan Lehman et al., eds., *Mothers in the Jewish Cultural Imagination* (Oxford: Littman Library of Jewish Civilization/Liverpool University Press, 2017); Mara H. Benjamin, *The Obligated Self: Maternal Subjectivity and Jewish Thought* (Bloomington: Indiana University Press, 2018).

40. One might read the repressed animal mother here in conjunction with the repressed animal father of the same-day slaughter materials—see chapter 3 of this volume and Ilan's argument that the Babylonian Talmud restores the repressed animal father, in *Massekhet Hullin*, 357.

41. Carol J. Adams, *The Sexual Politics of Meat: A Feminist-Vegetarian Critical Theory* (New York: Bloomsbury USA, 2015).

42. See chapter 1 of this volume on the impact of maternal separation on farm animals.

43. Annie Potts, ed., *Meat Culture*, Human-Animal Studies, vol. 17 (Leiden: Brill, 2016).

5. ANIMAL FATHERS AND OTHER CAREGIVERS

1. "Yonis Mom Does Shiluach Hakan," YouTube, July 6, 2018, www.youtube.com/watch?v=8MtSx8sRfj8; "Bubby Does Shiluach Hakan," YouTube, July 6, 2018, www.youtube.com/watch?v=kdDD1f7B-bs.

2. The correct pronunciation is *shiluah ha-ken*, but since the word *ken* appears in the biblical verse in construct state, it is traditionally pronounced as *kan;* see Natan Slifkin, "Shiluach haKein: The Transformation of a Mitzvah," Zoo Torah, www.zootorah.com/RationalistJudaism/ShiluachHaKein.pdf, 5. One would expect, in fact, for the mitzvah to be called *shiluah ha-em* (sending of the mother) rather than *shiluah ha-ken* (sending of the nest). For a discussion, see Joseph Tabory, "Shiluah ha-Ken: On the Relationship Between the Reason for the Mitzvah and Its Laws," in *Studies in Halakhah and Jewish Thought in*

Honor of Rav Menahem Immanuel Rackman on His 80th Birthday, ed. Moshe Beer (Ramat Gan, Israel: Bar-Ilan University, 1994), 130.

3. The promise is in reverse order in the decalogue; see the discussion in chapter 2 of this volume.

4. Yair Hoffman, "The Segulah of Shiluach HaKan," *Yeshiva World* (blog), September 18, 2016, www.theyeshivaworld.com/news/headlines-breaking-stories/464072/464072.html.

5. "Shiluach Haken 4 AV 5779," YouTube, August 5, 2019, www.youtube.com/watch?v=dBx7mu-HKf8.

6. Babylonian Talmud Hullin 139b.

7. On this type of rhetorical question in midrash, see Azzan Yadin-Israel, *Scripture and Tradition: Rabbi Akiva and the Triumph of Midrash* (Philadelphia: University of Pennsylvania Press, 2014), 53–55.

8. See Slifkin, "Shiluach haKein," 17–18

9. Tabory, "Shiluah ha-Ken," 133–41; Slifkin, "Shiluach haKein," 17–20, 26–31, 36; David Mevorach Seidenberg, "Sending the Mother Bird: A Window into the Soul of Judaism," *Times of Israel* (blog), https://blogs.timesofisrael.com/sending-the-mother-bird-a-window-into-the-soul-of-judaism/, 8. For a contemporary legal handbook on the mitzvah, see Naftali Weinberger, *A Practical Guide to the Mitzvah of Shiluach Hakan* (Jerusalem: Feldheim, 2007).

10. Matthew Calarco, "Being Toward Meat: Anthropocentrism, Indistinction, and Veganism," *Dialectical Anthropology* 38, no. 4 (2014): 415–29; Matthew Calarco, *Thinking Through Animals: Identity, Difference, Indistinction* (Palo Alto, CA: Stanford University Press, 2015), 48–69. My formulation here echoes the thinking of Ibram X. Kendi's distinction between nonracism and antiracism; see *How to Be an Antiracist* (New York: Random House, 2019).

11. Calarco, "Being Toward Meat," 423.

12. Calarco, *Thinking Through Animals*, 51.

13. See the discussion in chapter 2 of this volume.

14. Tosefta Hullin 10:16.

15. The Mishnah (12:5) is, by contrast, unrelentingly positive: "If in respect of so light a commandment, which deals with that which is worth but an issar, the Torah said, 'In order that you may fare well and have a long life,' how much more [must be the reward] for the observance of the more difficult commandments in the Torah!"

16. Hullin 142a. The manuscripts (Munich 95; Vatican 121, 122, 123b) abridge the tradition, omitting the tragic anecdote as well as the subsequent exchange.

17. On the figure of Elisha ben Abuya, see Alon Goshen-Gottstein, *The Sinner and the Amnesiac: The Rabbinic Invention of Elisha Ben Abuya and Eleazar Ben Arach* (Stanford, CA: Stanford University Press, 2000).

18. Penelope Green, "Twigitecture: Building Human Nests," *New York Times*, June 19, 2013, sec. Home and Garden, www.nytimes.com/2013/06/20/garden/twigitecture-building-human-nests.html.

19. Janine M. Benyus, *Biomimicry: Innovation Inspired by Nature* (New York: Perennial, 2002).

20. Green, "Twigitecture"; Hannah Waters, "Live Like a Bird in This Nest-Inspired Apartment," Audubon, January 13, 2016, www.audubon.org/news/live-bird-nest-inspired-apartment; "4 Nest-Inspired Designs for Humans," Inhabitat, https://inhabitat.com/4-nest-inspired-designs-for-humans/.

21. Peter Goodfellow, *Avian Architecture: How Birds Design, Engineer and Build* (Princeton: Princeton University Press, 2011).

22. Cited in Hullin 139b.

23. Goodfellow, *Avian Architecture*, 21, 29, 79. Steinsaltz's commentary explains that a pit is narrow and circular, a ditch is long and narrow, and a cave resembles a pit with a roof. Adin Steinsaltz, *Koren Talmud Bavli: The Noé Edition*, Hullin Part 2 (Jerusalem: Koren, 2016), 397.

24. Hullin 139b. Munich 95 and other Talmud manuscripts have *borot* (pits) instead of *birot* (buildings), making it more similar to the Tosefta. Munich 95 and other manuscripts add "and birds" *(ve-tziporim)* after mentioning the two types of pigeons.

25. Hullin 139b.

26. See, for example, the pied-billed grebe's aquatic nest in Goodfellow, *Avian Architecture*, 47.

27. Goodfellow, *Avian Architecture*, 46.

28. See the white stork nest in Goodfellow, *Avian Architecture*, 45, and the baya weaver's nest woven from live grasses on page 100.

29. Hullin 140b.

30. On the figure of Rabbi Yirmiyah and his questions, see Sarah Wolf, "'Haven't I Told You Not to Take Yourself Outside of the Law?': Rabbi Yirmiyah and the Characterization of a Scholastic," *AJS Review* 44, no. 2 (2020): 384–410. On nest-building techniques, see Nicholas E. Collias and Elsie C. Collias, *Nest Building and Bird Behavior* (Princeton University Press, 2014), 164–90.

31. Tim H. Clutton-Brock, *The Evolution of Parental Care* (Princeton: Princeton University Press, 1991), 132.

32. Sigal Balshine, "Patterns of Parental Care in Vertebrates," in *The Evolution of Parental Care*, ed. Nick J. Royle et al. (Oxford: Oxford University Press, 2012), 71. See also Natalie Angier, "Paternal Bonds, Special and Strange," *New York Times*, June 14, 2010, sec. Science, www.nytimes.com/2010/06/15/science/15fath.html.

33. T. Clutton-Brock, *Evolution of Parental Care*, 135.

34. Yehuda Feliks, *Ha-Hai ba-Mishnah* (Jerusalem: Institute for Mishna Research, 1982), 148–49. See also Philip J. K. McGowan and Guy M. Kirwan,

"Sand Partridge *(Ammoperdix heyi)*," in *Birds of the World*, ed. Josep del Hoyo et al. (Ithaca, NY: Cornell Lab of Ornithology, 2020); parallels in Sifre Deuteronomy 228 and Tosefta Hullin 10:9.

35. Curiously, the Cornell Lab of Ornithology site (McGowan and Kirwan, "Sand Partridge") describes sand partridges as practicing female-only incubation.

36. Mishnah Hullin 12:3. Parallels in Sifre Deuteronomy 227 and Tosefta Hullin 10:11.

37. Hullin 140b.

38. *D-g-r* in Aramaic refers to "gathering together as a brood" or "heaping together"; see Brown, *English Lexicon*, 186.

39. On the identification of the *kipoz*, see Menahem Dor, *Ha-Ḥai Bi-Yeme Ha-Miḳra, Ha-Mishnah Veha-Talmud* (Tel-Aviv: Sifre Grafor-Daftal, 1997), 110–11. Dor identifies the reference in Isaiah 34:15 as a European eagle owl.

40. Hullin 140b; Tosefta Hullin 10:9.

41. Hullin 140b. On the destabilizing character of Rabbi Yirmiyah's questions, see Wolf, "Haven't I Told You?" Ilan reads the question about the bird father being ridden by the female as comic; see Tal Ilan, *Massekhet Hullin: Text, Translation, and Commentary* (Tübingen, Germany: Mohr Siebeck, 2017), 606–8.

42. Walter D. Koenig and Janis L. Dickinson, eds., *Cooperative Breeding in Vertebrates* (New York: Cambridge University Press, 2016), 1; Alexander Frank Skutch, *Helpers at Birds' Nests: A Worldwide Survey of Cooperative Breeding and Related Behavior* (Iowa City: University of Iowa Press, 1999).

43. The classic study is Nick B. Davies and Michael de L. Brooke, "Cuckoos Versus Reed Warblers: Adaptations and Counteradaptations," *Animal Behaviour* 36, no. 1 (1988): 262–84. On the impact of this work and new directions, see Mary Caswell Stoddard and Rebecca M. Kilner, "The Past, Present and Future of 'Cuckoos Versus Reed Warblers,'" *Animal Behaviour* 85, no. 4 (2013): 693–99.

44. Mishnah Hullin 12:2.

45. Sifre Deuteronomy 227.

46. Tosefta Hullin 10:10.

47. Hullin 140b.

48. A *tasil* is a species similar to a pigeon, mentioned also in Hullin 62b.

49. In Munich 95: "Perhaps it is a female *qore!*"

50. The rabbinic nest speaks to the project of challenging "monomaternalism" articulated in Shelley M. Park, *Mothering Queerly, Queering Motherhood: Resisting Monomaternalism in Adoptive, Lesbian, Blended, and Polygamous Families* (Albany: State University of New York Press, 2013), 1.

51. On morality in other species, see Frans B. M. de Waal, *Good Natured: The Origins of Right and Wrong in Humans and Other Animals* (Cambridge, MA:

Harvard University Press, 1996); and Marc Bekoff, *Wild Justice: The Moral Lives of Animals* (Chicago: University of Chicago Press, 2009).

52. Michael Double and Andrew Cockburn, "Pre-dawn Infidelity: Females Control Extra-Pair Mating in Superb Fairy-Wrens," *Proceedings of the Royal Society of London: Series B; Biological Sciences* 267, no. 1442 (2000): 465–70.

53. Andrew Cockburn, "Evolution of Helping Behavior in Cooperatively Breeding Birds," *Annual Review of Ecology and Systematics* 29, no. 1 (1998): 141–77.

54. Sarah Blaffer Hrdy, *Mothers and Others: The Evolutionary Origins of Mutual Understanding* (Cambridge, MA: Harvard University Press, 2009), 191.

55. See Mishnah Nazir 4:3 and Tosefta Makkot 3:10.

56. The *moredet* and *mored* of Mishnah Ketubbot 5:7 are formulated with the same Hebrew root *m-r-d*. On these categories, see the discussion in Ruth Roded, "Islamic and Jewish Religious Feminists Tackle Islamic and Jewish Oral Law: Maintenance and Rebellion of Wives," *Comparative Islamic Studies* 11, no. 1 (2017): 35–63. See Hullin 139a–b for further references to rebelling birds.

57. Hullin 138b–39a. Some manuscripts omit "pure."

58. See my discussion of animal trials in Beth A. Berkowitz, *Animals and Animality in the Babylonian Talmud* (New York: Cambridge University Press, 2018), 63–88.

59. Darren Naish, "How Dangerous Are Cassowaries, Really?," *Scientific American Blog Network*, https://blogs.scientificamerican.com/tetrapod-zoology/how-dangerous-are-cassowaries-really/; Liam Stack, "A Giant Bird Killed Its Owner. Now It Could Be Yours," *New York Times*, April 24, 2019, www.nytimes.com/2019/04/24/us/cassowary-bird-florida.html; *Encyclopedia Britannica*, "6 of the World's Most Dangerous Birds," www.britannica.com/list/6-of-the-worlds-most-dangerous-birds.

60. See Feliks, *Ha-Hai ba-Mishnah*, 72–73.

61. Hullin 139b. The motif of sixteen rows appears also in Hullin 60b, where an obscure biblical people called Avvim are described as possessing sixteen rows of teeth. In both texts the number "sixteen" connotes a multitude in a grotesque and comical way. Sixteen is also used to signify averageness: the average width of a thoroughfare (Mishnah Bava Batra 6:7); the average distance a person can walk (Pesahim 94a); and the average number of meals eaten per week (Shabbat 118a).

The version in Munich 95 is more difficult to parse: "There was one who did not know. He said to his companion, 'Blind one, my master, my slave.' They brought her and slaughtered her." The version in Vatican 121 (and Vatican 122 is similar) makes more sense: "There was one who did not know to say it. Her companion said to her, 'Blind one, my master, my master.' She said, 'Blind one, my master, *kiri*.' They brought her and slaughtered her." *Kiri* is likely the word intended, but the printed version uses *biri*. See Eruvin 53b, whose subject is confusion about this word; see also Michael Sokoloff, *A Dictionary of Jewish Babylonian Aramaic of the Talmudic and Geonic Periods* (Baltimore: Johns Hopkins University Press, 2002), 578.

62. For a discussion, see Jeffrey L. Rubenstein, *Rabbinic Stories* (Mahwah, NJ: Paulist, 2002), 33–37; Yonatan Feintuch, "External Appearance Versus Internal Truth: The Aggadah of Herod in Bavli Bava Batra," *AJS Review* 35, no. 1 (2011): 85–104; and Jeffrey L. Rubenstein, "King Herod in Ardashir's Court: The Rabbinic Story of Herod (B. Bava Batra 3b–4a) in Light of Persian Sources," *AJS Review* 38, no. 2 (2014): 249–74.

63. The theme of blindness that is prominent in the original story is evoked here too in the birds' exchanges with each other. See Feintuch, "External Appearance." There is irony in Hullin's use of the theme given birds' keen vision. See Tim Birkhead, *Bird Sense: What It's Like to Be a Bird* (London: A&C Black, 2013), 1–32.

64. Ilan offers a gendered reading of the rebellion—the dove is female—in Ilan, *Massekhet Hullin*, 601–5.

65. Jason Hribal, *Fear of the Animal Planet: The Hidden History of Animal Resistance* (Oakland, CA: AK Press, 2010), 25–26.

66. Hullin 139b. Munich 95 features Rav Pappa, not Mattana, no doubt due to the similarity of Pappa to Pappunya.

67. On the Pappunyans, see also Bava Kamma 54b, where they appear in another discussion of entanglements between animals and people, this one addressing a variety of scriptural commandments related to animals. The Bava Kamma passage asks explicitly who the Pappunyans are and answers (unpersuasively) that the term refers to a single Rabbi, Rav Aha bar Yaakov (see also Kiddushin 35a). They appear as unsavory characters in Bava Kamma 115a, where a Pappunyan is part of a money-laundering scheme. See the discussion of Pappunya in Aharon Oppenheimer, *Babylonia Judaica in the Talmudic Period*, Beihefte Zum Tübinger Atlas Des Vorderen Orients (Wiesbaden, Germany: Reichert, 1983), 340–44.

68. Calarco, "Being Toward Meat," 422.

69. Calarco, 416.

6. ANIMAL ORPHANS

1. Ilan argues that the Mishnah's grouping of these laws in Hullin indicates that the Rabbis attribute to them a common moral principle related to parent-offspring relationships among animals, but the argument does not account for why the fourth law is not also treated and why other animal laws not having to do with parent-child relationships are. Tal Ilan, *Massekhet Hullin: Text, Translation, and Commentary* (Tübingen, Germany: Mohr Siebeck, 2017), 74.

2. Mekhilta de-Rashbi Tractate Nezikin on Exodus 22:21: "Why does Scripture state, 'widow or orphan' (Exod. 22:21)? [God is saying,] 'I will be quick to exact punishment on behalf of the widow and orphan more than for any person! For the wife receives [support] from her husband, and the child receives [support] from his father. But these have no one who will support them, except for Me alone!" Translation from W. David Nelson, ed., *Mekhilta De-Rabbi Shimon Bar Yoḥai* (Philadelphia: Jewish Publication Society, 2006), 249.

3. For a discussion, see Marjorie Garber, "Good to Think With," *Profession* (2008): 11–20.

4. On the Mishnah's relationship to scripture and its "commandment-based orientation," see Tzvi Michael Novick, "The Mishnah and the Bible," in *What Is the Mishnah? The State of the Question*, ed. Shaye J. D. Cohen, Jewish Law and Culture Series (Cambridge, MA: Harvard University Press, 2023), 3–22.

5. Mishnah Zevahim 14:2–3. Mekhilta de-Rabbi Yishmael Tractate Kaspa 19 establishes that the term *mehusar zeman* (lacking time) describes the baby animal in Exodus 22:29, though the Mishnah never itself defines the term that way. H. Saul Horovitz and Israel Abraham Rabin, eds., *Mechilta d'Rabbi Ismael* (Jerusalem: Wahrmann Books, 1970), 320.

6. The standard printed edition of the Mishnah presents a rabbinic consensus about exemptions.

7. For the treatment of time in early rabbinic literature, see Sarit Kattan Gribetz, *Time and Difference in Rabbinic Judaism* (Princeton: Princeton University Press, 2020). On sacrifice in early rabbinic literature, see Mira Balberg, *Blood for Thought: The Reinvention of Sacrifice in Early Rabbinic Literature* (Berkeley: University of California Press, 2017).

8. Mishnah Bekhorot 9:4. In the printed edition: "All enter *the fold (la-dir)* to be tithed." On the term "one who emerges from the side" and its relationship to the term orphan, see Ilan, *Massekhet Hullin*, 210–11. In many if not all cases the infant born from a C-section would presumably also be an orphan since the C-section reflects dire circumstances during delivery and a surgery from which the mother animal would not likely have been able to recover. See also the translation in Chaya Halberstam, "Tractate Bekhorot," in *The Oxford Annotated Mishnah: A New Translation of the Mishnah*, ed. Shaye J. D. Cohen et al., 3 vols. (New York: Oxford University Press, 2022), 3:209. Mishnah Bekhorot Chapter Nine begins with the same structure of binary legal applications—of in/outside the land of Israel; Temple/no Temple; meat/sacrifice—that launches the series of chapters in Mishnah Hullin, starting with Chapter Five, dealing with animal law. The common structure suggests that the Mishnah considers them connected and means to impress that connection on the audience.

9. The Kaufmann manuscript scribe fills in the other categories in a marginal note. In a parallel passage in Tosefta Bekhorot 7:3, the categories all appear, but they are split. The first two, mixed species and the *terefah*, are ascribed to Rabbi

Joshua, while Rabbi Akiva is said to exempt the C-section, the one lacking time, and the orphan. Later on Rabbi Shimon is said to disagree in the case of the one lacking time, who in his opinion should be included in the tithe.

10. Sifra Emor Parashah 8 Perek 7; Isaac Hirsch Weiss, ed., *Sifra Deve Rav: Hu Sefer Torat Kohanim* (New York: Om, 1946), 99. See also Bekhorot 57a.

11. The categories are the same in the Mishnah and the Sifra with the exception of the one "who resembles" *(nidmeh)*, which appears in the Sifra (though not in Vatican manuscript 66) but not in the Mishnah, and the *terefah*, which appears in the Mishnah but not in the Sifra.

12. Azzan Yadin-Israel's approach to the Akivan school of exegesis is that it is a form of "midrashic camouflage" with little serious effort made to anchor the reading convincingly in scripture. See *Scripture and Tradition: Rabbi Akiva and the Triumph of Midrash* (Philadelphia: University of Pennsylvania Press, 2014).

13. Oddly, Mishnah Zevahim never explicitly disqualifies the orphan animal from sacrifice even though midrash halakhah shows the tithe disqualification to be based on the sacrifice disqualification. See the extensive discussion by Ovadiah Bartenura in Mishnah Bekhorot 9:4, entry *"ve-yatom."*

14. According to the Tosefta, the disqualifications from tithes are Rabbi Akiva's view.

15. Mishnah Bekhorot 9:4. The formulation of this Mishnah in the Babylonian Talmud seems to be influenced by Hullin 38b: "or has been slaughtered and afterwards gave birth." In Mishneh Torah, Laws of Things Forbidden on the Altar 3:4, Maimonides follows this formulation, omitting the natural-death scenario, as does Rabbi Joshua in the Mishnah itself. The Mishnah's definition of an animal orphan is absent from the parallel Tosefta Bekhorot 7:6, which defines the other categories (the mixed-breed, the animal born from a C-section, and the infant in the first week of life), but not the orphan.

16. See Mekhilta de-Rabbi Shimon bar Yohai on Exodus 22:21, only in the manuscript of the Hoffmann edition; see David Hoffmann, ed., *Mekhilta De-Rabi Shim'on Ben Yoḥai 'al Sefer Shemot* (Frankfurt: Kaufmann, 1905), 150. See also Olympia Bobou: "In the Greco-Roman world, an orphan was any child who had lost a parent, especially his or her father. Only from the time of Justinian did the term signify a child who had lost both parents." "Orphans," *The Encyclopedia of Ancient History*, 2012, https://doi.org/10.1002/9781444338386.wbeah22213. See also John T. Fitzgerald, "Orphans in Mediterranean Antiquity and Early Christianity," *Acta Theologica* 36 (January 2016): 29–48.

17. Maia Kotrosits's question is apt here: "So the question is not only, How does objectification happen? It is also . . . what is happening when one carves up or cordons off dimensions of that forest of elements composing selfhood into distinguishable parts—a mouth from its voice, the voice from its speaker, the flesh from that which keeps its warm"? *The Lives of Objects: Material Culture,*

Experience, and the Real in the History of Early Christianity (Chicago: University of Chicago Press, 2020), 14.

18. See Mishnah Makhshirin 5:6 and Shabbat 4:2. Mishnah Avodah Zarah 2:7 uses the term in a conceptually similar way to refer to an olive stripped of its skin.

19. Bekhorot 57b. The Rabbi's name in the Oxford manuscript is Rabbi Yehoshua ben Satriel. In Vatican 119 it is Rabbi Yishmael ben Baterah.

20. Rashi: "Since the skin benefits the baby, he is like one whose mother exists." In a manuscript variant of Rashi, he explains that the skin is intended to warm the infant, an observation many other Mishnah and Talmud commentators also make.

21. See Donna Haraway, "Teddy Bear Patriarchy: Taxidermy in the Garden of Eden, New York City, 1908–1936," *Social Text*, no. 11 (January 1984): 20; and Steve Baker, *The Postmodern Animal* (London: Reaktion, 2000).

22. Jane Desmond, "Vivacious Remains: An Afterword on Taxidermy's Forms, Fictions, Facticity, and Futures," *Configurations* 27, no. 2 (2019): 261.

23. Baker, *Postmodern Animal*, is discussed in Helen Gregory and Anthony Purdy, "Present Signs, Dead Things: Indexical Authenticity and Taxidermy's Nonabsent Animal," *Configurations* 23, no. 1 (2015): 71.

24. Gregory and Purdy, 61, 64.

25. This testament can be seen in the cowhide in artist Nandipha Mntambo's 2013 work *Umfanekiso wesibuko (Mirror Image)*, reshaped into the form of a female human body. See Giovanni Aloi, "Speculative Taxidermy: Inscribing Vulnerability," *Configurations* 27, no. 2 (2019): 200–202.

26. Gregory and Purdy, "Present Signs," 73.

27. For this formulation, see Caroline Galambosova, "From Specimen to Contemporary Taxidermy," *DailyArt Magazine* (blog), January 29, 2024, www.dailyartmagazine.com/taxidermy-in-art/.

28. On the similarities between taxidermy and relics, see Gregory and Purdy, "Present Signs," 63. On the similarities between taxidermy and souvenirs, see Rachel Poliquin, *The Breathless Zoo: Taxidermy and the Cultures of Longing* (University Park: Pennsylvania State University Press, 2012), 7–8.

29. One might make the inference from Rabbi's response that before he heard this testimony he did not understand his own Mishnah! See the discussion of this passage's implications for Rabbi's editing of the Mishnah as well as the Talmudic portrayal of him in Jacob Nahum Epstein, *Mevo'ot Le-Sifrut Ha-Tana'im: Mishnah, Tosefta u-Midreshe Halakhah* [Introduction to the literature of the Tannaim: Mishnah, Tosefta, and Midrash Halakhah] (Tel Aviv: Devir, 1957), 188; Ezra Zion Melamed, *Pirke Mavo Le-Sifrut Ha-Talmud* [Introductory chapters to the literature of the Talmud] (Jerusalem, 1973), 119; and Ofra Meir, *Rabbi Yehudah Ha-Nasi: Deyokano shel Manhig be-Masorot Eretz-Yisrael u-Vavel* [Rabbi Judah the patriarch: Portrait of a leader in the traditions of the land of Israel and Babylonia] (Tel-Aviv: Ha-Kibbutz ha-Me'uḥad, 1999), 204.

30. See, for example, the magical divorce decree of M103 in Dan Levene, *A Corpus of Magic Bowls: Incantation Texts in Jewish Aramaic from Late Antiquity* (London: Kegan Paul, 2003), 51.

31. On the genre of rabbinic folklore, see Galit Hasan-Rokem and Haim Weiss, "Folklore in Antiquity," *Humanities* 7, no. 2 (2018): 47.

32. Other variants are Caesarea Arca and Caesarea ad Libanum. See Pinchas Neaman, *Encyclopedia of Talmudical Geography* (Tel Aviv: Chachik, 1972), 2:301–2. The entry is spelled with aleph in Marcus Jastrow, "Dictionary of the Targumim, the Talmud Babli and Yerushalmi, and the Midrashic Literature," Tyndale Archive, 125, www.tyndalearchive.com/TABS/Jastrow/.

33. See Neaman, *Encyclopedia of Talmudical Geography*, who says that Arqa is mentioned in the list of cities conquered by Thutmose III and in the Amarna letters.

34. Genesis Rabbah 37:8.

35. *Jewish War* 7:97; Flavius Josephus, *The Jewish War*, trans. Henry St. J. Thackeray, Loeb Classical Library 210 (Cambridge: Harvard University Press, 1928), 3:336–37.

36. Bekhorot 57b. On the *beit ha-meses*, or omasum, as the stomach of a ruminant, see Mishnah Hullin 3:1–2. The omasum is absent from the Oxford, London, and Vatican 120 manuscripts: "The lettuces in our locale have 600,000 leaves on them." Munich and Florence omit the word "leaves" as well: "The lettuces in our locale have 600,000 on them." The standard printed version with omasum would seem to be a more hyperbolic form since it describes the lettuces as having 600,000 leaves just in its core. At this point most of the manuscripts (Munich, Florence, London, Oxford, and Vatican 120) have an additional section describing giant mosquitoes very similar to the one about lettuces. This is the Munich manuscript version: "Mosquitoes *(yitushin)* in our locale have 600,000 on them, in its omasum." London and Oxford use the word for "leaves" *(kelafim)* that describes lettuce leaves in the previous section. That word can also refer to scales or scabs, suggesting an image of mosquitoes with an enormous number of wings.

37. Dan Ben-Amos, "Talmudic Tall-Tales," in *Folklore Today: A Festschrift for Richard M. Dorson*, ed. Richard M. Dorson et al. (Bloomington: Research Center for Language and Semiotic Studies, Indiana University, 1976), 35.

38. On the Ketubbot passage, see Jeffrey L. Rubenstein, "Grappling with the Merits of the Land of Israel: Analysis of the Sugya in BT Ketubot 110a–112b," in *Center and Diaspora: The Land of Israel and the Diasporas in the Period of the Second Temple, the Mishnah, and the Talmud [Merkaz u-Tefutsah: Erets Yisra'el ve-ha-Tefutsot be-Yeme Bayit Sheni, ha-Mishnah ve-ha-Talmud]*, ed. Isaiah Gafni (Jerusalem: Zalman Shazar Center, 2004), 159–88.

39. Deuteronomy 3:4 is likely the origin of the sixty-cities motif, which appears also in Kiddushin 66a.

40. Fans of *Game of Thrones* might consider also the colossal sculpture *(Titan of Braavos)* through which Arya enters the port of Braavos, an island where one could say that she is put in her place as she trains to be a "faceless man." "The House of Black and White," *Game of Thrones* (New York: HBO, 2015).

41. Herbert Marcuse, interview with Stuart Wrede, *Perspecta* 12 (1969): 75; Beth Py-Lieberman and Attilio Maranzano, "The Really Big Art of Claes Oldenburg," *Smithsonian* 26, no. 5 (1995): 78.

42. The human body as a method of measure is "one of the oldest and most solid notions." See Joan Kee and Emanuele Lugli, "Scale to Size: An Introduction," *Art History* 38, no. 2 (2015): 251, quoting Gregoire Muller. See pages 254–55 on Derrida's preference for the term "colossal" over "monumental," the more common term in art criticism, because of the association of "colossal" with transhuman dimensions.

43. Consider also the Gospel of Peter's giant Jesus, treated by Kotrosits, *Lives of Objects*, 27–28.

44. Ben-Amos details a structure common to Talmudic tall tales, according to which the phenomena described become increasingly implausible and then are capped by an ironic coda that contracts the narrative exaggeration ("Talmudic Tall-Tales," 35–40).

45. Kee and Lugli, "Scale to Size," 252.

46. The aim in Yoma 80a is to determine measurements by egg bulk, and the problem is the variability of egg size, with the *bar yokhani* representing the large end of the spectrum. In the parallel in Sukkah 5a, the measurement is of the thickness of the ark cover, and the basis is face size, but the principle is the same. The *bar yokhani* is invoked to contest rough measurements by analogy.

47. Pliny the Elder, *The Natural History*, www.perseus.tufts.edu/hopper/text?doc=urn:cts:latinLit:phi0978.phi001.perseus-eng1:10.1.

48. That being said, the portrait in Bekhorot of the *bar yokhani* weaponizing her large eggs bears echoes of Pliny's ostrich, who likewise is described as an aggressive creature prone to throwing things at people.

49. In Pahlavi texts the simorg nests on a tree whose shoots drop seeds that rain down on the earth and form its plant life. In the Rivayat accompanying the Dadestan i Denig, the simorg also plays a cosmos-creating role. In the Bundahisn, the simorg is destructive, causing the tree on which the nest rests to wither. The Bundahisn pairs the simorg with the kamak, who causes drought and death and devours men and animals, and the sen bird, who seems closer to a real bird, perhaps the ostrich, black vulture, or golden eagle. See Hanns-Peter Schmidt, "Simorg," *Encyclopaedia Iranica*, July 20, 2002, https://iranicaonline.org/articles/simorg; Reuven Kiperwasser and Dan D. Y. Shapira, "Irano-Talmudica II: Leviathan, Behemoth and the 'Domestication' of Iranian Mythological Creatures in Eschatological Narratives of the Babylonian Talmud," in *Shoshannat Yaakov: Jewish and Iranian Studies in Honor of Yaakov Elman*, ed. Shai Secunda and

Steven Fine (Leiden: Brill, 2012), 209, 212–13; and Kiperwasser and Shapira, "Irano-Talmudica III: Giant Mythological Creatures in Transition from the Avesta to the Babylonian Talmud," in *Orality and Textuality in the Iranian World*, ed. Julia Rubanovich (Leiden: Brill, 2015), 63–92. The key section from the Bundahisn—Chapter 24—is found in translation in Domenico Agostini and Samuel Thrope, eds., *The Bundahišn: A New Translation* (New York: Oxford University Press, 2020), 120–24.

50. Christa A. Tuczay, "Motifs in The Arabian Nights and in Ancient and Medieval European Literature: A Comparison," *Folklore* 116, no. 3 (2005): 276.

51. Daniel J. Frim, "'Those Who Descend upon the Sea Told Me...': Myth and Tall Tale in Baba Batra 73a–74b," *Jewish Quarterly Review* 107, no. 1 (2017): 28–29.

52. On demonic eggs, see Joseph Naveh and Shaul Shaked, *Magic Spells and Formulae: Aramaic Incantations of Late Antiquity* (Jerusalem: Magnes, 1993), 127–30; and Siam Bhayro et al., *Aramaic Magic Bowls in the Vorderasiatisches Museum in Berlin: Descriptive List and Edition of Selected Texts* (Leiden: Brill, 2018), 60–61. Eggs are represented in the incantations as forces that threaten the client. On inscribed eggshells used for magical purposes, see Bhayro et al., *Aramaic Magic Bowls*, 66; and Ortal-Paz Saar, *Jewish Love Magic: From Late Antiquity to the Middle Ages* (Leiden: Brill, 2017), 101–8.

53. Bekhorot 57b. The text shifts at this point from Hebrew to Aramaic. Most manuscripts (Venice, Florence, London, Vatican) read *sharya* (is permitted) instead of *shadya* (throw), an understandable variant, given the similarity of the letters *resh* and *dalet*. Both versions presume that it goes against the nature of the *kenaf renanim* for her to drop the egg.

54. Arthur Walker-Jones, "The So-Called Ostrich in the God Speeches of the Book of Job (Job 39, 13–18)," *Biblica* 86, no. 4 (2005): 494–535.

55. Job's characterization of the ostrich is inaccurate. "This notion that the ostrich abandons all the eggs she lays and does not stay to hatch them is no more than ancient folk zoology"; see Robert Alter, ed., *The Wisdom Books: Job, Proverbs, and Ecclesiastes: A Translation with Commentary* (New York: Norton, 2010), 165. See Peter Goodfellow, *Avian Architecture: How Birds Design, Engineer and Build* (Princeton: Princeton University Press, 2011), 18: "It's normal for the major hen to incubate by day and the male by night. The nest is usually so clearly in the open that the daytime incubating bird often lies with its neck stretched out along the ground in order to be less conspicuous. The chicks begin calling one or more days before hatching, thus establishing close contact with their parents, who care for them for up to a year after hatching."

56. Alter, *Wisdom Books*, 168.

57. In Walker-Jones's reading, the Talmud's sympathetic depiction of the bird is more aligned with the original intended meaning in Job, which is that the

sandgrouse mother sacrifices her own safety to protect the nest; see "So-Called Ostrich."

58. Menahot 66b is an important intertext for understanding the Talmud's depiction of the bird. Using the exegetical method of *notariqon*, Menahot 66b takes the enigmatic verb *ne'elasah* in the Job verse to be a melding together of three Hebrew words: "And it says, 'The *kenaf renanim* rejoices *[ne'elasah]*' (Job 39:13). [The word *ne'elasah* is a combination of the words:] Carries *(nos'e)*, goes up *(oleh)*, and places down *(venit'hata)*. [The bird carries the egg, flies upward, and places the egg down.]" In this creative rendering of Job 39:13, the *kenaf renanim* bird "carries, goes up, and places down," presumably relocating the egg from one nest to another. (Moving eggs around from one nest to another is not something birds typically do, but ornithological realism may not be the point here; in a personal communication on May 26, 2021, evolutionary biologist Jon Regosin said that most birds don't or can't fly with their eggs and wouldn't know if an egg was unfertilized unless perhaps the others have hatched.) On *notariqon*, see Yonah Frenkel, *Darkhe Ha-Agadah Veha-Midrash* [Studies in hermeneutics of Aggadah and Midrash] (Givatayim, Israel: Yad LaTalmud, 1991), 125–32. Frenkel discusses this passage on page 129.

59. Some gender ambiguity, however, surrounds the bird in this story. I am presuming that the *bar yokhani* is female—the grammar of *shadya* is feminine, as is the grammar used for the *kenaf renanim* of Job—but the masculine *bar* in the name *bar yokhani* does point potentially to a masculine meaning. *Bar yokhani* may operate, alternatively, more as a proper noun that would apply to both females and males of the species.

60. Sokoloff translates *muzarta* here as rotten and associates it with the adjective *madur* (Sokoloff, *Dictionary of Jewish Babylonian Aramaic*, 646). In light of the shared nesting habits of ostriches—one "major" female hen incubates not only her own eggs but also those of "minor" hens (two minor hens on average) and sometimes discards the eggs of the minor hens—it is possible to read *muzarta* in this instance as being related to *zar* and *mamzer* and to translate it as "foreign" or "bastard." In Hullin Chapter Twelve, the Rabbis show clear awareness of brood parasitism. See my discussion in chapter 5.

61. According to Goodfellow, "Many eggs fail to hatch. On average, only one chick [out of up to fifty eggs] survives to adulthood, which illustrates the vulnerability of ground nesting"; see *Avian Architecture*, 19.

62. The language attributed to Rav Ashi, *muzarta*, associates rotten eggs with sexual imagery. In a purportedly early rabbinic teaching cited in Sanhedrin 82a, the biblical Zimri is said to have had sex so many times—sixty (like the number of cities destroyed by *bar yokhani*'s yolk!)—that he became like a rotten egg *(ke-vetzah ha-muzeret)*. Niddah 35b compares seminal discharge to a rotten egg. See Saar, *Jewish Love Magic*, on associations between bird eggs and human sexual intercourse.

63. Dan Ben-Amos observes that only one rabbinic passage, Bekhorot 8b, explicitly names the tall tale, and it does so in connection with a story about a mule giving birth, which is a biological rarity ("Talmudic Tall-Tales," 28). It is striking to me that when the tall tale is identified explicitly within the Talmud as a literary genre, it is associated with animal motherhood, a theme also in the materials I am discussing here.

64. Tosefta Bekhorot 7:10; Moses Samuel Zuckermandel, ed., *Tosephta: Based on the Erfurt and Vienna Codices [Tosefta al-pi Kitve-yad 'Erfurṭ Vinah]* (Jerusalem: Wahrman, 1970), 542; Bekhorot 58b.

65. Bekhorot 58b.

66. Orphans and purchased animals are noted to be exempt.

67. Bekhorot 53a.

68. Dina Stein, *Textual Mirrors: Reflexivity, Midrash, and the Rabbinic Self* (Philadelphia: University of Pennsylvania Press, 2012), 58. Stein is drawing on Georges Van den Abbeele, *Travel as Metaphor: From Montaigne to Rousseau* (Minneapolis: University of Minnesota Press, 1992), xiii.

CONCLUSION: WHAT FAMILIES TEACH US ABOUT ANIMALS

1. The Masoretic Text has "hemorrhoids" in the tradition for recitation but "tumors" in the consonantal written version. See Robert Alter, *The David Story: A Translation with Commentary of 1 and 2 Samuel* (New York: Norton, 1999), 7.

2. Playing with the verb that describes the cows going straight ahead *(va-yisharnah)*, a third-person plural feminine form rare in biblical Hebrew, rabbinic midrash imagines the cows singing while they walked. See Shimon Bar-Efrat, *Shemu'el im Mavo u-Ferush* [Samuel, with an introduction and commentary] (Jerusalem: Magnes, 1996), 108. The root is *y-sh-r*, but the Rabbis read it as based on the similar root *shir*—"they recited a song" (Genesis Rabbah 54:4; Babylonian Talmud Avodah Zarah 24b).

3. This repetition is observed in Robert Polzin, *Samuel and the Deuteronomist: 1 Samuel* (Bloomington: Indiana University Press, 1993), 67; and Bar-Efrat, *Shemu'el*, 108.

4. As Polzin writes, "It is through 'leaders' devoid of progeny that the ark and Israel eventually will be brought home. Dynastic leadership had lost Israel its proper place; nondynastic leadership will restore it"; see *Samuel and the Deuteronomist*, 67.

5. The cows are not only suppressing their maternal attachment as they march to Bet-shemesh but also heading straight to their death, seeing as they are sacrificed upon arrival, having themselves drawn the wood that will be used. See Jan

P. Fokkelman, *Narrative Art and Poetry in the Books of Samuel: A Full Interpretation Based on Stylistic and Structural Analyses* (Assen, Netherlands: Van Gorcum, 1981), 4:282.

On the connection of this scene to the earlier one with Hannah and the recurring theme in Samuel of nursing mothers yearning for their young, see Alter, *David Story*, 7, 32–33. Fokkelman connects the scene also to the one in 1 Samuel 4:19–22, in which Eli's daughter-in-law gives birth and then dies (*Narrative Art and Poetry*, 282–83). Maria J. Metzler connects the milch cows to other "afflicted wombs" in Samuel and in ancient Greek literature; "The Ark of the Covenant and Divine Rage in the Hebrew Bible" (PhD diss., Harvard University, 2016), 235–36. This scene featuring crying animal mothers is suggestive also for the role that affect theory might play in reading the Bible's animals; see Ken Stone, *Reading the Hebrew Bible with Animal Studies* (Palo Alto, CA: Stanford University Press, 2017); and Sébastien Doane, *Reading the Bible amid the Environmental Crisis: Interdisciplinary Insights to Ecological Hermeneutics* (Lanham, MD: Lexington Books, 2024).

6. "Succession: Official Website for the HBO Series," HBO, www.hbo.com/succession.

7. "The choice of the sacrificial animal strikes an odd little echo with the two milch cows sacrificed at the end of the Ark narrative and with the emphasis on nursing and weaning in Samuel's own infancy." Alter, *David Story*, 38.

8. Alter, xxiv.

9. These words are according to the Kaufmann manuscript.

10. Since Exodus 22:30 forbids eating an animal "torn *(terefah)* in the field," which is rabbinically understood to mean that the animal cannot have died of natural causes, the cow who dies in childbirth would become *traif*, or not kosher.

11. Rabbi Shimon Ha-Shezuri is Rabbi Shezuri in the standard printed edition, which also states eight years old instead of five.

12. In the parallel Tosefta Hullin 4:5, Rabbi Meir and the Sages also debate the liability for gifts to the priest treated in Hullin 10. In the Tosefta the Sages offer exegetical backing for their exemption.

13. Tosefta Hullin 4:6: "Rabbi Shimon Shezuri says: Even if it is standing and ploughing on the furrow." Rabbi Shimon Ha-Shezuri does not specify age in this version but implies it through the act of ploughing. Moses Samuel Zuckermandel, ed., *Tosephta: Based on the Erfurt and Vienna Codices [Tosefta al-pi Kitve-yad 'Erfurṭ Vinah]* (Jerusalem: Wahrman, 1970), 506.

14. Hullin 75b. The Venice printed edition mistakenly has Ravina instead of Rabbi Hanina. The Vatican 122 manuscript has Abaye transmitting Zeiri, which is probably a scribal mistake carrying over the name from Abaye's teaching immediately before.

15. The chronological and geographic spread of speakers in the discussion is wide, from first- to sixth-generation Rabbis, from both Palestine and Babylonia:

Rav Kahana (first- or second-generation Babylonian Amora), Zeiri (second-generation Babylonian Amora), Rabbi Hanina (first-generation Palestinian Amora), Rabbi Yohanan (second-generation Palestinian Amora), Abaye (fourth-generation Babylonian Amora), Rav Mesharshiya (fifth-generation Babylonian Amora), and Rav Ashi (sixth-generation Babylonian Amora). (I do not discuss the final three positions).

16. On the establishment of the law according to Shimon Ha-Shezuri here and elsewhere, see Tal Ilan, *Massekhet Hullin: Text, Translation, and Commentary* (Tübingen, Germany: Mohr Siebeck, 2017), 342–47.

17. For the exemption from prohibitions on the sciatic nerve and forbidden fat, see Hullin 74b, which also addresses whether the prohibition on consumption of its blood applies. For a thorough discussion of relevant Jewish legal sources, guided by an agenda to permit the ben pekuah, see Meir G. Rabi, "Ben PeKuAh: A New Approach," Academia, January 1, 2022, www.academia.edu/91733806/Ben_PeKuAh_A_New_Approach.

18. See the comment *"koro"* in Hullin 74a.

19. The root *p-k-a* means to "rupture" or "tear open": Michael Sokoloff, *A Dictionary of Jewish Babylonian Aramaic of the Talmudic and Geonic Periods* (Baltimore: Johns Hopkins University Press, 2002), 925. My speculation is that the phrase ben pekuah was inspired by Hosea 14:1, *ve-hariyotav yevuqa'u* ("and their women with child ripped open"), with the consonants bet and peh swapped. The term applies also to the previous case in the Mishnah, not discussed here, in which an eight-month-old fetus (i.e., not full term) is retrieved alive from its dying mother. That fetus, the anonymous Mishnah rules, does not require slaughter. One need only "tear it out and extract its blood" to make it kosher to consume.

20. Maimonides, Mishneh Torah, Forbidden Foods 5:14; Shulhan Arukh, Yoreh Deah 13:2–4. The Shulhan Arukh follows the position attributed to Rabbi Mesharshiya on Hullin 75b that if the ben pekuah mates with an animal born under typical circumstances, then even kosher slaughter does not make the offspring kosher.

21. Nomi Kaltmann, "Why Is This Meat Different from All Other Meat?," *Tablet Magazine*, March 18, 2021, www.tabletmag.com/sections/food/articles/ben-pekuah-meat-that-isnt-meat. As of 2021, the founder was looking to revive the company. On halakhic opposition to the initiative, see Yair Hoffman, "The New Commercially-Produced Ben P'Kuah Meat," *Yeshiva World* (blog), January 7, 2016, www.theyeshivaworld.com/news/headlines-breaking-stories/374628/the-new-commercially-produced-ben-pkuah-meat.html; Hoffman, "The Ben P'Kuah Meat Controversy Continues: Video from Rav Chaim Kanievsky," *Yeshiva World* (blog), January 13, 2016, www.theyeshivaworld.com/news/headlines-breaking-stories/376120/the-ben-pkuah-meat-controversy.html.

22. Kawit is sometimes spelled Kauit, and Deir al-Bahari is sometimes spelled Bahri. Cattle images were common in tomb chapels of pharaonic civilization.

See Patrick F. Houlihan, "Animals in Egyptian Art and Hieroglyphs," in *A History of the Animal World in the Ancient Near East*, ed. Billie Jean Collins (Leiden: Brill, 2002), 105–6; Douglas J. Brewer, "Cattle," in *The Oxford Encyclopedia of Ancient Egypt*, ed. Donald B. Redford (New York: Oxford University Press, 2001); *Sarcophagus of Kawit*, JF 47397, Ministry of Tourism and Antiquities, https://egymonuments.gov.eg/collections/kawit-sarcophagus-4/.

23. The two cows are clearly both meant to be females since they are depicted with udders, though they would appear to be of different breeds. See the section on "Egyptian Breeds" in Brewer, "Cattle."

24. The scene of a cow shedding tears while being milked, with her calf tied beside or to her, was something of a stock image in ancient Egypt. See the section on "Cattle Care" in Brewer, who adds that a series of sticks found at Amarna were thought to be used as muzzles designed to prevent the calf from drinking the mother's milk.

25. Tommy Kane and Sylvia Ugga, *Vegan Art: A Book of Visual Protest* (London: HENI, 2022).

26. Edouard Naville et al., *The XIth Dynasty Temple at Deir El-Bahari* (London: Egypt Exploration Fund, 1907), 1:55.

27. The far more common depiction in tomb chapels is of the binding, slaughtering, and butchering of cattle. See Houlihan, "Animals in Egyptian Art," 106. While ancient Egypt imagery could therefore be said to normalize or routinize the use of domesticated animals, there is also an intriguing tradition in ancient Egyptian art, though mostly of a later vintage, of satiric depictions of animals in which they imitate and parody human behavior and reverse typical power relations. See Patrick F. Houlihan, *Wit and Humour in Ancient Egypt* (London: Rubicon, 2001); Jennifer Miyuki Babcock, *Ancient Egyptian Animal Fables: Tree Climbing Hippos and Ennobled Mice* (Leiden: Brill, 2022).

28. Othmar Keel, *Das Böcklein in Der Milch Seiner Mutter und Verwandtes: Im Lichte Eines Altorientalischen Bildmotivs* (Freiburg, Göttingen: Universitätsverlag/Vandenhoeck und Ruprecht, 1980). Keel reproduces the Kawit image on page 49. See also Oded Borowski, *Every Living Thing: Daily Use of Animals in Ancient Israel* (Walnut Creek, CA: AltaMira, 1998), 77–79. A sidebar to a piece by Jacob Milgrom (written seemingly by the *Bible Review* editors) surveys the motif of the animal mother in ancient Mediterranean art, pointing to its popularity among ivory workers active in ninth-century-BCE Syro-Palestine. See "You Shall Not Boil a Kid in Its Mother's Milk," *Bible Review* (Washington, DC) 1, no. 3 (1985). In the case of the Egyptian image, the reference would be to the cow goddess Hathor since Kawit is described in the tomb as a priestess of Hathor.

29. I refer to images stored in Credo; see Credo Reference, ed., *Credo* (London: Credo Reference, n.d.). I have not found a comprehensive treatment of this visual motif. For the Chagall painting, see Marc Chagall, "A la Russie, aux ânes et

aux autres," Centre Pompidou, www.centrepompidou.fr/en/ressources/oeuvre/6WhG2F1.

30. Hibiscus Paws, "Teeny Tiny Chihuahua Pup Nursing," YouTube, July 14, 2017, www.youtube.com/watch?v=dmgvu98jOiU.

31. Dodo, "Mama Dog Who Lost Her Puppies Was Heartbroken Until She Got Kittens," YouTube, January 2, 2022, www.youtube.com/watch?v=ByF7swYddEQ.

32. Bava Kamma 5:1, 9:1; Bava Batra 5:3.

33. Shabbat 128b; Pesahim 112a; Ta'anit 16a; Ketubbot 49b; Bava Batra 80a; Bekhorot 24a.

34. Aelian, *On Animals:* storks (3.23); pigeons (3.45); cocks (4.29); donkeys (4.52); catfish (12.14); hares (13.12); elephants (7.36); Libyan cows (14.11); cows (6.10.ii); ants (6.43); mares (3.8, 6.48). These passages are pulled from my own review of Aelian; I have not seen any studies of this theme in his work.

35. Michael J. Curley, trans., *Physiologus* (Chicago: University of Chicago Press, 2009), 4, 9–10, 30. See discussion in Patricia Cox Miller, *In the Eye of the Animal: Zoological Imagination in Ancient Christianity* (Philadelphia: University of Pennsylvania Press, 2018), 29–31, 68–74.

36. *Videvdad* 13.2.12. See Maria Macuch, "On the Treatment of Animals in Zoroastrian Law," in *Iranica Selecta: Studies in Honour of Professor Wojciech Skalmowski on the Occasion of His Seventieth Birthday*, ed. Alois van Tongerloo (Turnhout, Belgium: Brepols, 2003), 183–86.

37. Gabriel Blanco et al., "Video: How Our Reporter Learned to Love Bats," *New York Times*, July 8, 2024, sec. Podcasts, www.nytimes.com/video/podcasts/100000009553674/how-our-reporter-learned-to-love-bats.html.

EPILOGUE: FIVE WAYS TO SUPPORT
ANIMAL FAMILIES

1. Tom Hesse, "How Birds Represent a Poetic Glimpse of Life in Denver," Colorado Public Radio, July 12, 2023, www.cpr.org/show-segment/how-birds-represent-a-poetic-glimpse-of-life-in-denver/.

2. Bava Metzia 85a. See discussion in Beth A. Berkowitz and Marion Katz, "The Cowering Calf and the Thirsty Dog: Narrating and Legislating Kindness to Animals in Jewish and Islamic Texts," in *Islamic and Jewish Legal Reasoning: Encountering Our Legal Other*, ed. Anver M. Emon (London: Oneworld, 2016), 89–97.

3. "Nature," Green-Wood, www.green-wood.com/nature/.

4. U.S. Fish and Wildlife Service, "To Feed or Not to Feed Wild Birds," June 9, 2021, www.fws.gov/story/feed-or-not-feed-wild-birds.

5. Angela Nelson, "New Study Is First to Find Exposure to Neurotoxic Rodenticide Bromethalin in Birds of Prey," Tufts Now, July 11, 2023, https://now.tufts

.edu/2023/07/11/new-study-first-find-exposure-neurotoxic-rodenticide-bromethalin-birds-prey.

6. Alene Tchekmedyian and Alexandra E. Petri, "'We're Inundated': Animal Shelters Across the U.S. Are Overflowing," *Los Angeles Times*, December 3, 2023, www.latimes.com/california/story/2023-12-03/animal-shelters-overflow.

7. "Our Pets Are Part of the Climate Problem: These Tips Can Help You Minimize Their Carbon Pawprints," CNN, www.cnn.com/2022/09/15/us/pets-climate-impact-lbg-wellness/index.html.

8. Lukasz Aleksandrowicz et al. "The Impacts of Dietary Change on Greenhouse Gas Emissions, Land Use, Water Use, and Health: A Systematic Review." *PloS One* 11, no. 11 (2016): e0165797.

9. See, for example, Center for Jewish Food Ethics, "A Sustainable Food System for All," www.jewishfoodethics.org.

10. Animal Legal Defense Fund, "Roadside Zoos: Small, Unaccredited Zoos Where Wild and Exotic Animals Suffer in Captivity," https://aldf.org/issue/roadside-zoos/. On the animals in *Tiger King*, see Vanessa Bateman, "'I'm in a Cage': A Historical Perspective on *Tiger King*'s Animals," in *"Tiger King": Murder, Mayhem and Madness: A Docalogue*, ed. Jaimie Baron and Kristen Fuhs (New York: Routledge, 2021), 81–96.

11. *Guidelines for Reintroductions and Other Conservation Translocations*, IUCN, 2013, https://portals.iucn.org/library/node/10386.

12. Humane Society of the United States, "Animal Cruelty Facts and Statistics," www.humanesociety.org/issues/abuse_neglect/facts/animal_cruelty_facts_statistics.html.

13. Leaping Bunny Program, "Compassionate Shopping Guide," www.leapingbunny.org/shopping-guide.

14. Nonhuman Rights Project, "Ways to Help," www.nonhumanrights.org/ways-to-help/.

15. U.S. National Park Service, "How Wildlife Are Responding to a Warming Climate," www.nps.gov/articles/000/aps-22-1-5.htm; Lucinda C. Aulsebrook et al., "Reproduction in a Polluted World: Implications for Wildlife," *Reproduction* 160, no. 2 (2020): 1470–626; Liam R. Dougherty et al. "A Systematic Map of Studies Testing the Relationship Between Temperature and Animal Reproduction," *Ecological Solutions and Evidence* 5, no. 1 (2024): e12303.

16. Blaise Martay et al., *Climate Change and Migratory Species: A Review of Impacts, Conservation Actions, Indicators and Ecosystem Services: Part 1, Impacts of Climate* (Peterborough, UK: Joint Nature Conservation Committee, 2023), 65.

17. Sarah Reid, "How to Be a Responsible Wildlife Tourist," *Lonely Planet*, March 7, 2022, www.lonelyplanet.com/articles/responsible-wildlife-tourism.

18. World Animal Protection, "Calling Out the Travel Companies Failing Wildlife," www.worldanimalprotection.org/our-campaigns/wildlife/commercial-exploitation/travel-tourism/the-real-responsible-traveller/.

Bibliography

"4 Nest-Inspired Designs for Humans." Inhabitat. https://inhabitat.com/4-nest-inspired-designs-for-humans/.

Abu El-Haj, Nadia. *The Genealogical Science: The Search for Jewish Origins and the Politics of Epistemology*. Chicago Studies in Practices of Meaning. Chicago: University of Chicago Press, 2012.

Adams, Carol J. "The Absent Referent." https://caroljadams.com/the-absent-referent.

———. *The Pornography of Meat*. New York: Bloomsbury, 2020.

———. *The Sexual Politics of Meat: A Feminist-Vegetarian Critical Theory*. New York: Bloomsbury USA, 2015.

Adamson, Peter. "Human and Animal Nature in the Philosophy of the Islamic World." In *Animals: A History*, edited by Peter Adamson and G. Fay Edwards, 91–114. New York: Oxford University Press, 2018.

Agostini, Domenico, and Samuel Thrope, eds. *The Bundahišn: A New Translation*. New York: Oxford University Press, 2020.

Albeck, Chanoch. *Mavo La-Mishnah* [Introduction to the Mishnah]. Jerusalem: Bialik Institute, 1960.

Aleksandrowicz, Lukasz, Rosemary Green, Edward J. M. Joy, Pete Smith, and Andy Haines. "The Impacts of Dietary Change on Greenhouse Gas Emissions, Land Use, Water Use, and Health: A Systematic Review." *PloS One* 11, no. 11 (2016): e0165797.

Alexander, Elizabeth Shanks. *Transmitting Mishnah: The Shaping Influence of Oral Tradition.* New York: Cambridge University Press, 2006.

Allport, Susan. *A Natural History of Parenting: From Emperor Penguins to Reluctant Ewes, a Naturalist Looks at Parenting in the Animal World and Ours.* New York: Harmony Books, 1997.

Aloi, Giovanni. "Speculative Taxidermy: Inscribing Vulnerability." *Configurations* 27, no. 2 (2019): 187–209.

Alon, Gedalia. *The Jews in Their Land in the Talmudic Age, 70–640 C.E.* 2 vols. Jerusalem: Magnes, 1980.

Alter, Robert. *The David Story: A Translation with Commentary of 1 and 2 Samuel.* New York: Norton, 1999.

———. *The Wisdom Books: Job, Proverbs, and Ecclesiastes: A Translation with Commentary.* New York: Norton, 2010.

Altmann, Jeanne. *Baboon Mothers and Infants.* Cambridge, MA: Harvard University Press, 1981.

Alwishah, Ahmed. "Avicenna on Animal Self-Awareness, Cognition and Identity." *Arabic Sciences and Philosophy: A Historical Journal* 26, no. 1 (2016): 73–96.

American Humane Society. "History." www.americanhumane.org/about-us/history/.

American Kennel Club. "AKC Pedigree: How to Purchase a Document on Your Dog's Lineage." www.akc.org/register/pedigree/.

Amit, Aaron. "The 'Halakhic Kernel' as a Criterion for Dating Babylonian Aggadah: Bavli Ḥullin 110a–b and Parallels." *AJS Review* 36, no. 2 (2012): 187–205.

Ancestry. "Searching Public Family Trees." https://support.ancestry.com/s/article/Searching-Public-Family-Trees?language=en_US.

Animal Legal Defense Fund. "Roadside Zoos: Small, Unaccredited Zoos Where Wild and Exotic Animals Suffer in Captivity." https://aldf.org/issue/roadside-zoos/.

Antler, Joyce. *You Never Call! You Never Write! A History of the Jewish Mother.* Oxford: Oxford University Press, 2007.

Aranoff, Deena. "Mother's Milk: Child-Rearing and the Production of Jewish Culture." *Journal of Jewish Identities* 12, no. 1 (2019): 1–17.

Asad, Talal. "Reflections on Violence, Law, and Humanitarianism." *Critical Inquiry* 41, no. 2 (2015): 390–427.

Aulsebrook, Lucinda C., Michael G. Bertram, Jake M. Martin, et al. "Reproduction in a Polluted World: Implications for Wildlife." *Reproduction* 160, no. 2 (2020): 1470–626.

Awabdy, Mark A. *Leviticus: A Commentary on Leueitikon in Codex Vaticanus.* Septuagint Commentary Series. Boston: Brill, 2019.

Babcock, Jennifer Miyuki. *Ancient Egyptian Animal Fables: Tree Climbing Hippos and Ennobled Mice.* Leiden: Brill, 2022.

Badham, Paul. "Do Animals Have Immortal Souls?" In *Animals on the Agenda: Questions About Animals for Theology and Ethics*, edited by Andrew Linzey and Dorothy Yamamoto, 181–89. Urbana: University of Illinois Press, 1998.
Baker, Steve. *The Postmodern Animal*. London: Reaktion, 2000.
Balberg, Mira. *Blood for Thought: The Reinvention of Sacrifice in Early Rabbinic Literature*. Berkeley: University of California Press, 2017.
Balcombe, Jonathan. *The Exultant Ark: A Pictorial Tour of Animal Pleasure*. Berkeley: University of California Press, 2011.
Balentine, Samuel E. *Leviticus*. Louisville, KY: Westminster John Knox Press, 2002.
Balshine, Sigal. "Patterns of Parental Care in Vertebrates." In Royle, Smiseth, and Kölliker, *Evolution of Parental Care*, 62–80.
Bar-Efrat, Shimon. *Shemu'el im Mavo u-Ferush* [Samuel, with an introduction and commentary]. Jerusalem: Magnes, 1996.
Barnwell, Ashley. "Convict Shame to Convict Chic: Intergenerational Memory and Family Histories." *Memory Studies* 12, no. 4 (2019): 398–411.
Bateman, Vanessa. "'I'm in a Cage': A Historical Perspective on *Tiger King*'s Animals." In *"Tiger King": Murder, Mayhem and Madness: A Docalogue*, edited by Jaimie Baron and Kristen Fuhs, 81–96. New York: Routledge, 2021.
Baumgarten, Elisheva. *Mothers and Children: Jewish Family Life in Medieval Europe*. Jews, Christians, and Muslims from the Ancient to the Modern World. Princeton: Princeton University Press, 2004.
Bazer, Fuller W. "History of Maternal Recognition of Pregnancy." In *Regulation of Implantation and Establishment of Pregnancy in Mammals: Tribute to 45 Year Anniversary of Roger V. Short's Maternal Recognition of Pregnancy*, edited by Fuller W. Bazer and Rodney D. Geisert, 5–25. New York: Springer Berlin Heidelberg, 2015.
Bazer, Fuller W., G. Cliff Lamb, and Guoyao Wu, eds. *Animal Agriculture: Sustainability, Challenges and Innovations*. London: Academic Press, 2020.
Beaver, Annabelle, Rebecca K. Meagher, Marina A. G. von Keyserlingk, and Daniel M. Weary. "Invited Review: A Systematic Review of the Effects of Early Separation on Dairy Cow and Calf Health." *Journal of Dairy Science* 102, no. 7 (2019): 5784–810.
Beer, Moshe. *Amora'e Bavel: Peraḳim Be-Ḥaye Ha-Kalkalah* [Babylonian Amoraim: Aspects of Economic Life]. Ramat Gan, Israel: Bar Ilan University Press, 1974.
Bekoff, Marc. *The Emotional Lives of Animals: A Leading Scientist Explores Animal Joy, Sorrow, and Empathy—and Why They Matter*. Novato, CA: New World Library, 2008.
———. *Wild Justice: The Moral Lives of Animals*. Chicago: University of Chicago Press, 2009.

Ben-Amos, Dan. "Talmudic Tall-Tales." In *Folklore Today: A Festschrift for Richard M. Dorson*, edited by Richard M. Dorson, Linda Dégh, Henry Glassie, and Felix J. Oinas, 25–43. Bloomington: Research Center for Language and Semiotic Studies, Indiana University, 1976.

Benjamin, Mara H. *The Obligated Self: Maternal Subjectivity and Jewish Thought*. Bloomington: Indiana University Press, 2018.

Benyus, Janine M. *Biomimicry: Innovation Inspired by Nature*. New York: Perennial, 2002.

Berkovitch, Nitza, and Shlomit Manor. "Between Familism and Neoliberalism: The Case of Jewish Israeli Grandmothers." *Feminist Theory*, February 28, 2022, 1–21.

Berkowitz, Beth A. *Animals and Animality in the Babylonian Talmud*. New York: Cambridge University Press, 2018.

———. "Interpretation in the Anthropocene: Reading the Animal Family Laws of the Pentateuch." In *Studies in the History of Exegesis*, edited by Mark Elliott, Raleigh C. Heth, and Angela Zautcke, 39–52. Tübingen, Germany: Mohr Siebeck, 2022.

———. "Jews and Animals." *Oxford Bibliographies in Jewish Studies*. https://www.oxfordbibliographies.com/display/document/obo-9780199840731/obo-9780199840731-0229.xml.

Berkowitz, Beth A., and Marion Katz. "The Cowering Calf and the Thirsty Dog: Narrating and Legislating Kindness to Animals in Jewish and Islamic Texts." In *Islamic and Jewish Legal Reasoning: Encountering Our Legal Other*, edited by Anver M. Emon, 61–111. London: Oneworld, 2016.

Bernstein, Moshe J. "The Employment and Interpretation of Scripture in 4QMMT: Preliminary Observations." In *Reading and Re-reading Scripture at Qumran*, 2:554–74. Leiden: Brill, 2013.

Berthelot, Katell. "Philo and Kindness Towards Animals (De Virtutibus 125-147)." *Studia Philonica Annual*, no. 14 (2002): 48–65.

Bhayro, Siam, James Nathan Ford, Dan Levene, et al. *Aramaic Magic Bowls in the Vorderasiatisches Museum in Berlin: Descriptive List and Edition of Selected Texts*. Leiden: Brill, 2018.

Birkhead, Tim. *Bird Sense: What It's Like to Be a Bird*. London: A&C Black, 2013.

Bleasdale, Madeleine, Kristine Richter, Anneke Janzen, et al. "Ancient Proteins Provide Evidence of Dairy Consumption in Eastern Africa." *Nature Communications* 12, no. 1 (2021): 632.

Bo, Federico Dal. *Massekhet Keritot*. Tübingen, Germany: Mohr Siebeck, 2013.

Bobou, Olympia. "Orphans." *The Encyclopedia of Ancient History*. 2012. https://doi.org/10.1002/9781444338386.wbeah22213.

Boissy, Alain, Gerhard Mantueffel, Morten Bakken, and Isabelle Veissier. "Assessment of Positive Emotions in Animals to Improve Their Welfare:

Stress and Welfare in Farm Animals." *Physiology and Behavior* 92, no. 3 (2007): 375–97.

Borowski, Oded. *Every Living Thing: Daily Use of Animals in Ancient Israel.* Walnut Creek, CA: AltaMira, 1998.

Bosworth, David Alan. *Infant Weeping in Akkadian, Hebrew, and Greek Literature.* Winona Lake, IN: Eisenbrauns, 2016.

Boyd, Samuel L. "Deuteronomy's Prodigal Son: Deut. 21:18–21 and the Agenda of the D Source." *Biblical Interpretation* 28, no. 1 (2020): 15–33.

Breed, Michael D. "Kin and Nestmate Recognition: The Influence of W. D. Hamilton on 50 Years of Research." *Animal Behaviour* 92 (June 2014): 271–79.

Breier, Idan. "Animals in Biblical and Ancient Near Eastern Law: Tort and Ethical Laws." *Journal of Animal Ethics* 8, no. 2 (2018): 166–81.

Brettler, Marc Zvi, and Adele Berlin, eds. *The Jewish Study Bible: Featuring the Jewish Publication Society Tanakh Translation.* New York: Oxford University Press, 2014.

Brewer, Douglas J. "Cattle." In *The Oxford Encyclopedia of Ancient Egypt*, edited by Donald B. Redford. New York: Oxford University Press, 2001.

Brown, Francis. *The Brown, Driver, Briggs Hebrew and English Lexicon.* Peabody, MA: Hendrickson, 1996.

"Bubby Does Shiluach Hakan." YouTube. July 6, 2018. www.youtube.com/watch?v=kdDD1f7B-bs.

Busch, Gesa, Daniel M. Weary, Achim Spiller, and Marina A. G. von Keyserlingk. "American and German Attitudes Towards Cow-Calf Separation on Dairy Farms." *PloS One* 12, no. 3 (2017): e0174013.

Calarco, Matthew. *Animal Studies: The Key Concepts.* London: Routledge/Taylor and Francis, 2021.

———. "Being Toward Meat: Anthropocentrism, Indistinction, and Veganism." *Dialectical Anthropology* 38, no. 4 (2014): 415–29.

———. *Thinking Through Animals: Identity, Difference, Indistinction.* Palo Alto, CA: Stanford University Press, 2015.

Carmichael, Calum M. *Law and Narrative in the Bible: The Evidence of the Deuteronomic Laws and the Decalogue.* Ithaca: Cornell University Press, 1985.

———. *The Laws of Deuteronomy.* Ithaca: Cornell University Press, 1974.

Caro, Timothy M. *Antipredator Defenses in Birds and Mammals.* Interspecific Interactions. Chicago: University of Chicago Press, 2005.

Carr, David M. "Competing Construals of Human Relations with 'Animal' Others in the Primeval History (Genesis 1–11)." *Journal of Biblical Literature* 140, no. 2 (2021): 251–69.

———. *Genesis 1–11: International Exegetical Commentary on the Old Testament.* Stuttgart: Kohlhammer, 2021.

———. "Standing at the Edge of Reconstructable Transmission-History: Signs of a Secondary Sabbath-Oriented Stratum in Genesis 1:1–2:3." *Vetus Testamentum* 70, no. 1 (2020): 17–41.

Carsten, Janet. Introduction to *Ghosts of Memory: Essays on Remembrance and Relatedness*, edited by Janet Carsten, 1–35. Malden, MA: Blackwell, 2008.

Center for Jewish Food Ethics. "A Sustainable Food System for All." www.jewishfoodethics.org.

Chagall, Marc. "A la Russie, aux ânes et aux autres." Centre Pompidou. www.centrepompidou.fr/en/ressources/oeuvre/6WhG2F1.

Chapman, Cynthia R. *The House of the Mother: The Social Roles of Maternal Kin in Biblical Hebrew Narrative and Poetry*. New Haven, CT: Yale University Press, 2016.

Charlton, Sophy, Abigail Ramsøe, Matthew Collins, and Oliver E. Craig. "New Insights into Neolithic Milk Consumption Through Proteomic Analysis of Dental Calculus." *Archaeological and Anthropological Sciences* 11, no. 11 (2019): 6183–96.

Chavel, Charles B. *Commentary on the Torah by Nahmanides*. New York: Shilo, 1971.

Clarke, Caroline, and David Knights. "Milking It for All It's Worth: Unpalatable Practices, Dairy Cows and Veterinary Work?" *Journal of Business Ethics* 176, no. 4 (2021): 673–88.

Clement. *Stromateis*. Translated by John Ferguson. The Fathers of the Church. Vol. 85. Washington, DC: Catholic University of America Press, 1991.

Clementi, Federica K. *Holocaust Mothers and Daughters: Family, History, and Trauma*. HBI Series on Jewish Women. Waltham, MA: Brandeis University Press, 2013.

Clines, David J. A., ed. "Seh." In *The Dictionary of Classical Hebrew*, 8:115–16. Sheffield, England: Sheffield Academic Press, 1993.

Cloutier, Sylvie, Daniel M. Weary, and David Fraser. "Can Ambient Sound Reduce Distress in Piglets During Weaning and Restraint?" *Journal of Applied Animal Welfare Science* 3, no. 2 (2000): 107–16.

Clutton-Brock, Juliet. *Animals as Domesticates: A World View Through History*. East Lansing: Michigan State University Press, 2012.

Clutton-Brock, Tim H. *The Evolution of Parental Care*. Princeton: Princeton University Press, 1991.

Cockburn, Andrew. "Evolution of Helping Behavior in Cooperatively Breeding Birds." *Annual Review of Ecology and Systematics* 29, no. 1 (1998): 141–77.

Cockram, Sarah D. P. "Sleeve Cat and Lap Dog: Affection, Aesthetics and Proximity to Companion Animals in Renaissance Mantua." In *Interspecies Interactions: Animals and Humans Between the Middle Ages and Modernity*, edited by Sarah D. P. Cockram and Andrew Wells, 34–65. London: Routledge, Taylor and Francis Group, 2018.

Cohen, Mordechai Z. *Rashi, Biblical Interpretation, and Latin Learning in Medieval Europe: A New Perspective on an Exegetical Revolution*. Cambridge: Cambridge University Press, 2021.

Cohen, Shaye J. D. *The Beginnings of Jewishness: Boundaries, Varieties, Uncertainties*. Berkeley: University of California Press, 1999.

Cohen, Shaye J. D., Robert Goldenberg, and Hayim Lapin, eds. *The Oxford Annotated Mishnah: A New Translation of the Mishnah*. 3 vols. New York: Oxford University Press, 2022.

Collias, Nicholas E., and Elsie C. Collias. *Nest Building and Bird Behavior*. Princeton: Princeton University Press, 2014.

Collins, Billie Jean, ed. *The SBL Handbook of Style*. 2nd ed. Atlanta: Society of Biblical Literature Press, 2014.

Columella, Lucius Junius Moderatus. *On Agriculture*. Translated by Edward S. Forster and Edward H. Heffner. Loeb Classical Library 361. Cambridge, MA: Harvard University Press, 2014.

Cook, Johann. "Towards the Dating of the Tradition 'The Torah as Surrounding Fence.'" *Journal of Northwest Semitic Languages* 24, no. 2 (1998): 25–34.

Cooke, Steve. "The Ethics of Touch and the Importance of Nonhuman Relationships in Animal Agriculture." *Journal of Agricultural and Environmental Ethics* 34, no. 2 (2021): 12.

Cooper, Alan. "Once Again Seething a Kid in Its Mother's Milk." *Jewish Studies: An Internet Journal* 10 (2012): 109–43.

Crane, Jonathan K. *Eating Ethically: Religion and Science for a Better Diet*. New York: Columbia University Press, 2018.

Credo Reference, ed. *Credo*. London: Credo Reference, n.d.

Croney, Candace C., and Ruth C. Newberry. "Group Size and Cognitive Processes." *Applied Animal Behaviour Science* 103, no. 3 (2007): 215–28.

Curley, Michael J., trans. *Physiologus*. Chicago: University of Chicago Press, 2009.

Darwin, Charles. *The Expression of the Emotions in Man and Animals*. London: Murray, 1904.

"Dávid Kaufmann and His Collection." Mishnah. http://kaufmann.mtak.hu/en/ms50/ms50-coll1.htm.

Davies, Nick B., and Michael de L. Brooke. "Cuckoos Versus Reed Warblers: Adaptations and Counteradaptations." *Animal Behaviour* 36, no. 1 (1988): 262–84.

Davis, Janet M. *The Gospel of Kindness: Animal Welfare and the Making of Modern America*. Oxford: Oxford University Press, 2016.

Derry, Margaret E. *Made to Order: The Designing of Animals*. Toronto: University of Toronto Press, 2022.

Desmond, Jane. "Vivacious Remains: An Afterword on Taxidermy's Forms, Fictions, Facticity, and Futures." *Configurations* 27, no. 2 (2019): 257–66.

Doane, Sébastien. *Reading the Bible amid the Environmental Crisis: Interdisciplinary Insights to Ecological Hermeneutics.* Lanham, MD: Lexington Books, 2024.

Dodo. "Mama Dog Who Lost Her Puppies Was Heartbroken Until She Got Kittens." YouTube. January 2, 2022. www.youtube.com/watch?v=ByF7swYddEQ.

Dor, Menahem. *Ha-Ḥai Bi-Yeme Ha-Miḳra, Ha-Mishnah Veha-Talmud.* Tel-Aviv: Sifre Grafor-Daftal, 1997.

Double, Michael, and Andrew Cockburn. "Pre-dawn Infidelity: Females Control Extra-Pair Mating in Superb Fairy-Wrens." *Proceedings of the Royal Society of London: Series B; Biological Sciences* 267, no. 1442 (2000): 465–70.

Dougherty, Liam R., Fay Frost, Maarit I. Maenpaa, et al. "A Systematic Map of Studies Testing the Relationship Between Temperature and Animal Reproduction." *Ecological Solutions and Evidence* 5, no. 1 (2024): e12303.

Doyle, Rebecca, and John Moran. *Cow Talk: Understanding Dairy Cow Behaviour to Improve Their Welfare on Asian Farms.* Clayton, Victoria, Australia: CSIRO, n.d.

Dunne, Julie, Katharina Rebay-Salisbury, Roderick B. Salisbury, and Alexander Frisch. "Milk of Ruminants in Ceramic Baby Bottles from Prehistoric Child Graves." *Nature* (London) 574, no. 7777 (2019): 246–48.

Eckel, Jan, Samuel Moyn, and Alexander Street Press, eds. *The Breakthrough: Human Rights in the 1970s.* Philadelphia: University of Pennsylvania Press, 2014.

Eddy, Beverley D. *Felix Salten: Man of Many Faces.* Riverside, CA: Ariadne, 2010.

Edenburg, Cynthia. "The Book of the Covenant." In *The Oxford Handbook of Biblical Law,* edited by Pamela Barmash, 157–76. New York: Oxford University Press, 2019.

Ekman, Paul, ed. *Emotions Inside Out: 130 Years After Darwin's "The Expression of the Emotions in Man and Animals."* New York: New York Academy of Sciences, 2003.

The Elephant Whisperers. Documentary (Short). Netflix. 2022. www.imdb.com/title/tt23628262/.

Epstein, Jacob Nahum. *Mevo'ot Le-Sifrut Ha-Tana'im: Mishnah, Tosefta u-Midreshe Halakhah* [Introduction to the literature of the Tannaim: Mishnah, Tosefta, and Midrash Halakhah]. Tel Aviv: Devir, 1957.

Eriksson, Hanna, Nils Fall, Silvia Ivemeyer, and Ute Knierim. "Strategies for Keeping Dairy Cows and Calves Together: A Cross-Sectional Survey Study." *Animal* (Cambridge) 16, no. 9 (2022): 1–14.

Eshel, Ben Zion. *Yishuve ha-Yehudim be-Vavel bi-Tekufat ha-Talmud* [Jewish settlements in Babylonia during Talmudic times]. Jerusalem: Magnes, 1979.

Feh, Claudia, and Jeanne de Mazières. "Grooming at a Preferred Site Reduces Heart Rate in Horses." *Animal Behaviour* 46, no. 6 (1993): 1191–94.

Feintuch, Yonatan. "External Appearance Versus Internal Truth: The Aggadah of Herod in Bavli Bava Batra." *AJS Review* 35, no. 1 (2011): 85–104.
Feldhamer, George A., and William J. McShea. *Deer: The Animal Answer Guide*. Baltimore: Johns Hopkins University Press, 2012.
Feliks, Yehuda. *Ha-Hai ba-Mishnah*. Jerusalem: Institute for Mishna Research, 1982.
Fine, Gila. *The Madwoman in the Rabbi's Attic: Rereading the Women of the Talmud*. Jerusalem: Maggid, 2024.
Finkelstein, Jacob J. "The Goring Ox: Some Historical Perspectives on Deodands, Forfeitures, Wrongful Death and the Western Notion of Sovereignty." *Temple Law Quarterly* 46, no. 2 (1972): 169–290.
Fishbane, Michael A. *Biblical Interpretation in Ancient Israel*. New York: Oxford University Press, 1985.
Fitzgerald, John T. "Orphans in Mediterranean Antiquity and Early Christianity." *Acta Theologica* 36 (January 2016): 29–48.
Fleishman, Joseph. "Legal Innovation in Deuteronomy XXI 18–20." *Vetus Testamentum* 53, no. 3 (2003): 311–27.
———. *Parents and Children in Ancient Near Eastern Law and Biblical Law*. Jerusalem: Magnes, 1999.
Flower, Frances C., and Daniel M. Weary. "Effects of Early Separation on the Dairy Cow and Calf." *Applied Animal Behaviour Science* 70, no. 4 (2001): 275–84.
Fokkelman, Jan P. *Narrative Art and Poetry in the Books of Samuel: A Full Interpretation Based on Stylistic and Structural Analyses*. Vol. 4. Assen, Netherlands: Van Gorcum, 1981.
Foltz, Richard. *Animals in Islamic Tradition and Muslim Cultures*. Oxford: Oneworld, 2006.
Fonrobert, Charlotte Elisheva. *Menstrual Purity: Rabbinic and Christian Reconstructions of Biblical Gender*. Palo Alto, CA: Stanford University Press, 2002.
Fontes, Pedro L. P., Nicola Oosthuizen, and G. Cliff Lamb. "Reproductive Management of Beef Cattle." In Bazer, Lamb, and Wu, *Animal Agriculture*, 57–73.
Forbes, Scott. *A Natural History of Families*. Princeton: Princeton University Press, 2005.
"Former Beatle 'Inspired by Bambi.'" BBC. December 12, 2005. http://news.bbc.co.uk/2/hi/entertainment/4520658.stm.
Fortune Business Insights. "Animal Genetics Market Size and Growth: Global Report." www.fortunebusinessinsights.com/animal-genetics-market-105584.
Freitas-de-Melo, Aline, Agustín Orihuela, Maria José Hötzel, and Rodolfo Ungerfeld. "What Do We Know and Need to Know About Weaning in Sheep?

An Overview of Weaning Practices, Stress and Welfare." *Frontiers in Animal Science* 3 (February 2022): 1–17.

Frenḳel, Yonah. *Darkhe Ha-Agadah Veha-Midrash* [Studies in hermeneutics of Aggadah and Midrash]. Givatayim, Israel: Yad LaTalmud, 1991.

Freud, Sigmund. *Dora: An Analysis of a Case of Hysteria.* Edited by Philip Rieff. New York: Simon and Schuster, 1997.

———. *The Standard Edition of the Complete Psychological Works of Sigmund Freud.* Edited by James Strachey and Anna Freud. Vol. 10. London: Hogarth/Institute of Psycho-Analysis, 1995.

Friedberg Jewish Manuscript Society. "Hachi Garsinan: The Friedberg Project for Talmud Bavli Variants." https://bavli.genizah.org/Global/homepage?lan=eng&isPartial=False&isDoubleLogin=False&TractateID=0&DafID=0.

Frim, Daniel J. "'Those Who Descend upon the Sea Told Me . . . ': Myth and Tall Tale in Baba Batra 73a–74b." *Jewish Quarterly Review* 107, no. 1 (2017): 1–37.

Fudge, Erica. *Quick Cattle and Dying Wishes: People and Their Animals in Early Modern England.* Ithaca: Cornell University Press, 2018.

Galambosova, Caroline. "From Specimen to Contemporary Taxidermy." *DailyArt Magazine* (blog). January 29, 2024. www.dailyartmagazine.com/taxidermy-in-art/.

Garber, Marjorie. "Good to Think With." *Profession* (2008): 11–20.

Gates, Henry Louis, Jr. *Finding Your Roots*, Arlington, VA: PBS, 2012–25.

Gerstenberger, Erhard S. *Leviticus: A Commentary.* Old Testament Library. Louisville, KY: Westminster John Knox Press, 1996.

Gillespie, Kathryn. *The Cow with Ear Tag #1389.* Chicago: University of Chicago Press, 2018.

Goedicke, Hans. "Review of *Das Böcklein in Der Milch Seiner Mutter und Verwandtes* by Othmar Keel." *Journal of Near Eastern Studies* 42, no. 4 (1983): 302–3.

Goldin, Judah. *Studies in Midrash and Related Literature.* Edited by Barry L. Eichler and Jeffrey H. Tigay. Philadelphia: Jewish Publication Society, 1988.

Goodall, Jane. *In the Shadow of Man.* Boston: Mariner Books, 2009.

Goodfellow, Peter. *Avian Architecture: How Birds Design, Engineer and Build.* Princeton: Princeton University Press, 2011.

Goodman, Lenn E., and Richard McGregor, eds. *The Case of the Animals Versus Man Before the King of the Jinn.* New York: Oxford University Press, 2012.

Gopalakrishnan, Pratima. "Domestic Labor and Marital Obligations in the Ancient Jewish Household." PhD diss., Yale University, 2020.

Goshen-Gottstein, Alon. *The Sinner and the Amnesiac: The Rabbinic Invention of Elisha Ben Abuya and Eleazar Ben Arach.* Stanford, CA: Stanford University Press, 2000.

Grau-Sologestoa, Idoia, Maaike Groot, and Sabine Deschler-Erb. "Innovation and Intensification: The Use of Cattle in the Roman Rhine Region." *Envi-*

ronmental Archaeology: The Journal of Human Palaeoecology, June 23, 2022, 1–19.

Greenberg, Moshe. "Some Postulates of Biblical Criminal Law." In *Studies in the Bible and Jewish Thought*, edited by Moshe Greenberg, 25–42. Philadelphia: Jewish Publication Society, 1995.

Greenspoon, Leonard J., ed. *Mishpachah: The Jewish Family in Tradition and in Transition*. Studies in Jewish Civilization 27. West Lafayette, IN: Purdue University Press, 2016.

Gregory, Helen, and Anthony Purdy. "Present Signs, Dead Things: Indexical Authenticity and Taxidermy's Nonabsent Animal." *Configurations* 23, no. 1 (2015): 61–92.

Gribetz, Sarit Kattan. *Time and Difference in Rabbinic Judaism*. Princeton: Princeton University Press, 2020.

Griffin, Donald Redfield. *Animal Minds: Beyond Cognition to Consciousness*. Chicago: University of Chicago Press, 2013.

———. *The Question of Animal Awareness: Evolutionary Continuity of Mental Experience*. New York: Rockefeller University Press, 1981.

Gross, Aaron S. "Animals, Empathy, and Raḥamim in the Study of Religion: A Case Study of Jewish Opposition to Hunting." *Studies in Religion/Sciences Religieuses* 46, no. 4 (2017): 511–35.

———. *The Question of the Animal and Religion: Theoretical Stakes, Practical Implications*. New York: Columbia University Press, 2015.

Gross, Rachel B. *Beyond the Synagogue: Jewish Nostalgia as Religious Practice*. New York: New York University Press, 2021.

Gubernick, David J. "Parent and Infant Attachment in Mammals." In Gubernick and Klopfer, *Parental Care in Mammals*, 243–306.

Gubernick, David J., and Peter H. Klopfer, eds. *Parental Care in Mammals*. New York: Plenum, 1981.

Guidelines for Reintroductions and Other Conservation Translocations. IUCN. 2013. https://portals.iucn.org/library/node/10386.

Gulak, Asher. "Al ha-Ro'im u-Megadle Behemah Dakah bi-Tekufat Hurban Bayit Sheni [Shepherds and breeders of domestic cattle after the destruction of the Second Temple]." *Tarbiz* 12, no. 3 (1941): 181–89.

Halberstam, Chaya. "Tractate Bekhorot." In Cohen, Goldenberg, and Lapin, *Oxford Annotated Mishnah*, 3:168–212.

Halberstam, Judith. "Forgetting Family: Queer Alternatives to Oedipal Relations." In *A Companion to Lesbian, Gay, Bisexual, Transgender, and Queer Studies*, edited by George E. Haggerty and Molly McGarry, 315–24. Blackwell Companions in Cultural Studies. Malden, MA: Blackwell, 2007.

Hartman Halbertal, Tova. *Appropriately Subversive: Modern Mothers in Traditional Religions*. Cambridge, MA: Harvard University Press, 2002.

Halivni, David. *Midrash, Mishnah, and Gemara: The Jewish Predilection for Justified Law*. Cambridge, MA: Harvard University Press, 1986.

———. *Sources and Traditions: A Source Critical Commentary on the Talmud: Seder Moed, from Yoma to Hagiga (Meḳorot u-Masorot)*. Jerusalem: Jewish Theological Seminary of America, 1974.

Haran, Menahem. "Seething a Kid in Its Mother's Milk." *Journal of Jewish Studies* 30, no. 1 (1979): 23–35.

Haraway, Donna. "Teddy Bear Patriarchy: Taxidermy in the Garden of Eden, New York City, 1908–1936." *Social Text*, no. 11 (January 1984): 20–64.

Hartley, John E. *Leviticus*. Word Biblical Commentary. Vol. 4. Dallas: Word Books, 1992.

Hasan-Rokem, Galit, and Haim Weiss. "Folklore in Antiquity." *Humanities* 7, no. 2 (2018): 47.

Haskell, Ellen Davina. *Suckling at My Mother's Breasts: The Image of a Nursing God in Jewish Mysticism*. SUNY Series in Western Esoteric Traditions. New York: State University of New York Press, 2012.

Hatfield, Gary. "Animals." In *A Companion to Descartes*, edited by Janet Broughton and John Peter Carriero, 404–25. Blackwell Companions to Philosophy 38. Malden, MA: Blackwell, 2008.

Hawkes, Kristen, James F. O'Connell, Nichola G. Blurton Jones, and Helen Alvarez. "Grandmothering, Menopause, and the Evolution of Human Life Histories." *Proceedings of the National Academy of Sciences* 95, no. 3 (1998): 1336–39.

Hayes, Christine Elizabeth, ed. *The Literature of the Sages: A Re-visioning*. Leiden: Brill, 2022.

Hayes, Christine Elizabeth, and Jay Michael Harris, eds. *What Is the Talmud? The State of the Question*. Cambridge, MA: Harvard University Press, forthcoming.

Hebb, Donald O. "Emotion in Man and Animal: An Analysis of the Intuitive Processes of Recognition." *Psychological Review* 53, no. 2 (1946): 88–106.

Heinemann, Yizhak. *The Reasons for the Commandments in Jewish Thought: From the Bible to the Renaissance*. Translated by Leonard Levin. Boston: Academic Studies Press, 2008.

Hepper, Peter G., ed. *Kin Recognition*. Cambridge: Cambridge University Press, 2005.

Hernandez, Elein, Pol Llonch, and Patricia V. Turner. "Applied Animal Ethics in Industrial Food Animal Production: Exploring the Role of the Veterinarian." *Animals* (Basel) 12, no. 6 (2022): 678.

Hersher, Leonard, Julius B. Richmond, and A. Ulric Moore. "Maternal Behavior in Sheep and Goats." In *Maternal Behavior in Mammals*, edited by Harriet Lange Rheingold, 203–32. New York: Wiley, 1963.

Herzog, Hillary Hope. *Vienna Is Different: Jewish Writers in Austria from the Fin de Siècle to the Present*. Austrian and Habsburg Studies. Vol. 12. New York: Berghahn Books, 2011.
Hesse, Tom. "How Birds Represent a Poetic Glimpse of Life in Denver." Colorado Public Radio. July 12, 2023. www.cpr.org/show-segment/how-birds-represent-a-poetic-glimpse-of-life-in-denver/.
Hibiscus Paws. "Teeny Tiny Chihuahua Pup Nursing." YouTube. July 14, 2017. www.youtube.com/watch?v=dmgvu98jOiU.
Hinch, Geoff N., Justin J. Lynch, R. L. Elwin, and G. C. Green. "Long-Term Associations Between Merino Ewes and Their Offspring." *Applied Animal Behaviour Science* 27, no. 1 (1990): 93–103.
Hirshman, Marc. "Changing Focuses of Sanctity: Honi and His Grandchildren" *Tura* 1 (1989): 109–18.
Hoek, Annewies W. van den. *Clement of Alexandria and His Use of Philo in the Stromateis: An Early Christian Reshaping of a Jewish Model*. Leiden: Brill, 1988.
Hoffman, Yair. "The Ben P'Kuah Meat Controversy Continues: Video from Rav Chaim Kanievsky." *Yeshiva World* (blog). January 13, 2016. www.theyeshivaworld.com/news/headlines-breaking-stories/376120/the-ben-pkuah-meat-controversy.html.
———. "The New Commercially-Produced Ben P'Kuah Meat." *Yeshiva World* (blog). January 7, 2016. www.theyeshivaworld.com/news/headlines-breaking-stories/374628/the-new-commercially-produced-ben-pkuah-meat.html.
———. "The Segulah of Shiluach HaKan." *Yeshiva World* (blog). September 18, 2016. www.theyeshivaworld.com/news/headlines-breaking-stories/464072/464072.html.
Hoffmann, David, ed. *Mekhilta De-Rabi Shim'on Ben Yoḥai 'al Sefer Shemot*. Frankfurt: Kaufmann, 1905.
Holloway, Kali. "Angela Davis's Family History Is Remarkable—and Unexceptional for Black Americans." March 2, 2023. www.thenation.com/article/society/angela-davis-pbs-genealogy/.
Horovitz, H. Saul, and Israel Abraham Rabin, eds. *Mechilta d'Rabbi Ismael*. Jerusalem: Wahrmann Books, 1970.
Hötzel, Maria J., Clarissa S. Cardoso, Angélica Roslindo, and Marina A. G. von Keyserlingk. "Citizens' Views on the Practices of Zero-Grazing and Cow-Calf Separation in the Dairy Industry: Does Providing Information Increase Acceptability?" *Journal of Dairy Science* 100, no. 5 (2017): 4150–60.
Houlihan, Patrick F. "Animals in Egyptian Art and Hieroglyphs." In *A History of the Animal World in the Ancient Near East*, edited by Billie Jean Collins, 97–143. Leiden: Brill, 2002.
———. *Wit and Humour in Ancient Egypt*. London: Rubicon, 2001.
"The House of Black and White." *Game of Thrones*. New York: HBO, 2015.

Hrdy, Sarah Blaffer. *Mother Nature: A History of Mothers, Infants, and Natural Selection*. New York: Pantheon Books, 1999.

———. *Mothers and Others: The Evolutionary Origins of Mutual Understanding*. Cambridge, MA: Harvard University Press, 2009.

Hribal, Jason. *Fear of the Animal Planet: The Hidden History of Animal Resistance*. Oakland, CA: AK Press, 2010.

Humane Society of the United States. "Animal Cruelty Facts and Statistics." www.humanesociety.org/issues/abuse_neglect/facts/animal_cruelty_facts_statistics.html.

Ilan, Tal. *Massekhet Hullin: Text, Translation, and Commentary*. Tübingen, Germany: Mohr Siebeck, 2017.

———. *Mine and Yours Are Hers: Retrieving Women's History from Rabbinic Literature*. Leiden: Brill, 1997.

Illmann, Gudrun, Marek Špinka, Lars Schrader, and Pavel Šustr. "Acoustical Mother-Offspring Recognition in Pigs (Sus Scrofa Domestica)." *Behaviour* 139, no. 4 (2002): 487–505.

Insley, Stephen J. "Long-Term Vocal Recognition in the Northern Fur Seal." *Nature* (London) 406, no. 6794 (2000): 404–5.

———. "Mother-Offspring Vocal Recognition in Northern Fur Seals Is Mutual but Asymmetrical." *Animal Behaviour* 61, no. 1 (2001): 129–37.

Jacobsen, Lea. *The Legal Status of the Mother in the Ancient Near East and the Bible*. Jerusalem: Magnes, 2017.

Jaffee, Martin S. *Torah in the Mouth: Writing and Oral Tradition in Palestinian Judaism, 200 BCE–400 CE*. New York: Oxford University Press, 2001.

Jastrow, Marcus. "Dictionary of the Targumim, the Talmud Babli and Yerushalmi, and the Midrashic Literature." Tyndale Archive. www.tyndalearchive.com/TABS/Jastrow/.

Jhala, Angma Dey. Introduction to *Genealogy, Archive, Image: Interpreting Dynastic History in Western India, c. 1090–2016*, edited by Angma Dey Jhala and Jayasinhji Jhala, 1–20. Warsaw: De Gruyter Open, 2017.

Josephus, Flavius. *Flavius Josephus: Translation and Commentary*. Vol. 10, *Against Apion*. Translated by John M. G. Barclay. Leiden: Brill, 2007.

———. *Jewish Antiquities*. Translated by Henry St. J. Thackeray. Vol. 1. Loeb Classical Library 242. Cambridge, MA: Harvard University Press, 1930.

———. *The Jewish War*. Translated by Henry St. J. Thackeray. Vol. 3. Loeb Classical Library 210. Cambridge, MA: Harvard University Press, 1928.

———. *The Life; Against Apion*. Translated by Henry St. J. Thackeray. Loeb Classical Library 186. Cambridge, MA: Harvard University Press, 2014.

Kaltmann, Nomi. "Why Is This Meat Different from All Other Meat?" *Tablet Magazine*, March 18, 2021. www.tabletmag.com/sections/food/articles/ben-pekuah-meat-that-isnt-meat.

Kamionkowski, S. Tamar. *Leviticus*. Collegeville, MN: Liturgical Press, 2018.

Kanarfogel, Ephraim. "Shemu'el Ben Me'ir." In *The Oxford Dictionary of the Jewish Religion*, edited by Adele Berlin, 675–76. Oxford: Oxford University Press, 2011.

Kane, Tommy, and Sylvia Ugga. *Vegan Art: A Book of Visual Protest*. London: HENI, 2022.

Katz, Maya Balakirsky. "'Bambi' Abroad, 1924–1954." *AJS Review* 44, no. 2 (2020): 286–316.

Kavesh, Muhammad A. *Animal Enthusiasms: Life Beyond Cage and Leash in Rural Pakistan*. Abingdon, Oxon: Routledge, 2021.

Kee, Joan, and Emanuele Lugli. "Scale to Size: An Introduction." *Art History* 38, no. 2 (2015): 250–66.

Keel, Othmar. *Das Böcklein in Der Milch Seiner Mutter und Verwandtes: Im Lichte Eines Altorientalischen Bildmotivs*. Freiburg, Germany: Universitätsverlag/Vandenhoeck und Ruprecht, 1980.

Kendi, Ibram X. *How to Be an Antiracist*. New York: Random House, 2019.

Kendrick, Keith M., Frédéric Lévy, and Eric B. Keverne. "Importance of Vaginocervical Stimulation for the Formation of Maternal Bonding in Primiparous and Multiparous Parturient Ewes." *Physiology and Behavior* 50, no. 3 (1991): 595–600.

Kent, John P. "The Cow-Calf Relationship: From Maternal Responsiveness to the Maternal Bond and the Possibilities for Fostering." *Journal of Dairy Research* 87, no. S1 (2020): 101–7.

Keverne, Eric B., Frédéric Levy, Pascal Poindron, and David R. Lindsay. "Vaginal Stimulation: An Important Determinant of Maternal Bonding in Sheep." *Science* 219, no. 4580 (1983): 81–83.

Keverne, Eric B., Nicholas D. Martensz, and Bernadette Tuite. "Beta-Endorphin Concentrations in Cerebrospinal Fluid of Monkeys Are Influenced by Grooming Relationships." *Psychoneuroendocrinology* 14, no. 1 (1989): 155–61.

Keyserlingk, Marina A. G. von, and Daniel M. Weary. "Maternal Behavior in Cattle." *Hormones and Behavior* 52, no. 1 (2007): 106–13.

King, Barbara J. *How Animals Grieve*. Chicago: University of Chicago Press, 2013.

Kiperwasser, Reuven, and Dan D. Y. Shapira. "Irano-Talmudica II: Leviathan, Behemoth and the 'Domestication' of Iranian Mythological Creatures in Eschatological Narratives of the Babylonian Talmud." In *Shoshannat Yaakov: Jewish and Iranian Studies in Honor of Yaakov Elman*, edited by Shai Secunda and Steven Fine, 203–35. Leiden: Brill, 2012.

———. "Irano-Talmudica III: Giant Mythological Creatures in Transition from the Avesta to the Babylonian Talmud." In *Orality and Textuality in the Iranian World*, edited by Julia Rubanovich, 63–92. Leiden: Brill, 2015.

Kleiman, Devra G., and James R. Malcolm. "The Evolution of Male Parental Investment in Mammals." In Gubernick and Klopfer, *Parental Care in Mammals*, 347–87.

Klip, Hedda. *Biblical Genealogies: A Form-Critical Analysis, with a Special Focus on Women*. Leiden: Brill, 2022.

Klug, Hope, and Michael B. Bonsall. "When to Care For, Abandon, or Eat Your Offspring: The Evolution of Parental Care and Filial Cannibalism." *American Naturalist* 170, no. 6 (2007): 886–901.

Knauf, Ernst Axel. "Zur Herkunft und Sozialgeschichte Israels: 'Das Böckchen in Der Milch Seiner Mutter.'" *Biblica* 69, no. 2 (1988): 153–69.

Kober, Melanie, Fritz Trillmich, and Marc Naguib. "Vocal Mother-Pup Communication in Guinea Pigs: Effects of Call Familiarity and Female Reproductive State." *Animal Behaviour* 73, no. 5 (2007): 917–25.

Koenig, Walter D., and Janis L. Dickinson, eds. *Cooperative Breeding in Vertebrates*. New York: Cambridge University Press, 2016.

Kölliker, Mathias, Per T. Smiseth, and Nick J. Royle. "What Is Parental Care?" In Royle, Smiseth, and Kölliker, *Evolution of Parental Care*, 1–17.

Koren, Yedidah. "'Look Through Your Book and Make Me a Perfect Match': Talking About Genealogy in Amoraic Palestine and Babylonia." *Journal for the Study of Judaism in the Persian, Hellenistic, and Roman Period* 49, no. 3 (2018): 417–48.

———. "Policing Lineage in Rabbinic Literature." *Journal of Ancient Judaism* 11, no. 1 (2020): 76–115.

Kotrosits, Maia. *The Lives of Objects: Material Culture, Experience, and the Real in the History of Early Christianity*. Chicago: University of Chicago Press, 2020.

Kozlova, Ekaterina E. *Maternal Grief in the Hebrew Bible*. New York: Oxford University Press, 2017.

Kraemer, David Charles. *Jewish Eating and Identity Through the Ages*. New York: Routledge, 2007.

———, ed. *The Jewish Family: Metaphor and Memory*. New York: Oxford University Press, 1989.

Kron, Geoffrey. "Animal Husbandry, Hunting, Fishing and Pisciculture." In *Oxford Handbook of Engineering and Technology in the Classical World*, edited by John Peter Oleson, 175–224. Oxford: Oxford University Press, 2008.

Küçüküstel, Selcen. *Embracing Landscape: Living with Reindeer and Hunting Among Spirits in South Siberia*. New York: Berghahn Books, 2021.

Kugel, James L. *Traditions of the Bible: A Guide to the Bible as It Was at the Start of the Common Era*. Cambridge, MA: Harvard University Press, 1998.

Labuschagne, Casper J. "'You Shall Not Boil a Kid in Its Mother's Milk': A New Proposal for the Origin of the Prohibition." In *The Scriptures and the Scrolls*, edited by Florentino García Martínez, Anthony Hilhorst, and Casper J. Labuschagne, 6–17. Leiden: Brill, 1992.

Lapin, Hayim. *Rabbis as Romans: The Rabbinic Movement in Palestine, 100–400 CE*. New York: Oxford University Press, 2012.

Lavie, Smadar. *Wrapped in the Flag of Israel: Mizrahi Single Mothers and Bureaucratic Torture*. Rev. ed. Expanding Frontiers: Interdisciplinary Approaches to Studies of Women, Gender, and Sexuality. Lincoln: University of Nebraska Press, 2018.

Lawrence, Alistair B. "Mother-Daughter and Peer Relationships of Scottish Hill Sheep." *Animal Behaviour* 39, no. 3 (1990): 481–86.

Leaping Bunny Program. "Compassionate Shopping Guide." www.leapingbunny.org/shopping-guide.

Lehman, Marjorie Suzan, Jane L. Kanarek, and Simon J. Bronner, eds. *Mothers in the Jewish Cultural Imagination*. Oxford: Littman Library of Jewish Civilization/Liverpool University Press, 2017.

Lesmeister, John L., Peter J. Burfening, and R. L. Blackwell. "Date of First Calving in Beef Cows and Subsequent Calf Production." *Journal of Animal Science* 36, no. 1 (1973): 1–6.

Levene, Dan. *A Corpus of Magic Bowls: Incantation Texts in Jewish Aramaic from Late Antiquity*. London: Kegan Paul, 2003.

Levenson, Jon D. *The Death and Resurrection of the Beloved Son: The Transformation of Child Sacrifice in Judaism and Christianity*. New Haven, CT: Yale University Press, 1993.

Levinson, Bernard M. "Deuteronomy: Introduction and Annotations." In Brettler and Berlin, *Jewish Study Bible*, 339–428.

Lev-Tov, Justin. "Animal Husbandry: Meat, Milk, and More." In *T&T Clark Handbook of Food in the Hebrew Bible and Ancient Israel*, edited by Cynthia Shafer-Elliott, Janling Fu, and Carol L. Meyers, 77–98. London: T&T Clark, 2021.

———. "Diet, Hellenistic and Roman Period." *The Oxford Encyclopedia of the Bible and Archaeology*. Oxford University Press. 2013. https://www.oxfordreference.com/display/10.1093/acref:obso/9780199846535.001.0001/acref-9780199846535-e-35.

———. "'Upon What Meat Doth This Our Caesar Feed . . .?' A Dietary Perspective on Hellenistic and Roman Influence in Palestine." In *Signs of Text and Stone: Studies Towards an Archaeology of the New Testament*, ed. Stefan Alkier and Jürgen Zangenberg (Tübingen, Germany: Francke, 2003), 420–46.

Lévy, Frédéric. "Neuroendocrine Control of Maternal Behavior in Non-human and Human Mammals." *Annales d'endocrinologie* 77, no. 2 (2016): 114–25.

Liss, Hanna. *Creating Fictional Worlds: Peshaṭ-Exegesis and Narrativity in Rashbam's Commentary on the Torah*. Leiden: Brill, 2011.

Lockshin, Martin I. *Rashbam's Commentary on Exodus: An Annotated Translation*. Brown Judaic Studies 310. Atlanta: Scholars' Press, 1997.

Loeffler, James Benjamin. *Rooted Cosmopolitans: Jews and Human Rights in the Twentieth Century*. New Haven, CT: Yale University Press, 2018.

Lutts, Ralph H. "The Trouble with Bambi: Walt Disney's Bambi and the American Vision of Nature." *Forest and Conservation History* 36, no. 4 (1992): 160–71.

Lynch, Eilish, Mark McGee, and Bernadette Earley. "Weaning Management of Beef Calves with Implications for Animal Health and Welfare." *Journal of Applied Animal Research* 47, no. 1 (2019): 167–75.

"Ma'agarim." Historical Dictionary Project of the Academy of Hebrew Language. https://maagarim.hebrew-academy.org.il/Pages/PMain.aspx?mishibbur=18000&mm15=011008001000.

MacKinnon, Michael. "Cattle 'Breed' Variation and Improvement in Roman Italy: Connecting the Zooarchaeological and Ancient Textual Evidence." *World Archaeology* 42, no. 1 (2010): 55–73.

Macuch, Maria. "On the Treatment of Animals in Zoroastrian Law." In *Iranica Selecta: Studies in Honour of Professor Wojciech Skalmowski on the Occasion of His Seventieth Birthday*, edited by Alois van Tongerloo, 8:167–90. Turnhout, Belgium: Brepols, 2003.

Maimonides, Moses. *The Guide of the Perplexed*. Translated by Shlomo Pines. Vol. 2. Chicago: University of Chicago Press, 1963.

———. *Mishnah 'im Perush Rabenu Moshe Ben Maimon*. Translated by Yosef Kafaḥ. Vol. 1. Jerusalem: Rav Kook Institute, 1963.

Mandelbaum, Bernard, ed. *Pesikta de Rav Kahana: According to an Oxford Manuscript with Variants from All Known Manuscripts and Genizoth Fragments and Parallel Passages with Commentary and Introduction*. 2 vols. New York: Jewish Theological Seminary of America, 1962.

Margalioth, Mordechai, ed. *Encyclopedia of Talmudic and Geonic Literature*. 2 vols. Tel-Aviv: Chachik, 1960.

———. *Midrash Wayyikra Rabbah: A Critical Edition Based on Manuscripts and Genizah Fragments with Variants and Notes*. Jerusalem: Wahrmann Books, 1972.

Martay, Blaise, Kirsty H. Macphie, Katharine M. Bowgen, et al. *Climate Change and Migratory Species: A Review of Impacts, Conservation Actions, Indicators and Ecosystem Services: Part 1, Impacts of Climate*. Peterborough, UK: Joint Nature Conservation Committee, 2023.

Martinez, Florentino García, and Eibert J. C. Tigchelaar, eds. *Dead Sea Scrolls: Study Edition*. Grand Rapids, MI: Eerdmans, 1999.

Massumi, Brian. *What Animals Teach Us About Politics*. Durham, NC: Duke University Press, 2014.

Mateo, Jill M., and Warren G. Holmes. "Development of Alarm-Call Responses in Belding's Ground Squirrels: The Role of Dams." *Animal Behaviour* 54, no. 3 (1997): 509–24.

Mayberry, Lorel, and Jacqueline Daniel. "Birthgasm." *Journal of Holistic Nursing* 34, no. 4 (2016): 331–42.

McGowan, Philip J. K., and Guy M. Kirwan. "Sand Partridge *(Ammoperdix heyi)*." In *Birds of the World*, edited by Josep del Hoyo, Andrew Elliott, Jordi Sargatal, David A. Christie, and Eduardo de Juana. Ithaca, NY: Cornell Lab of Ornithology, 2020.

McNamara, Martin, Robert Hayward, and Michael Maher. *The Aramaic Bible: Leviticus*. Vol. 3. Collegeville, MN: Liturgical Press, 1994.

Mealy, J. Webb. "You Shall Not Boil a Kid in Its Mother's Milk (Exod. 23:19b; Exod. 34:26b; Deut. 14:21b)." *Biblical Interpretation* 20, no. 1 (2012): 35–72.

Meir, Ofra. *Rabbi Yehudah Ha-Nasi: Deyoḳano shel Manhig be-Masorot Eretz-Yisrael u-Vavel* [Rabbi Judah the patriarch: Portrait of a leader in the traditions of the land of Israel and Babylonia]. Tel-Aviv: Ha-Ḳibbutz ha-Meʼuḥad, 1999.

Melamed, Ezra Zion. *Pirḳe Mavo Le-Sifrut Ha-Talmud* [Introductory chapters to the literature of the Talmud]. Jerusalem, 1973.

Metzler, Maria J. "The Ark of the Covenant and Divine Rage in the Hebrew Bible." PhD diss., Harvard University, 2016.

Milanich, Nara B. *Paternity: The Elusive Quest for the Father*. Cambridge, MA: Harvard University Press, 2019.

Milgrom, Jacob. "HR in Leviticus and Elsewhere in the Torah." In *The Book of Leviticus: Composition and Reception*, edited by Rolf Rendtorff, Robert A. Kugler, and Sarah Smith Bartel, 24–40. Leiden: Brill, 2003.

———. *Leviticus 1–16: A New Translation with Introduction and Commentary*. Vol. 3A, *The Anchor Bible*. New York: Doubleday, 1991.

———. *Leviticus 17–22: A New Translation with Introduction and Commentary*. Vol. 3, *The Anchor Bible*. New York: Doubleday, 2000.

———. "You Shall Not Boil a Kid in Its Mother's Milk." *Bible Review* (Washington, DC) 1, no. 3 (1985): 48–55.

Miller, Michael R. "Descartes on Animals Revisited." *Journal of Philosophical Research* 38 (2013): 89–114.

Miller, Patricia Cox. *In the Eye of the Animal: Zoological Imagination in Ancient Christianity*. Philadelphia: University of Pennsylvania Press, 2018.

Moore, Susan, Doreen Rosenthal, and Rebecca Robinson. *The Psychology of Family History: Exploring Our Genealogy*. London: Routledge, 2021.

Muers, Rachel. "Setting Free the Mother Bird: On Reading a Strange Text." *Modern Theology* 22, no. 4 (2006): 555–76.

Musa, Aisha Y. "Raḥma: Universal Divine Mercy in the Qur'an and Hadith." *Journal of Islamic and Muslim Studies* 6, no. 1 (2021): 131–39.

Nagel, Thomas. "What Is It Like to Be a Bat?" *Philosophical Review* 83, no. 4 (1974): 435–50.

Naish, Darren. "How Dangerous Are Cassowaries, Really?" *Scientific American Blog Network*. https://blogs.scientificamerican.com/tetrapod-zoology/how-dangerous-are-cassowaries-really/.

Napolitano, Fabio, Andrea Bragaglio, Emilio Sabia, and Francesco Serrapica. "The Human–Animal Relationship in Dairy Animals." *Journal of Dairy Research* 87, no. S1 (2020): 47–52.

Napolitano, Fabio, Giuseppe De Rosa, and Agostino Sevi. "Welfare Implications of Artificial Rearing and Early Weaning in Sheep." *Applied Animal Behaviour Science* 110, no. 1 (2008): 58–72.

Napolitano, Fabio, Francesco Serrapica, Ada Braghieri, and Felicia Masucci. "Human-Animal Interactions in Dairy Buffalo Farms." *Animals* (Basel) 9, no. 5 (2019): 246.

Nash, Catherine. *Genetic Geographies: The Trouble with Ancestry*. Minneapolis: University of Minnesota Press, 2015.

"Nature." Green-Wood. www.green-wood.com/nature/.

Naveh, Joseph, and Shaul Shaked. *Magic Spells and Formulae: Aramaic Incantations of Late Antiquity*. Jerusalem: Magnes, 1993.

Naville, Edouard, Charles T. Currelly, Somers Clarke, Edward R. Ayrton, and Henry R. Hall. *The XIth Dynasty Temple at Deir El-Bahari*. Vol. 1. London: Egypt Exploration Fund, 1907.

Neaman, Pinchas. *Encyclopedia of Talmudical Geography*. Tel Aviv: Chachik, 1972.

Neis, Rafael Rachel. *When a Human Gives Birth to a Raven: Rabbis and the Reproduction of Species*. Oakland: University of California Press, 2023.

Nelson, Angela. "New Study Is First to Find Exposure to Neurotoxic Rodenticide Bromethalin in Birds of Prey." Tufts Now. July 11, 2023. https://now.tufts.edu/2023/07/11/new-study-first-find-exposure-neurotoxic-rodenticide-bromethalin-birds-prey.

Nelson, W. David, ed. *Mekhilta De-Rabbi Shimon Bar Yoḥai*. Philadelphia: Jewish Publication Society, 2006.

Newberry, Ruth C., and Janice C. Swanson. "Implications of Breaking Mother-Young Social Bonds." *Applied Animal Behaviour Science* 110, nos. 1–2 (2008): 3–23.

Niehoff, Maren. *Philo of Alexandria: An Intellectual Biography*. Anchor Yale Bible Reference Library. New Haven, CT: Yale University Press, 2018.

Nihan, Christophe. *From Priestly Torah to Pentateuch: A Study in the Composition of the Book of Leviticus*. Tübingen, Germany: Mohr Siebeck, 2007.

Nonhuman Rights Project. "Ways to Help." www.nonhumanrights.org/ways-to-help/.

Novick, Tzvi Michael. "The Mishnah and the Bible." In *What Is the Mishnah? The State of the Question*, edited by Shaye J. D. Cohen, 3–22. Jewish Law and Culture Series. Cambridge, MA: Harvard University Press, 2023.

Nowak, Raymond, Matthieu Keller, and Frédéric Lévy. "Mother-Young Relationships in Sheep: A Model for a Multidisciplinary Approach of the

Study of Attachment in Mammals." *Journal of Neuroendocrinology* 23, no. 11 (2011): 1042–53.

Olazábal, Daniel E., Mariana Pereira, Daniella Agrati, et al., "New Theoretical and Experimental Approaches on Maternal Motivation in Mammals." *Neuroscience and Biobehavioral Reviews* 37, no. 8 (2013): 1860–74.

Olyan, Saul M. *Animal Rights and the Hebrew Bible*. Oxford: Oxford University Press, 2023.

"One Health." World Health Organization. www.who.int/news-room/questions-and-answers/item/one-health.

Oppenheimer, Aharon. *Babylonia Judaica in the Talmudic Period*. Beihefte Zum Tübinger Atlas Des Vorderen Orients. Wiesbaden, Germany: Reichert, 1983.

Orgeur, Pierre, N. Mavric, Pierre Yvoré, et al., "Artificial Weaning in Sheep: Consequences on Behavioural, Hormonal and Immuno-pathological Indicators of Welfare." *Applied Animal Behaviour Science* 58, no. 1 (1998): 87–103.

Otto, Eckart. "Book of the Covenant." *The Oxford Encyclopedia of the Bible and Law*. Oxford University Press. https://www.oxfordreference.com/display/10.1093/acref:obso/9780199843305.001.0001/acref-9780199843305-e-11.

"Our Pets Are Part of the Climate Problem: These Tips Can Help You Minimize Their Carbon Pawprints." CNN. www.cnn.com/2022/09/15/us/pets-climate-impact-lbg-wellness/index.html.

Palladius, Rutilius Taurus Aemilianus. *The Work of Farming (Opus Agriculturae) and Poem on Grafting*. Translated by John G. Fitch. Totnes, UK: Prospect Books, 2013.

Panken, Aaron D. *The Rhetoric of Innovation: Self-Conscious Legal Change in Rabbinic Literature*. Lanham, MD: University Press of America, 2005.

Panksepp, Jaak. *Affective Neuroscience: The Foundations of Human and Animal Emotions*. New York: Oxford University Press, 1998.

Park, Shelley M. *Mothering Queerly, Queering Motherhood: Resisting Monomaternalism in Adoptive, Lesbian, Blended, and Polygamous Families*. Albany: State University of New York Press, 2013.

Parker, Julie F. *Valuable and Vulnerable: Children in the Hebrew Bible, Especially the Elisha Cycle*. Providence, RI: Brown Judaic Studies, 2013.

Payne, Charles M. *I've Got the Light of Freedom: The Organizing Tradition and the Mississippi Freedom Struggle*. Berkeley: University of California Press, 1995.

Payne, Richard E. *A State of Mixture: Christians, Zoroastrians, and Iranian Political Culture in Late Antiquity*. Berkeley: University of California Press, 2015.

Philo. *On the Decalogue.* Translated by Francis H. Colson. Vol. 7. Loeb Classical Library 320. Cambridge, MA: Harvard University Press, 1937.
———. *On the Virtues.* Translated by Francis Henry Colson. Vol. 8. Loeb Classical Library 341. Cambridge, MA: Harvard University Press, 2014.
———. *Philonis Alexandrini de Animalibus: The Armenian Text.* Translated by Abraham Terian. Chico, CA: Scholars' Press, 1981.
Pinillos, Rebeca García, Michael C. Appleby, Xavier Manteca, and Freda Scott-Park. "One Welfare: A Platform for Improving Human and Animal Welfare." *Veterinary Record* 179, no. 16 (2016): 412–13.
Placzek, Matthias, Inken Christoph-Schulz, and Kerstin Barth. "Public Attitude Towards Cow-Calf Separation and Other Common Practices of Calf Rearing in Dairy Farming: A Review." *Organic Agriculture* 11, no. 1 (2021): 41–50.
Pliny the Elder. *The Natural History.* www.perseus.tufts.edu/hopper/text?doc =urn:cts:latinLit:phi0978.phi001.perseus-eng1:10.1.
Poindron, Pascal, Mario Caba, P. Gomora Arrati, and Dwight Krehbiel. "Responses of Maternal and Non-maternal Ewes to Social and Mother-Young Separation." *Behavioural Processes* 31, no. 1 (1994): 97–110.
Poindron, Pascal, Gabriella Gilling, Horacio Hernandez, Norma Serafin, and Angélica Terrazas. "Early Recognition of Newborn Goat Kids by Their Mother: I. Nonolfactory Discrimination." *Developmental Psychobiology* 43, no. 2 (2003): 82–89.
Poindron, Pascal, Frédéric Lévy, and Matthieu Keller. "Maternal Responsiveness and Maternal Selectivity in Domestic Sheep and Goats: The Two Facets of Maternal Attachment." *Developmental Psychobiology* 49, no. 1 (2007): 54–70.
Poindron, Pascal, Angélica Terrazas, María de la Luz Navarro Montes de Oca, and Norma Serafín. "Sensory and Physiological Determinants of Maternal Behavior in the Goat (Capra Hircus)." *Hormones and Behavior* 52, no. 1 (2007): 99–105.
Poliquin, Rachel. *The Breathless Zoo: Taxidermy and the Cultures of Longing.* University Park: Pennsylvania State University Press, 2012.
Polzin, Robert. *Samuel and the Deuteronomist: 1 Samuel.* Bloomington: Indiana University Press, 1993.
Porter, Richard H. "Mutual Mother-Infant Recognition in Humans." In Hepper, *Kin Recognition,* 413–32.
Potts, Annie, ed. *Meat Culture.* Human-Animal Studies. Vol. 17. Leiden: Brill, 2016.
Price, Edward O., J. E. Harris, Reid E. Borgwardt, and Matthew L. Sween. "Fenceline Contact of Beef Calves with Their Dams at Weaning Reduces the Negative Effects of Separation on Behavior and Growth Rate." *Journal of Animal Science* 81, no. 1 (2003): 116–21.

Propp, William Henry. *Exodus 19–40: A New Translation with Introduction and Commentary*. New York: Doubleday, 2006.
Py-Lieberman, Beth, and Attilio Maranzano. "The Really Big Art of Claes Oldenburg." *Smithsonian* 26, no. 5 (1995): 78–83.
Qimron, Elisha, and John Strugnell, eds. *Qumrân Cave 4: Miqṣat Maʿaśe Ha-Torah. V.* Qumrân Cave 45. Oxford: Oxford University Press, 1994.
Rabi, Meir G. "Ben PeKuAh: A New Approach." Academia. January 1, 2022. www.academia.edu/91733806/Ben_PeKuAh_A_New_Approach.
Raucher, Michal. "Jewish Pronatalism: Policy and Praxis." *Religion Compass* 15, no. 7 (2021): e12398.
Rebanks, James. *Pastoral Song: A Farmer's Journey*. New York: HarperCollins, 2021.
Rebora, Simone, and Massimo Salgaro. "Is Felix Salten the Author of the Mutzenbacher Novel (1906)? Yes and No." *Language and Literature* 31, no. 2 (2022): 243–64.
Redden, Reid, and Jacob W. Thorne. "Reproductive Management of Sheep and Goats." In Bazer, Lamb, and Wu, *Animal Agriculture*, 211–30.
Reid, Sarah. "How to Be a Responsible Wildlife Tourist." *Lonely Planet*. March 7, 2022. www.lonelyplanet.com/articles/responsible-wildlife-tourism.
Reitter, Paul. *Bambi's Jewish Roots and Other Essays on German-Jewish Culture*. New York: Bloomsbury Academic, 2015.
Rhyder, Julia. *Centralizing the Cult: The Holiness Legislation in Leviticus 17–26*. Forschungen Zum Alten Testament 134. Tübingen, Germany: Mohr Siebeck, 2019.
Riggs, Damien W., and Elizabeth Peel. *Critical Kinship Studies: An Introduction to the Field*. London: Palgrave Macmillan, 2016.
Robinson, Scott R., and William P. Smotherman. "Fetal Learning: Implications for the Development of Kin Recognition." In Hepper, *Kin Recognition*, 308–34.
Roded, Ruth. "Islamic and Jewish Religious Feminists Tackle Islamic and Jewish Oral Law: Maintenance and Rebellion of Wives." *Comparative Islamic Studies* 11, no. 1 (2017): 35–63.
Rodolfo, Ungerfeld, Maria J. Hötzel, and Daniel Enríquez. "Minimising the Stress of Weaning of Beef Calves: A Review." *Acta Veterinaria Scandinavica* 53, no. 1 (2011): 28.
Rose, Anne C. *In the Hearts of the Beasts: How American Behavioral Scientists Rediscovered the Emotions of Animals*. Oxford: Oxford University Press, 2020.
Rosenbaum, Stacy, and Lee T. Gettler. "With a Little Help from Her Friends (and Family): Part I, The Ecology and Evolution of Non-maternal Care in Mammals." *Physiology and Behavior* 193 (September 2018): 1–11.

———. "With a Little Help from Her Friends (and Family): Part II, Non-maternal Caregiving Behavior and Physiology in Mammals." *Physiology and Behavior* 193 (September 2018): 12–24.

Rosenblum, Jordan. *The Jewish Dietary Laws in the Ancient World*. New York: Cambridge University Press, 2016.

———. "Tractate Hullin." In Cohen, Goldenberg, and Lapin, *Oxford Annotated Mishnah*, 3:120–67.

Rosenstock, Eva, Julia Ebert, and Alisa Scheibner. "Cultured Milk." *Current Anthropology* 62, no. S24 (2021): S256–75.

Royle, Nick J., Per T. Smiseth, and Mathias Kölliker, eds. *The Evolution of Parental Care*. Oxford: Oxford University Press, 2012.

Ruane, Nicole J. "Milk, Meat, and Mothers: The Problem of Motherhood in Some Ritual Food Laws." In *New Perspectives on Ritual in the Biblical World*, edited by Melissa Ramos and Laura Quick, 51–70. London: T&T Clark International, 2022.

———. *Sacrifice and Gender in Biblical Law*. New York: Cambridge University Press, 2013.

Rubenstein, Jeffrey L. *The Culture of the Babylonian Talmud*. Baltimore: Johns Hopkins University Press, 2005.

———. "Grappling with the Merits of the Land of Israel: Analysis of the Sugya in BT Ketubot 110a–112b." In *Center and Diaspora: The Land of Israel and the Diasporas in the Period of the Second Temple, the Mishnah, and the Talmud [Merkaz u-Tefutsah: Erets Yisra'el ve-ha-Tefutsot be-Yeme Bayit Sheni, ha-Mishnah ve-ha-Talmud]*, edited by Isaiah Gafni, 159–88. Jerusalem: Zalman Shazar Center, 2004.

———. "King Herod in Ardashir's Court: The Rabbinic Story of Herod (B. Bava Batra 3b–4a) in Light of Persian Sources." *AJS Review* 38, no. 2 (2014): 249–74.

———. *Rabbinic Stories*. Mahwah, NJ: Paulist, 2002.

Saar, Ortal-Paz. *Jewish Love Magic: From Late Antiquity to the Middle Ages*. Leiden: Brill, 2017.

Safina, Carl. *Beyond Words: What Animals Think and Feel*. London: Souvenir, 2016.

Safrai, Zeev. "Agriculture and Farming." In *The Oxford Handbook of Jewish Daily Life in Roman Palestine*, edited by Catherine Hezser, 246–63. New York: Oxford University Press, 2010.

———. *The Economy of Roman Palestine*. London: Routledge, 1994.

Salten, Felix. *Bambi: A Life in the Woods*. Translated by Whittaker Chambers. New York: Simon and Schuster, 1928.

Samely, Alexander. *Profiling Jewish Literature in Antiquity: An Inventory, from Second Temple Texts to the Talmuds*. Oxford: Oxford University Press, 2013.

Sandem, Agnethe-Irén, and Bjarne O. Braastad. "Effects of Cow-Calf Separation on Visible Eye White and Behaviour in Dairy Cows: A Brief Report." *Applied Animal Behaviour Science* 95, no. 3 (2005): 233–39.

Sapir-Hen, Lidar, Yuval Gadot, and Israel Finkelstein. "Environmental and Historical Impacts on Long Term Animal Economy: The Southern Levant in the Late Bronze and Iron Ages." *Journal of the Economic and Social History of the Orient* 57, no. 5 (2014): 703–44.

Sarcophagus of Kawit. JF 47397. Ministry of Tourism and Antiquities. https://egymonuments.gov.eg/collections/kawit-sarcophagus-4/.

Sarna, Nahum M. *Exodus = [Shemot]: The Traditional Hebrew Text with the New JPS Translation.* Philadelphia: Jewish Publication Society, 1991.

Sasson, Aharon. *Animal Husbandry in Ancient Israel: A Zooarchaeological Perspective on Livestock Exploitation, Herd Management and Economic Strategies.* London: Taylor and Francis, 2016.

Sasson, Jack M. "Ritual Wisdom? On 'Seething a Kid in Its Mother's Milk.'" In *Kein Land für sich allein: Studien zum Kulturkontakt in Kanaan, Israel/Palästina und Ebirnari für Manfred Weippert zum 65 Geburtstag,* edited by Manfred Weippert, Ulrich Hübner, and Ernst Axel Knauf, 294–308. Freiburg, Germany: Universitätsverlag; Vandenhoeck und Ruprecht, 2002.

Saul Lieberman Institute for Talmudic Research and CDI Systems, eds. *Sol and Evelyn Henkind Talmud Text Databank.* Jerusalem: CDI Systems, n.d.

Schaefer, Donovan O. *Religious Affects: Animality, Evolution, and Power.* Durham, NC: Duke University Press, 2015.

Schatten, Heide, and Gheorghe M. Constantinescu. *Comparative Reproductive Biology.* Hoboken, NJ: Wiley and Sons, 2008.

Schiffman, Lawrence H. "'Miqsat Ma'aseh Ha-Torah' and the 'Temple Scroll.'" *Revue de Qumrân* 14, no. 3 (1990): 435–57.

Schiffman, Lawrence H., and Andrew D. Gross. *The Temple Scroll: 11q19, 11q20, 11q21, 4q524, 5q21 with 4q365a.* Dead Sea Scrolls Editions 1. Boston: Brill, 2021.

Schmidt, Hanns-Peter. "Simorg." In *Encyclopaedia Iranica.* July 20, 2002. https://iranicaonline.org/articles/simorg.

Schorch, Stefan. "'A Young Goat in Its Mother's Milk'? Understanding an Ancient Prohibition." *Vetus Testamentum* 60, no. 1 (2010): 116–30.

Schroer, Sara Asu. "Breeding with Birds of Prey: Intimate Encounters." In *Domestication Gone Wild: Politics and Practices of Multispecies Relations,* edited by Heather Anne Swanson, Marianne E. Lien, and Gro Ween, 33–49. Durham: Duke University Press, 2018.

Schwartz, Baruch J. "Leviticus: Introduction and Annotations." In Brettler and Berlin, *Jewish Study Bible,* 193–266.

Schwartz, Seth. *Imperialism and Jewish Society, 200 B.C.E. to 640 C.E. Jews, Christians, and Muslims from the Ancient to the Modern World*. Princeton: Princeton University Press, 2001.

"Sefaria: A Living Library of Jewish Texts Online." Sefaria. www.sefaria.org/texts.

Segal, Alan F. *Two Powers in Heaven: Early Rabbinic Reports About Christianity and Gnosticism*. Leiden: Brill, 2002.

Segal, Eliezer. "Justice, Mercy and a Bird's Nest." *Journal of Jewish Studies* 42, no. 2 (1991): 176–95.

Seidenberg, David Mevorach. "Sending the Mother Bird: A Window into the Soul of Judaism." *Times of Israel* (blog). https://blogs.timesofisrael.com/sending-the-mother-bird-a-window-into-the-soul-of-judaism/.

Shemesh, Aharon. *Punishments and Sins: From the Bible to Rabbinic Literature (Onashim va-Hata'im: Min ha-Miqra le-Sifrut Hazal)*. Jerusalem: Magnes, 2003.

Sherman, Phillip Michael. "Animals." *The Oxford Encyclopedia of the Bible and Law*. Oxford University Press. 2015. https://www.oxfordreference.com/view/10.1093/acref:obso/9780199843305.001.0001/acref-9780199843305-e-5.

"Shiluach Haken 4 AV 5779." YouTube. August 5, 2019. www.youtube.com/watch?v=dBx7mu-HKf8.

Shyovitz, David I. *A Remembrance of His Wonders: Nature and the Supernatural in Medieval Ashkenaz*. Jewish Culture and Contexts. Philadelphia: University of Pennsylvania Press, 2017.

Sibiryakova, Olga V., Ilya A. Volodin, Vera A. Matrosova, and Elena V. Volodina. "The Power of Oral and Nasal Calls to Discriminate Individual Mothers and Offspring in Red Deer, Cervus Elaphus." *Frontiers in Zoology* 12 (January 2015): 2.

Singer, Peter. *Animal Liberation: The Definitive Classic of the Animal Movement*. New York: Ecco, 2009.

Sirovica, Lara V., Caroline Ritter, Jillian Hendricks, and Daniel M. Weary. "Public Attitude Toward and Perceptions of Dairy Cattle Welfare in Cow-Calf Management Systems Differing in Type of Social and Maternal Contact." *Journal of Dairy Science* 105, no. 4 (2022): 3248–68.

Skutch, Alexander Frank. *Helpers at Birds' Nests: A Worldwide Survey of Cooperative Breeding and Related Behavior*. Iowa City: University of Iowa Press, 1999.

Slifkin, Natan. "Shiluach haKein: The Transformation of a Mitzvah." Zoo Torah. www.zootorah.com/RationalistJudaism/ShiluachHaKein.pdf.

Smelik, Willem F. *Rabbis, Language and Translation in Late Antiquity*. Cambridge: Cambridge University Press, 2013.

Smith, D. Charles. *The Role of Mothers in the Genealogical Lists of Jacob's Sons*. Contributions to Biblical Exegesis and Theology 90. Leuven: Peeters, 2018.

Sokoloff, Michael. *A Dictionary of Jewish Babylonian Aramaic of the Talmudic and Geonic Periods*. Baltimore: Johns Hopkins University Press, 2002.
Soler, Jean. "The Semiotics of Food in the Bible." In *Food and Drink in History: Selections from the Annales; Économies, Sociétes, Civilisations*, edited by Robert Forster and Orest A. Ranum, 5:126–38. Baltimore: Johns Hopkins University Press, 1979.
Soloveitchik, Haym. "Rupture and Reconstruction: The Transformation of Contemporary Orthodoxy." *Tradition: A Journal of Orthodox Jewish Thought* 28, no. 4 (1994): 64–130.
Spinka, Marek, Ruth C. Newberry, and Marc Bekoff. "Mammalian Play: Training for the Unexpected." *Quarterly Review of Biology* 76, no. 2 (2001): 141–68.
Stackert, Jeffrey. "The Holiness Legislation and Its Pentateuchal Sources: Revision, Supplementation, and Replacement." In *The Strata to the Priestly Writings: Contemporary Debate and Future Directions*, edited by Sarah Shectman and Joel S. Baden, 187–204. Zürich: Theologischer, 2009.
Stěhulová, Ilona, Lena Lidfors, and Marek Špinka. "Response of Dairy Cows and Calves to Early Separation: Effect of Calf Age and Visual and Auditory Contact After Separation." *Applied Animal Behaviour Science* 110, no. 1 (2008): 144–65.
Stein, Dina. *Textual Mirrors: Reflexivity, Midrash, and the Rabbinic Self*. Philadelphia: University of Pennsylvania Press, 2012.
Stein, Siegfried. "The Concept of the 'Fence': Observations on Its Origin and Development." In *Studies in Jewish Religious and Intellectual History: Presented to Alexander Altmann on the Occasion of His Seventieth Birthday*, edited by Siegfried Stein and Raphael Loewe, 301–29. Tuscaloosa: University of Alabama Press, 1979.
Steinberg, Naomi A. *The World of the Child in the Hebrew Bible*. Sheffield: Sheffield Phoenix, 2013.
Steinmetz, Devora. *From Father to Son: Kinship, Conflict, and Continuity in Genesis*. Louisville, KY: Westminster John Knox Press, 1991.
Steinsaltz, Adin. *Koren Talmud Bavli: The Noé Edition*. Hullin Part 2. Jerusalem: Koren, 2016.
Stern, Josef. *Problems and Parables of Law: Maimonides and Nahmanides on Reasons for the Commandments (Ta'amei Ha-Mitzvot)*. Albany: State University of New York Press, 1998.
Stoddard, Mary Caswell, and Rebecca M. Kilner. "The Past, Present and Future of 'Cuckoos Versus Reed Warblers.'" *Animal Behaviour* 85, no. 4 (2013): 693–99.
Stone, Ken. *Reading the Hebrew Bible with Animal Studies*. Palo Alto, CA: Stanford University Press, 2017.
Stroumsa, Sarah. *Maimonides in His World: Portrait of a Mediterranean Thinker*. Jews, Christians, and Muslims from the Ancient to the Modern World. Princeton: Princeton University Press, 2009.

"Succession: Official Website for the HBO Series." HBO. www.hbo.com/succession.

Sussman, Yaacov, ed. *Talmud Yerushalmi According to Ms. Or. 4720 (Scal. 3) of the Leiden University Library with Restorations and Corrections*. Jerusalem: Academy of the Hebrew Language, 2001.

Svare, Bruce B. "Maternal Aggression in Mammals." In Gubernick and Klopfer, *Parental Care in Mammals*, 179–211.

Švaríčková-Slabáková, Radmila, ed. *Family Memory: Practices, Transmissions and Uses in a Global Perspective*. Memory and Narrative. New York: Routledge, 2021.

Tabory, Joseph. "Shiluah ha-Ken: On the Relationship Between the Reason for the Mitzvah and Its Laws." In *Studies in Halakhah and Jewish Thought in Honor of Rav Menahem Immanuel Rackman on His 80th Birthday*, edited by Moshe Beer, 121–41. Ramat Gan, Israel: Bar-Ilan University, 1994.

Tang, Akaysha C., Katherine G. Akers, Bethany C. Reeb, and Russell D. Romeo. "Programming Social, Cognitive, and Neuroendocrine Development by Early Exposure to Novelty." *Proceedings of the National Academy of Sciences* 103, no. 42 (2006): 15716–21.

Taylor, Laurel Koepf. *Give Me Children or I Shall Die: Children and Communal Survival in Biblical Literature*. Minneapolis: Fortress, 2013.

Terrazas, Angelica, Norma Serafin, Horacio Hernández, Raymond Nowak, and Pascal Poindron. "Early Recognition of Newborn Goat Kids by Their Mother: II. Auditory Recognition and Evidence of an Individual Acoustic Signature in the Neonate." *Developmental Psychobiology* 43, no. 4 (2003): 311–20.

Theodor, Julius, and Chanoch Albeck, eds. *Berischit Rabba, mit Kritischem Apparat und Kommentar*. 3 vols. Jerusalem: Wahrmann Books, 1965.

Thorhallsdottir, Anna G., Frederick D. Provenza, and David F. Balph. "The Role of the Mother in the Intake of Harmful Foods by Lambs." *Applied Animal Behaviour Science* 25, no. 1 (1990): 35–44.

Tigay, Jeffrey H. *Deuteronomy = [Devarim]: The Traditional Hebrew Text with the New JPS Translation*. Philadelphia: Jewish Publication Society, 1996.

Touitou, Elazar. *"Exegesis in Perpetual Motion": Studies in the Exegesis of Rashbam on the Torah*. Ramat-Gan, Israel: Bar Ilan University Press, 2003.

Tuczay, Christa A. "Motifs in *The Arabian Nights* and in Ancient and Medieval European Literature: A Comparison." *Folklore* 116, no. 3 (2005): 272–91.

U.S. Fish and Wildlife Service. "To Feed or Not to Feed Wild Birds." June 9, 2021. www.fws.gov/story/feed-or-not-feed-wild-birds.

U.S. National Park Service. "How Wildlife Are Responding to a Warming Climate." www.nps.gov/articles/000/aps-22-1-5.htm.

Valenze, Deborah. *Milk: A Local and Global History*. New Haven, CT: Yale University Press, 2011.

Val-Laillet, David, Raymond Nowak, Sandra Giraud, and Céline Tallet. "Nonnutritive Sucking: One of the Major Determinants of Filial Love." *Developmental Psychobiology* 48, no. 3 (2006): 220–32.

Val-Laillet, David, Maud Simon, and Raymond Nowak. "A Full Belly and Colostrum: Two Major Determinants of Filial Love." *Developmental Psychobiology* 45, no. 3 (2004): 163–73.

Van den Abbeele, Georges. *Travel as Metaphor: From Montaigne to Rousseau.* Minneapolis: University of Minnesota Press, 1992.

Van Seters, John. *A Law Book for the Diaspora: Revision in the Study of the Covenant Code.* New York: Oxford University Press, 2003.

Varro, Marcus Terentius. *On Agriculture.* Translated by Harrison Boyd Ash and William Davis Hooper. Loeb Classical Library 283. Cambridge, MA: Harvard University Press, 2014.

Veissier, Isabelle, Alain Boissy, Raymond Nowak, and Pierre Orgeur. "Ontogeny of Social Awareness in Domestic Herbivores." *Applied Animal Behaviour Science* 57, no. 3 (1998): 233–45.

Ventura, Beth A., Marina A. G. von Keyserlingk, Catherine A. Schuppli, and Daniel M. Weary. "Views on Contentious Practices in Dairy Farming: The Case of Early Cow-Calf Separation." *Journal of Dairy Science* 96, no. 9 (2013): 6105–16.

Ventura, Beth A., Marina A. G. von Keyserlingk, Hannah Wittman, and Daniel M. Weary. "What Difference Does a Visit Make? Changes in Animal Welfare Perceptions After Interested Citizens Tour a Dairy Farm." *PloS One* 11, no. 5 (2016): e0154733.

Vergil. *Eclogues and Georgics.* Translated by James Bradley Wells. Madison: University of Wisconsin Press, 2022.

Vermeersch, Shyama, Simone Riehl, Britt M. Starkovich, et al. "Animal Husbandry from the Middle Bronze Age Through the Iron Age in the Shephelah: Faunal Remains from the New Excavations at Lachish." *Archaeological and Anthropological Sciences* 13, no. 3 (2021): 38.

Vidas, Moulie. *Tradition and the Formation of the Talmud.* Princeton: Princeton University Press, 2014.

Vuolanto, Ville. "Grandmothers in Roman Egypt." *Greek, Roman and Byzantine Studies* 57, no. 2 (2017): 372–402.

Waal, Frans B. M. de. *Chimpanzee Politics: Power and Sex Among Apes.* New York: Harper and Row, 1982.

———. *Good Natured: The Origins of Right and Wrong in Humans and Other Animals.* Cambridge, MA: Harvard University Press, 1996.

———. *Mama's Last Hug: Animal Emotions and What They Tell Us About Ourselves.* New York: Norton, 2020.

Wagenaar, Jan Paul T. M., and J. Langhout. "Practical Implications of Increasing 'Natural Living' Through Suckling Systems in Organic Dairy Calf

Rearing." *NJAS: Wageningen Journal of Life Sciences* 54, no. 4 (2007): 375–86.

Wagner, Kathrin, Daniel Seitner, Kerstin Barth, and Rupert Palme. "Effects of Mother Versus Artificial Rearing During the First 12 Weeks of Life on Challenge Responses of Dairy Cows." *Applied Animal Behaviour Science* 164 (March 2015): 1–11.

Waiblinger, Susanne, Xavier Boivin, Vivi Pedersen, and Maria-Vittoria Tosi. "Assessing the Human-Animal Relationship in Farmed Species: A Critical Review." *Applied Animal Behaviour Science* 101, nos. 3–4 (2006): 185–242.

Waldman, Bruce. "The Ecology of Kin Recognition." *Annual Review of Ecology and Systematics* 19, no. 1 (1988): 543–71.

Walker-Jones, Arthur. "The So-Called Ostrich in the God Speeches of the Book of Job (Job 39, 13–18)." *Biblica* 86, no. 4 (2005): 494–535.

Wasserman, Mira Beth. *Jews, Gentiles, and Other Animals: The Talmud After the Humanities*. Philadelphia: University of Pennsylvania Press, 2017.

Waters, Hannah. "Live Like a Bird in This Nest-Inspired Apartment." Audubon. January 13, 2016. www.audubon.org/news/live-bird-nest-inspired-apartment.

Webster, John. *Management and Welfare of Farm Animals: The UFAW Farm Handbook*. Hoboken, NJ: Wiley and Sons, 2011.

Weinberger, Naftali. *A Practical Guide to the Mitzvah of Shiluach Hakan*. Jerusalem: Feldheim, 2007.

Weisberg, Dvora E. *Levirate Marriage and the Family in Ancient Judaism*. Waltham, MA: Brandeis University Press, 2009.

Weiss, Haim, and Shira Stav. *The Return of the Absent Father: A New Reading of a Chain of Stories from the Babylonian Talmud*. Translated by Batya Stein. Philadelphia: University of Pennsylvania Press, 2022.

Weiss, Isaac Hirsch, ed. *Sifra Deve Rav: Hu Sefer Torat Kohanim*. New York: Om, 1946.

Weiss, Roslyn. "Maimonides on 'Shilluaḥ Ha-Qen.'" *Jewish Quarterly Review* 79, no. 4 (1989): 345–66.

Weitzman, Steven. *The Origin of the Jews: The Quest for Roots in a Rootless Age*. Princeton: Princeton University Press, 2017.

Wierucka, Kaja, Benjamin J. Pitcher, Robert Harcourt, and Isabelle Charrier. "Multimodal Mother-Offspring Recognition: The Relative Importance of Sensory Cues in a Colonial Mammal." *Animal Behaviour* 146 (December 2018): 135–42.

Wolf, Sarah. "'Haven't I Told You Not to Take Yourself Outside of the Law?': Rabbi Yirmiyah and the Characterization of a Scholastic." *AJS Review* 44, no. 2 (2020): 384–410.

World Animal Protection. "Calling Out the Travel Companies Failing Wildlife." www.worldanimalprotection.org/our-campaigns/wildlife/commercial-exploitation/travel-tourism/the-real-responsible-traveller/.

Wright, David P. *Inventing God's Law: How the Covenant Code of the Bible Used and Revised the Laws of Hammurabi.* Oxford: Oxford University Press, 2009.

Wright, Elizabeth, and Catarina Ginja, eds. *Cattle and People: Interdisciplinary Approaches to an Ancient Relationship.* Archaeobiology 4. Columbus, GA: Lockwood, 2022.

Yadin, Yigael, ed. *The Temple Scroll.* Vol. 1. Jerusalem: Israel Exploration Society, 1983.

Yadin-Israel, Azzan. *Scripture and Tradition: Rabbi Akiva and the Triumph of Midrash.* Philadelphia: University of Pennsylvania Press, 2014.

"Yonis Mom Does Shiluach Hakan." YouTube. July 6, 2018. www.youtube.com/watch?v=8MtSx8sRfj8.

Zerubavel, Eviatar. *Ancestors and Relatives: Genealogy, Identity, and Community.* New York: Oxford University Press, 2012.

Ziyadah, Ma'an. "Ibn Bajja's Book Tadbir al-Mutawahhid: An Edition, Translation and Commentary." Master's thesis, McGill University, 1968.

Zuckermandel, Moses Samuel, ed. *Tosephta: Based on the Erfurt and Vienna Codices [Tosefta al-pi Kitve-yad 'Erfurṭ Vinah].* Jerusalem: Wahrman, 1970.

Index of Sources

HEBREW BIBLE

Genesis
  1:26-28, 12
  2:18, 13
  2:24, 13
  9:2, 180-181n25
  9:2-3, 12
  9:3, 43
  9:4-5, 43
  9:6, 43
  9:15-17, 13
  10:17, 132
  18:6-8, 174n87
  32:12, 180n25
  32:33, 74
Exodus
  6:6, 143
  11-15, 71
  12:5, 174n87
  13:1, 71
  20:10, 44
  20:12, 99
  21-22, 47
  21:28-32, 44, 76
  22:21, 206n2
  22:27, 47
  22:28-29, 47, 50, 71, 124
  22:29, 5, 19, 36, 65, 106, 122, 124, 126, 128, 206n5
  22:30, 214n10
  23:4-5, 44
  23:12, 44
  23:14-17, 45
  23:18, 46
  23:18-19, 46
  23:19, 5, 36, 45, 50, 56, 87, 106
  34:19-20, 72
  34:26, 5, 36, 45, 46, 50, 87, 106
Leviticus
  9:3, 174n87
  17:13, 74
  18:23, 76
  19:19, 69, 71
  20:15-16, 76
  22, 125
  22:6-7, 36
  22:17-25, 48, 71
  22:27, 5, 19, 36, 65, 71, 106, 122, 124, 126, 127, 128, 183n38
  22:27-28, 48, 51, 71, 124

Leviticus *(continued)*
  22:28, 5, 18, 36, 48, 51, 54, 55, 62, 63,
    65, 71–72, 73, 74, 106, 124, 126, 145,
    183n38
  22:32, 139
  27:26–27, 72
  27:32, 127, 128
  27:32–33, 127
  32:28, 180n25
Numbers
  6:7, 143
  6:9, 143
  6:14, 144
  7, 174n87
  7:9, 144
  13:21–24, 133
  13:25–33, 133
  18:15–18, 72
  19, 76, 87
  19:2, 143
Deuteronomy
  3:4, 209n39
  4:40, 180n22
  5:14, 44
  5:16, 49, 51, 99, 104, 180n22
  13:6, 117
  14:2, 184n47
  14:21, 5, 36, 45, 46, 50, 87, 106
  14:22–29, 178n11
  15:19–23, 72
  18:3, 74
  18:4, 74
  20, 50
  20:19, 49, 51
  21:1–4, 87
  21:10–14, 93
  21:18–21, 104
  22, 50
  22:1, 105
  22:1–4, 44, 104
  22:6, 53, 55, 64, 65, 105, 107, 109, 110,
    111, 180n25
  22:6–7, 5, 19, 49, 50, 61, 104, 111, 122,
    135
  22:7, 105, 180n22
  22:8, 104
  22:10, 44, 71
  22:11, 87
  22:55, 104
  22:78, 187n78
  25:4, 44
  25:5–10, 93
Judges
  6:19, 174n87
  13:15, 174n87
  15:1, 174n87
1 Samuel
  2:29, 144
  4–7:1, 142
  4:19–22, 213–214n5
  5:12, 143
  6, 142
  6:7–8, 143
  6:12, 143
2 Samuel
  15:32, 119, 120
2 Kings
  8:12, 183n43
Isaiah
  1:17, 123
  13:16, 183n43
  34:15, 113, 203n39
  43:16, 110
Jeremiah
  4:30, 197n14
  17:11, 113
Hosea
  10:1, 180n25
  10:14, 53, 55
  12:10, 55
  14:1, 183n43
Nahum
  3:16, 183n43
Psalms
  137:9, 183n43
  146:7, 198n22
Proverbs
  12:10, 53, 54
  30:5, 187n78
  30:19, 110
Job
  39, 136, 150
  39:13, 136, 137, 212n58
  39:13–18, 136
Esther
  3:13, 54, 55
1 Chronicles
  1:15, 132

DEUTEROCANONICAL WORKS

4 Maccabees
  14:14–18, 150

INDEX OF SOURCES 253

DEAD SEA SCROLLS

4QMMT Miqsat Ma'aseh Ha-Torah
  B36–38, 180n21
  B36–38 Column 1, 193n51
11QT Temple Scroll
  52:5–7, 180n21

ANCIENT JEWISH WRITERS

Josephus
  Antiquities
    3.9.4, 194n55
  The Jewish War
    7:97, 132
Philo
  On the Virtues
    129, 52, 182n35
    134, 182n36
    136, 53
    137–39, 180n21
    341, 194n54

NEW TESTAMENT

Matthew
  6:25, 62
  10:29, 62
Luke
  12:24, 62

RABBINIC LITERATURE

Mishnah
  Avodah Zarah
    1:6, 39
    2:7, 208n18
  Bava Batra
    6:7, 204n61
  Bava Kamma
    2:3, 175n99
    7:7, 38
    10:9, 39
  Bava Metzia
    5:5, 39
  Bekhorot
    1:1, 139

Bekhorot (*continued*)
    7:7, 82, 192n47
    9:4, 127, 128, 206n8, 207n13
  Berakhot
    5:3, 61, 64, 186n72
  Hullin
    2:4, 190n34
    3:1–2, 209n36
    4, 38, 144–145
    4:5, 82, 145, 192n47
    5, 73
    5:1, 73, 74, 75
    5:2, 190n33
    5:3, 76, 77
    6, 74
    6:1, 74
    7, 74
    7:1, 74
    8, 122
    8:3, 90
    10, 74
    12, 74
    12:1, 110
    12:2, 112, 114
    12:3, 112
    12:5, 201n15
  Keritot
    3:5, 79, 189–190n26
    5:1, 197n12
  Ketubbot
    3:2, 79
    3:5, 189–190n26
    5:7, 204n56
  Kiddushin
    4:4, 189n26
  Makhshirin
    5:6, 208n18
  Makkot
    3:12, 39
  Megillah
    4:9, 61, 65
  Pesahim
    4:1, 199n33
  Shabbat
    16:5, 39
  Sukkah
    2:8, 112
  Yevamot
    1:1, 79, 189n26
    7:5, 189n26
  Zevahim
    14:2–3, 125

Index of Sources

Tosefta
- Bava Metzia
  - 5:4, 176n101
- Bekhorot
  - 7:3, 206n9
  - 7:6, 207n15
  - 7:10, 138
- Hullin
  - 4:5, 214n12
  - 4:6, 214n13
  - 10:9, 113, 116
  - 10:10, 115
  - 10:13, 109
  - 10:16, 107
- Parah
  - 2:3, 38
- Shabbat
  - 15:2, 38

Palestinian Talmud
- Berakhot
  - 5:2 (9c), 63
  - 5:3 (9c), 185n67
- Kilayim
  - 8:2:2, 188n11
- Megillah
  - 4:10 (75c), 185n67, 186n70
- Yevamot
  - 11:1, 191n40

Babylonian Talmud
- Avodah Zarah
  - 20b, 188n11
- Bava Batra
  - 3b-4a, 118
  - 73-75, 133
  - 125b, 189-190n26
- Bava Kamma
  - 54b, 205n67
  - 80a-b, 199n27
  - 80b, 73
  - 115a, 205n67
- Bava Metzia
  - 30a, 176n103
  - 91a, 70, 188n11
  - 91b, 188n10
- Bekhorot
  - 17a, 73
  - 45b, 192n47
  - 53a, 139
  - 57b, 129, 132, 136, 211n53
  - 58b, 139
- Berakhot
  - 33b, 62, 185-186n67, 186n69
- Eruvin
  - 53b, 204n61
- Gittin
  - 53a, 176n103
- Hullin
  - 12, 19
  - 38b, 129, 207n15
  - 59b, 133
  - 60b, 133, 204n61
  - 62b, 203n48
  - 74b, 215n17
  - 75b, 73, 146, 215n19
  - 78b, 187n81
  - 80a, 191n35
  - 81b, 190n34
  - 82a, 78
  - 83a, 191n43
  - 100a-b, 98
  - 109a-110b, 19, 100
  - 109b, 91, 92, 93
  - 110a, 94, 95, 96, 97, 199n31
  - 110b, 99
  - 138b-39a, 117
  - 139b, 105, 110, 118, 119
  - 140b, 111, 113, 115
- Ketubbot
  - 62b-63a, 165n28
  - 111b, 133
- Kiddushin
  - 35a, 205n67
  - 66a, 209n39
- Megillah
  - 6b, 133
  - 25a, 62, 185-186n67, 186n69
- Menahot
  - 66b, 212n58
- Pesahim
  - 26a, 176n103
  - 94a, 204n61
- Shabbat
  - 118a, 204n61
- Sukkah
  - 5a, 210n46
- Yoma
  - 80a, 210n46

Mekhilta de-Rashbi
- Kaspa
  - 19, 206n5
- Nezikin
  - 249, 206n2

Sifra
- Emor
  - Parashah 8, Perek 7, 128
  - Parashah 8, Pereq 1 and 2, 83
  - Parshata 8:9-12, 187n81

Kedoshim
  Perek 4:13, 188n10
Sifre Deuteronomy
  227, 115
Genesis Rabbah
  44:1, 187n78
  76:12, 180n25
  77:26, 189–190n26
  86:2, 150
Leviticus Rabbah
  22:10, 198n22
  27:11, 53–54, 180n25
Deuteronomy Rabbah
  Ki Tetze 6:1, 183n44
Pesikta de–Rav Kahana
  9:11, 180n25, 183n38

CLASSICAL WRITINGS

Columella
  On Agriculture
    246–47, 175n96
    248–49, 37–38
Palladius
  The Work of Farming
    211, 175n94
Varro
  On Agriculture
    340–41, 37

On Agriculture (continued)
    342–43, 37
    348–49, 37
Vergil
  Georgics
    3:398–99, 175n96

MEDIEVAL WRITINGS

Maimonides
  Commentary on Mishnah Berakhot 5:3
    1:42, 64
  The Guide for the Perplexed
    2:599–600, 56–57
  Mishneh Torah, Laws of Prayer
    9:7, 65
  Mishneh Torah, Laws of Slaughter
    12:1, 190n32
    12:14, 191n43
    12:15, 191n44
  Mishneh Torah, Laws of Things Forbidden on the Altar
    3:4, 207n15
Shulhan Arukh
  Yoreh Deah
    13:2–4, 215n20
    16, 74
    16:2, 194n60

General Index

Abaye, 63, 97, 115, 214n14, 214-15n15
Abbahu, Rabbi, 113
Abraham, 11-12, 14
Absalom, 120
absent referent, 89
Adam, 14
Adams, Carol, 89, 100-101
Aelian, 150
affective neuroscience, 26-27
affect theory, 27
Affleck, Ben, 69
agency, 44
Agnon, Shmuel Yosef, 13
agriculture: ancient, 35-39; factory farms, 155-56; family separations, 18, 32-33, 34-35, 39-42, 101, 123, 175n96; industrial, 16, 174n83; Roman Empire, 37-39, 40
Agrippa, 132
Akedah, 12
Akiva, Rabbi, 207n14
Albeck, Chanoch, 193-94n53
Alter, Robert, 54, 144
American Humane Society, 59-60
American Kennel Club (AKC), 85
American Society for the Prevention of Cruelty to Animals (ASPCA), 59
Amoraim, 20, 21

Ancestry.com, 69
Ancient Kosher Ben Pekuah Australia, 147
Anderson, Sam, 151-52
Animal (podcast), 151
animal families: on the ark, 181n29; artistic depictions of, 148, 149*fig*., 150, 215-16nn22,23,24, 216nn27,28; descriptions of, 150-51; dynamics of, 3; encounters with, 151-52; generations, 18; human harms to, 3-4, 16, 58-59; integrity of, 58; language of, 79-81, 82, 191n40; as legal subjects, 80; in modern agriculture, 18, 32-33; nursing cows and the Davidic crown, 142-44, 213n2, 213n5; parental roles, 84; Pentateuch laws about, 5-7; separations, 18, 32-33, 34-35, 39-42, 101, 123, 151, 175n96; supporting, 153-58; terminology for, 6
animal-family laws: alternatives to humanitarian rationale for, 66-67; in Babylonian Talmud, 6-7; cooking a kid in his mother's milk prohibition, 19, 36, 45-46, 59-60, 106, 122, 189n21; development of, 18; evolution of, 50-51; as humane, 59-60; humanitarian rationale for, 51-61; Josephus on, 182n32; Maimonides on, 186n74, 187n78; in Mishnah, 5-7; objections to humanitarian rationale

257

GENERAL INDEX

animal-family laws *(continued)*
for, 61–66; in Pentateuch, 5–7, 44–45, 60, 182n32; Philo on, 52–53, 66, 182nn31,32; rabbinical interpretations of, 6; as *rahamim* traditions, 60, 61; same-day slaughter prohibition, 18, 36, 48, 55–56, 63, 65, 73–81, 82, 85–86, 106, 144–47, 186n69–70; sending off the mother bird, 5, 6–7, 19, 44, 49–50, 55–56, 58, 103–5, 122; separation of mother and baby in first week prohibition, 19, 36–39, 46–48, 106, 122; in Tosefta, 5–7; treated as a unit, 122, 205n1

animal hides, 130–31, 208n20

Animal Liberation (Singer), 27

animal rights, 13, 27, 44

animals: behavior, 9; in biblical law, 43–45; breeding, 69–70; captive, 156–57; companion, 154–55; domestication of, 40, 41, 84, 152, 177n116; farmed, 155–56; feelings and emotions, 25–28; genealogies, 69–70, 71–72, 85–86; God's covenant with, 13; in Hebrew Bible and rabbinic literature, 11–14; humane treatment of, 5, 60, 184n55; human relationships with, 7–8, 180–81n19; in Islamic thought, 57–58; and the Jewish family, 10–11; judicial trials for, 117; kinship, 7–9; natural habitats, 157–58; orphans, 128–30, 138–39; roles of, 10–11; as sacrifices, 12, 36, 124–26, 143–44, 174n87; suburban, 153–54; tithes, 126–28, 138–39; urban, 153–54; use of, 16–17; use of term, 23; what they teach about families, 14–17. *See also* animal families; animal-family laws

animal welfare, 44, 176n112

anthropocentrism, 14, 106, 107, 120–21

anthropodenial, 27

anthropomorphism, 26

antisemitism, 2

aquariums, 156–57

Arca Caesarea, 131

Ark of the Covenant, 142, 213n4

Arqa, 131–33

Arqat Leveinah, 131–32, 134, 140

artificial rearing, 33, 35

Ashi, Rav, 136, 199n29, 212n62, 214–15n15

assimilationism, 2

Assyria, 55

attachment, parent-child, 30–32, 33–34

Augustine, Saint, 66
Australia, 86
Avempace (Ibn Bājja), 57
Avicenna, 57
Avvim, 133

Babylonian Talmud, 20–22; animal breeding in, 69–70, 188n11; animal families in, 150; animal-family laws, 6–7, 182n32; animal grandparents in, 73; on animal tithes, 139; on ben pekuah, 146–47; bird's nest prayer formula, 62, 185–86n67; on consumption of udders, 19, 91–93, 197–98n20, 198n22; fathers in, 10; Hardisean dove story, 118–19, 204n61; head-bird-nest in, 120, 121; on same-day slaughter prohibition, 83; sending off the mother bird, 105, 108, 110; sending off the mother bird exemptions, 115

Baker, Steve, 130
Balcombe, Jonathan, 27
Bambi (film), 4, 207n11
Bambi (Salten), 1–5, 17, 151, 163n5, 163n9
Bambi's Children (Salten), 2
Baron, Devorah, 13
bar yokhani bird, 134–36, 137–38, 210n46, 210n48, 212n59
bats, 151–52
"beast-machine," 25
behavioral discrimination, 28
behavioral flexibility, 27
Beijing National Stadium, 109
Bekoff, Marc, 27
Ben-Amos, Dan, 210n44, 213n63
ben pekuah, 144–47, 215n16
Benyus, Janine, 109
Berekhiah, Rabbi, 54
Beth-shemesh, 143–44
biblical laws: dietary, 5, 6, 43; regarding animals, 43–44, 52, 69–70, 87. *See also* animal-family laws
Biblical Zoo, 13
Bilaam, 12
biodiversity, 154, 157–58
biomimicry, 109
birds: angry mothers, 136–38, 210n48–49; as babysitters, 114–16; brood parasitism, 114; as builders, 6–9, 19, 109–11; cooperative breeding, 114, 116; domesticated, 116–17; eggs, 17, 134–36, 210n46, 211n52; fathers, 111–14; giant, 133, 134–36, 210n46, 210n48; as hats, 119–

GENERAL INDEX 259

21; judicial trials for, 117–18; mothers, 107–9; queer families, 116; as rebels and killers, 116–19. *See also* nests; sending off the mother bird
birth, 126–28, 206nn8,9
Bobou, Olympia, 207n16
Book of the Covenant, 50, 124, 179n12
Bowlby, John, 33
breastfeeding, 10
breeding, 69–70, 84, 188n10
Brettler, Marc, 197n14
brooding, 113
brood parasitism, 114

Caesarea Libani, 131
Calarco, Matthew, 106, 120–21
Calvin, John, 66
Canaan, 133
captive animals, 156–57
caregiving relationships, 29–30
Carr, David, 180–81n25, 181n29
Carsten, Janet, 85
Center for Jewish History, 123
Chambers, Whittaker, 4
children: animal-family laws, 5–7; kin recognition, 28–30; mother-child separation, 33–35; orphans, 122–23; parent-child attachment, 30–32. *See also* parent-child relationships
children of Israel, 9
Chimpanzee Politics (de Waal), 14
Christianity, 3, 13, 20, 56, 60, 61, 66, 122, 132, 142, 150, 151
civilized behavior, 18, 56, 61, 184n47
Clement of Alexandria, 66
climate crisis, 12
Clines, J. A., 192n48
Cockburn, Andrew, 116
Code of Hammurabi, 50
cognitive ethology, 26
Cohen, Shaye, 84
colossal, use of term, 133–34, 210n42
Columella, 37–38, 70, 85, 175n96
coming-of-age tales: *Bambi*, 1–3; *Finding Nemo*, 15–16
companion animals, 154–55
conservation programs, 157–58
Cooke, Steve, 41
cooking a kid in his mother's milk prohibition, 19, 36, 45–46, 59–60, 189n21; lack of concern for animal families, 101–2; objection to humanitarian rationale for, 66; Philo on, 52, 87; related prohibitions, 88; udders as both milk and meat, 19, 90–102, 197–98n20; understandings of, 87–88, 195–96nn2,3,4
cooperative breeding, 114, 116
covenants, 13
"Covering the Blood" law, 74
cows, 29, 31, 32; in ancient agriculture, 34–35; ben pekuah, 144–47; domestication of, 40–41; on Kawit's sarcophagus, 49*fig.*, 148, 150, 215–16nn22,23,24; nursing cows and the Davidic crown, 142–43, 213n2, 213n5
critical animal studies, 8–9
crossbreeding, 69–70, 71, 188n10, 189n19
C-section births, 127–28, 206nn8,9
culling, 37

dairy industry, 16, 32–33, 41–42, 174n87
Daniel, 12
Daniel, Jacqueline, 30
Darwin, Charles, 25–26
David, 120
Davis, Angela, 69
Dead Sea Scrolls, 83
deer, 1–3, 29, 73
DeGeneres, Ellen, 16
Derrida, Jacques, 210n42
Descartes, René, 25, 26
Descent of Man (Darwin), 25
Deuteronomy, 20; animal-family laws, 5, 36, 50–51, 182n32; animal genealogies, 71–72; animal laws, 44; cooking a kid in his mother's milk prohibition, 45–46, 106; dietary laws, 46, 191n35; sending off the mother bird, 49–50, 104–5, 116, 138; warfare rules, 49–50
dietary laws, 5, 6, 46, 50–51, 91–93, 191n35
Disney, Walt, 4, 5
domestication, 40, 41, 84, 116–17, 152, 177n116
donation of firstborn, 46, 47, 71–72, 124–25, 126–28, 179n15
donkey, 12, 36, 38, 44, 69, 144, 188n10
Double, Michael, 116
Dukha people, 8

eggs, 134–36, 210n46, 211n52, 212nn60,61,62
Egypt: ancient, 148–50, 215–16nn22,23,24, 216n27; Roman, 73
Ekronites, 142–43
Elazar, Rabbi, 95

GENERAL INDEX

The Elephant Whisperers (film), 8
Eli, 144, 213–14n5
Eliezer, Rabbi, 112–13
Epistles of the Brethren of Purity, 58
ethical principles, 54–56
ethology, 9, 26–27
eugenics, 70
evolution, 26, 27, 28
Exodus, 20; animal-family laws, 5, 36, 50; animal genealogies, 71–72; animal laws, 44; animal sacrifice, 174n87; animals in, 12; Book of the Covenant, 50, 124, 179n12; cooking a kid in his mother's milk prohibition, 45–46, 106; the family in, 9; rules dealing with firsts, 47; separation of mother and baby in first week prohibition, 106, 122, 124; seven-day rules, 128
Expression of the Emotions in Man and Animals (Darwin), 25–26

facial expressions, 27
families: genealogies, 10, 68–69, 79–80, 85–86, 166n35; Jewish, 4, 9–11; language of, 79–81, 191n40; obliteration of Israelite, 55–56, 183n43; separations, 17; what animals teach about, 14–17
family myth, 24–25
fathers: in *Bambi*, 1–2; father birds, 111–14; in *Finding Nemo*, 15–16; and orphanhood, 129, 207n16; role of, 9–10, 84; as subject of same-day slaughter prohibition, 82–84, 192n47, 192n49, 194n60, 200n40
feelings and emotions: affective neuroscience, 26–27; of animals, 25–28; behaviorist model, 26; Cartesian perspective, 24, 25; family separations, 18, 39–42; filial, 24–25; grief, 10, 47, 179n16, 213–14n15; of humans towards animal family separations, 40–42, 176n106, 177n118; identifying, 27–28; impacts of animals' distress on humans, 177n123; love, 24–25, 28, 57–59; mother-child separation, 33–35; parental, 24–25
Feliks, Yehuda, 112
festival laws, 50–51; announcement of animal sales, 80–81; cooking a kid in his mother's milk prohibition, 45–46
Festival of Booths (Sukkot), 46
fetus from slaughtered mother, 144–47, 215nn19,20
filial cannibalism, 168n4
Finding Nemo (film), 15–16, 17

Finding Your Roots (Gates), 86
firstborn donations, 46, 47, 71–72, 124–25, 126–28, 179n15
"First of the Fleece" law, 74
"flesh of their flesh," 14
Forbes, Scott, 24–25
Freud, Sigmund, 2, 197n13
functional magnetic resonance imaging (fMRI), 28
fur seals, 29

Game of Thrones (TV show), 210n40
Gamliel, Rabban, 12
Gates, Henry Louis, Jr., 86
gender, grammatical use of, 22–23, 82–83, 192n48, 193n53, 212n59
genealogy: animals, 69–70, 71–72, 85–86; humans, 10, 68–69, 79–80, 85–86, 166n35; maternal, 84
Genesis, 28; animal laws, 43–44; animals in, 11, 13; covenants, 13; creation stories, 43, 178n1; the family in, 9; genealogy in, 69; young animals served as a delicacy, 174n87
Genesis Rabbah, 131
giant flora and fauna, 132–40
Gillespie, Kathryn, 42
gluttony, 52, 56, 61
goats, 12, 29, 31, 32, 37–39, 73, 176n101
God: covenants, 13; orphan's cry and, 123, 206n2; righteousness of, 55–56
Gonzaga family, 8
Goodall, Jane, 27
Goodfellow, Peter, 109, 110, 212n61
Gopalakrishnan, Pratima, 197n14
Governance of the Solitary (Ibn Bājja/Avempace), 57
grammar, use of, 22–23, 82–83, 192n48, 193n53, 212n59
grandparents, 189–90n26; animal, 73; grandfathers, 81–82, 84; grandmother hypothesis, 72–73; in Rabbinic literature, 73
grief, 10, 47, 179n16, 213–14n5
Griffin, Donald, 26
Gross, Aaron, 60, 61, 107
Gross, Rachel, 68, 84
Gubernick, David, 30
Guide for the Perplexed (Maimonides), 56–58, 65, 186–87n73
guinea pigs, 29

Halberstam, Jack, 14, 15–16
Haman, 55

Hananiah, Rabbi, 83
The Handmaid's Tale (TV show), 70, 123
Hanina, Rabbi, 146–47, 214n14, 214–15n15
Hannah, 144, 213–14n5
Haran, Menahem, 59, 60
Hardisean dove story, 118–19, 204n61, 205n63
Hebrew Bible: animal families in, 150; animals in, 11–14; laws regarding animals, 43–45
Hefer, Porky, 109
Heine, Heinrich, 13
Herod, 118–19
Herzl, Theodor, 2
"Him and His Child" law, 74, 75–76, 82–83, 125
Hisda, Rav, 97–99, 199n34, 200n38
Hiyya, Rabbi, 95
Hoffman, Melissa, 19
holiness, 51, 181n29
Holiness Legislation, 51, 71–72, 181n29, 189n19
Holocaust, 3, 5
holy lineage, 68–70, 71
hormones, maternal, 30–31
Hrdy, Sarah Blaffer, 116
Hribal, Jason, 119
human-animal dualism, 121
humane, defined, 59, 60
Humane Methods of Slaughter Act, 59–60
humaneness, 18
human exceptionalism, 14, 15, 120–21
humanitarian, defined, 59
humanitarianism, 6, 18, 60
humanitarian rationale: alternatives to, 66–67; Maimonides's objection to, 64–65; medieval, 56–59; modern, 59–61; modern objections to, 65–66; in Philo, 51–53; in rabbinic literature, 53–56; rabbinic objections to, 61–64; use of term, 45
human rights, 60
humans: body as method of measure, 210n41; feelings towards animal family separations, 40–42, 58–59, 176n106, 177n118; genealogies, 10, 68–69, 166n35; genealogy, 85–86; God's covenant with, 13; impacts of animals' distress on, 177n123; impacts of on animal families, 3–4, 16, 58–59; kin recognition, 28–29; milk consumption, 41, 176n113; murdered by birds, 117–18; relationships with animals, 7–8, 180–81n19; similarities to sheep, 40; ways to support animal families, 153–58
Huna, Rav, 139

Ibn Bājja (Avempace), 57
Ibn Ezra, Abraham, 69, 181n29, 184n47
Ilan, Tal, 203n41, 205n1
imaginative faculty, 57
incestuous rape, 73, 189n26
indistinction, 106–7
industrial agriculture, 16, 32–33, 174n83
intermarriage, 188n9
Iranian mythology, 135–36, 210n49
Isaac, 14, 28
Isaiah, 12, 113
Ishmael, 14
Islamic thought, 57–58, 61
Israel: animal family critical to beginnings of, 144; animals in, 13; giant flora and fauna in, 133; State of, 10
Israelites, 9; agricultural practices, 35–39; family obliteration by enemies, 55–56, 183n43; holiness, 51, 181n29; nursing cows and the Davidic crown, 142–44

Jacob, 12, 14
Jeremiah, 113
Jewish community, 10
Jewish continuity, 10
Jewish family: animals and, 10–11; as legal subjects, 80; precariousness of, 4; in rabbinic literature, 9–10; trauma experienced by, 10; vulnerability of, 9
Jewish people: ancient agricultural practices, 35–39; in Europe, 2–3; importance of genealogy, 10, 68–69, 166n35; matrilineal principle, 84; philanthropy, 51–53, 61; rebellion against rabbinic law, 117; in Roman Empire, 20, 21, 38–39
Jewish pronatalism, 10
Jewish Publication Society, 22
Job, 12, 136–38, 211n55, 211n57
Jonah, 12
Joseph, 12, 14
Josephus, 83, 182n32, 194n55
Joshua, Rabbi, 129, 130–31, 207n15
Joshua of Sikhnin, Rabbi, 182n38
Judges, 174n87

Kabak, Bernard, 167n51
Kafka, Franz, 13
Kahana, Rav, 146, 214–15n15

kamak bird, 210n49
Kamionkowski, S, Tamar, 192n49
Kawit's sarcophagus, 148, 149*fig.*, 150, 215–16nn22,23,24
kenaf renanim (bird), 136–37, 211n53, 211n57, 212n58
King, Barbara, 27
kinship: and animal-family laws, 105–6; elastic notion of, 7–8; "flesh of their flesh," 14; geographies, 179n15; history, 84–85; maternal units, 10; nature metaphors describing, 7; shared between animals, 8–9; shared between humans and animals, 7–8. *See also* animal families
kinship selection theory, 28
Kleiman, Devra, 84
Kotrosits, Maia, 207n17
Kraus, Karl, 163n5

lettuces, 132, 134, 209n36
Levi, Rabbi, 54–56, 62–63, 182n38
levirate marriage, 73, 79, 189n26
Lévi-Strauss, Claude, 123
Leviticus, 20; animal-family laws, 5, 36, 51; animal genealogies, 71–72; animal sacrifice, 174n87; crossbreeding prohibition, 69, 71; Holiness Legislation, 51, 71–72, 124, 181n29, 189n19; same-day slaughter prohibition, 18, 48, 63–64, 71–72, 106, 122, 125, 186n70; separation of mother and baby in first week prohibition, 47–48, 106, 122, 124–26; seven-day rules, 47–48, 71, 124–26, 128
Leviticus Rabbah, 53–54, 63
lineage confirmation, 73, 189n26
Lorenz, Konrad, 26
love: maternal, 57–59; parental, 24–25, 28
Luther, Martin, 66
Luzzatto, Samuel David, 193–94n53

MacKinnon, Michael, 70
Maimonides, 18, 61; on animal family laws, 186n74, 187n78; on cooking a kid in his mother's milk prohibition, 87; *Guide for the Perplexed*, 56–58, 65, 186–87n73; objection to humanitarian rationale, 64–65; on orphans, 207n15; on same-day slaughter prohibition, 57–59, 65, 83, 190n32
Malcolm, James, 84
Marcuse, Herbert, 134
Massumi, Brian, 14–15, 167n51

matrilineal principle, 84
Mattana, Rav, 119–20
Mayberry, Lorel, 30
McCartney, Paul, 4
meat industry, 16
Meir, Rabbi, 12, 76, 79, 145, 191n38
Mekhilta de-Rabbi Yishmael, 88
menopause, 72–73
Mesharshiya, Rav, 214–15n15
midrash halakhah, 20, 22
Milgrom, Jacob, 65–66
Miqsat Ma'aseh Ha-Torah, 83
Mishnah, 20; animal-family language, 79–81, 82; animal-family laws, 6–7; animal genealogies, 18, 85–86; animal grandparents in, 73; animal laws, 74–75; animals in, 12; on animal tithes, 139; on ben pekuah, 144–47, 215nn19,20; bird's nest prayer formula, 61–63; on birthing and rearing of animals, 38–39; cooking a kid in his mother's milk prohibition, 88; Hardisean dove story, 118–19, 204n61, 205n63; head-bird-nest in, 120, 121; holy lineage for animals, 71; on orphans, 128–30, 207n13, 207n15; same-day slaughter prohibition, 71–72, 73–81, 82, 85–86, 122, 124–25; sending off the mother bird, 110; seven-day rules, 125, 127; udders in, 90–91
monomaternalism, 203n50
moral accountability, 44
moral codes, 116
Moses, 9, 20
mother-bird mitzvah. *See* sending off the mother bird
mothers: as an absent referent, 89, 100, 200n40; angry, 136–38, 210n48–49; as attachment figures, 2; in *Bambi*, 1–3; bonding behaviors, 31–32; in *Finding Nemo*, 15–16; grief of, 10, 47, 179n16, 213–14n5; Jewish mother trope, 10; kin recognition, 28–30, 58, 170n31; love of, 24–25, 28, 57–59; maternal acceptance, 31; maternal dependency, 112; maternal motivation, 31; maternal recognition of pregnancy, 28–29; maternal responsiveness, 30, 34; matrilineal principle, 84; mother birds, 107–9; and orphanhood, 129–30, 140, 207n16; role of, 10, 30, 84; separation from child, 33–35; as subject of same-day slaughter prohibition, 82–84, 192n47, 192n49, 194n60; symbolized by udders, 88–91, 100–101;

traumatic witness of, 18; zombification of, 131
movement, 27
mules, 188n10, 189n19, 213n63
mutual inclusion, 14

Nagel, Thomas, 26
Nahman, Rav, 94–96
Nahmanides, 69, 107, 121, 187n78
Nazis, 3, 10
nefesh (soul), 54
nests: architecture and locations of, 6–7, 19, 109–11, 202n24; biomimicry, 109; building materials, 111; empty, 138–40; on heads, 119–21; mother-bird mitzvah as an industry, 17; in prayer formula, 61–63; as queer spaces, 116. *See also* sending off the mother bird
neural circuits, 27
Newberry, Ruth, 33–34
Ninevites, 150
Northern Israelite Kingdom, 55
Nowak, Raymond, 40
Numbers, 20, 174n87
nursing, 10, 31, 37

objectification, 207n17
Oedipus, 28
Oldenburg, Claes, 133–34
omasum, 132, 209n36
"One Welfare" agenda, 176n112
orphans, 7, 19, 122–23, 128–30, 138–40, 206n2, 213n66
ostriches, 118, 135, 136–37, 210n48, 211n55, 212n60

Palestine, 2; Byzantine, 21; Roman, 20, 38–39, 54
Palestinian Talmud, 20–21; bird's nests and prayer, 185n67; same-day slaughter prohibition, 63, 186n70
Palladius, 175n94
Panksepp, Jaak, 26–27, 28
Pappi, Rav, 96–97, 199n30
Pappunyans, 119–20, 205n67
parent-child relationships: animal-family laws, 5–7; in *Bambi*, 1–3; ben pekuah, 147; emotions characterizing, 24–25; family myth, 24–25; kin recognition, 28–30, 58, 170n31; maternal dependency, 112; signs of attachment, 30–32
parent-child relationships, honoring, 49, 51, 52, 180n22

parents, honoring, 49, 51, 52, 180n22
Passover, 46
Payne, Charles, 84
Payne, Richard, 20
Pentateuch: animal-family laws, 5–7, 44–45, 50–51, 60, 182n32; animal laws, 43–44
Perry, Michael, 109
PETA, 101
pets, 154–55
philanthropy, 18, 51–53, 61
Philistines, 142–43
Philo: on animal family laws, 52–53, 66, 182nn31,32; on cooking a kid in his mother's milk prohibition, 87, 182n36; humanitarian rationale, 51–53, 61, 107; on same-day slaughter prohibition, 83; *On the Virtues*, 51–53
Physiologus, 151
Pixar, 14, 15
plant-based diet, 155–56
Pliny, 135
polygamy, 79
Polzin, Robert, 213n4
positron-emission tomography (PET) scans, 28
posture, 27
pronatalism, 10
Prophet Muhammad, 58
Proverbs, 54–56
Psalms, 12

qore (bird), 112–13
queer families, 116

Rabbahi, 63
Rabbah bar bar Hanah, 133
rabbinic literature: alternatives to humanitarian rationale, 66–67; animals in, 11–14; background, 20–22; grandparents in, 73; humanitarian rationale in, 53–56; Jewish family in, 9–10; objections to humanitarian rationale in, 61–64; tall tales, 123, 132–40, 210n44, 213n63
Rabbis: animal-family law interpretations, 6, 53–56; on birthing and rearing of animals, 38–39; as fathers, 10; lineage, 20; literary output, 20; power of, 20; pure lineage prized by, 9–10; Romanization of, 20, 21, 70
Rachel, 37
rahamim traditions, 18, 60, 61, 107
Ramat-Gan Safari, 13
Rami bar Tamarei (Rami bar Dikulei), 97–99

Rashbam, 18, 56, 61, 66, 107, 183n45
Rashi, 64, 69, 78, 93, 96, 120, 136, 147, 176n104, 190n34, 191n44, 198n21, 208n20
rats, 26, 29
Ravina, 117
Reagan, Ronald, 5
Rebanks, James, 42
Rebecca, 37
recognition of kin, 28–30, 170n31
Regosin, Jon, 154
reinstatement behaviors, 34
Roman Empire: agriculture, 37–39, 40; animal breeding in, 70; giant flora and fauna in, 133; grandparent demographics, 73; intersections between humans and animals, 13; Jewish integration, 20, 21, 70
Rosenblum, Jordan, 190n34
Ruane, Nicole J., 192n49
rukk bird, 135–36

sacrifices, 12; cooking a kid in his mother's milk prohibition, 45–46; exemptions, 127–29, 207nn11,12,13, 213n66; lacking time as disqualification, 125–26, 206n5; nursing cows, 143–44, 213n5, 214n7; same-day slaughter prohibition, 124–25, 179n17; seven-day rules, 124–25; yearlings, 36, 174n87
Safina, Carl, 27
Salten, Felix, 1–5, 17, 163n9
same-day slaughter prohibition, 18, 48, 63, 106, 186n69–70; animal genealogy and, 71–72; announcement of animal sales, 80–81; applicability to fathers, 82–84, 192n47, 192n49, 194n60, 200n40; applicability to mothers, 82–84, 192n47, 192n49, 194n60; applicability to non-Jewish people, 191n43; applicability to pregnant animals, 48, 180n21, 192n47; ben pekuah exemption, 144–47, 215n16; in Dead Sea Scrolls, 83; Josephus on, 83, 194n55; Maimonides on, 57–59, 65, 83, 190n32; Mishnah on, 71–72, 73–81, 82, 85–86; objection to humanitarian rationale for, 65–66; parallels with violation of Israelite families, 55–56; penalties for violating, 75–76, 77–79, 190n31, 191n36; Philo on, 52–53, 83; temporality and, 77–79, 191n44; violation of and animal consumption, 75–77, 85–86, 190n34, 191n35
Samely, Alexander, 190n30

Samuel, 142–44, 213–14n5
sand partridge, 112, 203n35
Satriel, 131
Saul, 144
Saunders, Howard, 111
"Sciatic Nerve" law, 74
sculptures, 133–34, 210n40
sea lions, 29
Second Temple, destruction of, 20
Seidenberg, David, 105
sending off the mother bird, 5, 6–7, 19, 44, 49–50; applicability of to male qore, 112–13; in Babylonian Talmud, 105, 108; bird-centric approach to, 105–7; birds of different species exemption, 114–15; domesticated bird exemptions, 116–17; homicidal bird exemptions, 117–18; Maimonides on, 58; Mishnah law, 74; as mitzvah, 103–5, 107, 201n15; nest locations, 109–11; not applicable to fledged birds, 112; objection to humanitarian rationale for, 66; parallels with violation of Israelite families, 55–56; Prophet Muhammad on, 58; videos featuring, 103, 104
Sennacherib, 55
sensory systems, 27, 29
separation of mother and baby in first week prohibition, 19, 36–39, 46–48, 52, 106
Septuagint, 83
seven-day rules, 47, 52, 71, 124–28, 182n32
sexual intercourse, 70, 188n11, 212n62
sheep, 12, 29, 31, 32, 37–39, 40, 176n101
Shekhinah, 105
shelah (skin), 129, 208n18
Shiloh, 142
shiluach haken tradition, 19, 44, 103–4, 200n2. *See also* sending off the mother bird
Shimon, Rabbi, 76, 126
Shimon Ha-Shezuri, Rabbi, 145–46, 224n11
Shoah, 10
"Shoulder, Cheeks, and Stomach" law, 74
Shulhan Arukh: on ben pekuah, 147, 215n20; "The Law of 'Him and His Child'", 74; on same-day slaughter prohibition, 83–84
Sifra: animal-family language, 79–81; announcement of animal sales, 80–81; same-day slaughter prohibition, 83
Sifre Deuteronomy, 115
simorg bird, 135, 210n49
Singer, Peter, 12, 27, 101
Sirovica, Lara, 41

Skutch, Alexander, 114
Slifkin, Natan, 105
smell, 27, 29, 170n31
Smith, Suzi Q., 153-54
Society for Biblical Literature, 22
Sokoloff, Michael, 212n60
speciesism, 12-13
Stam/Stammaim, 21
Steinsaltz, Adin, 22
Stern, Josef, 184n55, 186n73
subjectivity, 44
suburban animals, 153-54
Sukkot (Festival of Booths), 46
Sumakhos, 79, 191n38
supersessionism, 60
Swanson, Janice, 33-34

Table of Nations, 132
tall tales, 123, 132-40, 210n44, 213n63
Talmud, 21-22
Tannaim, 20
Targum, 63, 83, 88
Tattlefush, 94-96, 198n23
taxidermy, 130-31, 208n25
Tel Arqa, 131
Temple Scroll, 83
Ten Commandments, 49, 52
Thomas Aquinas, 66
Tigay, Jeffrey, 59
Tinbergen, Niko, 26
tithes, 73, 126-28, 138-39, 189n26, 207n14
Titus, 12
Tolstoy, Leo, 15
Tosefta, 20; animal-family language, 79-80; animal-family laws, 6-7; on birthing and rearing of animals, 38-39; consumption of udders in, 92-93; sending off the mother bird, 109-10, 116; sending off the mother bird exemptions, 115
transliteration style, 22, 168n61

udders, 6; as both milk and meat, 90-93, 99-100, 197-98n20; consumption of, 19, 88-89, 91-93; Freud's associations, 197n13; as kosher way to eat meat and milk together, 94; Mishnah interest in, 90-91; Rav Pappi story, 96-97; Tattlefush story, 94-96; tearing open of, 91-92, 197n14; Yalta's story, 93-94, 96; Yom Kippur story, 97-99
urban animals, 153-54

vaginocervical stimulation (VCS), 30
Valenze, Deborah, 41
Varro, 37, 70
veganism, 7, 13, 16, 148-50, 155-56
Videvdad, 151
On the Virtues (Philo), 51-53
visual appearance, 170n31
vocalizations, 27, 29, 31, 34, 170n31

Waal, Frans de, 14, 27
wahm (estimation), 57
Walker-Jones, Arthur, 211n57
Wall-E (film), 123
warfare, rules of, 49-50
weaning, 32, 35, 37, 174n88
Weiss, Roslyn, 65, 184-85n55
What Animals Teach Us About Politics (Massumi), 14
"What Is It Like to Be a Bat?" (Nagel), 26
widows, 206n2
wildlife, 153-54
Winnicott, Donald W., 91
women, transmission of legal standards by, 93-94, 97, 100, 199n30

Yaakov, Rabbi, 107-8
Yadin-Israel, Azzan, 207n12
Yalta, 93-94, 96
Yehudah, Rabbi, 80-81, 98, 188n11, 191n44
Yehudah, Rav, 70
Yehudah Ha-Nasi, Rabbi, 154
Yerkes, Robert, 26
Yirmiyah, Rabbi, 111, 113, 203n41
Yishmael, Rabbi, 128
Yishmael ben Satriel, Rabbi, 130, 131, 132-34, 136-38, 140, 208n19, 208n29
Yitzhak bar Avudimi, Rav, 95
Yitzhak Nappaha, Rabbi, 97
Yohanan, Rabbi, 146, 214-15n15
Yom Kippur, 97-99
Yosi, Rabbi, 186n70
Yosi bar Abba, Rabbi, 95

Zeira, Rabbi, 92
Zeiri, 95, 146, 214n14, 214-15n15
Zerubavel, Eviatar, 7-9
Zionism, 2
Zohar, 105, 131
zoos, 156-57
Zoroastrianism, 151

Founded in 1893,
UNIVERSITY OF CALIFORNIA PRESS
publishes bold, progressive books and journals
on topics in the arts, humanities, social sciences,
and natural sciences—with a focus on social
justice issues—that inspire thought and action
among readers worldwide.

The UC PRESS FOUNDATION
raises funds to uphold the press's vital role
as an independent, nonprofit publisher, and
receives philanthropic support from a wide
range of individuals and institutions—and from
committed readers like you. To learn more, visit
ucpress.edu/supportus.

www.ingramcontent.com/pod-product-compliance
Lightning Source LLC
Chambersburg PA
CBHW021852230426
43671CB00006B/361